S0-AHM-125

PREHISTORY OF THE FAR WEST

Homes of Vanished Peoples

Frontispiece. Sandals excavated from Fort Rock Cave in south-central Oregon by the author's party in 1938. The sandals are twined with shredded sagebrush bark cords. They were radiocarbon dated at 9053±350 years ago. *Museum of Natural History, University of Oregon, photograph by author.*

PREHISTORY
OF THE FAR WEST
Homes of Vanished Peoples

L. S. Cressman

University of Utah Press
Salt Lake City, Utah

Permission to quote and/or reproduce figures whole or in part has been given by the following publishers:

American Association for the Advancement of Science: C. B. Hunt, "Quaternary Geology Reviewed," *Science,* vol. 150 (October 1, 1965), pp. 47–50, © 1965, A.A.A.S.

American Philosophical Society: L. S. Cressman, "Klamath Prehistory," *Transactions,* vol. 46, pt. 4 (1956), and "Cultural Sequences at The Dalles, Oregon," *Transactions,* vol. 50, pt. 10 (1960).

British Columbia Lands Service, Air Division, Victoria, B.C.: Photograph no. 58, roll no. B.C. 899.

Copley Books, Union-Tribune Publishing Co.: Richard F. Pourade, ed., *Ancient Hunters of the Far West,* © 1966.

D. C. Heath & Co., Boston, Mass.: W. C. Boyd, *Genetics and the Races of Man,* © 1950.

Princeton University Press: H. E. Wright, Jr., and David G. Frey, eds., *The Quaternary of the United States,* © 1965; Table 2, p. 227, Figure 4, p. 277, Figure 2, p. 274, Figure 14, p. 850, Figure 2, p. 725, and various short quotations.

Santa Barbara Museum of Natural History: Phil C. Orr, *Prehistory of Santa Rosa Island,* © 1968.

Stanford University Press: David M. Hopkins, ed., *The Bering Land Bridge,* © 1967.

The Wenner-Gren Foundation for Anthropological Research: J. C. Vogel, *Current Anthropology,* vol. 7, no. 1, pp. 46, 47.

John Wiley & Sons, Inc.: Richard Foster Flint, *Glacial Geology and the Pleistocene Epoch,* © 1966 (5th printing).

To Cecilia

(January 10, 1888–January 25, 1977)

For thy sweet love remember'd such wealth brings
That then I scorn to change my state with kings.

William Shakespeare, Sonnet XXIX

Contents

Illustrations

Figures

Maps

Tables

Foreword

Luther S. Cressman's *Prehistory of the Far West* is the first book-length synthesis of the prehistory of far-western North America. It is at the same time a scientific reminiscence exemplifying the period of its author's active life in the field when the archæological approaches and interpretations of today were being shaped. The synthesis incorporates the multidisciplinary approach in which Professor Cressman was a pioneer and the warm humanistic bent for which he is especially known among his students and colleagues.

Professor Cressman came to the University of Oregon in 1929 with a doctorate in Sociology taken at Columbia under Ogburn with collateral studies in Anthropology under Boas. He trained himself as an archæologist, founded the Department of Anthropology and later the Museum of Natural History at the University of Oregon, and remained active in archæological field research in the Northwest for four decades, until well past his official retirement in 1963. This book is the product, then, of long involvement and displays the unique and useful perspective of one who was present at the creation of viewpoints that still guide us in exploring the prehistory of the Far West.

Professor Cressman early became convinced of the high antiquity of human occupation in far-western North America through his explorations in Northern Great Basin caves. His collaboration with the geologists Ira S. Allison and Howel Williams was a pioneering step in the use of volcanic ash layers to date archæologic sites, and the results demonstrated that the simple hunting-gathering cultures of the Great Basin were indeed ancient. Previously, some had attributed the Great Basin cultures to diffusion from the rather late Basketmaker or pre-Basketmaker cultures of the Southwest. Cressman's work, later supported by radiocarbon evidence from sites in the Northern Great Basin and elsewhere, showed that the Great Basin culture was far more ancient than Basketmaker, and was in fact the Desert culture substratum out of which Basketmaker arose.

Professor Cressman was also one of the first archæologists in the West to reckon with the effects of postglacial environmental change on the human occupants of the region. His collaboration with Ernst Antevs and Henry P. Hansen brought to bear the insights of Recent geology and palynology on desert west archæology, a problem orientation that has grown and prospered and continues as a major focus of attention today.

Prehistory of the Far West draws together the evidence and insights earned during a long archæological career and will serve as a valuable stocktaking of western prehistory for archæologists now active in the field and students now in the colleges and graduate schools. It will prove interesting and informative as well to the general lay reader. Moreover, by the manner of his writing it, Professor Cressman exemplifies a humanism that, it may be hoped, will come to be as much emulated as the methodological orientations just mentioned. This is a time when American archæology is accused by some modern American Indians of exploitation of the remains of their ancestors. The genuine admiration and respect for his subjects that shows throughout the pages of Professor Cressman's book displays the archæological enterprise at its best: not as exploitation in any sense, but as a scientifically informed and humanistically focused presentation of the forgotten history, adventures, and contributions of a major segment of humanity.

C. Melvin Aikens
University of Oregon

Preface

I RETIRED FROM active status in the Department of Anthropology at the University of Oregon June 30, 1963, where I had been since September 1929 and went east for the next year. After some few months of adjustment to my new status, I decided it was time to make plans to continue the work in which I had been so long engaged. I corresponded with a number of former colleagues, and one of the suggestions I received was that I continue the study of the prehistoric culture relations of the Intermontane Region and the Pacific Coast, a project I had been working on actively since 1947. The suggestion appealed to me and, after some reflection, I decided to undertake the study.

I submitted an application to the National Science Foundation for support for a two-year project that was approved and funded as Grant GS–432. Parts of the Abstract—which outlined the plan of study, the hoped for results, and organized the subsequent work—follow.

> The objective of the proposed research is to assemble the existing data on cultural development in the region lying between the Rocky Mountains and the Sierra-Cascade mountain chain and in the adjacent Pacific Coast region and identify the major cultural processes and events involved in the prehistoric relationships between the two regions. . . . Problems to which particular attention will be given include priority of early cultural developments between the coastal and inland regions, the identification of the sequent phases of development of the distinctive maritime culture of the North Pacific Coast and the relationship of these phases to those of the contemporaneous inland peoples, and the possibility of archæological identification of the migrations within and into the area of Shoshoneans, Salishans, and Athapascans as inferred from linguistic data. Although it is by no means certain that these and other problems can be solved with existing information, it seems clear that assembling, ordering, and publishing the relevant data will, at a minimum, provide a significantly better basis for future identification of the sequent phases of development of the area.

I began work in September 1964 after my return to Eugene, Oregon, but it was not long before it became perfectly clear that the project as formulated in the Abstract had to have a wider orientation than that implied by the title "Prehistoric Cultural Relations between the Intermontane and the Pacific Coast Regions." These "relations" were but one aspect of the wider subject—far-western North American prehistory. The "relations" were functions of social, historical, and environmental factors through time and varied through time. This study is the result of the reorientation in the wider frame of reference. I believe that the objectives as stated in the Abstract have been reasonably well achieved. New information may require modification of points of view I have expressed. Such is the nature of this kind of study, a "Progress Report," as I state in the Introduction.

All opinions and conclusions are my own, unless otherwise indicated. Any book of this type is bound to reflect the personality of the writer. Opinions and evaluations of data are a part of the study, and when they are clearly presented as such, kept apart from the "hard facts," the results are no less "objective." I have presented here not a simple record of events or artifact descriptions and classifications, but an important segment of human experience as I see it after some forty years of active work in which I have tried to understand and appreciate its great human significance. To write meaningful prehistory, it seems to me, the scholar must establish empathy with the people who left the artifacts that we archæologists discover and describe. Artifacts are the means for the understanding, however partial, of the achievements, the experiences, the fears, the apprehensions, and the extraordinary courage of men and women. This book is, I hope, a small contribution to that end.

L. S. C.

Acknowledgments

MANY INDIVIDUALS and organizations have given significant help in the course of this study, and it is a pleasure to acknowledge my gratitude to them. I can acknowledge only a few of the many to whom I am indebted. The following have helped in various ways by making collections available and discussing them with me, by taking me to sites, by providing source material not otherwise readily available, and by corresponding with me: Charles E. Borden, Wilbur A. Davis, Carl L. Hubbs, Robert S. Kidd, C. W. Meighan, James R. Moriarty, David Sanger, A. C. Spaulding, and Emory Strong.

Bill McClure and Jack Nicolarsen gave permission to publish photographs of atlatls from their private collections. The Oregon State Highway Department, Travel Division, and the Nevada State Highway Department generously provided photographs. Figures 7 and 9 are the result of the help of four men, only one of whom I know personally, Robert P. Sharp of the California Institute of Technology. I wanted to illustrate the probable appearance of the British Columbia-Alaska coast at the time of the Vashon Stade of the Wisconsin Glaciation to parallel the illustration of interior glaciation, Figure 8. I wrote Dr. Sharp, who has extensive firsthand acquaintance with the glaciers of the British Columbia-Alaska region, and explained my problem. He referred me to W. O. Field of the American Geographic Society who in turn suggested I write to Charles Janda, Chief Ranger, Glacier Bay National Monument, and Austin S. Post. All these men not only took the time to correspond with me but sent me photographs for possible use. I chose two submitted by Austin S. Post. To these men, three of whom had probably never heard of me before receiving my S O S, and whose concern was the desire to help a fellow scientist, I am particularly grateful.

Various colleagues at the University of Oregon and elsewhere kindly read portions of the manuscript and gave helpful advice. Dr. L. K. Kittleman, Curator of Geology of the Museum of Natural History, University of Oregon, read critically the final sections dealing with geology to insure the accuracy of my treatment. Dr. C. Melvin Aikens of the Department of Anthropology, University of Oregon, read the manuscript before it was submitted for publication. After acceptance, the director of the University of Utah Press and I agreed on Mel as an editor to apply his skill to revisions. In any manuscript of this kind the author tends to include from the great mass of available information data which, at the time at least, seems interesting, important, and relevant. Only an outsider can approach the material and separate out the irrelevant from the relevant, and it requires an understanding person to do this without traumatic effect on the author. Mel carried out his task with great skill and I am greatly obligated to him; I suffered scarcely at all.

Mrs. Norma B. Mikkelsen, Director of the University of Utah Press, from the invitation to submit my manuscript to the finished book, has been most helpful and sympathetic to the author's problems. I also wish to thank the staff of the University of Utah Press for the tedious task of editorial preparation and production.

The National Science Foundation supported the early part of this study by Grant GS–432, and the University of Oregon provided office and laboratory space.

To express my indebtedness to my wife, Cecilia, I can only refer to my dedication.

PREHISTORY OF THE FAR WEST

Homes of Vanished Peoples

Introduction

Our knowledge is a torch of smoky pine
That lights the pathway but one step ahead.

George Santayana, Sonnets and Other Verses, III

MY OBJECTIVE in this study is to present a pre-history of human occupation in the far-western part of North America, an area approximately 1,900 miles in length and up to 700 in width, the topography of which includes almost all the features earth is heir to.

I see this segment of the record of human experience as a remarkable achievement in successfully meeting the challenges of extremely diverse and often difficult environments within the limits of the technological developments of the various cultures. As a natural environment, this area west of the Rocky Mountains posed probably the most difficult and diverse challenges of all areas of North America, except perhaps the Arctic, as a human habitat. Yet it is not all difficult, for over against the grudging desert environment must be set the genial climate of the Southern California coast with its wealth of marine resources used for both food and material objects. These western people during many thousands of years saw parts of their country covered by great depths of glacial ice, lakes forming in regions where there had been none, volcanic eruptions on both limited and catastrophic scales, deglaciation, and desiccation of vast areas of formerly favorable habitats. There is no clear evidence in the archæological record south of the glacial front that, once initial entry was achieved, there was any break in the continuity of occupation.

Some forty years of study of this western area, thirty-five of which have involved field experience in different environments, have impressed upon me the tremendous achievements of these people. I find in my thinking about them that wonder is a part of my reaction, and the following pages reflect this attitude. My book is an effort to describe some of these remarkable human achievements and the ways of life of these people of which the artifacts are mute evidence.

Human life is extremely complex, and many diverse methods of study are required to apprehend even a small amount of its richness. Archæology is one of these methods and, to me, is the anthropology of prehistoric people. Archæology also encompasses natural science, social science, and humanism, with the accent varying according to the objective and data at hand, and use of other fields of study is relevant when jointly directed toward the understanding of man and his works in prehistory. Use of the procedures of any school of research—cultural, historical, processual, or systems—will depend on the objectives one has in mind, and one may reasonably shift from one procedure to another. I think the methods of each of these schools are represented at various points in this study depending on the different objectives I have had in mind. The following general concepts are a more detailed presentation of the intellectual structure within which I work.

CULTURE—A DEPENDENT AND INDEPENDENT VARIABLE

A basic observation from which much of my thinking proceeds is that culture, at the stages of development discussed in this study, is largely a dependent variable. The independent variables are the natural environment and the biological character of man as reflected mainly in the mind of the individual man or woman. To be sure, I may be oversimplifying the situation, but I think the record is quite clear that the simpler the culture the more dependent it is on these other variables, particularly the environment. It is also true that aspects of the culture may become variables affecting its own development.

Consider an example. Sometime before 9,000 years ago Indians living in the Columbia River drainage began to take salmon from the Columbia, and in a short time this previously unexploited natural resource became a major food supply. It is possible that the salmon were not in the Columbia River before the Indians started taking them, or perhaps they were, but the Indians lacked the knowledge of their potential use and the means of exploiting their availability. Some evidence suggests that salmon were

1

not in the river (Cressman et al. 1960). Salmon were in the Fraser River by 9,000 years ago, but up to a relatively short period before that the Fraser River canyon was a solid mass of ice, which reached a depth of over a mile at the site of present-day Vancouver, British Columbia. Along the Columbia River, spears, harpoons, and dip nets were all used to take salmon, and for my immediate purpose it does not matter when they individually came into use. The important point is that some places were more favorable than others as fishing stations and that long stretches of the river offered no suitable sites for use of aboriginal fishing gear. The location of a rapids or a waterfall determined the best fishing sites.

Since salmon could be taken only at certain times of the year—during the "runs"—and at specific places, socialization or regularization of fishing activities had to develop to avoid anarchy. "Fishing rights" at various desirable localities became vested in families, and these rights were treated like any other property.

As salmon moved slowly up the Columbia to spawn, their numbers became progressively less as spawners dropped off at the streams of their birth, the goals to which their reproductive drive directed them. And, the fish, no longer feeding since they left salt water, provided less and less food value as they moved farther upstream. As a result, upriver Indian groups moved down the river to fish. The most striking ethnographic example are the Nez Percé (Walker 1967) who moved from their home in northeastern Oregon in the Wallowa Mountain area in the spring first to the Willamette River Falls (at present-day Oregon City), where the salmon swam in hordes and were in prime condition, and then, as the run passed, to The Dalles-Celilo Falls section of the river upstream east of the Cascade Mountains. Some eventually went as far up the river as Kettle Falls. They might be in The Dalles-Celilo area for a couple of months if there was a good run. Families came on these expeditions and surplus salmon were dried for future use. This kind of movement of groups from within the Columbia drainage to these favorite fishing sites, that is, into the territory held by the permanent inhabitants of those stretches of the river, required the development of a system of intergroup relations to avoid conflict. Intergroup marriage, by which this problem was largely solved, resulted in the establishment of a system of far-ranging kinship ties. A system of trading partners also developed at some point in the history. Both the kin ties and the trading partners assured friendly relations among the various groups even though many came from distant points. Peaceful relations among the people who shared this ecosystem based on the salmon subsistence pattern was the price for survival. The culture, or parts of it, became an independent variable affecting the development of other elements for this system based on a particular environment to survive. I discuss this subject more at the close of Chapter 7.

Environment as Limiting and Permissive

The role of environment in culture history, as I see it, is limiting and permissive. Anthropologists reacted violently against the excessive claims of the environmental determinists such as Huntingdon and Semple. The violence of their reaction often carried them off the deep end in the opposite direction, and any influence of the environment was for all practical purposes denied or at least ignored. In most cases people do not have to exploit all the opportunities of the natural environment to survive, but the more fully they exploit them, the higher the standard of living *within the limits imposed by the environment*. The full exploitation of the resources of the Great Basin, which had been carried on for 10 millenia, could never raise the standard of living above a mere subsistence level, although within that region there were more favorable niches; I call them oases. At these oases were found the slight upward curves in the otherwise monotonous, almost horizontal curve of Great Basin prehistory. The Columbia River drainage, the Pacific Northwest Coast of British Columbia, the delta area of Central California, and the Santa Barbara Mainland-Channel Islands are examples of progressively richer environments with higher levels of potential exploitation. Yet each one set a limit on aboriginal exploitation, and in each case the limit had been probably reached by their native populations. All the shamans in the world acting in concert could never change the salmon runs, make the pine groves with their nuts grow in a new environment, or change the season for the ripening of the nuts and their harvest. Cultural development by innovation or diffusion will enable a people to exploit more fully—eventually to the limit—particular environments.

Fishing requires certain basic types of instruments and weapons and illustrates how similar problems may lead to similar solutions with no historic connection between the areas concerned. The wounded land animal can be tracked and eventually, with luck, be retrieved. In contrast, the quarry in the water has to be held by the weapon, which killed or wounded it, or be caught in a net. Otherwise the fisherman spends a lot of time in fruitless effort. The spear has to pierce the body of the fish either entirely or turn in the wound for the hunter to retrieve his quarry. The leister spear is an excellent example of the effort to solve this problem in the use of the spear. The toggling harpoon with the retrieval line represents the best solution. The upshot of all this is that in environments where fishing is a basic subsistence activity, people are all faced with the same problem the retrieval of the fish from the water. Since there are a limited number of ways of doing this, one could reasonably expect the development in the different environments, quite independently of one another, of at least some of the same kinds of instruments to solve the same kinds of problems. The environment provides the resource and the opportunity for cultural response, which has to be made in terms of the problem to be solved. I have discussed this matter at some length to make my position clear, lest anyone draw unwarranted conclusions from Chapters 7 and 8 that I border on being an environmental determinist. I am not, but I do assign a very large role to the environment at the time level of cultural development about which I am writing. The archæological record from the diverse environments in which I have worked permits me no other interpretation. As earthbound biological creatures, our ways of life (culture) can never fully escape coming to some modus vivendi with the natural environment, a basic concept of cultural-ecological study.

The Individual as Biological Variable

The biological variable in this trinity of man, culture, and environment is fundamentally the individual. The group has a sociological reality, but whatever biological character is assigned to it must be in the sense of a reservoir of reproducing and behaving individuals. A small, isolated group may provide the complete gene pool for the genetic endowment of a future population. The smaller the group the less representative the gene pool sample will be, and there will be a smaller distribution of genes in the total population. As there is a genetic basis for various observable physical traits, so there is a genetic basis for potential intelligence, however it may be defined. If small groups gradually spread throughout the vast area of the Far West, separated from others for long periods of time, genetic drift would have been effective in producing diverse physical types. If this is true for the observable physical traits, I see no reason to doubt that there would have been the same kind of effect operative at the intellectual level, and the results would reflect the change in character from the initial gene pool of the group. It would be reasonable to expect differences in adaptive capacity among groups until population increase and changed mating patterns restricted the process of drift. I know of no way of validating these hypotheses from the archæological record, but a positive answer must be considered a real possibility.

It is the individual who innovates, makes the artifact, gets an idea—in sum, reacts to the culture. He has to do this within the permissive limits of the group to which he belongs. The individuals making up an aboriginal group differed from one another, as do we, both in genetic traits and in learned capacities. There were individuals who could perform brilliantly, others who were bumblers; some who were hard workers, others lazy; some truthful, others liars; and so on.

Numerous studies in modern society have shown that the period of the highest rate of creativity in the lifetime of an individual is in the early thirties. This characteristic probably reflects the nature of the human life processes. I see no reason to believe that the period of creativity in the populations I am writing about was any different from that of modern man, except perhaps it might have been slightly earlier since the great increase in life expectancy of the people living under the Euro-American culture system is a product of developments in science, health care, and medicine. One must remember, too, that these populations were young, probably having a life expectancy of about twenty years. A person in his thirties would have been old but still close to his period of maximum creativity. There is no reason to doubt that the selective processes under the rigorous conditions of aboriginal life would have favored the superior; the more intelligent; the more observant; those more able to make sound, quick decisions; those physically stronger; those who had more resistance to infection; and those who had patience when needed. Individuals who had the ingenuity to devise and use new and superior implements and had ways to meet new challenges, if my thinking is sound, would have been the leaders within the groups by the very fact of their survival.

VARIABILITY IN SKILLS PRODUCES VARIABILITY IN PRODUCTS

Since individuals for the most part made their own tools and weapons, and since motor skills are not equally distributed through a population, it is reasonable to expect that within the general pattern considerable variation would occur in the finished product. Projectile points provide a good example. Any large collection from a given site and the same time level in the Far West can be expected to provide a variety of point forms. Consider the side-notched point. There are many variants classified depending on where the notch is placed, its shape, direction, etc. Types are set up based on these attributes and others, and some of them may be valid. Consideration of these types, however, leads me to believe that many represent the results of sloppy individual performance and differential skill in fabrication. This can be specially true where sloppy work is the rule, and it sometimes was. It may be that the archæologist is fabricating types when he should be describing the products of differential individual abilities and performance levels.

CULTURE—BOTH PERMISSIVE AND LIMITING ENVIRONMENT FOR INNOVATOR

The innovator may have little chance in some cultures for his novel product to be accepted. On the other hand, a culture may put a premium on innovation. Consider the projectile point again. The Clovis point is found in a series of sites with little or no change over a period of 500 years and without competitors. A projectile point must not only be able to pierce its target but must be capable of being fastened effectively to a shaft. Actually, the significant variation in kinds of points is in the devices for hafting. The fluting on the Clovis point was apparently a hafting device, and because of its long use without competitive forms, one may reasonably infer that it was fairly effective; however, apparently other effective methods were in use in adjacent western areas even earlier and at the same time as Clovis. It may be that the psychological orientation of the Clovis culture was inimical to innovation, but firm supporting evidence is lacking.

The Great Basin, cultures, by contrast, seem to have given a high priority to innovation. Even at the earliest periods there are multiple kinds of points at the same site. These people seem to have been keenly interested in developing more efficient methods of hafting; at least the evidence of variation in form of the proximal end of the point certainly suggests this inference. A method that worked was not discarded when a new one was developed but continued in use as though the people were experimenting with the effectiveness of variant forms. Hogup Cave (Aikens, Harper, and Fry 1970) gives a firm record of one type lasting 5,000 years with another introduced and used at the same time for 2,000 years. Other also were in use. The invention of the notched forms in the Great Basin provided the most effective hafting device; and various modifications were made on the basic form, some of which clearly improved hafting, while others can only be explained as the result of an expression of an individual desire to be different, for they seem to offer no improvement whatever to the effectiveness of hafting.

To survive the Great Basin, people had to exploit successfully all the resources of that hard environment. The long archæological record from this region makes this abundantly clear. I believe that exploitation of the Great Basin environment provided a stimulating atmosphere for the innovator, one in which the individual was constantly pressured by the nature of the life to attempt to devise more effective ways of adaptation (Cressman 1966a).

What I have just said needs to be qualified to this extent. There is the probability of a different attitude toward artifacts that had a definite adaptive function and those lacking it—for example, between a projectile point and a decorative device used on basketry. In the latter case innovation was encouraged, but not always exploited to the full potential. An example will illustrate this point. When I studied the many kinds of fine-twined basketry some thirty years ago, which I had excavated from the south-central Oregon caves, I discovered there were two ways of producing the same decorative device—that is, a continuous line of overlay on a weft row on the outer surface of the basket. The most common method, and on this basis I think it the older, was to use two strands of *Xerophyllum*, one on each of the weft strands, and twist them with the wefts as they crossed and enclosed the warps. This produced a continuous overlay surface on both the inside and outside of the basket. The basket maker thus had to manipulate and keep in proper positions four strands, the two binding weft strands and the two decorative strands, in addition to the proper positioning of the warps. The other method I discovered was used when it was desired to produce a full overlay on the outside surface for a distance of three or four warps, for example, for a chevron design. The method was a wrapped-twined overlay. Only one overlay strand was used and was brought up vertically on the inside of the basket between the warps, then down diagonally on top of the outside weft as it crossed the warp. The design on the outer surface of the basket did not indicate which method had been used.

Stratigraphic evidence showing which method was the earlier is lacking largely because of the fragmentary nature of much of the basketry and the cache origin of the large pieces. The internal evidence of the use of the two methods, as inferred from the examination of numerous specimens, strongly suggested that the wrapped-twining method was a later innovation which gained social acceptance when used for a limited end—for example, the application of certain designs under limited conditions—but beyond that was used only occasionally by some individual who saw the possibilities in the method and did not worry about conforming to social pressure.

I think one can make a reasonable guess as to what happened, and it would run something like this. The use of the wrapped-twined method of applying continuous overlay reduced the needed amount of *Xerophyllum* by half. Also short pieces, leftovers, could be used. The arduous trips to collect the overlay material could be reduced in number. Instead of having to control two weft strands and the corresponding overlay with the proper twist between each pair of warps, only one overlay strand was needed, and it could be handled more easily than two. I imagine some bright woman, who used her head to save her feet and hands, invented this method of wrapped-twined overlay as she sat with her friends gossiping and making baskets. Perhaps she aimlessly played with the strands, her hands manipulating them, as hands do by their very nature in being hands, in the "play function"; perhaps her play led her to "see what she could do." Perhaps she looked at "the problem," how to provide a continuous overlay in a simpler way than that customarily followed, and devised wrapped-twining as the answer. The new method was obviously a labor-saving device. Within the basketmaking tradition, however, its use was largely limited to the production of designs. Occasionally it was used to produce a single, continuous line of overlay, but I do not recall a case where it was used for a complete circuit, yet there was nothing to prevent this but social pressure. It was all right to be lazy and different for the small designs but not for the larger ones. Neither of the two methods really had any preferential adaptive value over the other. The choice of one or the other must have been the responsibility of the individual within the limits of custom.

An experience some ten years after reaching this conclusion from my study of the basketry provided at least strongly suggestive support for my hypothesis. I had taken my field party onto the Klamath Indian Reservation to observe a demonstration of basketmaking by one of the few Klamath Indian survivors skilled in this craft, a Mrs. Jackson, now deceased for some years. Mrs. Jackson was explaining what she did, why, and the kinds and sources of materials she used. She was applying a two-strand overlay when she came to the end of one of the overlay pieces. To insert a new strand and fasten the starting end securely was a fairly intricate process. She looked up at me from the chair on which she was sitting, smiled, and asked if I would mind if she used the "lazy woman" method of continuing. "Of course not," I replied. The "lazy woman" method she used was *wrapped-twined overlay*. She simply took the long overlay strand and shifted from the two-strand twining to the wrapped overlay. Her characterization of the method, and the attitude of slight embarrassment as she spoke to me, clearly indicated that while the method was in use, it had a somewhat lower status than the two-strand kind. An individual could use it, but it really "was not the thing to do" in applying continuous overlay on a single weft strand. Many years of study of Klamath prehistory and their basketry has convinced me that Klamath basketry is the lineal descendant of that excavated from caves in adjacent areas.

I do not suppose any culture has ever offered full freedom to the people who share it to innovate without restriction in all aspects. Certainly cultures differed in this respect. And as cultures differed, so did the role of the individual and the production of novel devices, whether material artifacts or intangible ideas. In our efforts to understand and explain culture history from the archæological record, these conditions, of course, bear directly on the question of independent invention or diffusion. At an early level of culture, with the pressures for survival bearing so heavily on a group, it is reasonable to suppose that the "crust of custom" was less thick than later when conditions of life were less pressing. If this is so, then a premium would have been set on individual achievement which would have aided the exploitative activities. Following this line of thinking and reflection on the results of my fieldwork, I have come to believe that independent invention was much more important in early cultural development than most archæologists are willing to concede. As I pointed out above, there are certain problems common to the fisherman, wherever he may be, that have common solutions, which could be arrived at by a reasonably intelligent individual without having to wait to see how some other fisherman, perhaps a thousand miles away, solved the problem.

We archæologists have an extremely limited view of the life of the people whose artifacts we recover. We do not know their myths, which validated their value systems, or the tales by which their imaginative life was given play in fantasy. We should not substitute our limited knowledge for their reality. That

there was more to their lives than just the struggle to survive is shown by the care men lavished on weapons, women on basketry, the humblest of household goods, and the ceremonial objects they made. I have excavated weapons as have other archæologists, which could only have been given their elegant finish to delight the beholder. The artistry lavished by the maker did not increase the lethal capacity of the weapon. And I have dug from the dirt and filth of caves fragments of exquisite basketry that give pleasure because of the skill with which the originals were made and the elegance of the decoration applied. Simple, woven, undecorated baskets would have served the housekeeping needs, but these people went beyond that and added intricacy of fabrication and imaginative designs to give pleasure to themselves and others.

MEANS, ENDS, AND "SO WHAT?"

The importance of keeping means and ends separate in any intellectual pursuit should be self-evident. Obviously they shift in the course of work and the end of a piece of research may be the means by which to attack another problem. Taxonomy and classification are but means of ordering data for analysis, a necessary step in the verification of hypothesis; yet much archæological writing seems to confuse means and ends by treating taxonomy as the desired end of archæological research—really as an end in itself. The results for understanding human behavior (except that of the taxonomist) are practically nil. Even when we verify a hypothesis that is not the end of the task; we archæologists have to ask, as W. F. Ogburn liked to insist for social scientists, "What of it?" or "And so what?" as Clyde Kluckhohn stated. All my life I have been trained to ask "What is the significance of this act, of this institution, etc., for man?" Kipling's "six honest serving-men" have served me well, if sometimes to my distress. This intellectual orientation—scepticism if you will—is a part of my life and is reflected in the pages that follow.

SPECULATION OR THEORIZING IN ARCHAEOLOGICAL STUDY

Speculation or theorizing in the proper sense, not engaging in fantasy, is basic to all scientific thought.

Kluckhohn (1940:44) emphasizing the importance of theorizing wrote:

> As for the distinction between theory and method, Goring has expressed this with singular felicity: ". . . we must pass to some extent from the strict and narrow confines of ascertained certainty into the wider latitudes of theory, where the laws which govern the imagination in the construction of ideas are more paramount than those which regulate the intellect in its analysis of facts. The interpreting of fact involves operations different and distinct from those by which facts are established—it involves work of synthesis and exposition, not of analysis and discovery."

Speculation, which I equate here with theorizing as just defined, is denigrated as an intellectual activity by the majority of my colleagues probably because it is not understood. If one is to reflect on the meaning of data (to try to answer the question "And so what?"), he cannot avoid speculation. It is the way he formulates new hypotheses and exploits his data for meaning. Speculative thinking is of particular importance in the field of human prehistory. The artifactual record is always limited and the functions, meanings, and uses of many artifacts are often conjectural. But the prehistorian draws from the fields of geology, biology, psychology, ethnology, and even the fine arts for the help he needs to give all possible meaning to his artifacts and their significance in the human experience. Obviously, one works here in the field of probability, for that is the character of life itself, and he has to proceed by the method "If x is true, then y follows." His conclusion must be stated as a probability only, for it then becomes a hypothesis subject to verification or disproof.

All human prehistory, all infrahuman history, and all earth history is at any given time an incomplete record. Any assertion that a situation is such and such can be only as valid as the data and the scientist's methods. On the basis of the evidence at a given time a certain conclusion may appear justified. The history of science, however, abundantly demonstrates that any "conclusion" on any matter where some of the evidence is still out can be nothing but a temporary statement of what the situation appears to be. New evidence forces a new statement. The previous "conclusion" has been transcended by new evidence, as Robert Oppenheimer put it. So interpretations of the course of human prehistory at a particular time must, because so much evidence is still "out," be considered as "Progress Reports" which may shortly be transcended by the discovery of new evidence. This study is such a report.

IMPORTANCE OF ORIGINAL DATA

I have quoted, in some cases at length, from scarce original documents and very frequently from various authors. I quote at length from Boas's studies of the physical characteristics of the living populations of western North America. There are two reasons for this: (1) the record is important for this study and paraphrasing would not improve it; and (2) the original reports made more than half a century ago are not readily accessible in the many institutions in which work in anthropology has developed within the last twenty years.

When a writer has stated an opinion or presented a statement of fact, I believe it incumbent on the one who reports his work to be accurate. The best way to do this is by a direct quotation of what the person wrote. It happens too often that a paraphrase of an original statement comes out as something different from the original. Whether intentional or unintentional the harm has been done. I have been victimized by this practice as have many others, if the often vitriolic exchanges that occur in the "Facts and Comments" sections of the professional journals are to be taken at face value. Therefore, I have chosen to let an author speak for himself or to give the reference which a reader may look up.

I have worked mostly from original data in this study. In some cases where a review article has been drawn on and perhaps quoted I have gone back to original studies on which the article was based. Where I am in disagreement with the interpretation I say so. Chapters 3 and 8 are cases in point. Within my lifetime the quantity of original data in archæology has increased from a relatively small amount, which any competent graduate student could control, to an extraordinary number of site reports, etc., which no student can familiarize himself with in the course of his graduate work. He, therefore, tends to rely on "authorities" or secondary and even tertiary sources as an economical method of acquiring needed information. Unfortunately, well-known "authorities" do not always report the work of others correctly. The graduate student who has relied on his "authority" is misled. So, in addition to having drawn my data from original sources when I quote an author, I then present accurately what he said.

This then is the conceptual frame of reference that has organized my thinking on the subject of this study and the reasons for certain formal aspects of presentation. Some of the concepts mentioned here will be discussed later in an effort to give greater clarity and effectiveness to the discussion. In the chapters that follow I first describe the environment and the changes through which it went during the period of potential occupation. This is followed by a discussion of first human arrivals in this environment (Chapter 4), followed by an examination of the evidence for the physical types of the living and nonliving populations (Chapter 5). The evidence from linguistic prehistory (Chapter 6) provides a record of both macro- and micro-population shifts. The processes of adaptation to the various environmental challenges are next discussed (Chapter 7), followed by an examination of archæological work and the present results in the different parts of the region (Chapter 8). Finally, some conclusions and observations that seem reasonable at the present time are proposed (Chapter 9).

The Land

Who can number the sand of the sea,
and the drops of rain, and the days of eternity?
Who can find out the height of heaven,
and the breadth of the earth, and the deep?

Ecclesiasticus 1:2–3

THE GENERAL geographic area encompassed by this study extends from the Continental Divide of the Rocky Mountains on the east to the Pacific Ocean on the west and from 57° north latitude to the Mexican border on the south. I have fixed the northern limit of discussion to include the Peace River as a potential route for communication between the Alberta Plains and the Canadian Cordillera of British Columbia.

Purists may question my use of this area as a unit for discussion but, in my opinion, it is justifiable for the following reasons. The area for the most part has a climate the origin of which is maritime, that is, derived from the Pacific winds. Of course the manifestations of climate vary with the landforms, elevation, and longitude and latitude. East of the Rocky Mountains in the interior of the continent, on the other hand, while Pacific maritime winds are sometimes influential, the climate is continental, with the major influences deriving from Canada and the Gulf of Mexico.

The western Cordilleran system in conjunction with the Pacific Ocean provides the other major feature that establishes this area as distinct from the rest of North America. The visible landforms in the West are for the most part younger than those east of the Rocky Mountain system. Great areas of the West are given their character by Pliocene and Pleistocene volcanism (Williams 1944), the events of Pleistocene glaciation with its concomitant pluvial conditions, and the disappearance of both. Probably the most striking feature of the western Cordilleran system is the line of magnificent peaks marking the skyline of the Cascade-Sierra mountains, remnants of the volcanism so important in the building of these ranges (Figure 1). It is a region of great diversity "where the Middle Pleistocene orogeny of the Coast Ranges, eustatic changes in sea level, block faulting in the Great Basin, Pleistocene desiccation, and volcanism have changed habitats more rapidly and drastically than in other parts of North America" (Taylor

1956:597). Yet, as anyone who has crossed the Rocky Mountains knows, there is a unity in the western environment that transcends this great diversity.

LAND FORMS

British Columbia

British Columbia (Map 1), except the northeastern portion, lies within the Canadian Cordillera (Holland 1964). The northeastern portion starting just south of the 55th parallel and lying between the 120th meridian and the Rocky Mountains is a part of the Alberta Plains. Holland, on the basis of three sets of factors, (1) process, (2) character of bedrock, and (3) orogenic or structural history, divides the cordilleran part of the province into three major physiographic subdivisions, (1) Western System, (2) Interior System, and (3) Eastern System.

The Western System "consists essentially of the mountainous mainland coast, but included within the System are a number of low-lying areas along the coast, as well as the mountains of Vancouver Island and of the Queen Charlotte Islands" (Holland 1964:28). The Coastal Trough, a low-lying depression partly submerged beneath the sea, lies between the Insular Mountains and the Coast Mountains* and in its southward extension runs through Washington as the Puget Depression (Map 2).

---

* The name Coast Mountains should not be confused with the Coast Range of the United States. Fenneman (1931:442n.) clarifies the Canadian usage: "Unfortunately the term 'Coast Range of British Columbia' has been applied to the mountains lying east of this trough [Hecate and Georgia depressions]. If the name were merely a descriptive term this would be suitable enough since they occupy the coast of the mainland, but the term 'Coast Range' has come to be understood as a proper name rather than a common noun. As such it should have been applied to the mountains of Vancouver Island in order to be consistent with custom which applies it to the much better known Coast Ranges of the United States. The mountains of British Columbia, while not a continuation of the Cascade Range, are closely related to it and not to the Coast Ranges."

FIGURE 1. Summit of the Cascade Mountains looking north from Bachelor Butte west of Bend, Oregon, showing characteristic volcanic peaks. On viewer's right is Broken Top with a small cirque glacier under the rim's center. On the left are the Three Sisters, South, Middle, and North in that order. *Photograph by author.*

The Interior System lies between the Coast Mountains and the Rocky Mountains and consists of a great diversity of landforms. Holland (1964:46) divides the Interior System west of the Rocky Mountain Trench for convenience of discussion into Northern Plateau and Mountain Area, Central Plateau and Mountain Area, and Southern Plateau and Mountain Area. The Southern Plateau lies south of the 55th parallel and comprises most of the area where we find the greatest amount of archæological information. "The Southern Plateau and Mountain Area includes large areas of plateau in central and southern British Columbia and the highlands and mountains in the southeastern part of the Province"

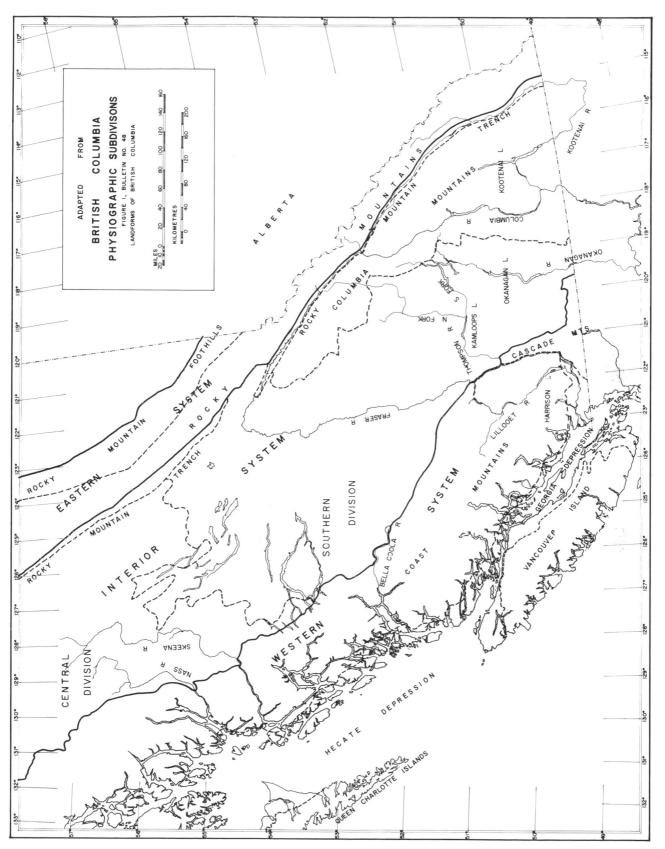

Map 1. Drainage and major mountain systems of British Columbia.

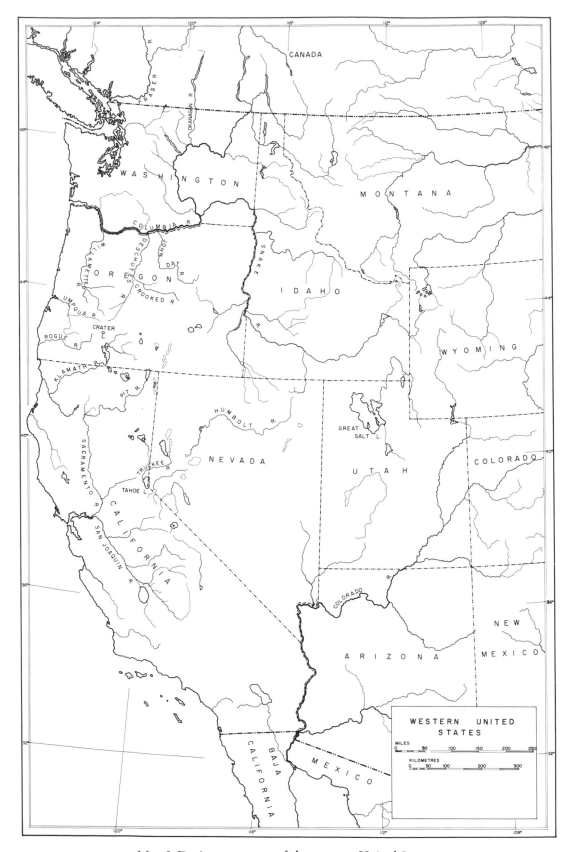

MAP 2. Drainage systems of the western United States.

(Holland 1964:46). "The Interior Plateau [of the Southern Plateau and Mountain Area] is almost entirely drained by the Fraser River and its tributaries; only minor drainage is to the Skeena, Peace, and Columbia Rivers" (Holland 1964:67).

The Rocky Mountain Trench completes the eastward extension of the Interior System for most of its length and is a remarkable topographic feature extending northwestward from the 49th parallel almost to the Liard River, a total distance of almost 900 miles. For the first 450 miles, from the Montana border to the McGregor River, the Rocky Mountain Trench is a continuous, somewhat sinuous valley lying between the Columbia Mountains on the west and the Rocky Mountains on the east. This valley is from 2 to 10 miles wide and is occupied by the southward-flowing Kootenay River, northward-flowing Columbia River, southward-flowing Canoe River, and northward-flowing Fraser River. The divides between the headwaters of these rivers are low. In this southern stretch, the eastern wall of the trench is the western front of the Rocky Mountains and the western wall of the trench is the eastern front of the Columbia Mountains.

> At the McGregor River, however, the line of the Rocky Mountains is breached, and the bold mountain front on the eastern side of the trench is offset about 14 miles northeast. At the same place the western wall of the trench disappears, and the trench merges in the Fraser Basin at an elevation of 2,000 feet. . . .
>
> The northern half of the Rocky Mountain Trench begins on the north side of the McGregor River, at the divide between James Creek and the Parsnip River, and continues northwestward to the point where, at the junction of the Kechika and Turnagain Rivers, the trench merges in the Liard Plain. . . .
>
> The trench is a structurally controlled erosional feature. . . . It developed as an erosional form during the Tertiary by streams whose courses were antecedent to the building of the Rocky Mountains. They were antecedent also to the uplift of the mountains on the western side of the trench. The erosion of the trench was completed by the end of the Pliocene. It was occupied by ice and its form modified, but the main effect of glacial occupation was the derangement of previously established drainage systems. The streams became established in their present courses with the waning of the ice, and during the postglacial period have incised themselves to varying depths into the deeply drift-filled floor of the trench (Holland 1964:65–66).

The Eastern System consists of the Rocky Mountains lying between the Rocky Mountain Trench on the west and the interior plains of central Canada on the east.

> The Rocky Mountains on the east are flanked by the Rocky Mountain Foothills, and . . . extend in a northwesterly direction along the eastern side of the Province for 850 miles between the 49th parallel and the Liard River. . . . The Rocky Mountains are underlain very largely by sedimentary and metamorphic rocks, which range from Proterozoic to Cretaceous in age. The youngest rocks are exposed in the foothills, and progressively older rocks lie to the west (Holland 1964:83–84).

The United States

The Cordilleran area of the United States is characterized by high relief (Map 3). "Three mountain ranges, the Rocky, the Cascade-Sierra, and the Coast Ranges, running roughly parallel to one another, are dominating features" (Cressman et al. 1960:9). The Coast Range bears southeastward, but in Southern California the trend is nearly west to east. Between the Rocky and Cascade-Sierra ranges lies the Intermontane Region, while the Coast Range is separated from the Cascade-Sierra by the Puget-Willamette Trough in Washington and Oregon and the great Central Valley in California. The Coast Range in much of its extent drops steeply to the Pacific shoreline. The coast is marked by spectacular sea cliffs, sandy beaches, and in some places a narrow coastal plain never more than a mile or two in width.

> *The Cascade-Sierra* mountain range consists in the Sierras mostly of Mesozoic igneous intrusives while their northern neighbors, the Cascades, are Tertiary and Quaternary volcanics. The Cascade-Sierra skyline is rugged and beautiful. Extinct volcanic peaks, many 3,000 m. [9,870 feet] high and some more than 1,000 m. [3,290 feet] higher, stand out starkly against the sky. The lower western slopes are mostly covered by rain forest while the eastern side supports yellow pine. The east slope of the Cascades extends gently to the high lava plateau while that of the Sierras ends abruptly with the fault escarpment [Figures 2-5] (Cressman et al. 1960:10).

The Cascade Range is divided physiographically into northern, central, and southern divisions (Fenneman 1931).

> The Coast Range mountains are mostly deformed Tertiary sedimentaries and volcanics with some Mesozoic meta-

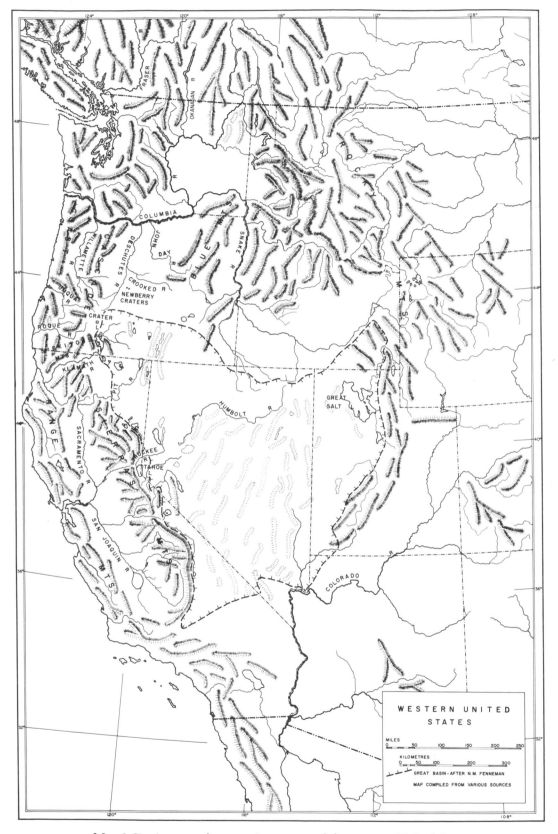

MAP 3. Drainage and mountain systems of the western United States.

FIGURE 2. The Cascade Mountains slope gently to the plateaus on the east. View southwest from Smith Rocks six miles north of Redmond, Deschutes County, Oregon, and three miles east of U.S. 97. Against the skyline from the right (north) are the North, Middle, and South Sister, Broken Top, and Bachelor Butte, all volcanic remnants. Airline distance from Smith Rocks to South Sister is about forty miles. Elevation of South Sister is 10,354 feet, and the plain at the base of Smith Rocks about 3,000 feet; Crooked River at lower left. Compare this with Figures 4 and 5. *Oregon State Highway, Travel Division Photograph #6067.*

morphics in the south. The highest point of the Coast Range, Mount Olympus, slightly more than 2,000 m. in elevation [6,580 feet], is a part of the Olympic uplift in northwestern Washington. Elsewhere the elevations run little more than 300 m. [987 feet] with occasional peaks extending slightly over 1,500 m. [4,935 feet] (Cressman et al. 1960:10).

The Intermontane Region is divided structurally into three subdivisions, the south centering on the Colorado drainage, the Great Basin in the center, and the Columbia River drainage system in the north. The rock system of the south consists in the main of (a) Pre-Cambrian intrusives, (b) Late Tertiary and Quaternary sedimentaries, and (c) some Tertiary igneous intrusives. It is an area of marked faulting. The early sedimentaries give rise to the characteristic mesa-arroyo topography. In the Great Basin, which extends approximately from 35° to 43° N latitude, there are (a) Late Tertiary and Quaternary sedimentaries, and (b) some intrusive igneous rocks. The region is characterized by north-south orographic features, aridity, extremes of temperature, and interior drainage. The

FIGURE 3. City of Bend, Deschutes County, Oregon, on U.S. 97. The elevation is 3,628 feet, and the Three Sisters and Broken Top are against the skyline to the west. Distance from Bend to South Sister is about twenty-three miles. View slightly north of west. *Oregon State Highway, Travel Division Photograph #5432.*

Columbia River drainage system consists mostly of (a) Tertiary volcanics, and (b) Mesozoic intrusives in the north extending into Canada. Volcanism occurred also in the post-Pleistocene (Libby 1955). This is the region of the great flows of Columbia River basalt. Extending like a great channel across Idaho is the Snake River Downwarp in the basalts extending to the headwaters of the Snake River (Cressman et al. 1960:10).

The Rocky Mountains, which form the eastern boundary of my area of discussion, need no further physiographic description than that given by Holland above for the Canadian portion of the range.

DRAINAGE PATTERNS

British Columbia

The Fraser River and its tributaries provide the most significant drainage system in British Columbia (Map 1) for the study of the prehistory of the region. The drainage basin is 89,310 square miles in extent entirely within the province, and almost all of it lies in the southern section (Southern Division) of the Interior System. Total length of the Fraser River is 850 miles.

"The Fraser River rises at Moose Lake in the Park (Main) Ranges of the Rocky Mountains, flows northwestward to the Rocky Mountains at Jackman [ca. 30 miles] and [north] along the Trench to Sinclair Mills [ca. 120 miles]. . . . Thence it swings around the north end of the Cariboo Mountains and flows southward through the Fraser Basin and Fraser Plateau" (Holland 1964:109).

Navigation of the upper Fraser was possible for about 100 miles south of Prince George. Thereafter its course followed deeply incised gorges and can-

FIGURE 4. The Sierra Nevada Mountains, in sharp contrast to the Cascade, terminate on the east in a marked escarpment. A characteristic scene on U.S. 395 in Nevada where the highway runs along the base of the escarpment. *Nevada State Highway Department Photograph*.

yons of the Fraser Plateau and the Coast Mountains, eventually turning southwest at Hope through the Fraser River canyon and the Fraser Lowland to the Strait of Georgia at the city of Vancouver.

In 1793 Alexander Mackenzie, seeking an overland route to the Pacific, went down the Fraser thinking it was the Columbia approximately to the junction of Narcosli Creek with the Fraser. On the advice of the Indians he met, that the Fraser was too difficult to traverse and that they followed an overland trail to the coast, he retraced his route and with Indian guides turned west along West Road River and followed the trail to the Bella Coola River and tidewater. This was the "grease trail" from the coast to the interior along which moved aboriginal trade, especially eulachon oil. How long it had been established is unknown.

In 1808 Simon Fraser, also thinking that he was on the Columbia River, followed the river to its mouth and returned, after incredible hardships, convinced by the bearings he took at the sea that the river was not the Columbia and also that it was unnavigable

(Sheppe 1962). His name was justifiably given the river.

Everywhere in the Interior Plateau south of the Peace River drainage, except for a small area of the Coast Mountains drained by the Bella Coola, the Skeena, and the Nass rivers to the Pacific and the limited drainage of the Columbia River and its two main tributaries, the drainage of the vast area of mountain and plateau was to the Fraser (Map 1).

The North Thompson River starts in the Columbia Mountains just south of the origin of the Fraser and flows in a general southerly direction to Kamloops Lake. This lake is drained by the Thompson River flowing west, then south to join the Fraser at Lytton. The Thompson and its confluents form the main drainage network of the Southern Division of the Interior System, and this made the Thompson of great importance in the movements of aboriginal peoples.

Other rivers of importance in the archæological picture in the Coast Mountains are the Lillooet, Bella Coola, Skeena, Nass, and Stikine. While all but the

FIGURE 5. A dramatic photograph of the Sierra escarpment (compare with Figure 3); Lake Tahoe at top and Carson City, Nevada, at bottom. The elevation of Lake Tahoe is 6,225 feet and Carson City is 4,660 feet. The airline distance from Lake Tahoe to Carson City is about six miles. Carson City, hemmed in by the desert on the east and the Sierras on the west, has to spread north and south, the same as the aboriginal line of movement. *Nevada State Highway Department Photograph.*

first start on the east side of the Coast Mountains, the drainage areas are comparatively small except for the Stikine. Their archæological importance lies in the fact that they breached the mountain barrier between the coast and the interior and thus offered means of communication between these areas. The aboriginal trade routes along these rivers show their importance in the prehistory of the coastal and interior areas.

A relatively small southeastern part of the interior is drained by the Columbia and Okanagan rivers with their tributaries. The Okanagan, flowing south from Lake Okanagan, crosses the international boundary and empties into the Columbia in north-central Washington (Map 2).

The main line of contact between the southern interior and the Columbia River drainage in the

United States seems to have been from the Kamloops Lake area to Lake Okanagan and then south on and along the Okanagan River to the Columbia. Following Simon Fraser's exploration of the Fraser in 1808, the Northwest Company established a route to the Columbia by canoe down the Fraser to Alexandria (approximately the point at which Mackenzie turned back), then overland to Lake Okanagan, and by canoe or boat from there down the Okanagan River to the Columbia. Since the routes of these explorers usually followed those used by Indians who were their guides, it is reasonable to conclude that the overland route of the Northwest Company closely approximated that of the Indians.

It should not be inferred from these remarks that the Fraser River was not used as a route to the coast by the Indians; however, the Fraser was not the main route from the coast into the interior. Jenness (1932: 351) writes: "The Lillooet were the westernmost of the five Interior Salish tribes, and the chief intermediaries in the trade with the coast people. . . ." He places them in the Lillooet River valley. The Lillooet were neighbors of fellow Salish speakers, the Thompson and Shuswap, and of the Athapascan-speaking Chilcotin on the north. The Shuswap controlled the Fraser River valley from Lillooet to Alexandria and east to the Rocky Mountains. The Thompson were on the Fraser from Yale to Lillooet and eastward on the Thompson to Ashcroft. Okanagan Indians occupied the lake and river of that name. The Lillooets, with an easier route over the Coast Range and a contact with the tribes controlling the interior along the main drainage systems, were thus in a most advantageous position to develop their role as middlemen, possibly via Harrison Lake to the lower Fraser River.

This drainage pattern of the Interior System, with access routes to the Plains and the Pacific together with the aboriginal trade routes adjusted to it, outlines the interior areas significant for the country's prehistory. The coastal area will be discussed as a separate section.

The Columbia Plateau

The drainage system of the Columbia River, which controls all the intermontane area north of the Great Basin (Maps 2 and 3), is described as follows:

[The] Columbia River rises in Columbia Lake, British Columbia, Dominion of Canada, and flows northwesterly parallel to the Rocky Mountains about 191 miles, then turns southward and flows about 271 miles to the international boundary, whence, in its course of about 745 miles in the United States, it flows generally southward across the State of Washington, skirting the Columbia Plateau on the northwest and west, to the Washington-Oregon state line, thence generally westward about 310 miles along the state line, passing through the Cascade and Coast Ranges, to its mouth at the Pacific Ocean near Astoria, Oregon. The river and its tributaries drain an area of 259,000 square miles consisting of rugged north-south trending mountain ranges separated by valley troughs and trenches, and the Columbia Plateau. The latter, formed by successive lava flows, is a great, generally treeless, semi-arid plateau covering over 100,000 square miles in the central portion of the basin and extending southerly beyond the basin boundary. About 39,500 square miles of the basin area lies in Canada. Elevations in the basin range from 8,500 to nearly 14,000 feet above sea level in the Rocky Mountain system on the east; 2,000 to 6,500 feet in the eastern valleys; 2,000 to 4,000 feet over the Columbia Plateau; 6,000 to 8,000 feet in the Cascade Range, with some summits exceeding 12,000 feet; sea level to 500 feet on the floor of the Puget Trough between the Cascade and Coast Ranges; and 2,000 to 4,500 feet in the Coast Range at the western edge of the basin. Stream slopes are steep in the mountain reaches and in canyons where the streams cut through mountain ranges [Figure 6]. Through valley reaches the slopes are relatively gentle and in the northern portion of the basin the streams flow through numerous lakes. The total fall of the main Columbia River from its source to the ocean is 2,652 feet but its major upper tributaries have much greater fall. The lower 140 miles of the river is tidal.

. . . Principal tributaries to the Columbia River and their drainage areas are, in downstream order: Kootenai River, 19,300 square miles; Clark Fork–Pend Oreille River, 25,960 square miles; Spokane River, 6,640 square miles; Yakima River, 5,970 square miles; Snake River, 109,000 square miles; and Willamette River, 11,200 square miles. Snake River, the largest tributary, drains the southeastern portion of the basin extending from northwestern Wyoming across Idaho, with small areas in northern Utah and Nevada, to eastern Oregon and southeastern Washington. It contributes slightly more than one-fifth of the mean annual run-off of the Columbia River. Kootenai and Clark Fork-Pend Oreille Rivers drain the northeastern section of the basin in Canada, Montana, northern Idaho, and northeastern Washington, contributing together an average annual run-off about equal to that of Snake River (United States Army Corps of Engineers 1952 1: 8–9).

FIGURE 6. The Columbia Plateau, Oregon. In the Columbia Plateau of north-central Oregon the rivers have incised deep canyons. The confluence of the Crooked and Deschutes rivers about ten miles southwest of Madras, Jefferson County, Oregon; Crooked River comes in from the viewer's left; depth of the canyon is from 800 to 1,000 feet. The view is southwest, and the Three Sisters can be seen against the skyline. An occupied cave on the west bank of the Deschutes just out of this photograph, upriver, produced a C-14 date of more than 8,000 years ago. The canyons are now occupied by the Round Butte hydroelectric dam. *Photograph by the author.*

The Great Basin

South of the Columbia Plateau is the Basin and Range Province lying between the Cascade-Sierra range on the west and the middle Rocky Mountains and the Colorado Plateau on the east. The province extends into Mexico. "Topographically it is distinguished by isolated, roughly parallel mountain ranges separated by desert basins, generally almost level" (Fenneman 1931:326). In the Great Basin, occupying most of the northern part of the province, drainage usually leads to enclosed basins but not always. The problem of drainage in the Great Basin is complicated by the different bases used to define it, physiographic and hydrographic. If the latter basis is used then the Pit River drainage of northeastern California and the Klamath Lake Basin of Oregon must be excluded. I use the physiographic basis for definition of the Great Basin in this study and thus include both the Pit River drainage and the Klamath Basin.

Klamath Lake at the eastern edge of the Cascade Range in southern Oregon is fed by the Williamson and Sprague rivers from the north and east and numerous springs and streams from the foot of the escarpment marking the eastern side of the lakes. Other smaller sources contribute water from the bordering Cascade Range. The Klamath River drains Klamath Lake and flows through the Cascade Range in southern Oregon, then across northwestern California to the Pacific Ocean. Its course follows deep canyons in many places, but it is easily traversable on foot. Archæological evidence (Cressman 1956b) shows that salmon ascended this river to spawn before the channel was obstructed by power dams.

The Pit River in northeastern California flows through the Sierra Nevada range into the Sacramento River in the area now occupied by the eastern arm of the Shasta Dam reservoir. Since the drainage area of the Pit River has an arid climate, the river's volume is not large. The Pit River has potential archæological significance because from time to time Goose Lake, a Great Basin lake of south-central Oregon and California, overflowed into it and thus had an outlet to the sea. Fenneman (1931:350) states that overflow occurred in 1869, and the structural features in the area indicate that the same kind of event occurred from time to time in the past.

The Colorado River Drainage Area

South of the Great Basin, in the Basin and Range Province relevant to this discussion, all drainage flows to the Colorado River (Map 2) and thence to the Gulf of California. The arid climate of the area precludes much runoff although, as in the Great Basin, during periods of climatic amelioration the precipitation was greater than now with consequent improvement of the habitat, as Ventana Cave and other archæological sites demonstrated.

The Coastal Trough of British Columbia

This is the Canadian section (Map 1) of the great depression between the Cascade-Sierra Nevada and the Coast ranges and extends from the southern end of the Central Valley of California into Alaskan waters, being interrupted only by the uplift of the Trinity and Klamath mountains of California and Oregon respectively. The Canadian Coastal Trough is distinctive in having its western side open to the sea except for the stretches occupied by Vancouver Island and the Queen Charlotte Islands where the continuation of the Coast Range appears as the

Insular Mountains. The trough's eastern side is formed by the Coast Mountains, related to the Cascade Mountains of the United States. The shoreline is essentially a glacially sculptured fiord coast protected in part from the open sea by Vancouver Island and the Queen Charlotte Islands. Numerous small islands close to the shoreline provide sheltered areas for human habitation. The mountainous eastern side is breached by the rivers mentioned above (pp. 17–19) that, with the exception of the Fraser River, flow into quiet fiords many miles from the open sea. Small rivers rise on the western flanks of the mountains to flow directly or indirectly into the sea. The Coastal Trough, with its rich marine and land fauna, its multiple access to the Interior Plateau via its transmontane flowing rivers, its many favorable sites for human settlement, and its equable maritime climate, is distinctive in the trough system and represents one of the most favorable human habitats in the far-western region.

The Puget Trough

The Puget Trough in Washington consists of Puget Sound and the adjacent lowlands between the sound and the Cascade Mountains. Some 35 to 40 miles south of the sound is an area of low relief which directs the course of the rivers to the Columbia River. The Skagit River, flowing from just across the international border south then west to the sound just north of the 48th parallel, is one of the potentially important rivers connecting the Puget Sound region with interior British Columbia. A series of other rivers rising in the western slopes of the Cascades follow short courses to the sound. The Coast Range and the Olympic Mountains provide drainage to the sound from the west. The courses of these rivers, like those from the western drainage of the Coast Mountains in British Columbia and those in the extension of the Puget Depression in Oregon (the Willamette Valley) and the Interior Valley of California, are short, rising in the nearby source mountains, but they provide, in at least some cases, access to passes for transmontane communication.

The Skagit River provided access to both British Columbia and the Okanagan Valley in Washington east of the Cascades and thence to the Columbia River. The Snoqualmie leads from the sound east to the Yakima drainage and on to the Columbia. The Lewis, Cowlitz, and Chehalis rivers, in that order from east to west, provided access between the Columbia River and the northward drainage to southern Puget Sound.

The Oregon part of the Puget Trough is the Willamette Valley drained by the Willamette River. It is fed by a series of short tributaries arising in the mountains on either side and flows into the Columbia at Portland. The lower 15 miles below the falls at Oregon City is almost like an extension of the Columbia as far as aboriginal use was concerned. On the east, passage over the Cascade Mountains was facilitated by the Santiam River and farther south by the headwater course of the Willamette River. At the time of white contact the Klamath Indians had a well-established line of communication by this route into the Willamette Valley. Passage to the south was relatively easy over the low divide into the Umpqua drainage, and in that area hunting and trading parties from the Willamette Valley came into contact with Indians from the Rogue River in the south and those from the coast. From the lower Willamette Valley access to the coast was up the Tualatin and Yamhill rivers and down the Trask or Nestucca rivers to the Tillamook Bay area.

The Willamette Valley is separated from the northern end of the Central Valley of California by the Klamath Mountains extending from the Cascade-Sierra range on the east to the Pacific Ocean on the west. Their approximate north-south extent is from 43° north to 40° north latitude. Two rivers, the Umpqua in the northern part of this region and the Rogue some 30 miles north of the Oregon-California border, have their sources near the Cascade Range summit and flow to the Pacific Ocean. Both of these rivers provided potential routes from east of the Cascades to the sea, and this potential was used in aboriginal times.

The California Trough

The California Trough (Central Valley) is a "low fluviatile plain" (Fenneman 1931, map, Physical Divisions of the United States). The northern portion of the trough forms the Sacramento Valley which is drained by the Sacramento River. South from latitude 40° north to where it flows into San Francisco

Bay, this river meanders broadly over the plain and has built up natural levees. The landscape as San Francisco Bay is approached "assumes the character of a composite delta built by streams from the north, south, and east" (Fenneman 1931:474). The rivers from the Sierra Nevada Mountains—the Feather and the American with others of less importance—are the main contributors to the Sacramento.

The southern part of the trough, the San Joaquin Valley, is drained by the San Joaquin River. It is similar to the Sacramento except for the effects of the greater aridity of the area, a condition resulting in overloading the river with silt; therefore, it winds and braids and is attended by a broad belt of swamps in much of its course, which is determined by the meeting of the slopes of the alluvial fans from each side of the valley. Since the confluent streams from the Sierras are stronger than those from the Coast Range, they have laid down larger alluvial fans than those on the western side, and the course of the river was pushed toward the west. There are no perennial streams flowing from the Coast Range into the San Joaquin River (Fenneman 1931:*passim*). As the river approaches its confluence with the Sacramento it forms a vast delta.

The southern portion of the San Joaquin Valley is the Tulare Basin. This basin is formed by the alluvial fan of Kings River which has cut off drainage to the San Joaquin. Tulare Lake is formed by Kings River, and farther south the alluvial fan of the Kern River obstructs the drainage and Buena Vista and Kern lakes are formed. All these lakes lack external drainage. The tributaries of the Kings and Kern rivers form numerous sloughs and swamps.

The Coast

The situation along the British Columbia coast has been discussed above (p. 21).

In general, the rivers along the Pacific Coast of the United States may be discussed as a unit. Those that arise in the Coast Range are generally short with drowned mouths, tides extending upstream 10 to 15 miles; however, from Bandon, Oregon, south into Northern California the rivers are not drowned, at least not to the same extent as the northern ones. In the Klamath Mountains the situation differs from that in the Coast Range proper. In the Coast Range in California, the Eel and Russian rivers differ from the usual transverse flowing Coast Range type in that they flow for long distances, the former north and the latter south, in north-south trending valleys before reaching the sea.

The short, seaward flowing Coast Range rivers, often separated from each other by exceedingly rough terrain covered by rain forest, provided the major settlement opportunities for the Indians of the coast. A settlement would generally occupy both sides of the river's mouth, and the pattern of movement was upriver into the mountains. Along the more rugged coastline this settlement pattern resulted in isolation of groups. When the coast was more open, as along the northern Oregon and southern Washington coastlines, movement was freer. Canoes could be launched more readily in the surf off sandy beaches than from rocky headlands. The linguistic distribution of the coastal inhabitants is clear evidence of the environmental influences I have, just briefly, pointed out. This discussion is a brief overview of the far-western environment in its present state. During the millennia of human occupation, many changes occurred affecting the quality of the environment as a human habitat and providing the geological sequence of events we now use to formulate a chronological system. There were climatic changes that produced glaciation and deglaciation, pluvial lakes and arid lake beds, and extensive coastal plains and land connections between separated land masses; and there were one-time events limited areally in their effects such as volcanism and catastrophic floods. These changes, their effects on the environment as habitat, and their use as time indicators will be discussed next.

Time and the Land

The years like great black oxen tread the world
And God, the herdsman, goads them on behind.

W. B. Yeats, The Countess Cathleen

MY MAJOR concern in this chapter will be the quality of our present chronological system since any study of culture history and cultural processes of adaptation requires a reliable method for the archæologist to use in ordering his data. The preservation of archæological evidence in the earth, not in a library or in the mind of living man, forces the archæologist to order his data chronologically by relating it to the geological frame of reference in which it is found. Thus the archæologist is forced to rely to a very large extent on the temporal dating sequences developed by geologists, and the accuracy of the archæologist's dating, in the absence of valid C-14 data, depends on the accuracy of the chronological systems of the geologists available to him. The record shows, however, wide differences of opinion among geologists on matters crucial to the formulation of a sound chronological system. The archæologist must critically examine the conflicting opinions and form his own as best he can.

GEOCHRONOLOGY

Two methods are available to establish the temporal occurrence of events: the calendrical system, with which we are familiar in the form of the Christian calendar, a man-made artifact, limited essentially to the period of recorded history, and the geochronological method. The latter is independent of the Christian calendar and may be stated in some such manner as "years before the present" or B.P. These results may be calibrated with the Christian calendar, but such calculations are not necessary and perhaps are even inadvisable when peoples of different religions are making use of the data.

The geochronological method on which the prehistorian must rely is constructed from information derived from the physical and natural sciences. When the word geochronology was first used late in the nineteenth century, it referred only to an orderly placement of geological events as demonstrated by the geologic column. The "law of superposition" stated that the age of the strata was determined by their primary position in the geologic column; the lowest formation is the earliest and each succeeding overlying one is respectively younger. Zeuner (1950: 5) changed the concept from a strictly geological one and pointed out that "geochronology employs methods which are derived from the physical and natural sciences."

> At the University of Arizona, geochronology is given the definition of being a field of study encompassing *all scientific methods which can be applied to the dating of terrestrial events*. These include events of anthropomorphic as well as geomorphic origin. . . . Purely terrestrial events which are either prehistoric or unrecorded can never be "dated" in the strict sense of the word, but may rather be placed in a bracket of time during which they could have occurred (Smiley 1955:9).

Examples of the last are Upper Pleistocene, Third Interglacial, Radiocarbon Age, etc.

The chronological problems, however, of the geologist and archæologist are different in that they involve utterly different magnitudes of time. The geologist deals with periods of hundreds of thousands and millions of years, while the Old-World prehistorian only with some hundreds of thousands of years at the most, and in the New World only now is the firm human record being pushed beyond 12,000 or 15,000 years ago. The archæologist is thus forced to have a critical interest in smaller units of time. Small units of possibly major significance to the archæologist are lost in the great time intervals of the geologists' interest. It is a working assumption of geology that significant events, such as waxing and waning of a glaciation, were contemporaneous throughout the world—"an assumption that, while not correct, is sufficiently so for indicating the approximate scale of the phenomenon" (Smith 1937: 90).

Glaciological theory holds, and field evidence validates it, that growth and decline of different glaciers is not synchronous and that a single ice sheet may be advancing in one area while retreating in another. The causes of the variation are meteorological—differences in precipitation, in altitude and latitude of the source ice, in temperature, in topography, etc. Since these effective factors are not the same for any given period of time over the whole continent, distinct regional variations may reasonably be expected in such phenomena as time of maximum expansion, beginning and rates of expansion and retreat, and oscillations in these movements. Such variations, in the main, account for the exceptions to the "assumption" mentioned immediately above. It is, therefore, a hazardous method to assign a chronology, or a particular event in glacial history, to one area by extrapolating from another area of a quite different kind. Firm evidence for the local occurrence and date of a phenomenon, such as a short warm interval, must be derived from pertinent field study and reliable C-14 dating, if possible, and not by extrapolation from broad generalizations of continental scope. The relatively short period of human prehistory in the New World and the necessity for precise dates to order events require the archæologist to work within the demonstrated variability in time and space of geological phenomena rather than according to the general working "assumptions" of the geologists.

The need for a more refined method of dating by both the prehistorian and the Pleistocene geologist was met by the development of *radiocarbon dating* by W. F. Libby (1952) in the late 1940s. This method is limited in its use to specimens containing carbon that have lived within the last 40,000 years. Since Libby's important discovery, various relatively precise methods of dating geological and archæological events have been developed based on the phenomena of thermoluminescence, fission tracks, K:Ar (potassium-argon), obsidian hydration, and paleo- and archæomagnetism. (The interested reader is referred to Michael and Ralph 1971.) Because the radiocarbon method of dating has been the one most widely used by archæologists and geologists studying events within the last 40,000 years in the Far West (as elsewhere), it is worthwhile to review here several considerations important in the evaluation of given C-14 dates.

Carbon has three principal isotopes, C-12, C-13, and C-14. Each has the same number of protons, 6, but differs in the number of neutrons, having 6, 7, and 8 respectively. The sum of the number of protons and neutrons identifies the particular isotope. The C-14 isotope is formed when a neutron, produced by primary cosmic rays entering our atmosphere, reacts with a nitrogen atom (7 protons and 7 neutrons) by "knocking out" a proton from the nitrogen nucleus to produce an atom consisting of 6 protons and 8 neutrons or C-14.

C-12 and C-13 are stable, not disintegrating radioactively, but C-14 is unstable and disintegrates by releasing an electron, called a beta ray, from its nucleus, while one of the excess neutrons is converted into a proton to produce the nitrogen atom of 7 protons and 7 neutrons. The C-14 in the atmosphere is absorbed through the carbon cycle. When the organism dies, assimilation of carbon ends and the C-14 atoms in the organism continue to disintegrate with total intensity that is proportional to the number of C-14 atoms present; this is determined by the measurement of the beta-ray emissions. Thus the larger the number of C-14 atoms present, the more intense will be the beta-ray emission. The rate of disintegration is expressed by the "halflife" concept, that is, the period of time required for half the number of atoms remaining at any given time to disintegrate. The "halflife" of C-14 is 5,570 years*—so 5,570 years after the death of the organism half of the C-14

---

* The early studies of the halflife of the C-14 isotope resulted in a range of values. Libby (1952) calculated the weighted mean, 5,568±30, of three values, one derived by his laboratory and one by each of two others, as the value most nearly reflecting the true halflife. He emphasized the need for further studies. These studies have indicated a more accurate halflife is 5,730 years. Thus all dates calculated from the 5,568 year halflife are too young by a factor of 1.03. Obviously there had arisen a problem of which date to use. If the new value was used then there would be a discrepancy between all dates calculated from the earlier value and from the later value. To resolve this problem the Sixth Radiocarbon Dating Conference at Pullman, Washington, in 1965 decided to continue the use of the original halflife value to avoid confusion. All calculated and published dates, unless otherwise indicated, are based on the 5,568 value (frequently given as 5,570). Anyone can make the correction to the true date by multiplying the calculated value by 1.03. Also the base year from which all dates are calculated is A.D. 1950; thus 1950 is the base year indicated by the "Present" in a

atoms will have distintegrated and half of the remainder will disintegrate in the next 5,570 years and so on. Thus the C-14 content of the sample, as a percentage of the modern standard in living organisms, may be translated into an estimated age, the number of C-14 years ago the organism died.

The C-14 date is an estimated date of the sample. The age value always is given with what is called the standard error, that is, a measure of the reliability of the sample. Thus a reading of 7,000±150 means that the chances are about 67 out of 100 that the estimated date, 7,000±150 (that is ± one standard error), includes the true date. Increasing the time bracket to two standard errors would increase the chances for the inclusion of the correct date to about 95 percent.

Radiocarbon dating has been the most important geochronological technique for archæologists, but nevertheless must be used with caution. Not all organic materials are equally satisfactory for dating; possibility of contamination exists both in the field and in the laboratory, and there is the problem of being certain that the dated sample is actually the same age as the event which it is used to date. J. C. Vogel of the famous Groningen Laboratory has commented as follows on C-14 dating:

> In the age range under discussion [>30,000 years], small quantities of recent carbon in the sample cause great changes in the apparent age. For instance, if the true age of a sample is 37,000 years it still contains 1 per cent of its original C-14, and the addition of only 1 per cent by weight of recent carbon is enough to make it appear nearly 6,000 years too young. Experience shows that contamination of this magnitude frequently occurs—in the form of rootlets and infiltrated humic substance—and it is not surprising to find considerable spread to younger values in different samples of the same age. As results accumulate, however, the dates can be expected to cluster about a certain maximum value which will then represent the true age of the event being dated.
>
> It thus follows that correlations based on only a few dates, without due consideration of the nature of the samples, will be liable to error. . . .
>
> It has been mentioned above that not all materials give radiocarbon dates of equal reliability. Large pieces of well

preserved wood and charcoal (in the strict sense, i.e., charred wood) give the best (oldest) results while all other types of material are to be considered suspect. The reason is that wood and charcoal can rigorously be treated with chemicals to remove all traces of foreign humic substances. In the case of peat and what is described as "burnt bone and ash" this is seldom the case. It is therefore important to remember that results obtained from wood and charcoal carry considerably more weight than other dates (Vogel 1966:46–47).

Shell, antler, bone, and burned soil have all been used for attempted C-14 dating with varying degrees of success. One cannot accept the results with confidence unless they are checked by corresponding dates for the same event or one closely related to it derived from wood.

Further studies of potential chronological sources, both in the field and the laboratory, are essential to validate proposed dates for various events.

GLACIATION AND DEGLACIATION*

General Aspects of the Cordilleran Ice Sheet

The Cordilleran ice sheet began its growth from a number of sources in British Columbia in a succession from cirque to mountain to valley glaciers, the flow of which was directed by the underlying topography. Valley glaciers coalesced to form larger ice fields which in turn grew in size and depth until only the highest peaks, those above 8,000 feet elevation, were above the ice, islands (nunataks) in a vast sea of ice.

In British Columbia (Figures 7–9) the Laurentide ice sheet, emanating from eastern Canada, contributed to the glaciation reaching to the eastern foothills of the Rocky Mountains and in some areas thrusting westward onto the foothills and mountains. Northeastern British Columbia was covered by this sheet to the Laird Plateau. The Laurentide ice apparently receded some time before the advance of the Cordil-

---

date given as 3000 years B.P. (Before Present). Any discrepancies caused by these conventions are small and well within the range of C-14 accuracy. At any rate, anyone by a little arithmetic can make his own corrections, if he desires.

---

* "By *glaciation* is usually meant the alteration of any part of the earth's surface (usually by means of erosion or deposition) in consequence of glacier ice passing over it. Erosional alteration may consist of anything from the inscribing of minor scratches to the profound excavation of valleys: depositional alternation may range from the lodgement of a single foreign stone to the building of a thick mantle of glacial sediments. By *deglaciation* is meant the uncovering of any areas as a result of glacier shrinkage" (Flint 1947:64).

FIGURE 7. Talbot Glacier, southeast Ellesmere Island, Canada. The probable kind of environment which extended during the maximum of the Vashon Stade from Cook Inlet, Alaska, to Juan de Fuca Strait, south of Vancouver Island, a distance of over 1,000 miles. The photograph "shows rough glacier ice descending mountain valleys and iceberg and flow littered sea in the foreground. . . . The eastern coast of Ellesmere Island is uninhabited today" (Austin Post, personal communication, April 15, 1968). *Photograph by Austin Post, University of Washington.*

leran down the east slope of the Rocky Mountains, as shown by the moraines of the latter overlying those of the former, but how long before is unknown. The

distribution and time span of the Laurentide ice and that of the Cordilleran border is pertinent to any question of the movement of aboriginal people

FIGURE 8. British Columbia interior glaciation. Looking west over Llewellyn Glacier in the Boundary ranges at the south end of Atlin Lake; elevation of the ice in the distance is 6,000 feet. During the Pleistocene (Vashon Stade) all of British Columbia was covered by ice to a greater extent than is here illustrated. *Holland 1964: Plate XLIA; British Columbia Government Air Photograph.*

through the Alberta Plains during the period of the ice sheet.

The Cordilleran ice sheet at its maximum extended from the eastern flank of the Rocky Mountains to the Pacific Ocean, from southwestern Alaska, and, in general, from the southern boundary of the Yukon River basin to southern Puget Sound in the state of Washington west of the Cascade Mountains. A series of lobes reached to the Columbia River east of that range and the Okanagan Lobe even crossed the river. The coalesced ice sheet is estimated to have covered 2,200,000 square kilometers at its final maximum

FIGURE 9. Glaciation, Makinson Inlet, Ellesmere Island, Canada. This shows the probable condition of the British Columbia coastline when "the ice had melted back from the outer coast and glaciers ended in big fiords. Travel by boat would probably be possible for a few months each year.... Eskimos do not live in this region" (Austin Post, personal communication, April 15, 1968). *Photograph by Austin Post, University of Washington.*

(Flint 1957:53). Mountain glaciers occurred south of the ice sheet in the Rocky and Cascade-Sierra Nevada mountains.

Differences in precipitation, latitude, elevation, length of summer, and summer temperatures are all local factors affecting glacial growth and decline; the diversified environment of British Columbia and the relevant parts of the state of Washington reflect these in their glacial history. The most intensively studied region is the Fraser Lowland-Puget Sound area. Aerial reconnaissance and mapping from surface features, determined by aerial photography, provide the main evidence at present for the extent of glaciation in the interior of British Columbia.

Fraser Lowland and Puget Sound Area*

Reasonably precise information on the succession of climatic changes, the extent of the ice, its thick-

* "(i) A glaciation was a climatic episode during which extensive glaciers developed, attained a maximum extent, and receded. (ii) An interglaciation was an episode during which the climate was incompatible with the wide extent of glaciers that characterized a glaciation. (iii) A stade was a climatic episode within a glaciation during which a secondary advance of glaciers took place. (iv) An interstade was a climatic episode within a glaciation during which a secondary recession or stillstand of glaciers took place" (American Commission on Stratigraphic Nomenclature 1961:660).

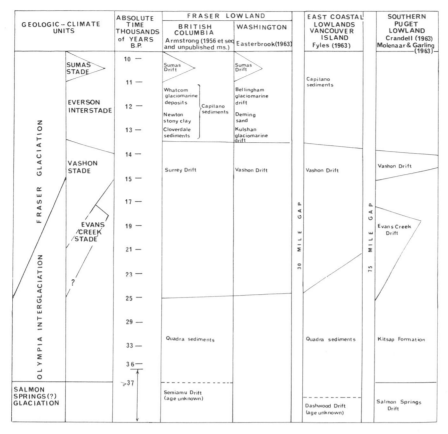

FIGURE 10. Late Pleistocene geologic-climate subdivisions and stratigraphic units in southwestern British Columbia and northwestern Washington. *Armstrong et al. 1965:Figure 2.*

ness, and the time of its recession is available for the Fraser Lowland-Puget Sound area.

> During the Vashon Stade the Cordilleran glacier covered the Coast Mountains near the city of Vancouver to altitudes of at least 5,500 feet. Further north in the Coast Mountains the ice probably reached altitudes of 7,500 feet or more. . . . Proceeding south from the Canada-United States border the ice sheet progressively thinned from about 5,500 feet to 3,000 feet in the Seattle area. . . (Armstrong et al. 1965:327).

The land in the area was depressed by the weight of the overlying ice. "The submergence of the land surface (Fraser Lowland) based on the occurrence of marine fossils amounted to 575 feet and is interpreted to have been as much as 1,000 feet during the Vashon glaciation" (Holland 1964:37). Isostatic depression to a less extent occurred to the southern margins of the ice; north along the coast mountains marine beaches far above present sea level, some of which have been

dated by the radiocarbon method, attest to the fact of depression and rebound.

The accepted sequence of Pleistocene climatic events in the Pacific Northwest following the Sangamon (Third) Interglacial from late to early follows:

The Fraser Glaciation
The Sumas Stade
The Everson Interstade
The Vashon Stade
No interstade recognized
The Evans Creek Stade
The Olympic Interglaciation
The Salmon Springs Glaciation
A younger glacial episode
A nonglacial interval
An older glacial episode

The archæologist at present is concerned mostly with the chronology of events of the Fraser Glaciation,

TABLE 1
CLIMATIC SUBDIVISIONS WITH C-14 DATES BY AREA AND SAMPLE SOURCE
WESTERN BRITISH COLUMBIA AND WESTERN WASHINGTON

Climatic Subdivisions	Area[1]				C-14 Dates by Sample Material			Age Range B.P. all Samples
	F.E.	F.W.	V.I.	P.L.	Shell	Wood	Peat	
Sumas S.	X					11,500		11,000-11,500
	X					11,000		(500)
Everson In.[2]								
	X				11,680			10,950-11,930
	X					11,700		(980)
	X					10,950		
	X				11,930			
		X				11,800		11,640-12,090
						10,370		(450)
		X					12,090	
		X				11,640		
		X			11,660			
Vashon S.			X[3]					15,000-25,000
		X				24,500		(10,000)
			X[4]			19,000		
				X[5]		15,000		
Evans Cr. S.					None	None	None	
		X						19,150-35,400
			X					18,100-22,400
			X					15,000-24,300
			X					27,000-34,700
			X				26,850±1700	
		X					36,200± 500 [6]	24,600-36,200

[1] F.E.—Fraser Lowland East; F.W.—F.L. West; V.I.—Vancouver Is.; P.L.—Puget Lowland
[2] Arranged in stratigraphic sequence; oldest on bottom. Three units recognized in F.W., 125' thick, 6 units in F.E., 500' thick, but samples are lacking from units 2, 3, and 5, with unit 1 as the oldest.
[3] N. end of Strait of Georgia—maximum limiting date
[4] S.E. end of Vancouver Is.—maximum limiting date
[5] S. end of Puget Sound
[6] Peat lying on till
SOURCE: Compiled from Armstrong et al. 1965.

but, as I point out in the next chapter, he may eventually have to push the limits of his interest back beyond the Olympic Interglaciation. Figure 10 presents the presently accepted geological sequence and the chronology assigned to coastal British Columbia and western Washington.

*The Olympic Interglaciation** in the Fraser Lowland extended from 36,000 to 24,500 years ago; on the eastern Vancouver Island lowlands from 35,000 to 19,000 years ago, and in the southern Puget Sound from 35,000 to 15,000 years ago. All dates are approximate and limiting; it is possible that the beginnings of the interglaciation are older than these dates. The variation in the dates for the termination of the interglacial period reflects, in the main, the relative closeness of the particular area to the main source of the ice formation on mainland British Columbia which

_____

* Table 1 presents a list of significant C-14 dates by area and sample.

marked the beginning of the Fraser Glaciation. Limited palynological evidence suggests that the climate was somewhat cooler than at present.

The Evans Creek Stade is defined as the climatic episode in the Fraser Glaciation during which large alpine glaciers formed and reached their maximum extents and deposited drift in the mountains of western Washington adjoining the southern Puget Lowland. This growth was probably contemporaneous with initial development of the Cordilleran ice sheet in the mountains of the mainland of Western British Columbia. Continued expansion of alpine glaciers in British Columbia apparently resulted in ice sheet formation; whereas, to the south, growth of alpine glaciers was interrupted before the ice sheet phase was reached, and individual glaciers began to retreat (Armstrong et al. 1956:326–27).

There are no C-14 dates for the Evans Creek Stade. How long after the termination of the Olympic Interglaciation the alpine glaciers began to form is unknown. All that is firmly known is that the glacial moraine at the Evans Creek type locality on the northwest side of Mt. Rainier is buried in the sediments of a proglacial lake of the Vashon Stade and is overlaid with Vashon drift. It is inferred that by the time of deposition of the Vashon drift the Evans Creek glacier had retreated far toward its source, but the length of time involved in the recession is unknown. The Vashon ice reached Evans Creek about 15,000 years ago, so the recession was well before then. Since it is assumed that the birth of the Evans Creek glacier was a response to the same climatic conditions which initiated the growth of the Cordilleran ice sheet after the Olympic Interglaciation, the beginning date must have been not less than 25,000 years ago and perhaps more.

Vashon Stade continental ice, originating in the mountains of mainland British Columbia, entered the northern end of the Strait of Georgia about 25,000 years ago (Figure 7). C-14 dates indicate that by 24,500 years ago the ice was in the Fraser Lowland, on southeast Vancouver Island by 19,000, but it did not reach its maximum extent, about 15 miles south of Olympia, Washington, until 15,000 years ago. The Puget Lobe, as this segment of the ice sheet is called, extended laterally from the Cascade Mountains to the Coast Range, and the ice in the Seattle area was 3,000 feet thick.

Recession of the Puget Lobe was rapid. A C-14 date from peat at Lake Washington, Seattle, indicates that marine sediments were being deposited before 13,500 years ago, and the Fraser Lowland was free of the continental ice by 13,000 years ago. Thus the recession to the Fraser Lowland took about 2,000 years in contrast to the 10,000 years for the advance.

The Everson Interstade, best represented in the Fraser Lowland, is a period of climatic amelioration which terminated the Vashon Stade. The type locality is at Everson, about 15 miles northeast of Bellingham, Washington, where the sedimentary sequence is approximately 125 feet thick. The sequence in the eastern Fraser Lowland is thicker, over 500 feet, and is more complex than at Everson. It

began with the invasion of the lowlands by the sea and apparently ended in the eastern half of the Fraser Lowland during the advance of the Sumas ice [11,000 B.P.]. Elsewhere it ended with the withdrawal of the sea from most of the area and the disappearance of floating ice. The relative position of the land and sea fluctuated from 600 feet or more above sea level, to present sea level or below. During this period of deposition glacier ice did not cover the lowlands, although floating ice was present during part or most of it. The ice was chiefly in the form of bergs, but probably also included shelf ice or sea ice or both (Armstrong et al. 1965:327–28).

The Everson Interstade lasted about 2,000 years in the Fraser Lowland but would have begun at least 500 years earlier in the southern Puget Sound area as shown by the 13,500 B.P. C-14 date from Lake Washington. The presence of bergs and other float ice shows that the climate was colder than at present.

The Sumas Stade (Figure 9) is the climatic episode that terminated the Everson Interstade. During the Sumas Stade a valley glacier, thought to have been a lobe of the Cordilleran ice, occupied the Fraser Lowland as far west as the town of Sumas on the Canadian-United States border. "In an area covering 250 square miles Sumas Drift overlies glaciomarine deposits of Everson age, thus indicating a probable readvance of Cordilleran ice." Radiocarbon dates from Sumas till and underlying sediments "suggest the advance of Sumas ice began about 11,000 B.P." (Armstrong et al. 1965:329). No firm dates are available to indicate the close of the stade, but, since Indians were using the Fraser River canyon at Yale 9,000 years ago, probably for salmon fishing (Borden 1960a), the closing date for the Sumas Stade, in that region at least, should be placed before that time.

Interior British Columbia

This region (Figure 8) experienced "at least two major advances of the Cordilleran ice-sheet, separated by an interglacial stage, and . . . in some peripheral areas there were three or more" (Holland 1964:103). These are apparently correlates of the similar sequence demonstrated for the coastal area. The major advance of the final glaciation is a part of the same climatic episode represented by the Vashon Stade in the west.

> In southern British Columbia the main gathering grounds for the Cordilleran ice sheet appears to be the Coast Mountains, Selkirk Mountains, and probably the Cariboo Mountains and the ice moved southerly across the southern interior plateau and westerly through the Coast Mountains. In view of the above it is quite obvious that the Cordilleran ice sheet had no center of accumulation, but several major centers and numerous minor centers, the location of each being governed by precipitation and topography. Possibly the greatest areas of ice accumulation were in the portions of the Coast Mountains lying opposite Queen Charlotte Sound and Dixon Entrance, the only parts of the Coast Mountains not protected by islands to the west and, consequently, areas of great precipitation. The ice flowing easterly from these areas greatly exceeded in mass any other sources of ice and overrode them. Nowhere else in British Columbia did ice flow to the east for such a great distance (Armstrong and Tipper 1948:309).

The southern section of the Cordilleran ice sheet moved southward by a series of river valley lobes, which eventually coalesced, to the Columbia River in Washington, and the Okanagan Lobe even crossed over it. It is not known if these lobes began their advances at the same time nor when they reached their maximum extent. Radiocarbon dates for the area are almost totally lacking, and temporal correlations are made for the Washington drift with the Rocky Mountain Pinedale and Bull Lake sequences. One date, however, 12,000±300 B.P. (WSU-155) from fresh-water mollusk shells, is thought to represent the Everson Interstade (Fryxell 1965:1290). The shells were secured from deposits of a lake formed by an ice dam (at least vestigial) on the Columbia River.

Two radiocarbon dates from the Kamloops Lake area of interior British Columbia suggest a maximum age limit for the appearance of glaciation there. Sample GSC-173, "woody plant detritus" dated at 21,500± 300 B.P., is from a deposit beneath glacial till that is considered to be either "interstadial or interglacial." Sample GSC-79, derived from "fresh water shells from clayey silt beneath till (?)," is dated at 25,200± 460 B.P. At Shuswap Lake, about 60 miles east and north from Kamloops Lake, a sample of "woody materials" found "about 75 feet above the lake and 5 feet above the base of a 30 ft. sequence of lacustrine sand and silt," gave a date of 20,230±270 B.P. (GSC-194). This sample is said to supply a maximum date for the latest glacial advance there (W.D. Dyck, J. G. Fyles, and W. Blake, Jr. 1965:33). The two dates from "woody plant" materials correspond fairly closely, but the date from "fresh water shells" is approximately 5,000 years older. One could hazard a guess on the time of the beginning of glaciation in the area at 23,000 or more years ago.

The character, or even the existence, of the Everson Interstade (13,000–11,000 B.P.) in interior British Columbia is largely conjectural, but some important facts are available. During the Cordilleran ice sheet maximum, the Columbia River was diverted through the Grand Coulee, but it subsequently returned to its old channel, after which a lake formed behind an ice dam in the Grand Coulee. Glacier Peak volcanic ash, dated at 12,000 C-14 years ago, was deposited in this lake, indicating that the lake had formed prior to this time. Glacier Peak ash is also found on the highest terrace of the Okanagan and Columbia rivers in the area of their confluence, but is not found on the younger terraces within the valleys, suggesting that the central parts of the valleys were still occupied by ice and that stagnant ice still existed at the lower end of the Okanagan Valley 12,000 C-14 years ago (Fryxell 1965:1290).

Early and late glacio-marine deposits in the Fraser Lowland, including evidence of bergs derived from the Coast Mountains, clearly indicate that glaciation continued there during the Everson Interstade, even though probably on a reduced scale. In view of the important role of the Coast Mountains as a source of ice in interior British Columbia and the likely presence of ice at the lower end of the Okanagan

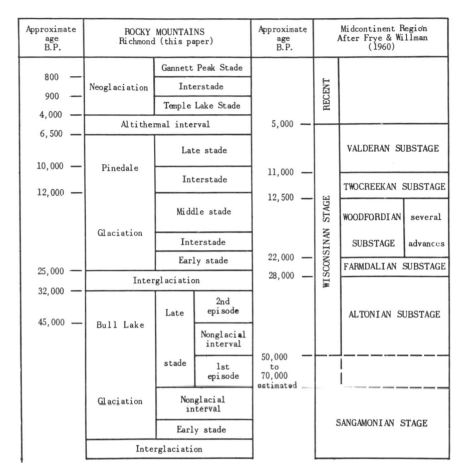

Approximate age B.P.	ROCKY MOUNTAINS Richmond (this paper)			Approximate age B.P.	Midcontinent Region After Frye & Willman (1960)		
800 —	Neoglaciation		Gannett Peak Stade		RECENT		
900 —			Interstade				
4,000 —			Temple Lake Stade				
6,500 —	Altithermal interval			5,000 —			
			Late stade			VALDERAN SUBSTAGE	
10,000 —	Pinedale			11,000 —			
			Interstade			TWOCREEKAN SUBSTAGE	
12,000 —				12,500 —			
	Glaciation		Middle stade		WISCONSINAN STAGE	WOODFORDIAN	several
			Interstade			SUBSTAGE	advances
			Early stade	22,000 —		FARMDALIAN SUBSTAGE	
25,000 —	Interglaciation			28,000 —			
32,000 —							
	Bull Lake	Late stade	2nd episode			ALTONIAN SUBSTAGE	
45,000 —			Nonglacial interval				
			1st episode	50,000 to 70,000 estimated			
	Glaciation		Nonglacial interval			SANGAMONIAN STAGE	
			Early stade				
	Interglaciation						

FIGURE 11. Correlation of Rocky Mountain and mid-continent glaciations. *Richmond 1965:227, Figure 2.*

Valley at 12,000 C-14 years ago, it is a strain on one's credulity to believe that southern interior British Columbia was ice free during the Everson Interstade, as some have suggested (cf. Fryxell 1962a:118).

The extent and intensity of the Sumas Stade in interior British Columbia is unknown, but perhaps 9,500 to 10,000 years ago would be a fair conjecture for a terminal date.

Deglaciation began with the cessation of accumulation of ice in the source areas. Stagnation occurred and the ice wasted away in place. In the Nechako Plateau and the Fraser basin, a vast wastage area extending practically from the Rocky to the Coast mountains is recorded by the presence of many lakes and the remains of numerous glacial lakes, now dry. This area must have been for centuries a most inhospitable environment and an effective barrier to human movement even though the ice sheet, as such,

had disappeared. Firm dates are completely lacking for the time when this habitat became available for human use.

The Rocky Mountains

Since the northern Rocky Mountain glaciation sequence is used as the chronological referent for the Cordilleran ice sheet in eastern Washington (Richmond et al. 1965:231–42, Figure 1) and for pluvial lake fluctuations in the Great Basin (see Pluvial Lakes, below), a brief consideration of the proposed glacial chronology of the Rocky Mountain sequence is in order (Figure 11). The Sangamon (Third) Interglacial is followed in order by the Bull Lake glacial episode, an interglacial, and the Pinedale Glaciation. The Bull Lake, like the Salmon Springs Glaciation, is separated by a nonglacial period into two glacial advances. An interglacial episode corresponds to the Olympic Interglaciation. The Pinedale Glaciation consists of three stades, Pinedale I, II, and III, or Early, Middle, and Late, separated by interstades corresponding taxonomically to the Fraser Glaciation of the Fraser Lowland-Puget Sound area. A close chronological correspondence has not been demonstrated, at least not one that fits the needs of the archæologist.

Richmond (1965:225) briefly summarizes the chronological evidence, and it is important to remember that most of the dates have been derived from calcareous sources (tufa and shells) which are not considered very reliable materials for radiocarbon dating:

> Very few C-14 dates are available from Pinedale deposits and *none are from till* [emphasis added]. Dates from deposits of Lake Bonneville, considered correlative with the early and middle stades of Pinedale Glaciation, range from 25,400 to 11,300 years B.P. (Broecker and Orr, 1958; Rubin and Alexander, 1958, 1960). One lake rise to the Bonneville shoreline, dated at 23,150±1,000 B.P. (L-363-H) (Broecker and Orr, 1958), may approximate the maximum of the early stade. The interstade separating the middle and late stades may be dated from marl and snails in kettles in early and middle Pinedale outwash and from charcoal in occupation sites of Folsom man that separate middle and late Pinedale alluvial deposits.

Finally, if man was in North America before the Fraser-Pinedale episode, as now appears likely, then the area of north-central Washington, like the Canadian-Washington coast and perhaps part of interior British Columbia, would have been a favorable habitat during the previous interglaciation. Firm dates, however, for these climatic episodes within the limits significant for the archæologist are lacking.

In sum, the archæologist in the Pacific Northwest has to work within the geochronological framework just discussed, and while on the whole the structure is generally satisfactory, there are many unanswered questions. The crucial problem for the archæologist concerned with land use is the availability of the land as a human habitat. For example, the southern Puget Lowland must have been a suitable human habitat for several thousand years during the Evans Creek Stade, although it is not certain. If man was in the New World before the advance of the Vashon ice then the Puget Lowland could well have been inhabited until the advancing Puget Lobe destroyed the ecosystems of which man would have been a part. In this case the archæologist would like to know precisely when the established ecosystem deteriorated and disappeared before the worsening climatic conditions of the approaching stade. Again, while it is geochronologically correct to say that the land in the Seattle area was once more free of the Puget Lobe ice by 13,500 years ago, it does not follow that the land was habitable; the sedimentary sequence of the Everson Interstade shows clearly that while the Fraser Lowland was free of Cordilleran ice by 13,000 years ago, it certainly was unsuitable as a habitat for any human population at the cultural level known for the New World at the time. The case of interior British Columbia is similar; the date at which the area became habitable by human beings following deglaciation is not yet known. The archæologist needs to know how long it took the postglacial climate to ameliorate sufficiently for an ecosystem capable of supporting human life at the expectable level of cultural development to become established.

Thus there are dates within the larger geochonological framework that are critical for the archæologist and that still remain to be determined; these problems constitute a research frontier in the prehistory of the area.*

---

* Comments by geologists engaged in the study of Pacific Northwest glacial history and its correlation with glacial episodes in other areas bring the problem into sharp focus. Mullineaux, Waldron, and Rubin (1965:7) write: "Until recently, the Vashon generally has been regarded as possibly correlative with the 'Classical' Wisconsin ice advance of the Midwest, which apparently began some 25,000 years or more ago and reached a maximum 18,000–20,000 years ago. The dates from the Seattle area, however, suggest that nonglacial conditions prevailed in this part of the Puget Sound lowland throughout the advance and much of the retreat of the ice sheet in the Midwest. It is not known yet whether or not the whole lowland was ice free throughout all this time. It is known that some valley glaciers in the Cascade Range and the Olympic Mountains reached their maximum extents and retreated before the Puget lobe reached its maximum extent in the lowland."

Easterbrook (1966:766) comments: "Relative to Rocky Mountain terminology the Vashon appears to be equivalent to the middle stadial of the Pinedale glaciation but might also include all or a part of the early Pinedale. Another possibility is that the early Pinedale may be equivalent to the Evans Creek stadial."

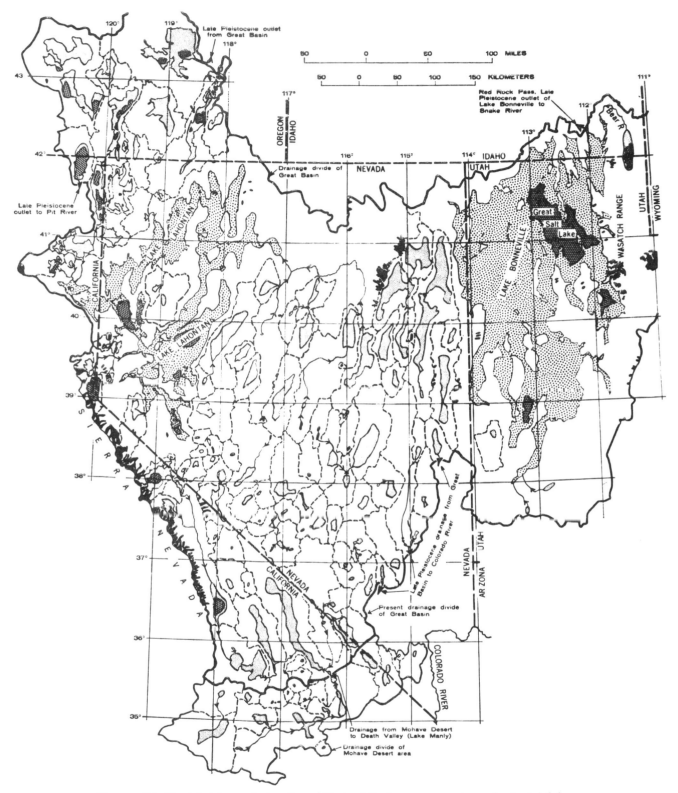

FIGURE 12. Pluvial lakes of the Great Basin. Maximum extension of pluvial lakes and glaciers (black) during post-Sangamon time. Existing lakes in darkest stipple, pluvial lakes in lighter; dashed lines mark drainage basins; solid lines with arrows indicate overflow connections between basins. *Morrison 1965:266, Figure 1.*

Pluvial Lakes

General Considerations

During the Pleistocene period, two vast pluvial lakes, Lake Bonneville and Lake Lahontan, dominated the Eastern and Western Great Basin respectively. The Northern Great Basin of south-central Oregon was characterized by a series of lakes, generally formed in fault basins, from Klamath Lake on the west to Lake Alvord on the east. In the southwestern part of the Great Basin was a lake complex consisting of lakes Mohave, Manly, Searles, Mono, and others. The distribution of pluvial lakes in the Great Basin has been mapped by Meinzer (1922), Hubbs and Miller (1948), and Morrison (1965), among others (Figure 12).

A century ago (Flint 1947:6–7) it was recognized that there was a generally synchronous relationship between glaciation, deglaciation, and the rise and fall of lakes in the arid intermountain area. Gilbert (1890) showed that the end moraines of the Wasatch Mountain glaciers underlay the highest shoreline of Lake Bonneville. Richmond (1964) provided more precision to the relation discussed by Gilbert. Since the rise and decline of pluvial lakes in the Great Basin profoundly affected the region as a human habitat, the archæologist is vitally concerned with the chronology of these events; moreover, it is frequently only by the association of artifacts and lake terraces that he can hope to date his material. The initial geochronological problem, then, is the identification of a particular lake terrace, representing a stillstand of the lake, with its related glaciation. It must be kept in mind that glaciation and deglaciation are correlates, not causes, of the rise and fall of pluvial lakes. The common cause is climatic change, and my preceding discussion of glaciation and deglaciation made abundantly clear that a climatic condition varies in its expression both in time and space. The sources of water that affect the viability of the lakes must also be considered. The presence of inflowing, perennial rivers may provide a minimal constant water supply, as in the case of Lake Bonneville. And in an area of pronounced faulting there will likely be major springs along the fault scarp where formerly deeply buried aquifers are brought close to the surface, as in the Northern Great Basin and along the Sierra-

Cascade escarpment. Of runoff from the glaciers themselves, Morrison (1965:281) points out "that most pluvial lakes in the Great Basin did not have glaciers within their drainage areas, and that for the few lake basins that contained glaciers the influence of glacial melt-water was minor."

Thus, while the theory of correlation of glaciation and lake presence is sound, it does not necessarily follow that glacial episodes and related episodes of rise and decline in the level of pluvial lakes will be consistently on the same time level throughout the whole Great Basin. This caution must be borne in mind in reading the following pages and also in assessing the validity of age ascriptions that Great Basin archæologists commonly make upon such bases (Chapter 8).

Lake Bonneville

This, the largest pluvial lake, covered at its greatest extent approximately 20,000 square miles and had a depth of 1,100 feet. The depression of the earth's crust by the weight of the water and its subsequent upwarping after evaporation of the water (Figure 13) was approximately 210 feet at its maximum (King 1965:850, Figure 14). Great Salt Lake is all that remains of this once vast body of water. Most of the lake was in Utah, but it extended into northeastern Nevada and slightly into southern Idaho. The eastern shoreline abutted against the Wasatch Range of the Rocky Mountains while the western extended slightly beyond 114° west longitude. The divide between Lake Bonneville and Lake Lahontan was but a few miles farther west, although the most easterly segment of Lake Lahontan did not extend east of 117° west longitude. The small area in Idaho includes Red Rock Pass, the overflow outlet for Lake Bonneville at 112° west longitude, and approximately 42° 30′ north latitude into the Snake River. Bear River flows into Lake Bonneville basin in Idaho some few miles south and east of Red Rock Pass; it "contributes 43.5% of the present inflow to Great Salt Lake" (Morrison 1965:276). Lake Bonneville was thus strongly oriented toward the Rocky Mountain area.

Figure 14 presents Morrison's correlation of Lake Bonneville history with Rocky Mountain glacial episodes, based on the excellent though not wholly un-

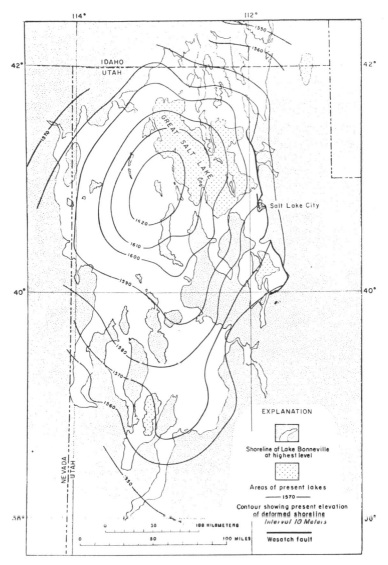

FIGURE 13. Map of northwestern Utah showing maximum area of Lake Bonneville and deformation of its highest shoreline. *King 1965:850, Figure 11.*

equivocal stratigraphic sequence exposed in Little Cottonwood and Bells canyons at the foot of the Wasatch Range south and east of Salt Lake City. There are three major terraces representing stillstands of the lake: the Bonneville, at an elevation of 5,100 feet; the Provo, at 4,775 feet; and the Stansbury, at 4,470 feet. The present surface level of the Great Salt Lake is 4,200 feet. The status of radiometric age determinations for the terraces, and the difficulty of relating the dates to stratigraphic and glacial chronologies, are best described by Morrison (1966:96–97), a recognized authority on the history of Lakes Bonneville and Lahontan:

Isotopic dating of deposits of Lake Bonneville age. About 90 radiocarbon and 3 uranium-series (Th^{230}–U^{234}) age determinations have been made from the sediments of Lake Bonneville and contemporaneous subaerial sediments. . . . With respect to the radiocarbon dates, certain baffling problems commonly appear when one tries to compare the dates from the same stratigraphic unit in the same or different parts of the lake basin, and also when one compares the dates from different units that have been precisely differentiated and correlated in the basis of geologic-stratigraphic methods. . . . In general, the dates from most subaerial and shallow-lake interlacustrine deposits fit well into a chronology based on linking the Lake Bonneville succession with the well-dated Midwestern glacial succession by geologic correla-

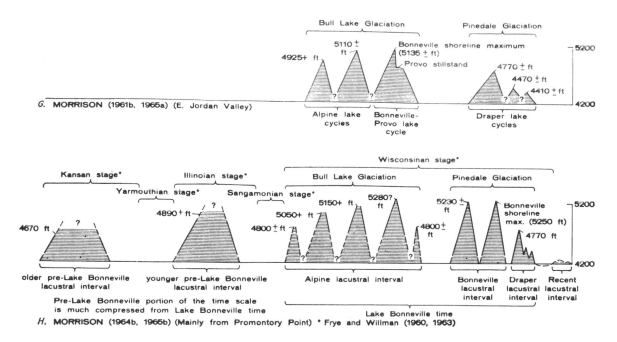

FIGURE 14. Interpretation of Lake Bonneville history. *Morrison 1965:274, Figure 2.*

tion methods, including soil stratigraphy. . . . On the other hand, dates from lacustrine carbonates (algal tufas, mollusk shells, marl) deposited during intermediate-to-high lake levels are erratic—some "fit" the correlation-chronology, others from the same stratigraphic horizon and altitude commonly differ by 2,000 to more than 5,000 years. For example, three determinations (all from tufa) within 50 feet vertically of the Bonneville shore-line . . . gave ages of 23,150, 15,650, and 12,500 years; however, four determinations (from snail shells) within a few feet of this shoreline in northern Cache Valley gave an average age of about 18,000 years (Meyer Rubin, U.S. Geol. Survey, oral commun., 1965). [The range of this series should have been given.] The latter four deter-minations are compatible with the correlation chronology, whereas the others are not.

Although the three uranium-series dates agree well with radiocarbon dates from the same samples, this is not in-variably true. . . . In the light of the meager data pre-sently available on uranium-series dates, it would appear that these dates are fraught with at least as much uncer-tainty as radiocarbon dates.

Because of the difficulties in detailed reconciliation of the radiometric dates with one another and with the geologic correlations, I have preferred to utilize these dates as subsidiary, rather than a primary means of cor-relation. In attempting to establish an approximate "ab-solute" chronology, . . . I have restored to a "subjective control of an objective effort" by selecting certain critical radiometric dates (mainly from interlacustral deposits) that appear to be most valid, and extrapolating the rest

of the chronology on the basis of the lake history that can be inferred from the stratigraphic succession.

There is no firm date accepted by the majority of geologists for the Bonneville Terrace at 5,100 feet elevation. The dating problem is complicated by the overflow of Lake Bonneville (Lake Bonneville Flood) through Red Rock Pass into the Snake River, an event I shall discuss briefly later, and the conflict-ing C-14 dates for the flood. Some C-14 dates are com-patible with the geological stratigraphy, but other dates, which should be equally reliable and pertinent, are not. The inferred dates of the flood are 30,000 years ago, proposed by Malde, and 18,000 by Bright and Rubin. The Bonneville Terrace was cut sub-sequent to the flood so the terrace, until the con-flict is resolved, may be given either date. Slow down-cutting of the outlet followed after the pass had been cut to bedrock. Eventually the lake level was stabilized for a period of approximately 3,000 years at 4,775 feet elevation, the Provo Terrace, for which a reasonably firm date exists.

The conflict of dates for the Bonneville Terrace is more than an academic problem for the archæologist. Since man has probably been in the Far West of North America for 25,000 years, and perhaps many more, it is possible for his remains to be found associated with that terrace. Which date would the archæologist choose for his artifacts?

The Provo Terrace formation and subsequent lake level changes have been dated by Bright's paleoecological study (1966) at Swan Lake, which was formed in a shallow depression in the outlet of Lake Bonneville about 4.5 miles south of Red Rock Pass after the lake level had dropped permanently below the Provo level at about 4,775 feet elevation.

The pollen profile from a core from Swan Lake should provide a reasonable record of climatic change for the area from the lake's beginning. The core indicates that the lake began to form before 12,090, perhaps by 13,000, years ago for there are about 1.55 meters of deposits below the level of the C-14 date (8.0 meters) of 12,090±300 (W-1338) years ago. The appearance of this lake marks the end of the Red Rock Pass downcutting. A second C-14 date (W-1339) 2 meters above the other is 10,190±250 years ago. Between these dates the coniferous forest was much more abundant than now and of different composition with *Pinus contorta* and *P. flexilis* being more plentiful. The lower limit of the forest was at lower elevation than at present and "the climate was colder and probably wetter than now" (Bright 1966: *passim*). The Provo Terrace may thus be dated at about 13,000 years ago.

The Stansbury Terrace, at 4,470±feet elevation, marks the last stillstand of Lake Bonneville. The water level was then approximately 160 feet above the floor of Danger Cave, an archæological site on the northern Utah-Nevada border that provides the best C-14 dated reference point for the latest stage of Lake Bonneville history. No firm date can be presently assigned to the Stansbury Terrace, but a C-14 date of approximately 11,000 years B.P. from the earliest level of human occupation on water-laid sediments in Danger Cave shows that the Stansbury Terrace is older than 11,000 C-14 years ago by the amount of time that it took the lake to recede 160 feet from the Stansbury level to a point below the mouth of the cave, opening it for occupation.

Lake Lahontan

Russell first described Lake Lahontan (Figure 15), and Morrison (1964:2) follows him, "as the series of deep-lake fluctuations (lake cycles) of Pleistocene age whose deposits and shore features are prominently exposed in the highlands, together with intervening lake recessions, but excluding earlier lake fluctuations that are poorly recorded, earlier lake recessions, and subsequent very shallow lakes of recent age." The drainage basin includes that of the Humboldt River, traversing the area from east to west, and Walker, Carson, and Truckee rivers flowing from the Sierra Nevada Mountains on the west. Except for a small, wedge-shaped portion in California between approximately 40° and 40° 45′ north latitude and a narrow finger extending some 10 to 15 miles into southeastern Oregon just east of 118° west longitude, the lake lies within western Nevada. At its maximum extent in the Early Wisconsin, Lake Lahontan covered an area of 8,665 square miles and had a maximum depth of 700 feet. Crustal depression and subsequent upwarping was between 20 and 30 feet. Honey, Pyramid, and Warner lakes, strung out north to south along the Sierra escarpment, are the modern remnants of former Lake Lahontan.

All studies report two periods of high lake level, one in the Early and another in the Late Wisconsin, separated by a period of desiccation, the Lahontan interlacustrine period. The Early Wisconsin lake, characterized by the Eetza Formation, is thought to have experienced two main periods of high-water levels interrupted by a series of three to four low-water levels that have been termed "interlacustrine diastems." The Late Wisconsin lake, characterized by the Sehoo Formation, is of particular interest to archæologists as a chronological referent (Chapter 8). Three terraces exist, at 4,370, 4,200, and 4,000 feet. The 4,000 foot terrace is the highest one bearing evidence of human occupation. It is thought that the lake rose twice to the 4,000 foot terrace in late Sehoo time.

Stratigraphically this sequence corresponds to the Pacific Northwest and Rocky Mountain glacial sequences. The Eetza Formation corresponds to the Salmon Springs and Bull Lake glaciations, and the Sehoo Formation to the Fraser and Pinedale glaciations. The Lahontan interlacustrine period correlates with the Olympic and Bull Lake-Pinedale interglacial periods. Obviously the fluctuations in the lacustrine record indicate a complex problem of causation and correlation with the glacial phenomena (Figure 16).

Figure 15. Bar of Lake Lahontan. Produced during the last high stand of the lake, it is now used as a source for highway gravel. The cattle in the foreground give some idea of the scale. The photograph was taken about thirty miles west and south of McDermitt on the Oregon-Nevada border in September of 1949. *Photograph by author.*

Only two reliable radiocarbon dates are available for dating episodes of Lake Lahontan history. One sample, from the base of a bat guano deposit resting on "Pleistocene gravels" at the Leonard Rockshelter, is 11,199±570 radiocarbon years old (C-599). The second date, derived from wood associated with human occupation and extinct fauna in Fishbone Cave on the shoreline of pluvial lake Winnemucca, is 10,900±300 radiocarbon years (no sample number available). Morrison points out that the significance of these dates for late Lahontan valley chronology is "uncertain, as the material directly beneath the dated samples cannot be correlated accurately. The samples may represent either the late or the middle Sehoo lake maximum" (Morrison 1964:112–13).

The upshot of this discussion is that as far as the archæologist is concerned there is at present practically no firm chronological data by which he can ac-

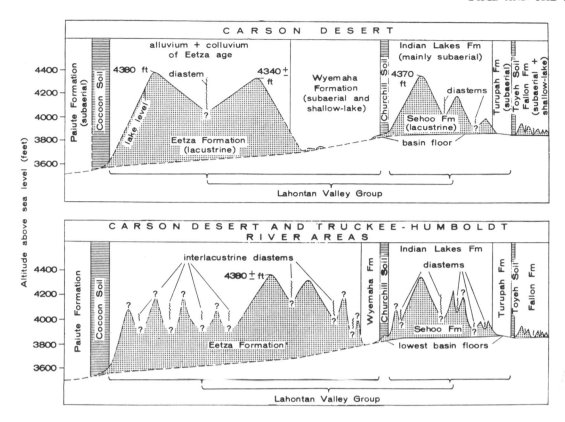

FIGURE 16. Interpretations of Lake Lahontan history. *Morrison 1965:277, Figure 4.*

curately date an archæological occurrence by association with a phase of Lake Lahontan's Late Pleistocene history.

Southeastern California

In southeastern California there was a continuous system of pluvial lakes. A southern leg of this system flowed into Lake Mohave which in turn drained into Lake Manly. Early Man left his artifacts on the high terraces of Lake Mohave. These terraces had to be cut while the lake stood high enough to overflow into Lake Manly. More than a dozen radiocarbon dates derived from shell samples indicate that the overflow ceased between 6000 to 7000 B.C. (see Chapter 8). This date for the terrace bearing the Early Man remains provides a limiting upper date for those artifacts but does not indicate an actual age. They may or may not be considerably younger.

The Northern Great Basin

The pluvial Fort Rock Lake basin in south-central Oregon provides an instructive archæological application of lake-terrace dating. The lake was formed in a depression formed by a depressed fault block. The remains of a volcano, called Fort Rock, rise from the lake bed. The south and east portion of this generally circular structure was breached by wave action. On the walls at each side of the breach are a series of terraces cut into the rock. On the west side is a section lacking talus; there are only the wave-cut platforms in the rock. These of course provide a referent for terrace elevations throughout the basin. Transit determined elevations are 4,430, 4,419, 4,406, and 4,386 feet. This lowest terrace represents the final stand of the lake. After the lake dropped below that level only scattered small lakes and ponds remained, as determined by the basin's topography.

Shells from a beach at 4,386 feet elevation some 12 miles distant from Fort Rock were dated at 12,980± 213 (GaK 1752) C-14 years ago. Correction for fractionation ($\delta^{13}C = -0.8$) gives a date of 13,380±230 B.P. The possible skewing of this date by ancient carbonates cannot be determined, but any effect is probably negligible because of the igneous rocks comprising the area. To verify the identification of this beach with the Fort Rock terrace at that elevation, a level was run by transit and stadia rod from the beach to Fort Rock. The identification was verified.

Fort Rock Cave, in a low volcanic butte about 1.5 miles west of Fort Rock, had been first occupied at 13,200±720 C-14 years ago (GaK 1738—sample; charcoal from hearth). Originally the butte was an island in the lake; when the lake level dropped sufficiently, a bar formed a connection to the shoreline on the west. Thus the bar had to exist by 13,200 years ago for the cave to be occupied. The level of the lake 13,380 years ago was sufficiently below the level of the bar for the land connection to be used by the cave occupants. The dates of the beach and earliest cave occupation are thus conformable, and the beach may be considered a firm chronological referent. What the dates of the older terraces are is unknown.

The date of this last stillstand of pluvial Fort Rock Lake corresponds in time with the Everson Interstade of the Pacific Northwest and the Provo Terrace of Lake Bonneville as described above. There is no lake, only remnants of a once large one, to correlate with the Sumas Stade of the Pacific Northwest or Pinedale III of the Rocky Mountain stratigraphic sequence.

This review of the Late Pleistocene history of the Great Basin pluvial lakes as presently known warrants the conclusion that there is great variation among them in actual events and no doubt also in the times at which similar episodes occurred. Certainly this is true within the time segments significant to the archæologist. It must be recognized that although a workable stratigraphic correlation may be established between events in major lake systems or between lacustrine events and glacial episodes, such a relationship is not necessarily a precise chronological one. Morrison's statement (1965:281) that "the pluvial lakes in the Great Basin were the chief phenomena resulting from the pluvial cycles, and the mountain glaciers were relatively incidental" is very important. It throws the emphasis on conditions of precipitation and temperature as causes of the growth and decline of the lakes, and these vary widely in a region when differential storm paths are operative, as in the Intermontane Region. Each lake system must be studied in its own terms of reference and it is unsound (although frequently done: cf.

Chapter 8) for the archæologist to cross-date terraces from one lake system to another, even though apparent stratigraphic correlation exists. The last lake level at pluvial Fort Rock Lake is dated 13,000 years ago, the same time as the Provo Terrace of Lake Bonneville, but following the Provo is the Stansbury with no correlate at Fort Rock. Long-distance stratigraphic correlation cannot be used by the archæologist as a dating device, although stratigraphic correlations within single lake systems can be of great importance, as in the Fort Rock example.

The Altithermal

The growth and decline of the pluvial lakes markedly affected the Great Basin as a human habitat. The intensity of the periods of arid climate and their duration are thus of special importance to the archæologist. Antevs (1948:8–9) proposed the term Neothermal as the name for the postglacial period based on the argument that temperature was the most significant factor in accounting for the environment of the period. He divided the Neothermal into three subdivisions, the Anathermal, the Altithermal, and the Medithermal. The Anathermal designates the period of increasing warmth from the end of the Pleistocene until about 7,500 years ago, when a period of marked rise in temperature and greater aridity began. This period, the Altithermal (high temperature), lasted until about 4,500 or 4,000 years ago. It was then followed by the Medithermal (temperature in the middle range) which lasted until the present (Figure 17). The first 2,000 years of the Medithermal were somewhat colder than the present, and this period correlates with the Little Ice Age of the Rocky Mountains. It is thought that most of the glaciers on the Rocky Mountains and the Cascade-Sierra ranges in the United States completely melted during the Altithermal, and that those now there are remnants of those formed during the Little Ice Age.

Martin and others (1961) and Aschmann (1958) have called into question the Neothermal climatic sequence proposed by Antevs, but the worldwide evidence from glacial and palynological studies and recent studies by Haynes (1968b) support the validity of the sequence proposed by Antevs, although C-14 dates indicate, as is to be expected, that the time

FIGURE 17. Abert Lake, Lake County Oregon. A pluvial lake probably at a climatic equilibrium at the Medithermal level. A high terrace can be seen running along the famous escarpment, the Abert Rim, on the east. *Photograph by author.*

brackets are not everywhere the same. That there have been local fluctuations in the conditions of Great Basin lakes, and presumably in local climatic conditions, is documented by historical records. Fenneman (1931) reports, for example, that in 1869 Goose Lake filled sufficiently to overflow into the Pit River. Local topographic and physiographic features in addition to local climatic variations are sufficient to account for diversity in the general picture, and it would be unreasonable to expect that the beginning and ending dates offered for the Neothermal periods are anything more than approximations or average dates.

The evidence from Danger and Hogup caves in western Utah, the Leonard Rockshelter of western Nevada, and the Fort Rock basin caves of Oregon clearly indicates that occupation of the Great Basin continued through the Altithermal, although the paucity of sites at this period clearly indicates that there was an unfavorable habitat with occupation in the pluvial lake basins limited to a few oasis areas. The work of Swanson in the Birch Creek Valley (1961, 1962b) of southeastern Idaho indicates during the Altithermal a movement of population into higher elevations of the surrounding mountains where the habitat was more favorable, an adaptive device apparently also used by plants and animals other than man.

Only a few cave sites preserve the occupation record over a long enough period of time—that is encompassing the Neothermal—to include the beginning and end of the Altithermal. The most complete record comes from the cluster of a half-dozen or more caves and shelters in the Fort Rock basin. While pollen is not preserved in the cave fill or in deposits outside the caves, for some unknown reason, the charcoal from the numerous hearths selected from the samples, which were dated for stratigraphic controls, was identified and gave a record of critical vegetation cover (critical in that it illustrated the vegetation-climatic relation). In sum, this evidence showed a slow, progressive deterioration of the climate in which shrubs and trees in the area gave way to those accommodated to a drier climate. Piñon (*Pinus edulis*) was replaced by juniper (*Juniperus*) by probably 7,500 years ago, and saltbush (*Atriplex*), the common shrub of the dry alkali soils of the Great Basin lake beds, appeared about 7,200 years ago. Then, at 7,000 years ago, practically all organic evidence disappeared from the record for about 2,000 years—probably a result of the eruption of Mt. Mazama imposed on an already deteriorating climate. By about 4,700 C-14 years ago the caves were reoccupied showing that a limited habitat at least was available in the lake basin. By 4,000 C-14 years ago the present habitat was reestablished, and for the next 1,000 years the caves were again used as habitation sites with an intensity approximating that of the period about 7,200 to 7,300 C-14 years ago. Occupation thereafter apparently was like that of the ethnographic horizon.

Limited evidence—pollen grains extracted from the sole of a sandal I excavated from the Fort Rock Cave in 1965 and C-14 dated at 8,500±140 C-14 years ago (I-1917)—indicates a moister climate then than at anytime since. Pollen, "composed primarily of pine, sagebush and other compositae with minor amounts of Graminea and Chenopodoacae . . . single grains of *Tsuga* (hemlock), *Betula* (birch) or *Corylus, Ostrya* (hop hornbean) and two grains of *Alnus* (alder)" (Bedwell and Cressman 1971), was found. This small sample is indicative of the vegetation around the area of the lake where this hunter moved.

The last four species are not now found in the area. A precipitation at that time of 9 to 10 inches per year, heavier than now found in the area, is indicated.

That the cave abandonment is not just some change in settlement patterns of the population, unrelated to habitat condition, is shown by the phytolith profile from a 2.8 meter section from 4 meters outside Connley Cave No. 4 and correlated with the stratigraphic sequence inside the cave by means of the layer of Mt. Mazama ash. The phytolith column started four levels (40 centimeters) below the ash, but the cave occupation began nine levels below with a C-14 date of 10,600 years ago.

Grasses absorb silica from the soil which in turn is precipitated in the form of grass opal or phytoliths. At the death of the plant the phytoliths are released into the earth where they are preserved. The greater the amount of grasses in an area, the greater should be the amount of phytoliths. Therefore the phytolith record should be an indication of variation in climatic conditions. The samples were selected by 10 centimeter levels to correlate with the excavation levels in the cave. Phytolith percentages for four levels below the Mt. Mazama ash varied from just over 1 percent to just over 2 percent. Five levels *immediately above* the ash contained only about 0.1 percent. The percentages for the next four levels varied, then steadied to a situation about like that before the Mt. Mazama eruption. From about 3,000 C-14 years ago there is the highest percentage of phytoliths averaging about 2.5 percent per level.

In sum, the evidence from all presently available sources shows the concept of an Altithermal to be valid and useful to the archæologist as a time referent if properly used. It also shows that this period of climatic change, like glaciation, varied in its expression in both space and time, and that no single time bracket applies to the whole Great Basin; this fact becomes more evident as more refined methods of study are applied to the problem. Human response took various forms of adaptive response to the deteriorating climate according to the opportunity afforded by local conditions. The dates used for the beginning and end of the Altithermal must be determined, if at all possible, for the area of the Great Basin in which the archæologist works.

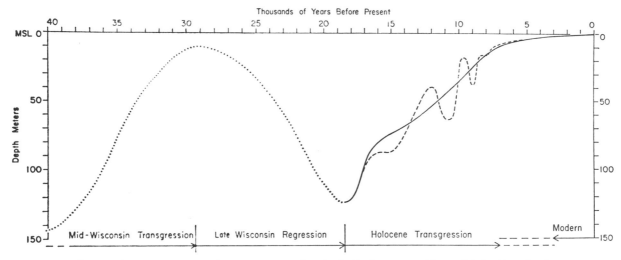

Thousands of Years Before Present

FIGURE 18. Quaternary changes in sea level. C-14 dates provide a fairly firm basis for interpretations up to 18,000 years ago. Before that the curve is much less certain, being based on a few C-14 dates and correspondence with continental features. *Curray 1965:725, Figure 2.*

SEA LEVEL CHANGES

Changes in sea level are important in New World prehistory for two reasons: (1) they produce new habitats for long periods of time along exposed coastlines and in turn destroy them; and (2) they expose and submerge land connections—land bridges —between Asia and North America. The times at which these changes occur are obviously of critical importance to the archæologist.

Sea level changes generally may be thought to occur in response to the long, slow rhythm of changing climate. Recession of the sea occurs during glaciation when the vast ice fields impound precipitation as snow and ice; transgression of the sea onto the land occurs when the impounded water is returned to the sea during deglaciation. This apparent synchroneity is not as close as the general theory suggests. It is thought that regression of the sea follows closely on the waxing of glaciers, but that transgression precedes deglaciation by an unknown period of time. The latter effect is interpreted as being due to the earlier melting of the ice in the center of the ice sheet than at the periphery so that melt water returns to the sea and the sea level rises while the outer boundaries of the ice sheet remain—for a time—unchanged.

Other factors being equal (but they never are), there should be a worldwide series of ocean terraces or beaches marking the stand of the sea at particular

times at appropriate levels. Two factors prevent this uniformity from being achieved: isostatic adjustment of the earth's crust—depression in response to the weight of the ice and rebound when the weight is removed—and tectonic changes or crustal deformation.

Isostatic adjustment occurs only in the area of marked glaciation, such as the Fraser Lowland of British Columbia and the Puget Lowland of northwest Washington. Human occupation, which occurs along early strandlines, may in the course of a few thousand years be found on these beaches far inland and above the present sea level as the glaciers melt. Radiocarbon dating of these ancient shorelines enables the archæologist to date his associated material, and the archæologist may be able to help the geologist, if he can date his material by the radiocarbon method, for he then provides a date for the beach. Unfortunately there is no constant rate that can be applied to the process of isostatic adjustment.

Tectonic changes—changes in the earth's crust caused by deformation such as faulting and earthquakes—are of limited value in assessing most archæological questions. However, in relation to the problems of land connections, deformation may be of significant importance. A news article by the United Press International reporting a study of effects of the Alaskan earthquake of 1964 by the U.S. Coast and

FIGURE 19. Underwater archæology off La Jolla, California. *Photograph courtesy of James R. Moriarty.*

Geodetic Survey states that "the ocean floor between Kodiak and Montague Island (ca. 275 miles distant) rose about 50 feet, the greatest such rise ever recorded" (*Eugene Register Guard,* July 9, 1969). It is quite possible that such events have occurred before in the unstable Pacific Rim during the time of man's occupancy.

Chronological information pertinent to sea level changes is derived from a variety of sources: C-14 dates from organic material in drill cores; dating of beaches by contained shells; or wood or other organic material from partially submerged archæological sites secured by scuba divers. Numerous

C-14 dates have been obtained from the Bering Sea and Strait and provide information for determining the late phases of the Bering Land Bridge.

Curray (1965:725, Figure 2) provides a curve for sea level changes plotted against time during the last 40,000 years (Figure 18). He evaluates the significance of his data as follows:

This portion of the curve [prior to 18,000 B.P.—dotted line, Figure 18] is *largely speculation* [emphasis added]. It is based on a few dates suggesting an interstadial high stand of sea level sometime between about 22,000 and 35,000 B.P. (Curray 1961, and unpublished dates; Shepard 1963b) and on correlation with continental Pleistocene events. This interstadial stand of sea level probably lay

FIGURE 20. Mortar resting on ocean floor off La Jolla, California. *Photograph courtesy of James R. Moriarty.*

slightly below present sea level. On the basis of indirect geological evidence, it is suggested that the maximum lowering of sea level during the early-Wisconsin glaciation was about -145 m, but the time of this lowering is not known. . . .

The maximum late-Wisconsin low stand of sea level occurred between about 20,000 and 17,000 B.P. at a level of about -120 to -125 m (Curray 1961; Curray and Moore 1964). The sea-level evidence agrees well with late-Wisconsin continental glacial chronology. Depth of the low stand is not well established, however, but it appears that the maximum lowering was at least 110 m. Figure 1 shows my estimate of -124 m (Curray 1965:724).

It is clear from the evidence that there has been a progressive, if uneven, rate in rise of sea level for the last 18,000 years correlated with the gradual reduction of the amount of glacial ice. A progressive rise continued and reached a high point of about -50 meters 12,000 years ago followed by a drop to about -70 meters at 11,000 B.P. A sharp but small rise occurs at 10,000 and then drops at 9,000 B.P. The curve then rises sharply to the 7,000 B.P. level. Shortly after 10,000 years ago, the rate of rise of sea level begins markedly to slow down and after 7,000 years it rises very slowly. This rise since 10,000 years ago has significance for the archæologist studying human prehistory in coastal areas (Shepard 1964).

Evidence of change in sea level within the last 10,000 years is shown by underwater archæology, Figures 19 and 20 (Marshall and Moriarty 1964: Figure 14), and by archæological excavation (Beardsley 1948; Newman 1959) in which occupation sites are partially or fully under the rising sea. For example, at Willow Creek (sites Mnt-281 and Mnt-282, University of California Archæological Survey) about 30 miles south of Big Sur, California, present-day beach gravels overlie 4.5 feet of archæological shell midden deposit indicating subsidence of the shore since the site was formed. Libby (1955:113, 115) gives C-14 dates of 1,879±250 (C-628) and 1,840±400 (C-695) years ago for charcoal from this midden.

It is not clear that there was any stand of sea level higher than the present shoreline in post-Pleistocene time. Those who assert such a higher stand would correlate it with the Altithermal period between about 7,500 and 4,000 years ago. But with opinions on both sides of the issue, the question must be left unanswered, although the more convincing arguments seem to be against a higher level than at present.

NONCLIMATIC TIME MARKERS

Two types of events are considered, floods and volcanism. Each is a single event caused by nonclimatic factors and may be useful within limited areas as a time marker for the archæologist.

Glacial Lake Missoula Flood

The most recent catastrophic flood in the Pacific Northwest was that caused by the sudden breaking of the ice dam that impounded the water of a vast glacial lake in western Montana and adjacent portions of Idaho. Estimates of the amount of water released range as high as 500 cubic miles. It devastated much of southeastern Washington producing the eroded area known as the "channeled scablands." Water was funneled into the Columbia River, and the tremendous volume of water left great deposits of gravel and boulders high above the present level of the river, some as far west as Portland, Oregon. Had humans lived in the area before the flood, clearly all evidence would have been destroyed or transported, perhaps to lodge in some bed of gravel downstream where it might be later found and recognized as a man-made object. I found a basalt knife (to be described later) in 1953 in the gravels of this flood on the west side of the John Day River more than 200 feet above the Columbia River where the John Day joins it. The presence of this artifact is valid evidence of man's presence in the area antedating the flood.

The flood, the youngest of these, is correlated with the post maximum of the early Pinedale Stade because the waters scoured moraines and other deposits of Early Pinedale age, and the flood debris in turn is covered by deposits of Middle Pinedale age (Richmond et al. 1965:239). A radiocarbon date of 32,700± 900 years (UW-9) was derived from "wood and fragments of dried peat-like muck" collected by Fryxell in August 1960 from "excavation of gravels during construction of Wanapum Dam, six miles south of Vantage [central] Washington, . . . between the present channel of the Columbia River and the west wall of the valley" (Fryxell 1962). "[S]amples of what appeared to be peat or muck with high organic content were collected from torrential fore-sets in the basaltic gravel" (Fryxell 1962:*passim*).*

The radiocarbon date from the gravels of Wanapum and the dates for the early Pinedale Stade are obviously in conflict. The former is in the time range of the Olympia Interglaciation (35,000–25,000 years ago) while the latter ranges from about 25,000 to 14,000 years ago, depending on the place of measurement. Fryxell (1962b:9) resolves this conflict by theorizing that the dated material does not represent the date of the flood. "[I]t must be concluded that the wood and peat are reworked deposits from an interstadial bog formed during the interval preceding the last Wisconsin advance of the Okanagan lobe." Fryxell (personal communication, R. Fryxell to L. S. Cressman, February 16, 1966) wrote: "[M]y best guess on the age of the major flood episode would be between 18,000–23,000 years ago."

---

* The original date for this sample is 31,600±900 radiocarbon years ago, but the age was recalculated on the half-life 5,730 years base to give 32,700±900. Since the 5,570 year half-life is conventionally used, as pointed out above, for comparative purposes, the original date is preferable.

There are various unanswered problems connected with this dating, but they need not be discussed here. The archæologist still does not have any reasonably precise date for the flood. The important conclusion from the incorporation of this artifact in the flood gravels is that man was in the area before the last major advance of the ice sheet into the area, but how long before is problematical.

The Bonneville Flood

This has been recognized for a long time as a violent overflow from Lake Bonneville into the Snake River, but only lately has firm evidence begun to be produced relative to the time of this episode and its causes. These studies, as Malde says, are "inconclusive" in details but nevertheless clarify to some extent lake history which in turn should eventually provide a firmer chronological basis for archæology in the lake basin.

What happened, without going into unnecessary detail, is this. Bear River in southeastern Idaho originally flowed into the Snake River via the Portneuf River (Bright 1963). About 34,000 years ago it was diverted by a lava flow and Lake Thatcher was formed. Subsequent faulting and volcanism caused Lake Thatcher, which previously drained into the Snake River, to change its outlet and to rise sufficiently to spill across a divide into Cache Valley, a part of the Lake Bonneville basin. Subsequently the divide between Cache Valley and Lake Thatcher was eroded to a minimum elevation of 4,600 feet; Lake Thatcher became an arm of Lake Bonneville, and Bonneville sediments were deposited over those of Lake Thatcher in Thatcher Basin (Bright and Rubin 1965; Morrison 1966). Subsequent to the establishment of the Bear River drainage into Lake Bonneville, that lake rose to a level of 5,135 feet, 30 or 35 feet above the later formed Bonneville Terrace, and overflowed. Rapid downcutting occurred resulting in a catastrophic flood along the lower Portneuf River and the Snake River. Relative stabilization was achieved when the surficial material was eroded to bedrock at 5,100 feet elevation. Gradual downcutting then eroded the pass to the Provo Terrace level. A probable maximum rate of discharge has been calculated of more than "one-third cubic mile per hour . . . [or] four or five times the average discharge of the Amazon River,"

for an available volume of 380 cubic miles of water (Malde and Trimble 1965:*passim*; Malde 1968). Thus the volume of the Bonneville Flood was smaller than that of the glacial Lake Missoula Flood, and, on comparative figures of estimated rate of discharge, the latter's rate of discharge was probably greater than the former. Both, however, were catastrophic. "I infer that the major effects of the Bonneville Flood probably were produced in a few days (certainly in less than a month) and that voluminous discharge continued for at least a year" (Malde 1968:13).

Geologists, however, differ sharply on the date of the flood. One group's view based on study of the flood in the Snake River valley places the date at about 30,000 years ago, while another whose studies have been in the Red Rock Pass and the Bear River–Thatcher Lake areas, prefers a date of about 18,000 years ago (International Association For Quaternary Research, VII Congress 1965:106).

In favor of the 30,000 years ago position is a C-14 date

of 29,700±1000 years (sample W-731) for mollusks from an alluvial terrace somewhat younger than the maximum flood, which probably formed as the flood waned and diminished in height (Trimble and Carr, 1961:1746). Although this date stands unsupported by others, it pertains to the only samples intimately tied to the flood deposits and must be considered in any reckoning of age (Malde 1968:11).

Further reliance is placed on the presence of soil mounds in lower Marsh Creek valley, downstream from Red Rock Pass, on lava denuded by the floodwaters. These mounds are similar to those in the western Snake River basin that are attributed to Late Pleistocene periglacial climate. If this attribution to a cold climate is correct, then it must have been a response to the Pinedale Glaciation, and the denuded surface must be correspondingly older than Pinedale.

Those who argue for the 18,000-years-ago date for the flood visualize the diversion of Bear River into Lake Bonneville basin as a relatively unimportant element in the rise of the lake to its overflow position. They interpret the rise of the lake as having taken place mainly in response to climatic conditions. Morrison (1966) reports a single radiocarbon date from "mollusk shells" (no code number given) of 27,000 years ago as marking the time of diversion of Lake Thatcher into Cache Valley. The 18,000-years-ago date for the flood is probably derived by correlation with an estimated middle Pinedale Stade maximum and two C-14 dates from Lake Thatcher.

The date of the Bonneville Terrace at 5,100 feet elevation is critical for archæologists. It is clear that man was in the Intermontane Region before the Pinedale Glaciation. If remains of human occupation are found firmly associated with the Bonneville Terrace, it makes a great deal of difference to the archæologist whether the date of that terrace is 18,000 or 30,000 years ago. But the evidence is inconclusive. One can only ask which argument is the more convincing.

Volcanism

Volcanism as an environmental attribute is important to the archæologist for two reasons: (1) it influences the environment as habitat, and (2) it serves as a time marker to which human events may be related for dating.

> Western North America is dotted with volcanoes that from time to time have discharged great quantities of volcanic ash. The ash is spread widely by wind, commonly over much of the continent, although ordinarily it accumulates as a thick blanket only near its source. The frequency of ash eruptions and their wide distribution, as indicated by the stratigraphic record, suggest that they are important geologic events to be considered seriously in reconstructing past environments (Malde 1964b:8).

The most important eruption for the purpose of this study is that of Mt. Mazama, in the Oregon Cascade Mountains, forming the caldera in which Crater Lake now lies. The eruption occurred about 7,000 years ago and threw out some 11 cubic miles of pumice and related materials, which were carried by the prevailing winds and the force of the explosions over vast distances. The ash has been identified in geological sections and exposures in Oregon, Washington west of the Cascade Mountains, from the Northern Great Basin to British Columbia, Alberta, and Montana. Our stratigraphic sections from the pluvial Fort Rock Lake basin show that the ash mantle there was about 6 inches thick. An arc about 20 miles from the vent marks the line of the one-foot-deep mantle. Of course the farther from the vent the thinner the mantle becomes. Archæologists have used this ash deposit only as a time marker, but our work in the Fort Rock area in 1967 clearly indicated that the eruption had a marked, probably catastrophic effect on the immediate habitat.

The agencies affecting the environment are chemical and mechanical. "The gases that are frequently expelled by volcanoes include water vapor, carbon dioxide, chlorine, fluorine, ammonia, the oxides of sulfur, and various acids: hydrochloric, hydrofluoric, and sulfuric. Plants are damaged by most of these gases, the only fumes having no marked effect being water and carbon dioxide" (Malde 1964b:7). Heavy deposits will overload and smother vegetation. Abrasive particles of ash on plants may be lethal to animals using the plants for food. Ash washed into streams long after the eruption may carry acids lethal to fish and the smaller organisms on which they feed. The effects, both short and long term, on the food chain may seriously damage a favorable environment as a habitat for both human and nonhuman life.

The eruption of Paricutin volcano in western Mexico in 1943 provided geologists an excellent chance to observe the effects of the eruption on the food chain.

> The ash rapidly reduced the local animal population. Deer, rabbits, and coyotes disappeared first, as their food supplies were destroyed. Squirrels and jays remained until the pine cones and acorns vanished. Myriad bugs, blown into the area, were battered to the ground by falling ash, thus furnishing a temporary source of food for the crows, foxes, and mice that managed to hang on. Lizards and snakes found the loose ash hard going. Trees of the surrounding forest lost their leaves, although some herbaceous plants flourished. Crop damage was especially severe: fine ash that sifted into avocado blossoms inhibited pollenization; sweet potato plantings failed to set tubers; and ash abrasion of sugar cane allowed invasion by fungi (Malde 1964b:10).

The carefully controlled excavations in the Fort Rock Lake area show that the Mt. Mazama eruption occurred some time, perhaps more than 100 years, after the onset of the Altithermal, and some of the deteriorating aspects of the environment resulting from the aridity were already in evidence; consequently the effects of the climatic condition and the eruption are confused. However, immediately after the eruption what had been a gradual environmental change became a sudden change, and this situation lasted for nearly 2,000 years in the lake basin. The evidence from the Fort Rock area suggests, in view of the evidence of the effects of volcanic eruption from widely scattered sources, that perhaps archæologists in the Pacific Northwest need to include with the climatic deterioration of the Altithermal the ecological damage of the Mt. Mazama eruption as a significant factor in what appears to be a decline in the level of human use of the area.* The opinion my colleagues and I advanced in 1940, that the eruption was just another event having but emotional significance to the inhabitants, must be discarded (Cressman, Williams, and Krieger 1940).

Volcanic Ash as a Stratigraphic Horizon Marker

"A mantle of volcanic ash, deposited over a region during a moment of geologic time and thereupon buried, constitutes an ideal stratigraphic marker. This forms the basis of *volcanic-ash chronology,* or, more generally, *volcanic-ejecta chronology*" (Wilcox 1965:807).

The Pacific Northwest, with its history of volcanism throughout the quaternary and until as late as 1917 at Mt. Lassen in California, offers an excellent opportunity for the application of volcanic ash chronology. The first opportunity in the Northwest for the use of this method was at the Wikiup Damsite on the Deschutes River some 30 miles south of Bend, Oregon (Cressman 1937a). A workman making soil tests for the contractor found a number of scrapers or knives under stratified deposits in turn overlaid by 2½ feet of pumice, which was identified by two geologists as having come from the climactic eruption of Mt. Mazama. At the time it was thought that the eruption had occurred about 25,000 years ago in the terminal Pleistocene. Since archæological opinion then placed the arrival of man in the New

World much later than 25,000 years ago, this discovery raised more problems than it solved.

The Paisley-Five-Mile Point caves in south-central Oregon and Fort Rock Cave 50 miles distant to the northwest were excavated in 1938 and contained occupation materials separated by unbroken layers of pumice; and one shelter produced a hearth, artifacts, and *Equus,* camel, and other bones, well beneath the pumice (Cressman 1939, 1940a, b; Cressman et al. 1942; Cressman, Williams, and Krieger 1940). Howel Williams (1942), who was then studying the geology of Mt. Mazama at Crater Lake National Park at my invitation, studied the pumice deposits in situ in both caves and took samples for later laboratory analysis. He identified the pumice in Paisley Cave as having been deposited by the Mt. Mazama eruption and that in Fort Rock Cave as being from a Newberry volcano eruption, a source 20 miles to the north. On the basis of his geological studies of Mt. Mazama, he estimated the date of the eruption at sometime between 4,000 and 10,000 years ago. Williams's study was long before the development of the radiocarbon method of dating and he had to use the methods available to the geologist at that time—rates of sedimentation, weathering, etc. The upshot of these studies proved conclusively that man was living in the area when the eruption of Mt. Mazama occurred and that pumice of that eruption could be used as a horizon marker to date a stage in human prehistory. The time spread of the possible dates, however, made the event of little help to the archæologist in precisely dating his material.

In the meantime Hansen (1947) had been studying the postglacial forest succession in the Pacific Northwest by using the record of pollen preserved in peat bogs. A by-product of this study was the demonstration by practically each core that a layer of volcanic ash of varying thickness had been deposited over the area; the volcanic ash horizon marker was far more widely distributed than had earlier been thought.

Now that it has become clear that there might be multiple sources of volcanic ash, the problem of source identification is of the greatest importance. The development of more refined methods of laboratory analysis of pumice along with improved field methods and the availability and application of radio-

* Hansen in 1942 reported on the effect of the Mt. Mazama eruption upon the forest succession as indicated by the pollen profile from a bog approximately 13 miles west of Bend, Oregon, in the Cascade Mountains. There were two pumice strata, one of which was derived from the Mt. Mazama eruption. "The occurrence of the pumice strata is significant, because the change in the edaphic conditions due to the deposition of the pumice in this region evidently had a marked influence upon the forest succession as suggested by the pollen profiles" (Hansen 1942:214). Little or no attention seems to have been paid to Hansen's observations at the time, but the Fort Rock study shows that he had correctly assessed the ecological importance of volcanic ash falls.

carbon methods of dating have brought us a long way toward solution of the problems of using volcanic ash as an archæological marker. Pumice previously thought to have been from Glacier Peak is now recognized as Mt. Mazama ash and dated about 7,000 years ago. It is probable that the pumice in Fort Rock Cave originally thought to have been derived from the Newberry volcano is really from the Mt. Mazama eruptions.

Identification of the pumice falls is not simple and the results are not always conclusive. Randle ct al. (1971:280, 281) have approached the problem in the Northwest by examining both the chemical composition and the petrographic characteristics of volcanic ejecta:

> Elemental abundances obtainable by instrumental neutron activation analyses are of great potential value in characterizing volcanic ashes, especially when some attention is given to geochemical characteristics of the elements determined, and to the likely effects of post-eruptive fractionation and contamination process....
>
> One should note especially the possibilities for confusion between ashes erupted from the same vent but at times which, on an archæological scale, are vastly different .... Nevertheless, by continuing activation analyses with good field control and at least preliminary petrographic work, it became possible to look through the overprint of a wide variety of post-eruptional effects to perceive the essential character of the ash stratum.

Continued research of this sort promises to greatly increase the accuracy and reliability of the identifications that the archæologist as geochronologist has to work with, even though the authors quite properly emphasize the persistent complexities and ambiguities inherent in the problem. Their last caution is well illustrated by their analysis of the volcanic ash deposits critical for the dating of early remains from Mexico. "Our work on volcaniclastic deposits near Puebla indicates that products of a succession of eruptions of La Malinche volcano over at least 18,000 years cannot be distinguished from one another by the approach we are using here" (Randle et al. 1971: 273). A similar situation is also reported from Crater Lake in which, had it not been for the field evidence, ash-flow tuff, discharged from the main cone many thousands of years earlier, was unlikely to have been distinguished from recent specimens even by the sophisticated methods used.

Dating the Pumice Horizon

Since pumice is inorganic, it cannot be dated directly by the radiocarbon method but only by association with dateable organic material (very old pumice, in the range of hundreds of thousands of years, may be dated directly by the potassium-argon method). Association should be direct and complete. Growing trees in a forest overwhelmed by a glowing avalanche of pumice, fired and reduced to charcoal by the overriding ash, as happened during the eruption of Mt. Mazama, provide a classic example of perfect association. A second sort of association is found in peat bogs when the ash is recorded in the peat profile and radiocarbon dated from the overlying and underlying peat. A third association is archæological—where again the ash may be radiocarbon dated by material above and below the deposit.

In such situations as peat bogs and archæological sites, one must first determine whether the ash is primary or not—that is, whether it lies where it fell or whether it has been reworked by air or water transport.* Then there is the question of how close the association actually is between the ash and the organic material dated. Obviously these cases are not like the perfect association described above. Peat bracketing pumice will certainly give zones of mixture both above and below the contact, and there will be a certain time lapse separating the time of the pumice deposition from that of the dated peat above and below it. Similarly, the archæologist who dates the ash in a site by artifacts or charcoal from "just above" or "just below" the pumice is not being precise. Rates of sedimentation vary. Occupational debris will build up more rapidly than nonoccupational;

---

* A secondary or reworked deposit may date any time from a few days to several thousand years after the eruption depending primarily on local topographic features and elements such as wind and weather. While redeposition may take place in a relatively short period after the eruption, this is not always true. The Weis Rockshelter (Butler 1962a) in western Idaho contains two deposits of Mt. Mazama pumice, a thin earlier one and a heavier later one. There is a C-14 date (TBN-319) from charcoal just below the earlier pumice of 7,340±140 years ago indicating possibly a primary deposit. The upper bed, averaging 30 centimeters thick, is dated from associated charcoal (TBN-322) at 4,640 years ago. Here 2,700 years separate the deposition of the two, a significant time interval for the archæologist.

and occupational material with much organic debris, like matting, basketry, etc., will accumulate much more rapidly than that limited to stone and bone objects.

The writer, in company with Dr. Ira Allison, then Professor of Geology at Oregon State College, and Dr. George Ruhle, Chief Naturalist of Crater Lake National Park, on July 31, 1949, collected the first charcoal sample for radiocarbon dating of the Mt. Mazama eruption. Ruhle took us to a highway cut on Muir Creek that had exposed charred trees embedded in the pumice. Under the direction of Allison I made my way up the face of the cut and secured a large collection of charcoal from a tree apparently still nearly upright but completely covered. Libby, using then the solid carbon method, dated the charcoal (C-247) at 6,453±250 C-14 years ago (an average of four runs). The University of Michigan Laboratory, to help calibrate their instruments, was given charcoal by Libby from the large supply I had sent him and calculated a date, average of two runs, of 6,500±500 C-14 years ago (personal communication, W. F. Libby to L. S. Cressman). The use of newer methods, such as gas counting rather than solid carbon, would probably have increased these dates by 200 or more years. Since these dates were determined there have been other improvements in the laboratory processes toward the elimination of contamination, etc.

Because of the increasing accuracy in the determination of C-14 dates, the great variation in dates for Mt. Mazama pumice from peat bogs and archæological sites, and the improved techniques of pumice identification, Dr. L. K. Kittleman, Curator of Geology, Museum of Natural History, University of Oregon, and I returned on October 19, 1965, to the same road cut from which I had secured the original charcoal sample to get another for dating. Kittleman carefully examined the site and determined that, except for an area close to the surface, there was no evidence of any disturbance of the original deposit. I located within the original deposit a portion of a branch of a tree and collected a charcoal sample. Kittleman collected a pumice sample from immediate contact with the charcoal sample.

Kittleman's laboratory study of the pumice showed that it was from the ash flow (glowing avalanche)

phase of the Mt. Mazama eruption. Two separate dates were secured independently by laboratories, neither knowing the result of the other's work. One date (GaK-1124) is 7,010±120 C-14 years ago; the other (TX-487) is 6,940±120 C-14 years ago. These two dates, supported by the earlier Chicago and Michigan dates, indicate that 7,000±120 C-14 years ago is a reasonably firm date for the eruption and may be used at present to date the Mt. Mazama Volcanic Ash Horizon.

A problem not yet resolved in the dating of the Mt. Mazama ashfall is the conflict between dates from open sites and dates from caves or dry sources. Dates from open sites, mostly peat bogs, range from 5,390±60 years ago to 7,000±200 C-14 years ago. On the other hand, dates from dry caves fall mostly just under 8,000 C-14 years ago. As I pointed out above, both sources of samples require the same use of relative association in dating. I am at a loss to explain the pattern of difference in the dates, and if the difference is not due to an error in collecting samples for dating, then there must be some undiscovered source of contamination to which the open sites are exposed. All these sites are wet, including the one at Muir Creek where water seeps through even late in the summer, and one can only ask if there may be a presently undetected contaminating factor associated with direct exposure to water.

In this chapter I have discussed the methods of determining a chronological order and its application to changes in the environment to which human phenomena may be related. The methods are those of geochronology. Radiocarbon dating has given us the most precise tool for age determination of a specimen or event occurring within the last 40,000 years. It is widely used by archæologists and Pleistocene geologists, though of course it is not foolproof and requires the utmost care in the handling of the sample from its collection to the final dating and interpretation of the result. In the absence of direct radiocarbon dating of archæological events, the archæologist is dependent for a chronology on the conclusions of geology. He must relate his data to the appropriate geological phenomenon and deduce a date for his material. The strengths or weaknesses of the chronological affirmations of the geologist will, therefore, apply equally to the archæologist's deductions.

I pointed out also that the geologist has a quite different time orientation than the archæologist since he is dealing in vast spans of time. Stratigraphic correlation charts for the continent are based on this, and the straight lines connecting the beginnings of these episodes at a given date on the time axis, say 25,000 years ago, derive from this assumption. This obscures the local variations so significant for the archæologist.

The tenor of this chapter is not defeatist; it is candidly critical of our methods and their results in the formulation of a chronological system useful to the prehistorian where a time bracket of a hundred years may be crucial for his purpose. It has attempted to set forth the limits of tolerance with which we are presently faced. By candidly facing the strengths and weaknesses of our knowledge we can evaluate objectively the validity of positions and see what needs to be done to get more light than that from a "torch of smoky pine" to light our pathway ahead.

The Wanderers

We are the Pilgrims, master; we shall go
Always a little further: it may be
Beyond that last blue mountain barred with snow,
Across that angry or that glimmering sea.

. . . .

We travel not for trafficking alone:
By hotter winds our fiery hearts are fanned:
For lust of knowing what should not be known
We make the Golden Journey to Samarkand.

. . . .

It was ever thus.
Men are unwise and curiously planned.

James Elroy Flecker, The Golden Journey to Samarkand

O UT OF ASIA an unknown number of centuries ago came these Wanderers, the first to set foot on the Western Hemisphere. Omnivorous Pleistocene predators, they followed their prey as it moved and sought new sources in a land that was to them only an extension of the country with which they had been long familiar—a land we now conveniently call a land bridge. Wanderers they were whose basic objective was survival, but there must have been accessory motivations less readily definable which moved them on. Flecker, in the words I quoted above, felicitously expresses both the variety and often indefinable quality of human motivation. Generation after generation of men must have come and gone before foot was ever set by any human on the land of North America. And in the expanse of tundra 1,000 miles wide with low, rolling hills that was the Bering Land Bridge were probably numerous small bands operating with many not aware of the existence of others. Probably, as time passed, additional population sources sent out new movements of people differing both in physical type and in material and nonmaterial cultural achievements with which they adapted to new environments. As confluent streams add their burden to the volume of a large river, so these human confluents flowed at special times and places into the larger stream of human history. I am concerned in this chapter with the problem of the source in place and time of the earliest part of this segment of history. So little of the relevant information is firm and so rapidly are new discoveries being made that any discussion must be in terms of probabilities, that is "if such and such is so, then this conclusion follows."

Significant discussion of this problem requires four bodies of information or variables: (1) the availability of a population reservoir in the source area; (2) the existence of a land connection between northeast Asia and Alaska; (3) an ice-free corridor from Alaska into the interior of the continent, either east of the Rocky Mountains or via interior British Columbia and the Intermontane Region, or both; and (4) the evidence of human presence validated by both stratigraphic provenience and precise methods of dating, such as radiocarbon dating. The interrelation of these factors provides the means of analysis. Consider a hypothetical example. If there was a population reservoir in northeast Asia 70,000 years ago but there was no land connection before 30,000 years ago, then man could not be expected to have been in the Western Hemisphere before 30,000 years ago. And if he did arrive by 30,000 years ago but there was no ice-free route to the continental interior for the next 15,000 years, his presence south of Alaska has to date from after that time. Change the time referent for any of these variables and the whole problem assumes a different aspect. If, given this general model, a *validated* (I emphasize *validated*) site of greater age is found than indicated as probable by the other variables, then the implication is that the data derived from one or more of the other variables is in error. An analogy may be taken from plane geometry. A circle is a closed plane curve each point of which is equidistant from a point, the center. On the other hand, a noncircular plane figure is defined by the location of a number of points, and if one is changed the whole configuration changes. The problem of the arrival of man in the Western Hemisphere is analogous to a non-circular plane figure whose shape is determined by the location of a number of points.

The relatively few survivors in the ranks of archæologists who have been actively engaged in this aspect of American archæology for the last 40 years are well aware of the great changes that have occurred in the thinking on this problem. A vast amount of new information—geological, climatological, biological, and cultural—has accumulated. New and relatively precise means of dating events which occurred 30,000 years ago have been developed. The parameters of the problem have undergone restatement. It is ironical that while we know a great deal more on all these matters than ever before, the knowledge does not lead to final decision but, in my opinion, only toward a recognition of the great complexity of the problem and the imperative for an open, critical, and exploring mind.

Sometimes, I think, we are tricked by words or expressions into failure to visualize the real situation, for example, by the expressions "land bridge" and "ice-free corridor." In our culture a bridge is a reasonably firm structure across a body of water connecting roads or multiple-lane highways coming from definite places and going to places equally known as objectives. To speak of a land bridge across the Bering Strait cannot but help carry some of the connotations the word has in our language. Land connection would be a much better phrase since it suggests a piece of land that connects two other bodies of land. If that land connection was a tundra 1,000 miles wide or 20 miles wide, the problem of survival, as anyone who has firsthand knowledge of the tundra knows, appears in a different form than when the image of a land bridge is evoked.

An ice-free corridor may sound like a well-cleared winter highway. How wide is the corridor? How continuous is it? Around the edges of ice there are bogs, probably masses of relict ice often of great size, and ephemeral lakes, all comprising the "wastage area" of the melting glacier. How wide does such a corridor have to be to support the life on which human hunters must rely to survive? The drainage from the runoff of melting ice as the Cordilleran and the Laurentide ice sheets drew apart must have produced a monstrous bog or bogs until the distance of separation was sufficient to permit new drainage systems to carry the runoff from the melting glaciers. The extensive muskeg of the western Canadian plains bears witness to these conditions. Expressions can be dramatic but semantically misleading.

Our thinking on this particular problem, as on many others, is influenced, I think, by what is probably a human if hardly a scientific trait, and usually it is unconscious at that. I mean the *resistance to "the new"* which may call into question established values or accepted intellectual positions if the new discovery is validated or accepted. This attitude leads, too often, not to an honest effort to validate the new discovery but to discredit it, for if this can be done "the old" remains and we still possess assurance. The qualifications of the discoverer may be denigrated, absurdly high levels of validation may be required when the same are not asked in another case, or the evidence may just be "not accepted"—and often without convincing evidence, or even any evidence for that matter, being offered as to why it should be rejected

Perhaps the bludgeons wielded as late as the 1930s by W. H. Holmes and Aleš Hrdlička, archæologist and physical anthropologist, respectively, of the United States National Museum and highly regarded scholars, have left unrecognized intellectual wounds on the body of archæological thought concerned with the antiquity of man in the New World—wounds that make us draw back from cognitive activity which might unconsciously recall the ugly blows delivered to the intellectual explorers of the past. But surely this amazing aspect of human history—the entrance of small bands of Wanderers into a new world of immensely diverse environmental challenges, the conquest of that world by their descendants and followers—requires no less from us than that we should push ourselves to the utmost to develop full empathy with these men, women, and children who lived this great epic of the human experience. Only then can we approach the study of this extremely complex and utterly fascinating problem with the sympathetic understanding and appreciation worthy of it.

It is a commonplace of archæological thought, fully justified by all available empirical and theoretical information, that some place or places of northeastern Asia were the homeland of these Wanderers. The evidence of physical anthropology, geology, biogeography, and culture all fits together to support this conclusion. The exact part of northeastern Asia, however, as the homeland is in dispute. One group argues strongly for the vast Lake Baikal area, using the expression as synonymous with northeastern Siberia, while a somewhat smaller group, to which I belong, sees the Pacific Ocean side of China as the more likely source of origin. The problem is complex and the evidence fragmentary. Pertinent evidence is required from physical anthropology, geology, and culture, but the evaluation of this evidence in terms of the weight to be given to each area and the question of cultural relationships (which is very much unanswered) provides answers only in terms of probabilities.

THE POPULATION RESERVOIR

The Probable New-World Early Population

Deductions from the knowledge and theory of the physical composition of the American Indian populations together with pitifully few samples of ancient skeletal material provide the working body of knowledge in this field (Stewart 1960). Stewart asserts a basic homogeneity, both genotypically and phenotypically, for the American Indian, and interprets such phenotypic variations as do exist as environmental adaptations of a single, basic genetic type. Blood-group studies provide one body of evidence of this genetic homogeneity. Blood-type O is most characteristic of the Indian populations, and where type B occurs in American Indians, it is usually assumed to be the result of Indian-white intermixture or faulty technique of the investigator. The populations of the Far North are partial exceptions to this generalization, however, and types B and A, which occur in the Eskimos, Aleuts, and Athapascans, are asserted to be the result of late waves of migration of Eskimos and Athapascans into the New World, with the Eskimo-Aleut source being closely related to the evolved Mongoloid of northeast Asia.

But Algonkians also have appreciable amounts of type A, for example, the Blackfoot (p. 84, below), and they would have to be included in the late arrivals.

Stewart (1960) chooses the Midland skull from Texas (see Wendorf et al. 1955) as his referent for American Indian skulls of some antiquity. While there are other remains "none has been proved to be older or more primitive" (Stewart 1960:261). This skull he described as representing "a long-headed Indian type." The Midland skull has a possible age ranging from 10,000 to 20,000 years ago, and Stewart accepts the latter as possible. Stewart sums up the evidence as he evaluates it (1960:261): "All this simply bears out the point I am trying to make, namely, at present the skeletal evidence from the hemisphere as a whole indicates nothing but the modern form of man going back over a span of about 20,000 years." Stewart thus sees the American Indian as a homogeneous population and views with considerable skepticism any evidence which seems to suggest the contrary. If there were areas of population before 20,000 years ago (Stewart's cutoff date), as I am convinced there were, then the problem of American Indian diversity or homogeneity is still open.

Skeletal material from the Tranquility Site, in the San Joaquin Valley about 24 miles from Fresno, California, may be used to support an argument for greater heterogeneity among early populations than is allowed by Stewart. This material was excavated during the years 1939–42 and further excavations were carried out in 1944 (Hewes 1946). Final publication of the results of the excavations has been held up because Satterthwaite, who conducted the final excavations, is not convinced that a perfect case has been made for the association of the skeletal and artifactual material with the fossil fauna, *Camelops, Equus,* and *Bison,* which suggests a Late Pleistocene age for the site. Angel (1966) thinks that the evidence strongly supports the association and, therefore, he has made available the results of his study of the skeletal materials.*

While fragments of over thirty individuals were

_____

* In spite of sophisticated methods of analysis, the association of the fossil human and nonhuman skeletal material and the dates applicable to each are still in dispute (Berger et al. 1971:47–48).

found, only "3 male and 4 female adults are usably complete" (Angel 1966:1). Angel compares these skulls, which may be contemporary with the Midland skull, with other Paleo-Indian and east Asiatic types which I discuss next. I quote from his summary:

> The robust skulls are long and extremely high, with somewhat pinched foreheads and broad and strong-jawed faces having low-rooted broad noses. They differ little from the East Asiatic Pleistocene Proto-Mongoloid norm so far established or from modern groups in the southern San Joaquin Valley. The Tranquility skulls differ more from other California groups and from other Paleo-american series as would be expected if microevolution in America over the past 20,000 years has involved sampling accident (drift) as well as isolation and selection. (Angel 1966:17).

The Tranquility skeletons may comprise evidence of an early population distinct from that represented by Stewart's examples and possibly derived from a different influx of New-World immigrants.

Old-World Population Reservoir

I pointed out earlier that there were two theories of the areas of origin of the early populations for the New World—the vast Lake Baikal area and the China-Pacific coast area. Consider the Lake Baikal area first. The earliest cultures excavated there are generally thought to be related to those of the European Late Paleolithic, and the assumption implicit in the writings is that a non-Mongoloid, European population produced the Lake Baikal area cultures. This may be true, but there is no direct evidence to support it. Chard (1958:3), writing of the "oldest stage, characterized by its general similarity to the classic Upper Paleolithic of Europe," reports at the Irkutsk Military Hospital site the presence "of a small number of crude, massive stone artifacts without western analogies in at least one early site. . . [and this] suggests that an east Asiatic element may have been present in the area from the beginning. *Unfortunately, we have no evidence of the racial type of these oldest Siberians* [emphasis added]. A child burial was found at Mal'ta, but the material has never been studied." Describing the somewhat later Stage II he writes: "A cranial fragment indentified as 'Mongoloid' gives added ground for postulating that the new culture represents *the absorption*

of the previous European population by invaders from eastern Asia [emphasis added]" (Chard 1958: 4). A single cranial fragment identified as "Mongoloid" here is used to represent an invading population, and the absorbed population is definitely stated to have been European. The evidence is inadequate basis for the postulate. The truth of the matter is that we have no reliable evidence at all of what the populations were like with either cultural stage—the conclusion to be drawn from Chard's evidence, if not his words.

China has provided important evidence even if limited in amount. It must be remembered that even though at the time of European discovery the American Indian population represented a homogeneous isolate, it is not likely that the the first Wanderers who entered the continent did. They certainly did not all come at once, and the populations that may have comprised the source reservoir in China, given the type of subsistence pattern and the environmental diversity existing at that time, must have consisted of a variety of breeding isolates. Evidence of considerable variability in the population in China during the late Upper Pleistocene comes from a number of skeletons of adults of both sexes and of children excavated from the Upper Cave at Choukoutien just above the famous deposits containing Peking Man and his debris. Weidenreich saw in the skeletal remains specimens suggesting the Old-World racial types, Cro-Magnon, Melanesian of New Guinea, and Eskimo, and he thought that "they might represent the ancestors of the Amerindian peoples already on the march towards the New World" (Boule and Vallois 1957:387).

Neumann (1956:380) writes concerning the possible relation of the Upper Cave skulls to early American Indians:

> With the accumulation of datable skeletal material from the earlier archæological horizon from both North and South America, the Upper Paleolithic cranial remains of five individuals from the Upper Cave at Choukoutien gain new significance as possible Proto-Mongoloid ancestral forms to the American Indian. . . . A detailed morphological and metrical reexamination of the available casts reveals that the particular traits, for which possible mixture has been invoked, are at the most only vaguely suggestive of Europeans, Melanesians, and Eskimos. All the traits in question appear repeatedly in various early

American Indian populations and should be regarded as expressive of the natural variability of the group.

Workmen, excavating for a bridge abutment in Szechwan province about 800 miles southwest of Peking in 1951, found a human skull representing Tzeyang Man reported on by Woo (1958). The fossil mammalian fauna from the site were classified by Pei into two groups, one from the Late Pleistocene (Third Interglacial-Fourth Glacial) and the other from the Middle Pleistocene (Second Interglacial-Third Glacial). In the Late Pleistocene group were *Homo sapiens, Equus sp., Mammonteus primigenius,* among others, while in the second group were *Stegodon orientalis, Cervus (Rusa) unicolor,* and *Rhinoceros sinensis.* The Late Pleistocene group specimens are "all lightly fossilized, not worn by water and contain small percentages of flourine." The Middle Pleistocene specimens are "all strongly mineralized, water rolled, and contain greater flourine percentages. *Hyena sp., Felis tigris, Sus sp., Hystris sp.,* and *Rhizomys sp.* are perhaps present in both groups."

The age of the human skull is asserted to be "earlier Late Pleistocene" (Woo 1958: *passim*) which would put it in the Third Interglacial, but the author is no more specific than that. The age was established from the associated mammalian fossils, the geological stratigraphy, and the morphological characters of the skull itself.

Woo writes in summary,

> The importance of the discovery lies in the fact that it is the first fossil human skull found in South China, while other human fossils such as *Sinanthropus,* the Ordos tooth and the Upper Cave people were all found in North China. However, the Tzeyang skull bears some resemblance to the Upper Cave Man on the one hand and with *Sinanthropus* on the other. This new discovery provides new data on the origin of the Chinese people and the distribution of Paleolithic man in China (Woo 1958:470–71).

Two other representatives of fossil man, probably from the Late Pleistocene, need to be mentioned. First is the skull of *Liukiang Man,* found in a cave near Liuehow in Kwangsi-Chuwang province of southern China. The fossil fauna consists of both Middle and Late Pleistocene types. Because of the apparent association of the fossilized hominid skull with that of *Ailuropoda,* the giant panda (both speci-

mens were encased in the same "reddish matrix" which is different from the yellowish sediments containing the other fossils), it is inferred that the skull dates from the Late Pleistocene. Woo states "chronologically, they are Late Pleistocene in age" (Woo 1959:116).

The other specimen consists of a fragmentary skullcap found in 1958 "in a limestone cave in the 'Lion Hill' at Mapa village, Shaquan Municipality (formerly Chukiang District) of Kwangtung Province. . ." (Woo 1959:176). Fauna associated with the specimen indicate the age, said to be "either late Middle Pleistocene or early Late Pleistocene" (Woo 1959:181). This skull is more primitive than the other two and apparently older. Woo (1959:181) writes that it "is the earliest human fossil so far found in China with the exception of *Sinanthropus.* This new discovery indicates that in the time of middle Pleistocene, not only North China but also South China are inhabited by early hominids. Thus it greatly extends the distribution of Paleolithic man in China" (Stewart 1960:268).

What is the significance of these fossil hominid remains, especially those that are definitely *H. sapiens,* for the problem of the relation of northeastern Asia to the settlement of the New World? The Lake Baikal area so far lacks both culture and fossil remains of the antiquity of these from China. The Upper Cave people and these others provide evidence from widely separated areas of China of available populations living in probably the early Late Pleistocene that could have served as reservoirs from which the Wanderers could have come. Further, the evidence seems to be that these fossil specimens represent early forms of the evolving Mongoloid stock. Neuman (quoted above) sees the Upper Cave people as possible Proto-Mongoloid ancestors of the American Indians. Stewart sees close similarities between the Tzeyang skull and certain high-vaulted skulls of American Indians and in reference to Liukiang Man writes: "In my opinion the skull type, which is moderately low vaulted with wide, short face, is not very different from that of some California Indians" (1960:268). This evidence, in my opinion, heavily weights the probabilities in favor of northeastern China over the Lake Baikal region as the source for the earliest Wanderers into the New World.

THE LAND CONNECTION

Beringia (Map 4), the name used for the vast low-land consisting of western Alaska, northeastern Siberia, and the shallow parts of the Bering and Chuckchi seas, is the area pertinent to the discussion of land connections between the continents in the Late Pleistocene when a human population reservoir was available in northeastern Asia.

The usual model for the appearance and disappearance of the land connection is pretty simplistic: the connection and its disappearance were functions of climatic conditions that produced glaciation and deglaciation, alternately decreasing and increasing the amount of water in the seas, and, consequently, submerged surfaces were exposed and again submerged resulting alternately in land connections and open seaways. While the broad relationship between climatic conditions and the land connection is simple and well established, the actual history of the phenomenon is more complex. Without entering into detailed discussion, its complexity may be illustrated by evidence indicating that in the late Miocene, between 12,000,000 and 10,000,000 years ago, and again in the late Pliocene, between approximately 4,000,000 and 3,500,000 years ago, seaways interrupted the land connection. The latter of these is called the "Beringian Transgression" which "evidently began during Pliocene time, but . . . was not terminated by a eustatic reduction in sea level until well after the Quaternary Period had begun" (Hopkins 1967:49). Thus, previous to the Pleistocene, land connections came and went without benefit of glaciation and deglaciation. Crustal instability is a well-known characteristic of the Beringian area, as of the whole Pacific rim, and may have been at various times an important contributor to the appearance and disappearance of the land connection during the great cycles of eustatic change.

Hopkins points out that "critical details of this [sea level] history remain uncertain or unknown" (1967: 461). Changes in topography, regional uplift, deposition of glacial moraines, and other sedimentation during interglacial or interstadial periods, which reduced the extent of the lowering of sea level necessary to produce a land connection, are important. In addition, it should be kept in mind that the Bering Land Bridge did not suddenly collapse like London Bridge, but that the land connection was slowly and probably unevenly exposed and later submerged. Vast swamps and bogs with surface ice would have been present for long periods of time. The land connection as human habitat, the significant aspect for human prehistory, is thus the product of a number of variables, and the possibility of several or all working in concert requires that suggested dates for the land connection's history are but approximations based upon the best information presently available.

With these cautions in mind, drawing upon Hopkins and others, I submit the following land connection chronology:

Land Connection	Years B.P.	Glaciations and Interglaciations
1. Open seaway	100,000– 70,000	Illinoisan-Wisconsin Interglacial; Sangamon Interglacial
2. Land connection	70,000– 35,000	Salmon Springs Glaciation; Early Wisconsin Glaciation
3. Open seaway	35,000– 25,000	Olympic Interglaciation; Mid-Wisconsin Interglaciation
4. Land connection	25,000– 10,000	Fraser Glaciation; Late Wisconsin Glaciation
5. Open seaway	10,000– present	Postglacial

It is not certain whether the land connection was exposed throughout the entire length of period 2, and it is possible, but uncertain, that there might have been only very limited land connection during the last 4,000 years of period 4, once about 13,000 or 14,000 years ago and once again at 11,000 years ago. If such were the case, the limited character of the connection would hardly have qualified it as a human habitat.

The Late Pleistocene land connections, 1,000 miles in width at maximum extent, were for the most part monotonous landscapes of low relief broken only by low hills, represented now by the islands of the Bering Sea. The snow- and ice-clad mountains of Siberia and Alaska would have been visible from many points on a clear day. Bison, horse, and mammoth grazed and were hunted by man. The landscape suggests an ideal habitat for the hunter until the climate is considered, and then the picture changes.

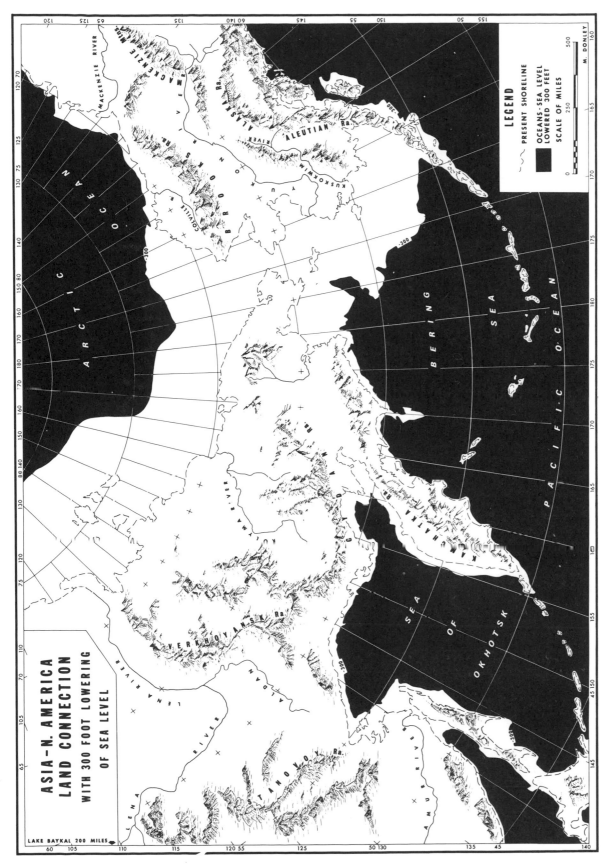

Map 4. Land connections between northeast Asia and northwest North America; polar projection.

Colinvaux (1964a, b; 1967) has studied the climatic conditions of Arctic Alaska and the intercontinental land connection by means of pollen analyses. His first study (1964a) was concerned with the "environment of the Bering Land Bridge." He took pollen cores from Imuruk Lake near the western end of the Seward Peninsula because it was close to the submerged platform and the lake apparently dates from the Middle Pleistocene. In addition, he used cores from St. Lawrence Island and one, provided by the University of Washington, from the Kotzebue Sound about 75 to 80 airline miles northwest of Imuruk Lake. The 1964b study was based on pollen samples collected at Point Barrow, one other site on the Arctic coastal plain, and two sites in the foothills to the south. The third study was carried out on Saint Paul Island in the Pribilofs, which is near the southern limit of the submerged platform.

These studies, insofar as the profiles overlap, corroborate one another. The Imuruk Lake profile records the longest period of deposition, and "Twice during the history of Imuruk Lake there occurred glaciations capable of lowering sea level from 300 to 450 feet. These resulted in Seward Peninsula becoming a part of a land mass connecting Alaska with Asia" (Colinvaux 1964a:323). Whether the climatic changes recorded in the Imuruk Lake profile are assignable entirely to the Wisconsin period, as Hopkins has argued, or whether the earliest is attributable to the Illinoian and only the later to the Wisconsin, as Colinvaux believes, the conclusions regarding the climate of the Bering land connection are significant.

> Vegetation was reduced to the most frigid form of arctic tundra, a tussockless, grassy expanse, spotted with frost scars and loess deposits and devoid of all trees and shrubs except willows. Only the most cold adapted animals and men could live in such a place. . . . The lowland climate probably allowed a milder form of tundra to grow but even if it allowed a rich tussock tundra, comparable with that at modern Imuruk Lake, it would still represent a cold, arctic environment. The absence of these elements, spruce and alder coupled with the extreme frigidity of the Imuruk Lake climate, demonstrates that the climate of the northern land bridge was everywhere truly arctic (Colinvaux 1964a:323).

The study on the Arctic coast, while it does not cover as long a record as the Imuruk Lake core, only

14,000 years, generally supports the evidence from that source. "This record of the arctic coastal plain tundras of the last 14,000 years implies an uninterrupted succession of cold climates, in which the present inclement weather of the place must be regarded as comparatively mild. The trend over the whole period has been one of warming" (Colinvaux 1964b: 708).

The pollen record from Saint Paul Island in the Pribilofs is of particular interest for the information it presents on environmental conditions of the southern portion of the land bridge from perhaps 35,000 years ago to the present. Birch, alder, and spruce do not now grow on Saint Paul Island. In the pollen rain at present on the island, alder may reach 5 percent of the total while birch and spruce each provide less than 1 percent. These falls must come from Alaska and Siberia some hundreds of miles away. Spruce does occur in significant amounts in the profile from perhaps 35,000 years ago, reaching a maximum of 20 percent between 10,000 and 9,000 years ago. Birch and alder maxima coincide with spruce. Mainland studies generally use the rule that for 20 percent spruce pollen to be deposited in the spectra the source trees must be not more than 50 kilometers distant. Applying this rule to Saint Paul, the conclusion may be drawn that, as the Wisconsin approached its end, spruce trees were a part of the ground cover on the land bridge to within 50 kilometers of the lake on the island from which the cores were taken. The sharp termination of the spruce record in the profile indicates the submergence of the land connection, and Colinvaux suggests that this first occurred on the Alaskan side.

"For the student of the land-bridge environment, this record shows that the southern plains of the land bridge, during the life of the bridge, probably supported local groves of alders. Scrubby outliers of the spruce forest were to be encountered along the flanks of the bridge. The environment was still arctic" (Colinvaux 1967:383).

The environmental evidence shows the land connection as an appallingly rigorous habitat. We have no information on what kinds of clothing these people wore; they had no caves for shelter as did the Paleolithic inhabitants of Europe; nor were there significant forested areas for shelter. In the demanding challenge of this environment were bred and selected through many generations the sturdy and durable men and women who were later to conquer a new continent.

THE ICE-FREE CORRIDOR

It is conventionally held that during a glacial period or stade severe enough to produce a land connection between the continents, there would also have been an extensive ice barrier formed by the coalescence of the Cordilleran and the Laurentide ice sheets, which would have blocked passage south into the continental interior. In Alaska the higher elevations of the Brooks Range in the north were covered with glaciers except for the extreme western part. The Aleutian Range, and the Alaskan Range bordering the Yukon-Kuskokwim plain on the south, were also ice covered. Only the Arctic shoreline extending eastward to the Mackenzie delta and the vast basin of the Yukon River were ice free. The eastern boundary of the ice-free area was at approximately 136° west longitude, the southern boundary at 62° north latitude. East and south stretched the glacial ice. Smith (1937:91) writes:

> None of these old glaciers on the Alaskan and Brooks ranges deployed far into the lowland beyond the fronts of these ranges, so that practically the entire central part of the Territory, an area several hundred miles from north to south and nearly 1,000 miles from east to west, at no time during the Quaternary was glaciated. This area, roughly about three-fifths of the Territory, may well have been a haven and place of refuge for animals and plants forced from other regions by the growing ice sheets of the Pleistocene.

Humans and other animals crossing the Bering Land Bridge during the late Wisconsin period of emergence, about 25,000-11,000 years ago, would thus have been directed into this huge cul-de-sac or refuge area, but their emergence to the east or south would have been blocked for an unknown period of time by the enclosing ice. The problem of an ice-free corridor, therefore, is where and when did an escape route exist out of the Alaskan cul-de-sac.

Theory concerning the ice-free corridor generally places it in the western plains along the eastern flank of the Rocky Mountains, although another possibility is sometimes considered, namely, the interior of British Columbia and into the Intermontane Region to the south. Information is required on two main problems: (1) the extent and times of glaciation, and (2) the character and times of deglaciation as these affect the corridor area. Precise field and laboratory studies of the glacial record and paleoecological evidence of the biota at the appropriate time levels provide the kind of evidence needed for answers to the corridor problem.

What is the evidence?

The glacial history of the area is not unequivocal. The Glacial Map of Canada (Geological Association of Canada 1962) shows that at a number of places the Cordilleran moraines overlie those of the Laurentide ice and extend some distance to the east. At other places the moraines are in contact indicating the probable coalescence of the two ice fronts. In the case of the overlap, it is not known at present what stage of glaciation is represented by the underlying moraines. They may represent an earlier glacial episode or only an advance of the Cordilleran after the retreat of the Laurentide of the same episode. It is not clear precisely how these overlaps are to be interpreted, and only careful field studies will clear the matter up, but these are so far lacking. At any rate, vast areas where the moraines were in contact, suggesting coalescence of the two ice sheets, lie between the problematical regions where the moraines overlap.

Hansen (1949), in a pioneering study, collected peat sections from four bogs along the Edmonton-Jasper highway which runs nearly due west from Edmonton; the bogs are about 30, 55, 85, and 125 miles distant, respectively, from that place. They thus form a transect from east to west between Edmonton and the Rocky Mountains. Hansen's conclusions are that

> Pollen analysis of four peat sections from bogs lying between Edmonton and the Rockies in west central Alberta, reveal that lodgepole pine and spruce have been the predominant forest tree species in adjacent areas during the time represented by the sedimentary columns. Since these bogs lie west of the border of the Altamont (Late Wisconsin) moraine and on older Keewatin [Laurentide] drift, but *probably* [emphasis added] east of the Late Wisconsin Cordilleran ice border, it is possible that they record pre-Late-Wisconsin forests, that had persisted in an ice-free corridor during this glacial stage (Hansen 1949:288).

The same author in a later paper states, "Apparently an ice-free corridor, 100 or more miles in width, existed between the Keewatin and Cordilleran ice during the Late Wisconsin glaciation" (Hansen 1950:420).

Hansen's study of the transect west of Edmonton does not indicate that there was an ice-free corridor from north to south in Late Wisconsin time. The significance of his pollen record is much more restricted. Assuming that the geological record is sound as he interprets it, the only valid conclusion that can be drawn from his profiles is that forests existed close enough to the particular bogs from which his samples were taken to permit the pollen rain to fall on them. Unless it can be demonstrated by north-south transects through the area in question, and others on an east-west axis, that the whole area of the corridor was deglaciated, no conclusion about a corridor can be drawn—perhaps about, refugia, but not about an ice-free corridor.

Heusser (1960:202) shows "unglaciated lacuna" in a sketch map of northwestern North America. He shows a lacuna in southwestern Alberta, one across northeastern British Columbia, and another east of the Mackenzie River. Terasmae states that about 10,000 to 12,000 years ago "some areas in southern Saskatachewan were covered by boreal forest" (1961: 668). He also suggests that tundra conditions should be expected to precede the boreal forest in deglaciated areas.

The most important current evidence, admittedly inadequate, concerning the problem of an ice-free corridor comes from the Altamont Moraine, which runs from North Dakota in a northwesterly direction across southwest Saskatchewan, across Alberta east of Edmonton to the Rocky Mountains, and marks the final stand of the Laurentide ice in that area. Wendorf (1966) presents two radiocarbon dates from beneath the moraine, one of 11,050±200 B.C. and one of 10,190±240 B.C. Thirteen other dates from above the till of the moraine range from 10,150±160 B.C. to 9530±300 B.C. and younger. Wendorf (1966: 260) writes: "These dates indicate that around 10,000 B.C. the southern margin of the Keewatin [Laurentide] ice sheet extended unbroken from the Rocky Mountains across southern Alberta and Saskatchewan. . . . No corridor could have existed until after 10,000 B.C. or approximately until the Two Creeks Interval." Others also have suggested the Two Creeks Interval as the time of an ice-free corridor.*

The radiocarbon dates obtained by Wendorf suggest that an ice-free corridor was exposed by around 11,000 years ago, but it probably became habitable only some time later. The wastage of the Cordilleran and Laurentide ice must have made the land bordering the eastern side of the Rocky Mountains uninhabitable for a very long time after the ice receded from the Altamont Moraine, and perhaps a reasonable guess for the time of a habitable ice-free corridor might be on the order of 10,000 years ago.

The mass of glacial ice covering British Columbia until the end of the last glaciation closed that area as a possible migration route (Figure 8). If, however, the Sumas Stade (Valders equivalent) were not a true stade but only a limited advance of certain mountain glaciers, as Borden has suggested (personal communication, C. E. Borden to L. S. Cressman), then possibly a route through the Interior Plateau leading into the Intermontane Region to the south would have been available by about 12,000 years ago. Present geological opinion generally accepts the Sumas Stade as a valid episode and holds that the southern Interior Plateau was deglaciated by 9,000–10,000 years ago. The earliest evidence of human occupation in the interior of British Columbia is dated at 5580±270 B.C. (GSC-530) at the Drynoch Slide site about 36 miles up the Thompson River from Lytton (Sanger 1967). Any interstadial evidence would probably have been obliterated by subsequent glacial action.

The Vashon Stade (Mankato equivalent) ice effectually blocked any route to the coast (Figures 7–9). Ice covered Vancouver Island and the Straits of Juan de Fuca so that any passage along the edge of the ice sheet would have had to be in the open sea of the stormy north Pacific. There is no evidence that it was possible to make such a journey.

* The period of the Altamont Moraine, however, is not the *critical evidence* to demonstrate the time of an ice-free corridor. All it actually shows is the time of an *ice-free area south of the moraine*. The Mackenzie Mountains area (Craig and Fyles 1960), extending several hundred miles north of the Altamont Moraine and Rocky Mountains contact, is critical for the study of the problem of the time of a fully ice-free corridor into the interior of the continent.

This review shows that the currently available geological and climatological evidence bearing on the problem of access to the continental interior of North America during Late Pleistocene times is far from unequivocal. For example, it indicates to Hopkins (Hopkins 1967:467–68) the probable existence of an ice-free corridor some time during a mid-Wisconsin episode of mild climate between 35,000 and 25,000 years ago, followed by a closure lasting until "at least 14,000 years ago and possibly until almost 10,000 years ago." In my own opinion, there is no convincing evidence for an ice-free corridor from the unglaciated area of the Far North into the high plains of the United States during the whole of the last glaciation, before probably 11,000 years ago. The weight of the presently available evidence is against its existence. This does not mean that there were no small ice-free areas, which interrupted the continuity of the ice sheet, but the existence of refugia (Hansen 1949, 1950; Heusser 1960; Terasmae 1961) is far different from the existence of a continuous ice-free landscape.

It remains to be noted that if, as Hopkins and others (1965:1113) suggest, there were land connections across Bering Strait during the Illinoian-Wisconsin (Sangamon) Interglacial period, then the whole picture presented above changes. There would at that time have been no cul-de-sac or refugium in the Far North, for there would have been no ice fields to form enclosing barriers and various routes would have led into the interior. If man crossed the Bering Land Bridge during the Sangamon Interglacial, much of the foregoing discussion is largely irrelevant. In such a case, if people were in the Northwest in pre-Wisconsin times, then occupation along the coast of Southern California would have been greatly facilitated by the lowered sea level of the ensuing glaciation. In the interior in the Puget-Willamette Trough, in the Intermontane Region, and east of the Rocky Mountains there would also have been favorable environments south of the Wisconsin ice where human life could have flourished.

The Cultural Evidence for Man's Arrival

Among archæologists there is disagreement over the possible time at which, on the basis of present evidence, the first people might have arrived in the New World. Even though some of the material discussed below is not accepted as valid by the majority of archæologists, it is essential that this evidence at least be considered since it seems convincing to other archæologists as well as myself. A great deal of evidence that is accepted now was quite unacceptable to professional archæologists before J. D. Figgins in 1927 discovered chipped stone points in unequivocal association with the bones of extinct bison near Folsom, New Mexico, and opened up a whole new perspective on the antiquity of man in the New World. I believe that the sites described below will someday be widely accepted as valid evidence of Early Man once a new and deeper time perspective is achieved (even deeper than that opened up by Figgins's discovery) among New-World archæologists.

Sites Whose Validity Has Been Questioned or Ignored

The Texas Street site at San Diego was discovered and reported on by Carter (1957). There is a C-14 date of greater than 35,000 years ago (L–299D) for charcoal from this site (Broecker and Kulp 1957: 1328). While most archæologists reject this site as representing human activity, I am not convinced that the rejection is well founded. I visited this site in the spring of 1965 under the guidance of Dr. Carl L. Hubbs of the Scripps Institution of Oceanography who has been familiar with the area throughout the period of the study by Carter and since. In a face of Texas Street deposit exposed by construction, but not in quite the same place that Carter discussed, Hubbs found what appeared to be a "hearth" similar to those described by Carter. We carefully cleared the area, and, after photographing it, collected what appeared to be charcoal. This "hearth" was about 25–30 centimeters long and 10 centimeters thick and showed some distortion, apparently because of earth movement. Hubbs examined the "charcoal" sample in the laboratory and reported to me that it was true charcoal.

True charcoal has to come from fire, but fire can be caused either by natural causes or by human methods. If the former, the most likely source is lightning that either sets fire to a single tree or starts a forest or grass fire. In the former case, if the tree burns down to its roots, the charcoal leaves a telltale pattern derived from the roots. In the case of a forest fire there is generally a mantle of charred debris—ash, charcoal, and often the earth is reddened from the heat of the fire. Forest fires burn not only surface material but burn down into the "duff" of the forest floor. Forest fire fighters push their arms up to the elbows into the burned areas to make sure there is no fire smoldering below the surface in the forest duff. Obviously one can expect a fairly continuous mantle of burned debris in an area of a forest fire. I have had personal experience with the results of both forest and grass fires caused by nature and have excavated through the mantle of burned material of a forest fire, including burned stumps. I have also excavated innumerable hearths in valid sites. On the basis of the information I have just given and the situation I examined at Texas Street in 1965, my opinion is that the probabilities favor the "hearth" being a true or man-made one.

At the time of the discovery of the Texas Street site,* archæologists should have organized an excavation project to seek further evidence, as was done at the Valsequillo site to be discussed later, instead of attacking both the validity of the site and the competence of the discoverer. It is probably too late for that now, but at any rate, in my opinion, the case is not only *not* closed, but the probabilities are in favor of the validity of the site as representing human use —a view supported by the evidence from the Scripps Campus and Santa Rosa Island sites.

The Scripps Campus site is composed of a number of apparently basin-shaped hearths exposed in a cliff face of the terrace fill at the Scripps Campus a short distance north of La Jolla. I have not examined these "hearths" in detail but am familiar with the area. Carl Hubbs of the Scripps Institution of Oceanography is probably the person most familiar with the situation, and I shall let him describe it.

> The terrace-fill here at Scripps Institution, roughly 50 feet deep, gives somewhat tenuous evidence throughout of human occupation, in the form of apparent hearthsites marked by saucer-shaped areas of burned clay, often associated with charcoal and bone fragments. A charcoal sample from about one-third the height down was dated by Dr. Suess at 21,500±700 years ago. It is our belief that

this terrace-fill encompasses the Wisconsin Period, and rests on a beach of Sangamon Interglacial age. The evidences of fire extend down to the old storm beach, but, significantly, do not appear in the older generations of terrace-fill alluvium in this region. The evidence parallels that on Santa Rosa Island, where human occupation is now definitely documented for about ten millenia, and is hypothetically indicated for the whole Wisconsin period (Hubbs 1961:3-4).

Krieger (1964:46) examined and described this site: "it does have some thin lenses of char and burned earth which contain bits of charred bone and shell, and small flakes, indicating a camp site."

Santa Rosa Island, off the Southern California coast southwest of Santa Barbara, has produced what is to some scientists, at least, convincing evidence of man's presence contemporary with that at the Scripps Campus site and in the same kind of formation, Pleistocene alluvial flood plain. Other archæologists doubt the validity of the evidence or ignore it and add it to the increasing pile under the rug and out of sight. But it obstinately refuses to stay there.

In 1960 Fay-Cooper Cole was a trustee of the Santa Barbara Museum of Natural History. At that time Phil C. Orr, as curator, had been carrying out the long period of study on Santa Rosa. Cole, in his life-long manner of asking "What are the facts?" arranged for a field conference on Santa Rosa Island in the summer of 1960 for a firsthand study of the evidence. The conference membership was composed of archæologists, geographers, geologists, and paleontologists. The conference met in two groups some weeks apart because of limited facilities on the island. Because of the tight security protecting the island, Orr had been able to leave sites exposed with the objects in situ with no fear of disturbance. If any member of the first group picked up an object from a site he returned it to the exact spot from where he had lifted it. Thus the second group had the same conditions for observation. I had the good fortune to be a member of the second group. Other members were James B. Griffin and Wilbur A. Davis, archæologists; K. O. Emery, geologist who had studied the underwater geology of the islands; Phil C. Orr, paleontologist; and Fay-Cooper Cole, anthropologist.

I was very skeptical of the claims of validity for the sites before I attended the conference. After the field study and the discussions, I was convinced that

---

* Cf. note at end of this chapter.

the sites provided valid evidence for man's presence on the island as claimed by Orr on the basis of numerous C-14 dates.

An experience during the conference is of interest as illustrating a bias that is shared by many North American archæologists. We were examining an apparent site with scattered stones of varying size and charcoal. I knelt down and examined the stones, one by one, with extreme care. Cole and Orr stood above me watching the results of my scrutiny. I finally pointed to two specimens, picked each up in turn, examined them, and carefully returned them to the spot from which I had lifted them. I then said that if these had been found in an undoubted cultural context they would certainly be accepted as artifacts and that I so accepted them here. Both Cole and Orr laughed and, somewhat miffed, I asked what was the matter. I was told that the first field group when visiting this site had several archæologists pick out the same stones as artifacts. Then one of them asked how old the site was. When told about 27,000 years he said without hesitation that they then *could not be artifacts*. I said at the time, and I still hold to the opinion, that they were artifacts.

What is the evidence from Santa Rosa Island?

Santa Rosa Island, the next to the largest of the Channel Islands, is separated from the mainland by the Santa Barbara Channel and is 31 miles southwest of Santa Barbara. The islands lie along an almost due east-west axis. The coastline from Point Hueneme, on the south, curves slightly to the northwest until just east of Santa Barbara where it runs practically west to Point Conception. The islands lie generally parallel to the east-west coastline. From west to east the islands are San Miguel, Santa Rosa, Santa Cruz, the largest, and Las Anacapas. The last is approximately 10 miles from the coast at Point Hueneme, the point where an ancient land connection with the mainland would have been established. At the maximum lowering of sea level during glaciation, the islands formed a single land mass for which Orr (1968:17) proposed the name "Santarosae." A precipitous mountain range runs the long length of the island, about the middle, and the underlying geology is composed of shales and sandstones. A broad floodplain has been shown by undersea geology to have extended about 5 miles seaward around

Santarosae. On Santa Rosa Island the remnant of this floodplain, called the Tecolote member of the Santa Rosa Formation, thought to comprise the whole of Wisconsin time, is from 50 to 100 feet thick where it is now exposed in the sea cliffs. It is in this member in a 2 square mile section on the northwest coast where most of the evidence of human occupation with which I am concerned occurs. The time period involved is indicated by a list of radiocarbon dates in Table 2.

Biological studies have shown that the islands must have been separated from the mainland for a very long time because none of the large Pleistocene fauna, herbivores, and predators found as fossils on the mainland, have been found on the islands. The endemic terrestrial fauna of the islands, and limited to them, consists only of the following three genera: "the fox (*Urocyon littoralis santarosae*), spotted skunk (*Spilogale gracilis amphialus*), and the mouse (*Peromyscus maniculatus streatori*)" Orr (1968:41). Other species of mice, however, exist on the other islands. Only one fossil of the dwarf fox has been found, but numerous bones of mice have been recovered. *Most striking, however, in the fossil record are the numerous bones of the dwarf mammoth*, named by Stock and Furlong, *Elephas exilis* and classified by Osborn as *Archidiskodon exilis*. The dwarf mammoth ranged in height from about 4 to 8 feet; it is possible that there was more than one species.

The archæological problem derives from the evidence, convincing to many competent authorities, that man was on Santa Rosa Island more than 37,000 years ago and that he killed, cooked, and ate dwarf mammoths. Three factors have caused many archæologists to question the validity of the evidence for the antiquity of man on Santa Rosa Island: (1) the evidence suggesting lack of a land connection for a very long time, (2) the great age of the hearths, and (3) skepticism concerning the validity of the evidence of *human* activity at the hearths.

Orr and Berger (1966:1681) present evidence concerning the land connections:

> The question of a connection between the mainland and the islands during the last 100,000 years cannot be unequivocally answered at present. At a greatest depression of 100 m, modern maps show a distance of less than 4 km between the 50 fathom contour lines, and a greatest depth

TABLE 2

RADIOCARBON DATES, SANTA ROSA ISLAND

	C-14 Age B.P.	Lab. No.	Sample	Location Data
1.	11,300±160	UCLA 748	Charcoal	3 m. deep in Tecolote member and seaward from UCLA-106
2.	11,800±800	UCLA-106	Charcoal	Arlington Canyon, 6.7 m. below valley terrace; fire area in direct contact with dwarf mammoth bones
3.	12,500±250	L-290-T	Charred bone	Just east of Tecolote Canyon mouth; 2.75 m. below cliff surface
4.	16,000±280	L-244	Cypress wood	Tecolote Canyon, 800 m. inland; 1 m. below fire area; 12 m. below surface
5.	16,700±1500	M-599	Charcoal	At edge of Pleistocene beds, 2.45 m. below surface; coll. by Carl Hubbs
6.	27,000±180	UCLA-746	Charcoal	Near Otter Point; 2.75 m. below Tecolote surface; about 100 m. west of M-599
7.	>25,000	M-1132	Charcoal	Survey Pt., 4.5 ft. (1.37 m.) above base of Tecolote member, 11 ft. (3.35 m.) above charred mammoth dated 29,700 (L-290-R). Coll. by J.B. Griffin, L.S. Cressman, W.A. Davis, K.O. Emery, P.C. Orr
8.	29,700±3000	L-290-R	Charred bone	Survey Pt.; 11.5 m. from top of cliff. Note that M-1132 supports this date
9.	>37,000	UCLA-749	Charcoal	Fire area 1 m. in dia.; 2.5 m. above Miocene shale on which Tecolote member rests; east of Arlington Canyon

SOURCE: M-1132 compiled from Orr 1962; others Orr and Berger 1966.

of *ca* 100 fathoms (1 fathom = 6 ft. = 1.83 m) with respect to the modern ocean level. An argument against a land bridge during the last several tens of thousands of years is the absence of fossil wildlife on Santa Rosa that is found on the mainland. On the other hand, a narrow channel of several kilometers is not an insurmountable distance to man. Finally, it is difficult at present to assess the action against a land bridge of the Santa Clara River *via* its path along the Hueneme submarine canyon, the waves driven by the predominant northwest winds, and tectonic movements. Earlier connections must have occurred, though, as documented by dwarf mammoth remains.

The root question about these sites is "Were the fires that burned the mammoth bones and the exposed surfaces of the fire pits deep red man-caused or nature-caused?" Orr (1968) has explored in detail all the possibilities and firmly concluded that man caused the fires. The probabilities certainly favor man as the causative agent. My own examination convinced me that they were fire pits made and used by man. Of course, if one simply categorically denies

that the fires were man made no further discussion is fruitful.

The pattern of reoccurrence of sites with dates of from 20,000 to more than 34,000 years in Southern California and on Santa Rosa Island in the Pleistocene coastal alluvium, even though questioned by some scientists, provides strong support for their validity. *Randomly* occuring events do not form *coherent patterns*. Two other locations far to the north, the Taber site in southwestern Alberta and the findspot of a stone knife from the glacial Lake Missoula Flood gravel in north-central Oregon, although they have received little attention, extend the distribution of the pattern of very early dates for human presence in the Far West.

Evidence of human presence should be progressively earlier as one backtracks along the line of movement into the continent. In the area of the ice sheets, however, there is little chance that the overriding glaciers spared earlier sites. The Taber Early Man site in southwestern Alberta provides a fortunate exception and suggests the possibility, though faint, that interior British Columbia may preserve similar evidence.

The Taber Early Man site designation refers to a locality in the cliff "on the east bank of the Oldman River about 3 mi. due north of Taber [Canada]" (Stalker 1969:425–28). In 1962, Stalker's field party, as part of the Geological Survey of Canada, discovered some bones which, after cleaning and study in the laboratory, were identified as those of a child under two years of age. The discovery was reported, but the possible significance of the discovery was not recognized at the time.

The bones lay in about the middle of a bed of alluvium approximately 30 feet thick, directly under about 60 feet of overlying glacial till of the Late (Classical) Wisconsin Stade. Consequently, the alluvium and the contained bones are stratigraphically older than the till.

No datable material was found associated with the bones. Two geological sections, however, in the same vicinity, similar to that containing the bones, provided pieces of wood in closely similar stratigraphic positions. These were dated at >32,000 (S–65), 36,000 (GSC–728), and >37,000 (GSC–888) C–14 years ago. Sample GSC–728 is thought to have been contaminated by plant rootlets and to be, therefore, too young. Since the other two samples came from about the same distance above the bottom of the alluvial bed as the bones, these dates should apply to the bones. The true age of the bones lies beyond the limits of C-14 dating, but how far is uncertain. "In the author's opinion they are considerably older than that [37,000], and perhaps as old as 60,000 years. Determination of their exact age, however, must await discovery of material suitable for dating from the bone site itself" (Stalker 1969:428).

Glacial Lake Missoula flood knife. In the early fifties while I was planning the excavations of sites in The Dalles dam reservoir area on the Columbia River, I examined the exposed face of gravel in a barrow pit about 100 yards upstream from the mouth of the John Day River some 200 feet above the present level of the Columbia River and about the same distance above the John Day. My purpose in this search was to look for fossils deposited by a Wisconsin-period flood, then called, after Bretz, the Spokane Flood, which might date the gravel bed.

I found no fossils, but I did find a basalt knife embedded tightly about the middle of the 20-foot gravel face exposed above the talus slope (Cressman et al. 1960). The object was verified as an artifact independently by four professional archæologists, three of whom were unaware of the source and its implications. After the identification in each case I told the person the source but none changed his opinion.

The knife was flaked by percussion to produce a zigzag cutting edge. I later returned to the site and examined numerous pieces of gravel, both large and small, to compare the fracture scars on them with those on the knife. Every piece examined bore only randomly distributed scars while the knife had a definite pattern of flake scars and, in addition, a small number of random scars from blows presumably received in the rolling gravel. Furthermore, the flake scars on the knife had been smoothed, as had other parts, by abrasion, either by water action or airborne sand.

In the course of the flood the knife had been picked up by the torrential water and eventually deposited—how far from its source no one knows. The flood, as I pointed out in the previous chapter, is dated by Fryxell at between 18,000 and 23,000 years ago. This date, which is a limiting one, means that man had been living in the flood area before that time. He was south of the Cordilleran ice sheet, meaning that he had to have come south into this area before the ice-free corridor into the continental interior was closed by ice about 25,000 years ago.

Sites Accepted as Valid and Firmly Dated

The Valsequillo area south of the city of Puebla, Mexico, has provided evidence of the greatest importance bearing on the time of the arrival of the earliest inhabitants in North America (Malde and Irwin-Williams 1967; Irwin-Williams 1967b). The correlation of cultural, geological, and paleontological information, and the great age of human presence indicated, give this area its outstanding importance. The Pleistocene fluviatile sediments, called the Valsequillo Gravels, have long been known as a rich source of fossil fauna, and, occasionally, objects thought to have been made by man have been found in the course of studies by Mexican paleontologists and particularly by Professor Juan Armenta Camacho of the University of Puebla. Professor Camacho and Irwin-Williams made a detailed survey of the area in 1962 (Irwin-Williams 1967b) and located four places where the association of artifacts and fossil fauna was unquestionable. In 1964, a joint project of the Peabody Museum of Harvard University and the University of Puebla, funded by the National Science Foundation, undertook the excavation of these sites. The project staff included Harold Malde of the United States Geological Survey for geological studies and Clayton Ray of the United States National Museum for paleontological studies.

The age of the artifacts was determined by dating the containing beds. Shells, charcoal, and buried soils provided the C-14 samples. The validity of the shells as a C-14 dating sample was confirmed by dating present-day shells from the area. Since they gave a "modern" date it was concluded that no radiocarbon-deficient contaminant was present in the older shells and that they could be used as a valid source for dating. Charcoal from trees burned by a glowing cloud of volcanic ash was used to date an ashfall, called the Rio Frio ash, which it was hoped could be used as a time horizon marker for the area. The shell dates are compatible and conformable with the geological stratigraphy. The buried soil dates, however, are incompatible with one another and do not conform to the stratigraphy. Erosional channels, none large in width, interrupt the continuity of the Valsequillo beds and complicate the problem of geological stratigraphy and dating.

Shells useable as C-14 samples for dating the older beds did not occur in the gravels at the oldest artifact locations but did occur in

> barrancas graded to the main body of Valsequillo from the North. . . . To extrapolate these radiocarbon dates from the barrancas southward to the exposures of the Valsequillo Gravel at Tetela [the area of the sites] involves some guesswork because the inferred continuity of the deposits is now interrupted by occasional gaps. Nevertheless, the missing parts are short, and the lithologic similarities permit gross correlations (Malde and Irwin-Williams 1967:6–7).

One of the barrancas, Caulapan, preserved an archæ-

ological locality in an apparently unbroken section of the gravels. They derived C-14 dates from this section—one date from near the top, giving a final date to the occupation of the area; one at some depth in the section that dated a stone scraper close by at 21,850±850 C-14 years ago (W-1895); and others from the base of the section giving a date of more than 35,000 years ago. Since the "gravelly base of the Valsequillo" in the barrancas is more than 35,000 years old (W-1899, W-1901, W-1898), at Tetela, the main area, the base of the deposit "is probably also more than 35,000 years old" (Malde and Irwin-Williams 1967:7).

The Rio Frio ash has a C-14 date of more than 40,000 years (W-1995), and, on the basis of petrographic examination, various ash exposures in the Tetela sites were tentatively indentified with the Rio Frio ash. The ash layers thus could be used as reference points in tentatively dating some archæological localities. Neutron activation analysis of the ash, however, has not supported the identification (personal communication, G. Giles to L. S. Cressman; Randle, Goles, and Kittleman 1971).

A detailed discussion of the cultural features of the Valsequillo Gravels excavations is outside of the field of this study, but because of the profound significance of this site in New World prehistory and its bearings on cultural origins, I shall give a brief summary. Three periods of occupation occur at Hueyatlaco, "which is situated ten meters below the top of the Valsequillo Gravel" (Malde and Irwin-Williams 1967:3). Artifacts of the two younger periods can be differentiated from those of the older, and the latter are similar to those from all the lower Valsequillo sites. An unconformity separates the older from the younger beds at Hueyatlaco, but the basal section of the column there seems to correlate with that in the barranca Caulapan and should be of the same age. The younger assemblages contain well-made bifacial stone tools—namely, stemmed and bi-pointed projectile points and knives, scrapers and perforators, burins, true blades and cores, and artifacts exhibiting prepared striking platforms. *A bifacial technology has developed.* The oldest sites represent a somewhat "less sophisticated method of working stone" than the younger, but contain projectile points and scrapers made on blades and flakes by edge trimming by percussion and pressure. Prepared striking platforms were used. At El Horno, a basal gravel site, burins were found but no blades, although the prepared striking platform was in use. *All artifacts here are unifacial.*

The younger levels with the bifacial tools are apparently the stratigraphic equivalents of the section in the barranca Caulapan containing the scraper dated at 22,000 years ago, while the older level corresponds to the basal gravel dated at more than 35,000 years ago.

The Tlapacoya site in the Valley of Mexico, state of Mexico, has provided what must be acceptable in terms of any reasonable theory of probability as firm evidence of man in that area by 24,000 years ago (Haynes 1968a). This site is on a shoreline of ancient Lake Chalco. Numerous bones of bear, horse, bison, and other Pleistocene animals occur in the site area. What is reported as a "true blade" has been found along with the usual hunting and butchering equipment, much of which has little diagnostic value. What is clearly a hearth has been dated from the contained charcoal at 24,000±4,000 years ago (A-794B). Haynes evaluates this site with extreme caution:

> Therefore, even if the stone artifacts are excluded from consideration, the concentration of charcoal within the small depression formed by the removal of beach gravel 24,000 years ago constitutes the best evidence I have seen for the presence of man in the New World more than 12,000 years ago, although as at Valsequillo and Wilson Butte Cave, the evidence is not so conclusive that it precludes other interpretations (Haynes 1967:49).

The Valsequillo and Tlapacoya dates have very important implications for the sites from Santa Rosa Island and the San Diego area of Southern California. If sites 22,000 or more than 35,000 years old exist in Puebla and a site 24,000 years old exists at Tlapacoya, then there must be older ones to the north along the route used in the southward movement into the New World. The questioned California sites fall into a reasonable pattern formed by these supporting dates. These early dates are further corroborated by two important sites in the Pacific Northwest, which have considerably younger C-14 dates, but which nevertheless indicate clearly, if the conclusions drawn in preceding pages about the dates

of the ice-free corridor are correct, that man had reached the interior of the continent before the last advance of the ice—about 25,000 years ago.

Wilson Butte Cave, in the Snake River plain of south-central Idaho, contains a basal stratum dated at 15,000±800 B.P. (M-1410) (Gruhn 1965). The authenticity as an artifact of a bone object from this stratum has been questioned, but I have examined this specimen through the courtesy of Dr. Gruhn and am convinced it is a tool because of what I am sure is use-faceting at one end. The faceting is similar to that on innumerable similar bone tools I have excavated. Even if those of us who accept this tool as a true artifact are in error, unquestionable chipped-stone artifacts from an overlying stratum dated at 14,500±500 years ago (M-1409) indicate the presence of man in the Northwest while the interior area from the Columbia River north to Alaska was under the Cordilleran ice.

Fort Rock Cave in south-central Oregon in the Northern Great Basin in a pluvial lake environment has a firm date of 13,200±720 B.P. (GaK-1738) for the earliest occupation (Bedwell 1969; Bedwell and Cressman 1971). This date was derived from charcoal in a hearth. Associated is a bifacial lithic assemblage including a Lake Mohave-type point and a rather simple crescent. Projectile points are present. A shelter a few miles distant at Cougar Mountain in the same environment was occupied at 11,950±350 B.P. (GaK-1751). This date, too, was derived from hearth charcoal. Since the butte containing Fort Rock Cave was an island until the lake level dropped sufficiently to provide connection with the shoreline, it is clear that the area around the lake must have been occupied before the cave became available. The people who occupied this area of Fort Rock more than 13,200 years ago, like those at Wilson Butte, are evidence of a population that had arrived in the Northwest before the Vashon Stade of the Fraser Glaciation.

Ventana Cave (Haury et al. 1950) in southwestern Arizona is a final though less definitive case in point. The cave was dug long before the development of C-14 dating, and so conventional dating methods were used drawing upon the geological and paleoecological evidence. While the lowest stratum, the

Conglomerate, was practically sterile, it did contain tenuous evidence of human presence in the form of bits of charcoal, a flake, and what probably was a basalt hammer stone. The overlying stratum, the Volcanic Debris, contained two projectile points and an assemblage of hunting and butchering tools. Since the two layers apparently represented the same climatic environment, Haury inferred that there was no essential time difference between them and so disregarded the two doubtful specimens from the Conglomerate. One of the two projectile points from the volcanic debris layer is shaped generally like a Folsom point but lacks the channel flake removal. There appears, from Haury's illustration, to have been some effort to thin the basal edge for hafting. The other point is leaf shaped and has bilateral notching; it is slight but there, just where the edges meet the straight base to form a slight stem. Haury suggested a time bracket for the two lower strata between 10,000 and 25,000 years ago.

Later, scattered charcoal picked from the Volcanic Debris for C-14 dating gave a date of 11,300±1,200 C-14 years ago (A-203) (Damon and Long 1962). How much earlier the underlying Conglomerate is it is impossible to say; it may be much or little. If the Conglomerate were 1,000 to 1,500 years older than the Volcanic Debris, the implication is clear that this area was also occupied when the north was still under ice.

This body of information from valid sites firmly dated, supported by that from those questioned by some, indicates man was distributed in the Far West from the Columbia River in the north to Puebla in the south before the last advance of the Cordilleran ice sheet about 25,000 years ago. Since the period between 35,000 and 25,000 years ago was a warm interstade, it is reasonable to accept the conclusion of Hopkins et al. (1967:467–68) that there was no Asian-American land connection during that time, but that there was an ice-free passage out of Alaska through which a population already there could have moved into the continent. The forebears of that population would have had to reach the New World on a land connection in existence before 35,000 years ago during the Early Wisconsin Stade.

Dr. Charles B. Hunt in his review of *The Quaternary of the United States* (1965) makes a comment that supports this interpretation:

> In the first place, Pleistocene mollusks along the arctic coast of Alaska have Atlantic rather than Pacific Ocean affiinities, suggesting that the bridge existed during much or all of Pleistocene time and cut off contact between the Arctic and Pacific Oceans. There is no need to labor the point about a bridge developing because of lowered sea level; the bridge was there, but it just was not used (according to doctrine) until the last glacial maximum. At that time, that area must have been a bleak, permanently frozen ground and immigration across it would have been the original ice folly. To this observer it would seem that one of two archæological doctrines will have to go— either man reached North America by a route other than the Bering Land Bridge, or George Carter has been right in saying that man arrived on this continent before the last glacial maximum (Hunt 1965:47–50).

If archæologists involved in the study of Early Man in the New World wish to make significant contributions to the elucidation of this problem, they need to undertake systematic studies of Pleistocene sediments for evidence of man. Practically nothing of this kind has been done. The nearest to such a study is Irwin-Williams's work in the Valsequillo Gravels, but this area was discovered by paleontologists and reported by them as a probable site of human occupation. Since it is established that man was a Pleistocene predator in northeast Asia, the Pleistocene sediments of the New World should be the place where his earliest remains here are to be found. In the Pleistocene sediments of Santa Rosa Island, San Diego County of Southern California, the Valsequillo Gravels, the Taber site, and the glacial Lake Missoula Flood gravel, some significant remains of Early Man have already been found. The caves and terraces of the pluvial lakes cannot furnish any evidence from a time earlier than the period when, as a result of growing post-Pleistocene aridity, they became habitable (a point made as long ago as 1940 by Julian Steward but ignored by most archæologists).* Yet the people who occupied these places when they became habitable, and their ancestors for an unknown period of time, had been occupying the area around the lakes. It is the habitat of these people for which diligent search must be made. Unfortu-

---

* Fort Rock Cave is an exception to this generalization with its date, 13,200 years B.P., placing it at the end of the Vashon Stade. The reason for the exception is to be found in the cave's unique position (p. 73, above).

nately uneroded Pleistocene sediments are limited, but the remnants are likely places to hold significant evidence for our study.

The present time depth of human occupation of the New World, and the technological skills in stone working clearly demonstrated at Valsequillo by 25,000 and probably more years ago, forces re-examination of various theories of the origin and development of early New-World culture. Most students of the problems approach with fear and trembling the idea of New-World origins for such things as projectile points, bifacial flaking, blades, burins, etc. All had to come from Asia where Lake Baikal serves as a kind of "Ur of the Chaldees." Bryan (1965) has argued persuasively for a New-World origin of projectile points, but his represents a minority viewpoint, at least at present.

The Clovis fluted point is the most discussed of the averred Asiatic imports, though it is not claimed that it necessarily arrived in the New World in a fully developed form. The earliest date for a Clovis site is about 11,600 years ago. Broecker and Farrand (1963) report a C-14 date for the Two Creeks Interstade of 11,850±300 B.P. and place this interstade within the period approximately 12,000 to 11,700 years ago. The time relation between the earliest Clovis site and the Two Creeks Interstade would, if Two Creeks is accepted as marking a period when an ice-free corridor* was available, permit the carriers of the Clovis flaking tradition to enter the continental interior from the north. Additional factors are, however, involved. The Kogruk Complex from Anaktuvuk Pass in the Brooks Range of northern Alaska, excavated and described by Campbell (1962b), has been postulated as a possible Alaskan source for the Clovis tradition, but Porter (1964) has shown that the Kogruk Complex cannot be more than about 7,000 radiocarbon years old. Further, the few occurrences of Clovis points in Alberta or elsewhere in the north are best accounted for by northward diffusion rather than northern origin (Wormington and Forbis 1965; MacNeish 1962). The preponderance of evidence presently available suggests a New-World

origin of the Clovis fluted point and a number of other sophisticated flaking techniques. But a great many more frames of very clear and sharp exposure are needed to complete the picture of Early Man in the New World.

I have been writing history without people, but it is essential, if one wishes to grasp something of the full meaning of this human experience, to explore it imaginatively in terms of problems met and solved or unsolved and in terms of the experiences faced by men, women, and their children. The thousands of miles of often frightful landscape, which they eventually crossed and even lived in, are part of the scene. We talk of tundra, taiga, mountains, ice-free corridors, predators and the lack of them, but the effects of these on the human experience escapes us or we avoid their consideration. This man/environment relation adds a proper dimension to this series of events of epic proportion. I can but suggest some of them: fears of the known—the dire wolf, the saber-toothed tiger, the jaguar, and other predators; and fears of the unknown—the seemingly limitless bogs, dark forests, deserts, volcanic eruptions, ice fields, and even "that angry or that glimmering sea," were as much a part of the Wanderers's world as the comprehended objects giving rise to their fears. Hardships and genial environments are part of the picture.

To help cope with these hardships and for assurance, the Wanderers certainly imposed a framework of imaginative fantasy on the perceptual world to give it meaning. What these myths were no one will ever know, but one can be sure that their acceptance provided an orderly world in which life was tolerable They must have learned early, as Shelley so eloquently writes, "To look through thin and rainbow wings upon the shape of death." The shaman must many times have been far more important to the individual and social group than the hunter. These were human beings whose epic behavior provides our problem, and its true dimensions become meaningful only if that salient fact is kept in mind.†

---

* It is not known how widely the climatic effects reflected in the Two Creeks episode of the northern mid-continent extended.

† I wish to call attention to three contributions that have appeared since my manuscript was submitted to the publisher:

1. Wade, with a reply by Haynes, briefly summarizes the significant positions taken in regard to the controversial

Calico Hills site in Southern California. The minimum age is reported to be greater than 50,000 radiocarbon years ago, while the maximum age is in controversy. Other sources suggest it may be as much as 100,000 C-14 years old. The other basic controversy is were the "tools" made by man or nature. The majority of competent professional opinion leans toward man as the fabricator, but some, including Haynes, disagree (Wade 1973:1371; Haynes 1973:1371–72).

2. Steen-McIntyre et al., using the method of age determination based on the amount of water "accumulated in closed vesicles of glass shards [in the tephra beds] during weathering," state that the amount of water in the Hueyatlaco vesicles (one-tenth filled) "implies an age as great as 250,000 years ago." This would appear to date the bifacial tools. "These findings accentuate the dilemma already recognized that so great an age for bifacial tools in the New World seems archæologically unreasonable" (Steen-McIntyre, Fryxell, and Malde 1973:820–21).

3. Bada et al. conclude: "It would appear, based on the limited number of dates we have obtained that man might have migrated to the New World during this time [ca. 70,000 B.P.]" (Bada, Schroeder, and Carter 1974:791–93).

The People

And I saw the glory of all dead men
In the shadow that went by the side of me.

John Drinkwater, Symbols

THE PREHISTORIAN cannot describe with any high degree of assurance the physical characteristics of the different populations who occupied the Far West in ancient times because he lacks sufficient skeletons to provide representative samples of the populations. Some physical anthropologists, in spite of limited samples, have drawn sweeping conclusions about physical types and their wide-ranging relations (cf. Hrdlička 1906; Heizer in Preface to Kennedy 1959). But in fact, on current evidence about all that the archæologist can reliably say is that certain individuals having certain physical characteristics lived at a few particular places and times.

This chapter reviews some of the major anthropometric and genetic studies that have been made in the Far West, indicates the major points of significance within this presently limited area of inquiry, and concludes on a note at once negative and positive —that while the prospect for gaining a detailed knowledge of the physical anthropology of ancient far westerners is not bright, the prospect for understanding the great *cultural* achievements of these people does not depend on such knowledge.

ANTHROPOMETRIC STUDIES ON LIVING POPULATIONS

Boas (1891, 1895a) made studies on the living populations of the Pacific Northwest for the British Association for the Advancement of Science under "The Committee appointed to investigate the physical characters, languages, and industrial and social condition of the North-Western Tribes of the Dominion of Canada." The "principal results" reported by Boas in 1895 show the diversity of the populations studied at that time as well as certain trends and suggestions of possible relationships which may have historical significance:

> It will be seen . . . that the statures of men and women of the different tribes are nearly arranged in the same order, differences appearing only in cases where the number of observations is very small. I have given the averages of the various series, not because I consider the averages as the typical values of the tribes, but because they give a convenient index for purposes of comparison. The table shows a gradual decrease in stature as we go southward along the coast from Alaska to Fraser River. In the series for men the stature decreases from 173 cm. among the Tlingit to 169 cm. among the Haida and Tsimshian; while the Nass River tribes, who live farther inland, and who are probably mixed Tinneh tribes of the interior, are only 167 cm. tall, the Tinneh of the interior being in their turn only 164 cm. tall. As we proceed southward, the stature decreases to 166 cm. among the Bilqula, 164 among the Kwakiutl, 162 in the delta of Fraser River and reaches its minimum of 158 cm. on the shores of Harrison Lake. As we go southward, the stature increases again, but its distribution becomes very irregular. The Salish tribes of Puget Sound and the Yakonan, Tinneh, and other tribes of Oregon have a stature of 165 cm. It seems that the Clallam and Nanaimo represent a taller people, but I am not quite certain of this, as some of the taller half-breeds may have been included in these series. On the Columbia River the Chinook, who extend from Dalles to the coast, represent a taller type of a stature of 169 cm., which may be considered as a continuation of the tall Sahaptin type, which has a stature of 170 cm. South of the Oregonian Tinneh the stature increases slightly, reaching 168 cm. among the Klamath, and sinking again to 166 among the Hoopa. The tribes of California, who lived north of San Francisco, and who are gathered on the Round Valley Reservation, near Cape Mendocino, represent a very short type of 162 cm. only, which is also distinguished by its elongated head. When we consider the stature of the inland tribes, we may say that the stature decreases north and south from Columbia River. The Sahaptin, a people of 170 cm., represent the tallest type; northward we find the Spokane and Okanogan 168 cm. tall, the Shuswap of South Thompson River of the same stature, while those of North Thompson River measure 167 cm. only. The Chilcotin measure only 164 cm. Along the Columbia River the tall stature extends to the sea. In the part of Oregon east of the Cascade Range, and in Western Nevada, we find statures of 168 cm., while Shoshone tribes of Idaho and Utah measure 166 cm. only (p. 529).

During the years 1891–92, extensive anthropometric studies were made under Boas's supervision for the program of the Anthropological Department of the World Columbian Exposition under authority of Professor F. W. Putnam, Chief of the Department. (The stimulus this program gave to anthropological investigation is analogous to that given to archæology by the Salvage Program.)*

Boas (1899:751, 753) reported briefly on studies of Shoshonean tribes. "The tribes included in these statistics are the Shoshone, the Bannock, and the Uintah, White River, Uncompagre, Moache, Capote, and Weeminuche Ute. The total series embraces 294 individuals, including 33 half bloods." The published data are not separated by tribes (except for a table of stature and head measurements that is probably for males) possibly due to the fact that in all measurements except one, the width of face among the Utes of Colorado, "the various tribes represent a uniform type. . . ." The cephalic index of 151 adults was 79.5, the average stature of 109 adult males was 166.1 cm., and 21 adult females 152.8 cm.

During the winter of probably 1894–95 (the paper was presented at the meeting of the American Association for the Advancement of Science, August-September 1895 and Boas speaks of "during the past winter"), Boas, under a grant from the AAAS, studied the Mission Indians of Southern California (1896). There were three linguistic stocks represented: the Shoshonean with four groups; the Yuman, San Diego Indians with one; and the Mariposan with one group, the Tule Indians. For some unexplained reason the San Diego Indians are not included in the summary tables although the individual measurements are given. All measurements were taken by Boas except for a few stature measurements taken by Mr. A. J. Street in 1892, which Boas incorporated (1896:292).

The statures of the tribes are nearly the same. There is a small amount of variation that may very well be due, as Boas (1896:263) points out, to the small samples available. The average stature for adult males 20 to 60 years of age is 169.3 centimeters

and for females 17 to 59 years of age 157.2 centimeters.

> The conclusion seems justified that all these tribes are tall, the average stature of the men being nearly 1700 mm. The average stature of the women is 92.8% of that of the men. . . . The most frequent index [cephalic] is 82, corresponding very nearly to that of the Yuma and Mojave. *The Indians differ therefore entirely in type from the former inhabitants of Santa Barbara and the islands of Southern California* [emphasis added]. The difference in type between these two neighboring peoples could hardly be greater than it is; the Mission Indians, tall, brachycephalic, with rather large and broad faces; the Indians of the islands, short, extremely dolichocephalic, with narrow faces and noses. It is of interest to note that a secondary maximum of frequency of length-breadth index of the Mission Indians is found at 79, and that it is most strongly developed among the Indians of San Luis Rey, who lived in the closest proximity to the long-headed islanders. It is quite probable that this maximum may be due to intermixture.
>
> It is worth remarking that the Mission Indians whom we found to belong to one and the same physical type, belong to three distinct linguistic stocks, and that other members of the Shoshonean stock belong to quite distinct physical types. We have, therefore, in this region, another excellent instance of the fact that the same language may be spoken by people representing quite distinct types, and that people belonging to the same type may speak quite distinct languages, that is to say that linguistic classification and racial classification are by no means identical (Boas 1896:263, 268–69).

Dr. Roland B. Dixon in 1899 and 1900, in connection with the Huntington California Expedition of the American Museum of Natural History, and Mr. V. K. Chesnut in 1892–93, for the World's Columbian Exposition, made anthropometric studies in Central California. Boas reports on some of the results of these studies as they tended to define the California population types.

> [T]he Yuki differ in type from all the neighboring tribes. They are short of stature, the average being 159 cm. for men, and 149 cm. for women. Their heads are elongated, which is due to great narrowness of the head; the cephalic index is about 77.5. The face is small, being both narrow and low. This type seems to be also present among the Maidu of the Foot-Hill region, but farther to the north and east it disappears. It is much less frequent among the Pomo than among the Maidu of the Foot-Hill region. Towards the interior and among the Pomo a type prevails which is similar to that of the Indians of the plateaus of Nevada and Utah. Their stature

---

*Boas (1895a) published the most comprehensive series of anthropometric measurements on the North American Indians. The material used from other of Boas's publications provides more or less summary statements for groups of tribes in the area of discussion in this paper. Additional data are to be found in the 1895 publication.

reaches 168 cm. among men, and 156 cm. among women, while the cephalic index is about 83. The width of face has the characteristic high value of the eastern Indians, being, on the average, 149. Among the Pit River Indians excessively short heads are found. I am doubtful if they may not be in part due to flattening of the occiput, although they seem to arise rather from excessive width than excessive shortness of the head.

It seems plausible that the type represented by the Yuki may be related to the very short and long-headed type of the islands of California, which, in its most pronounced form, was found on the most southern islands; while northward, towards Santa Barbara, its most striking characteristics become less marked. It would seem, that, if this relationship exists, the Yuki would resemble the ancient inhabitants of Santa Barbara.

The occurrence of this peculiar type among other types of the Pacific Coast is very remarkable. *It is another instance of the irregularity of distribution of types along this coast, and analogous to the irregularities of distribution that are found along the coast farther to the north* [emphasis added] (Boas 1905:356–57).

Gifford (1926) has provided the only other significant anthropometric study on living populations in the Far West but limited to California. The measurements were made during the first quarter of the century by various members of the Department of Anthropology at the University of California at Berkeley. Gifford was responsible for the ordering and analysis of the data as shown in Figures 21, 22, and 23.

He divides the living aborigines of California into two main groups, one low-faced, the other high-faced (Figure 24). The low-faced type is the *Yuki* type of Boas (p. 78, above), to which he adds further characteristics, a high nasal index, relatively low cephalic index, and short stature.

The high-faced group is variable in cephalic index and nasal indices and ranges from medium stature to tall stature. . . . The high-faced group may be divided into a broad-headed subgroup of wide distribution, which I have called the *Californian* type, and a narrow-headed, narrow-nosed subgroup restricted to the *Western Mono* and called the *Western Mono* type.

The *Californian* type is divisible into three subtypes. One, which I have called the *Narrow-nosed* subtype, is found in the mountainous portions of extreme northern California, in the Sierra Nevada region, and in extreme southern California. A second subtype, characterized by great size and relatively broad nose, inhabits the Colorado valley between Needles and the Gulf of California. I have called it the *Tall* subtype. The third subtype, found chiefly in north central California and among the Yurok

and Wiyot of northwestern California, I have designated the *Broad-nosed* subtype.

Summing up, then, we have among the living three main types, *Yuki, Mono,* and *Californian,* the last named being divisible into three subtypes, *Narrow-nosed, Broad-nosed,* and *Tall* (Gifford 1926:224).

Gifford (1926), on the basis of more cases and the elimination of some half-breeds, finds that the Yuki type is more distinctive than Boas indicated. He finds a bimodal curve for cephalic index, which suggests to him intermixture. Otherwise Gifford's results corroborate those of Boas where they overlap. In some cases the list of measurements used by Gifford is amplified by those made by other investigators. I have included for reference Gifford's map of Californian peoples in Figure 21. There are some minor bibliographic sources drawn on by Gifford, which I have used only indirectly, but I have included them in the bibliography.

These early anthropometric studies, while not in any sense comprehensive, offer a picture of the range of variations in stature and cranial indices among the native far-western peoples of historic times. The factors underlying the variations and patterns within the data are usually assumed to be genetic but are in fact not clearly understood and probably include dietary and cultural factors as well. Because the forces which shaped the data are not understood, the use of them in historical reconstruction would not be defensible, and I refrain from attempting any further conclusions here.

ANTHROPOMETRIC STUDIES ON THE NONLIVING

Examination of the major studies of skeletal material taken from archæological contexts leads to the discouraging realization that little in the way of reliable conclusions can be based on them. A brief review will indicate the nature of the problems involved and the reason for this pessimism.

Oetteking (1930) presented a detailed and extensive study of 75 crania from seven different tribal areas of the Northwest, which were collected by the Jesup North Pacific Expedition under Boas. The material was treated voluminously, but because of the small sample size, the lack of information on the antiquity of the specimens, and the artificial deformation of many of the skulls, the study is not an

Athabascan
1a. Rogue River (uninhabited)
1b. Tolowa
1c. Hupa
1d. Chilula
1e. Whilkut
1f. Mattole
1g. Nongatl
1h. Lassik
1i. Sinkyone
1j. Wailaki
1k. Kato
Yurok
2a. Yurok
2b. Coast Yurok
3. Wiyot
Yukian
4a. Yuki
4b. Huchnom
4c. Coast Yuki
4d. Wappo
Lutuamian
5. Modoc

Shastan
6a. Shasta
6b. New River Shasta
6c. Konomihu
6d. Okwanuchu
6e. Achomawi (Pit River)
6f. Atsugewi (Hat Creek)
Yana
7a. Northern Yana (Noze)
7b. Central Yana (Noze)
7c. Southern Yana
7d. Yahi
8. Karok
9. Chimariko
Pomo
10a. Northern
10b. Central
10c. Eastern
10d. Southeastern
10e. Northeastern
10f. Southern
10g. Southwestern
11. Washo
12. Esselen
Salinan
13a. Antoniano
13b. Migueleño
13c. Playano (doubtful)
Chumash
14a. Obispeño
14b. Purisimeño
14c. Ynezeño
14d. Barbareño
14e. Ventureño
14f. Emigdiano
14g. Interior (doubtful)
14h. Island

Yuman
15a. Northern Diegueño
15b. Southern Diegueño
15c. Kamia (doubtful)
15d. Yuma
15e. Halchidhoma (now Cheme-huevi)
15f. Mohave
Wintun
16a Northern
16b. Nomlaki
16c. Valley Patwin
16d. Hill Patwin
Maidu
17a. Northeastern
17b. Northwestern (Valley and Hill)
17c. Southern (Nishinam)
Miwok
18a. Coast
18b. Lake
18c. Plains
18d. Northern
18e. Central
18f. Southern
Costanoan
19a. Saklan (doubtful)
19b. San Francisco
19c. Santa Clara
19d. Santa Cruz
19e. San Juan Bautista (Mutsun)
19f. Monterey (Rumsen)
19g. Soledad
Yokuts
20a. Northern Valley (Chulam-ni, Chauchila, etc.)
20b. Southern Valley (Tachi, Yauelmani, etc.)
20c. Northern Hill (Chuk-chansi, etc.)

20d. Kings River (Choinimni, etc.)
20e. Tule-Kaweah (Yaudanchi, etc.)
20f. Poso Creek (Paleuyami)
20g. Buena Vista (Tulamni, etc.)

Shoshonean
21a. Northern Paiute (Paviotso)
21b. Eastern Mono (Paiute)
21c. Western Mono
21d. Koso (Panamint, Shoshone)
21e. Chemehuevi (Southern Paiute)
21f. Kawaiisu (Tehachapi)

21g. Tübatulabal (and Bankalachi)
21h. Kitanemuk (Tejon)
21i. Alliklik
21j. Vanyume (Möhineyam)
21k. Serrano
21l. Fernandeño
21m. Gabrielino
21n. Nicoleño
21o. Juaneño
21p. Luiseño
21q. Cupeño
21r. Pass Cahuilla
21s. Mountain Cahuilla
21t. Desert Cahuilla

FIGURE 21. Key map of Californian peoples. *Gifford 1926:222, Map 1.*

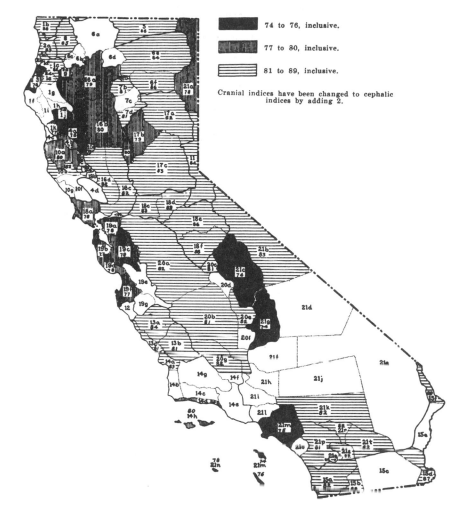

FIGURE 22. Average cephalic indices (living and cranial combined) for Californian peoples. *Gifford 1926:250, Map 2.*

adequate basis for inference about prehistoric Northwest populations.

Gifford (1926) presented the first comprehensive anthropometric study of the prehistoric population of California. He had at his disposal cranial series from the University of California and other sources and measurements furnished by Hooton on crania in the Peabody Museum, Harvard University, which came from the Santa Barbara region. Unfortunately, for historical purposes, Gifford faced the same problem of lack of precise time depth information as did Oetteking. In addition, he was faced with small samples. "The only regions which are anywhere near adequately represented by cranial material are the shores of San Francisco Bay, the Sacramento-San

Joaquin delta, the southern San Joaquin Valley, and the Santa Barbara coast and islands. The remainder of the state is represented by but a few scattering [of] crania" (Gifford 1926:241). The problem of comparing the cranial populations with living ones was also complicated by the different distribution of the two sources of material. Gifford writes:

> Unfortunately for comparative purposes, it is from those regions best represented by cranial material that no measurements of the living are forthcoming, and from the regions best represented by the living that but scanty cranial material has been derived. A comparison of ancient and modern Indian populations of identical areas is therefore largely impossible (Gifford 1926:249).

In view of the methodological weaknesses of his

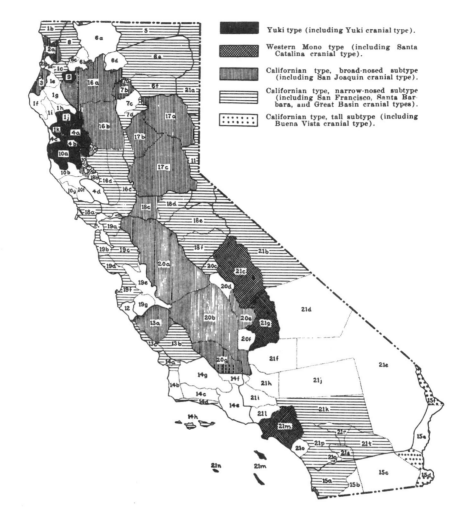

FIGURE 23. Physical types (living and cranial data combined) for Californian peoples. *Gifford 1926:252, Map 3.*

study, I do not summarize Gifford's conclusions here, and I feel that it is unwise on my part to attempt to draw any historical conclusions from his data.

Kennedy (1959) has made the most extensive study of Great Basin physical types to date, basing his work on materials in the Museum of Anthropology at the University of California, Berkeley, and on the published data of various authors, including Gifford. In addition, he used a series of measurements on living Great Basin peoples made by Hrdlička (Kennedy 1959:1–2). Despite the fact that Kennedy's attempt encompasses virtually the entire range of data available on the subject, his conclusions are rendered unreliable by the same problems that affected earlier

studies of far-western material: the skeletal remains are poorly dated, if dated at all; the sample sizes are impossibly small in all instances; and, in some cases, even the geographical provenience of the specimens is uncertain. Again, because of my strong reservations about the validity of inferences based on such data, I do not summarize Kennedy's conclusions.

Many other treatments of very small collections of skeletal material from the Far West can be cited (e.g., Hill-Tout 1895; Smith 1909b; Cressman 1933, 1950; Hegrenes 1955; Laughlin in Cressman 1956), but in every case the samples are too small, and in most cases the dating too poorly controlled, to yield reliable generalizations. It must be reluctantly concluded that the unlikelihood of ever obtaining suffi-

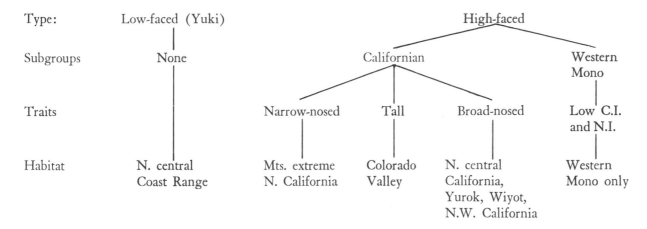

Type:	Low-faced (Yuki)			High-faced	
Subgroups	None		Californian		Western Mono
Traits		Narrow-nosed	Tall	Broad-nosed	Low C.I. and N.I.
Habitat	N. central Coast Range	Mts. extreme N. California	Colorado Valley	N. central California, Yurok, Wiyot, N.W. California	Western Mono only

FIGURE 24. Proposed types of living California Indians and their distribution. *Compiled from Gifford 1926:224–25.*

ciently large and well-dated samples of human skeletal material from far-western sites makes the investigation of the anthropometric characteristics of the ancient populations an unpromising line of inquiry.

GENETIC STUDIES

During the years following the discovery of blood groups in World War I, many studies were made of different populations to determine the blood groups to which they belonged. Table 3, slightly edited, presents results of some of these studies (Laughlin in Cressman 1950). The appearance of this new method for determining genetic relationship, the ease of its use, and its apparent simplicity caused it to be accepted with enthusiasm. The first applications of the method were pretty crude because not enough was known about the genetics of the groups and the conditions controlling their distribution, such as mating patterns, etc. As knowledge of the genetics of blood groups has increased, studies have become more sophisticated and complex, and at the same time some limitations in their use have become more fully recognized.

Archæologists and others also initially accepted the validity of a process for determining blood types from skeletal material. This method of genetic identification would have allowed detection of the direction of gene flow over time, provided enough firmly dated skeletons could be found, but Thieme and Otten (1957) and Gray (1958) indicate that the

blood types derived from skeletal material are equivocal because the antigen for type A occurs in the soil, and bone may be contaminated by absorption of the substance from the earth in which it is buried. It is interesting that most skeletal material has been identified as representing blood-type A. This work makes it clear that further discussion of results of this kind of genetic study is not warranted.

Hulse (1955, 1957, 1960) has provided recent data for the Pacific Northwest, though mostly for coastal populations. He has been concerned with the dynamics of distribution of gene frequencies: the effect of marriage patterns, the apparent gene flow of allele A from the Rocky Mountains and western Canada toward the Pacific Coast, and the relative strength of geographic and linguistic barriers affecting gene flow. If these factors affect the gene frequencies of living populations, there is no reason to doubt that they did in the past. A westward direction of gene flow indicates some movement of population elements in that direction, when or why we do not know at present, but recent archæological evidence, to be discussed later, tends to corroborate this directional movement at a period of considerable antiquity.*

---

* Simply stated, the hypothetical history of the ABO blood-group types in the New World is this: the first entrants belonged to the O group; later arrivals (Algonkians and Athapascans) introduced the allele for A; and the last arrivals, the Eskimos, introduced the B blood type. The presence of the allele for type B among Indian groups not

TABLE 3

SHORT TABLE OF BLOOD GROUPS OF NORTH AMERICAN POPULATIONS*

People	Place	Investigators	No.	O	A	B	AB	P	q	r	D/o
ESKIMO:											
Nanortalik (slight mixture with Europeans)	Greenland	Fabricius-Hansen 1939	419	48.92	44.39	4.29	2.38	.271	.034	.699	.99
Aleuts	Aleutians	Laughlin 1948	132	48.5	44.7	4.5	2.3	.269	.032	.696	.441
NORTH AM. INDIANS:											
Athapascans	Peace Riv., Canada	Grant 1936	61	62.0	38.0	0	0	.213	—	.787	—
Navajo	Ft. Defiance and St. Michaels, Ariz.	Nigg 1926	457	72.9	26.9	0.2	0.2	.145	.001	.854	—
Stoney	Alberta, Canada	Grant 1938	158	67.1	32.3	0	0.6	.178	—	.819	—
Blackfeet	Montana	Matson and Schrader 1933	115	23.5	76.5	0	0	.515	0	.485	—
Blackfeet	Browning, Mont.	Matson, Levine and Schrader 1936	103	24.3	74.8	0	1.0	.503	0	.493	—
Piegan	Brocket, Alberta	Matson 1938	42	19.1	80.9	0	0	.563	0	.437	—
Flatheads (Salish)	W. Montana	Matson and Schrader 1933	258	51.5	42.2	4.7	1.6	.250	.032	.718	0.3†
Salish	Coast, B. C.	Gates and Darby 1934 and Ride and Furahata 1935	50	80.0	20.0	0	0	.205	0	.895	—
Kwakiutl	Bella Bella Br. Columbia	Gates and Darby 1934	94	92.6	7.4	0	0	0.37	0	.963	—
Tsimshian	Coast, B. C.	Gates and Darby 1934 and Ride and Furahata 1935	54	72.2	27.8	0	0	.150	0	.850	—
Tsimshian and Kwakiutl	Haskell Inst. Lawrence, Kans.	Landsteiner and Levine 1929	124	66.1	33.9	0	0	.186	0	.814	—
Shoshone	S. Agency, Ft. Washakie, Wyo.	Snyder 1926	60	51.6	45.0	1.6	1.6	.264	.011	.718	—

* All data for Aleuts, Laughlin 1948; all others from Boyd's unpublished data, 1939a, 1939b.
† Less than.
SOURCE: Laughlin in Cressman 1950.

Hulse (1955) gives the most up-to-date information on the distribution of gene frequencies among the Northwest Coast Indians and in his work has made every effort to control the variable, hybridization. Tables 4 and 5 summarize his work.

Inspection of entries for the ABO group shows that six out of eighteen are type O with frequencies between 90 and 98 percent inclusive. These are the extreme peripheral populations on the Pacific Coast from the Nootka of the west coast of Vancouver Island on the north to Quilleute on Cape Flattery of

in contact with Eskimos is attributed to European contact. The descendants of the earliest arrivals should belong to the O group, and the presence of peoples exhibiting both A and O types indicated the introduction of the allele for A into a population of the O type.

TABLE 4

ABO FREQUENCIES, BY POPULATION GROUPS

Population Group	Numbers Typed				Gene Frequencies		
	O	A	B	AB	p (a)	q (b)	r (o)
Haida	6	2			.13		.87
Tsimshian	37	12	1		.13	.01	.86
Kwakiutl	21	10			.18		.82
Gulf Salish	36	10	1		.11	.01	.88
Nootka: Indian	267	9			.016		.984
Mixed	48	16			.13		.87
Central	225	9			.02		.98
Nitinat	91	16			.07		.93
Makah-Nitinat	35	6	3		.07	.035	.89
Makah: Indian	100	11	1		.05	.004	.946
Mixed	60	24	3		.15	.02	.83
Makah-Quilleute	33	5			.07		.93
Quilleute	27	2			.04		.96
Makah-Klallam	14	8			.20		.80
Port Madison	56	23	3	4	.15	.03	.82
Tulalip: Indian	68	13	8		.08	.05	.87
Mixed	64	11	9	1	.072	.058	.87
Muckleshoot	57	23		2	.16	.007	.833

SOURCE: Hulse 1955:96.

northwest Washington on the south. The remaining groups have frequencies ranging from 80 to 89 percent. MN frequencies occur in about the usual percentage rate common to the American Indians but showing considerable intertribal variation. The Kwakiutl divergence from the pattern, however, is worth noting: "Among the groups which appear to be relatively free of Caucasian inter-mixture, only the Kwakiutl have any considerable percentage of the allele for A and the allele for N" (Hulse 1955:97).

Hulse's hypothesis of gene flow is that the original blood-group type of the coastal area was O and that this was diluted by a gradual flow of the allele for type A from the east. Such gene flow could be in the form of migration of gene carriers or by slow injection of the new substance through various forms of contact providing for interbreeding. Archæological evidence shows that the interior of British Columbia was occupied at least 7,000 years ago by peoples with two different cultural traditions (cf. Chapter 8), one evidently derived from Alaska (Athapascan?) and the other from Alberta (Algonkian?). Both areas

had populations with a mixture of the A and O blood types.

Hulse tentatively suggests, on the basis of very slight evidence, that the route of type A gene flow was down the Columbia River from the northern Rocky Mountain area where the Blackfoot and Piegan have the allele for type A in excess of 50 percent. His evidence is the presence in a skeletal population in the Columbia River valley in northeastern Washington of the allele for type A and the allele for type O about midway of the ratios for the two types found in the Coast Salish and the Rocky Mountain tribes mentioned. The suggestion of direction of gene flow based on this evidence can now be rejected because of the unreliability of buried skeletal material as a blood-typing source, as mentioned above. I propose that the earliest populations of interior British Columbia probably provided the source for the allele for type A, if the archæologist's identification of population sources is correct, and carried it to the coast when movements from the interior occurred (cf. Chapter 6).

TABLE 5

MN FREQUENCIES, BY POPULATION GROUPS

Population Group	Numbers Typed			Gene Frequencies	
	M	MN	N	m	n
Haida	7	1		.94	.06
Tsimshian	41	9		.91	.09
Kwakiutl	21	7	3	.79	.21
Gulf Salish	26	16	5	.72	.28
Nootka: Indian	213	33	30	.83	.17
Mixed	50	13	1	.88	.12
Central	182	31	21	.84	.16
Nitinat	86	13	8	.87	.13
Makah-Nitinat	12	7		.82	.18
Makah: Indian	63	21	3	.85	.15
Mixed	38	8	1	.89	.11
Makah-Quilleute	16	2	1	.89	.11
Quilleute	24	1	1	.94	.06
Makah-Klallam	3	2		.80	.20
Port Madison	52	18	14	.73	.27
Tulalip: Indian	73	13	1	.92	.08
Mixed	69	8	6	.88	.12
Muckleshoot	53	9	1	.91	.09

SOURCE: Hulse 1955:97.

The extreme peripheral people with 96 to 98 percent of the allele for type O could represent either descendents of an early type O population in an original habitat and relatively untouched by the gene flow from the east, or they could be viewed as a part of an original Gulf of Georgia population which moved to the western coast to avoid contact with incoming eastern migrants. Archæology at present makes no contribution to the solution of this problem.

Hulse also considers the possibility that the allele for type A came from a European source, but thinks a more likely origin is an aboriginal one and suggests the Blackfoot and Blood of the Rocky Mountain area, "which have a higher proportion of the allele for A than has any European group" (Hulse 1955: 99).

Hulse also concluded that linguistic barriers were more of an obstacle to gene flow than geographic ones. He compared two Salish-speaking groups, the Swinomish of Puget Sound and the Okanagan of the Okanagan Valley of northern Washington and British Columbia, with the Yakima, a Sahaptin-speaking population living in the Yakima River area. The Yakima and the Okanagan are both Plateau cultural groups. The results of the study indicated that

In this particular case, at any rate, the linguistic barrier would appear to be the stronger. The Okanogan differ from the Yakima in the MN system of blood groups. They differ even more markedly in the RH system. The Okanogan differ much less, in either system, from the Swinomish, despite paucity of contact between these tribes in recent centuries. The two Plateau groups resemble one another in the ABO system, but this can be most readily explained by contacts in each case with more easterly tribes of its own linguistic stock, rather than by interbreeding between them (Hulse 1957:224).

Hulse's study of the Hupa, a small Athapascan-speaking group living on the lower reaches of the Trinity River in northwestern California far removed from the Athapascan homeland in the north, indicated marked changes in blood-group types. He writes:

Comparison with other Athapaskan tribes show that the Hupa have a greater incidence of blood-group O than any other people of the same linguistic stock. Most Athapaskans have a higher frequency of A than their neighbors, but we are unable to say this of the Hupa. Rather in their low incidence of A, the Hupa-Yurok-Karok group resemble such other Pacific Coast people as the Nootka and Coast Salish to the north and the Diegeño in southern California. . . (Hulse 1960:150; see Pantin: 1953 for data on the Diegeño).

Hulse makes clear that the Hupa do not resemble the blood-type frequencies of other Athapascan-speaking groups and suggests that "the influence of Northwest Coast culture, even in its attenuated form, led to such extensive and long continued intermarriage that the original Hupa gene-pool merged in another, larger one long ago" (Hulse 1960:151).

The genetic studies of far-western peoples carried out to date offer some provocative suggestions of migration and of prehistoric mergings of peoples for the archæologist to consider and for which he may seek archæological correlatives (see Chapter 8). As such studies become more fully developed, they may provide the archæologist with some of the insight he has hoped for but has not been able to gain from the older anthropometric studies.

In closing this chapter it seems important to focus on some of the reasons why so much of the material discussed above has left us with no satisfactory picture of the physical anthropology of prehistoric far-western peoples. By directing attention to certain basic concepts that tend to be ignored in our search for answers to this question, we may make clearer the requirements for successful future approaches to at least some aspects of this vexing problem.

1. The human physical type, as with other organisms, changes in response to different environmental pressures in ways that are not understood. Boas's study of the changes in head form of European immigrants to the United States was the first work to show the instability of physical type. The idea was shocking in its impact and strenuously opposed but not disproved. He called attention (1895b:375) to the increase in stature of the Cherokees in Oklahoma in comparison to those Cherokees who remained behind in the mountains of western North Carolina, but suggested that there might have been some intermixture to account for the increased height. There were other studies that confirmed Boas's results. Shapiro (1939) proved conclusively that the physical type changed not only in stature

but in many aspects of the body. Parts of the head, parts of the appendages, etc., changed although the explanation was not understood. Cressman (1931) called attention to the fact that the particular conditions of an environment, in this case mineral deficiency, could affect the body and performance in different ways. Boyd (1950:87) writes, "The phenotype is always the resultant of the interaction between a certain genotype and a certain environment. The end result depends upon both factors. Different genotypes may react in some environments to produce similar phenotypes. So dissimilarity of phenotypes is not necessarily proof of dissimilarity of genotypes." Boyd's statement demonstrates the *instability of physical type* since it is the result of a dynamic relation between organism and physical environment.

2. Any effort to relate the physical type of a modern population to that of a supposed ancestral group must depend to some extent on a knowledge of the habitat conditions of the supposed ancestral group. The ancestral group could have lived in a different environment from that of the modern group, and the phenotype represented by the skeletal population might be quite different from that of the modern group. We tend to compare similar phenotypes reflected by skeletal populations diverse in time and space, and if they share a series of attributes anthropometrically determined, the tendency is to equate the population in a historical sequence. Conclusions so arrived at are not defensible.

3. There is also the influence of genetic drift. For many thousands of years much of the Indian population, especially in an environment as differentiated as the western United States, must have been composed of small groups of hunters and gatherers who wandered within customarily defined areas with little contact with other groups. This kind of a situation would undoubtedly have favored genetic drift by which certain genes were lost in various groups, and not always the same genes either, so that on the one hand genotypes would diverge, and on the other hand originally diverse groups might by the same process become more alike. With population increase and more frequent contacts between groups, gene flow would be resumed, but the components of the current would depend on the genotypes then present in the meeting populations.

4. Surely over the many millennia man has been in the New World natural selection must have brought about some changes in the physical types. The very diversity of environments argues for this result.

Both the substantive and the theoretical material I have just summarily referred to, which indicates the instability of physical type because of the dynamic relationship it always bears to the environment, requires that evidence of diverse environments in space and their changes through time, discussed in Chapters 2 and 3, should always be part of the data if we even hope to understand the physical types of the populations of the aboriginal West. Some of the desired information is available in archæological reports in which skeletal materials are discussed. Yet when the bones are studied, it seems that they are usually considered to exist without reference to such factors.

What, then, of a positive nature are we able to offer from this review of uncertain and fragmentary knowledge? Just this: certainly there were many population types at any given time segment of the millennia represented in far-western prehistory; certainly there was no single "far-western type" just as there never was a single "American Indian type"; natural and social selection and other factors mentioned above changed these types through time; the differences in physical types, which have been demon-

strated for early historic times, are *not* correlated with differences in accomplishments.

Beyond this, perhaps the remarkable thing to consider about "The People" is that they conquered a continent. What they looked like is certainly a legitimate scientific concern but perhaps tangential to the more important fact of their accomplishments. I do not mean that the study of the physical characteristics of a population is without merit; the study of the archæologist's limited samples may contribute certain relevant kinds of useful information and should be continued. I think, however, that the prehistorian as *humanist* might more profitably seek his reward in exploration of the psychological characteristics of his people. He would find them to have been durable under extreme environmental demands, imaginative in meeting challenges, sensitive to the need to satisfy the æsthetic sense, capable of love and devotion as well, and possessors of other traits both admirable and detestable in our value system. These traits are neither revealed nor measured by calipers. The archæological record when sensitively analyzed provides ample evidence for the quest I urge. Perhaps the prehistorian as humanist would contribute more to the understanding of his people and their part in the human experience if he approached them in the spirit of the poet who sang in Ecclesiasticus 44:1:

> Let us now praise famous men
> And our fathers that begat us.

Linguistic Prehistory

He gave man speech, and speech created thought,
Which is the measure of the universe.

Percy Bysshe Shelley, Prometheus Unbound, Act III, Scene IV

RECONSTRUCTION OF linguistic prehistory may follow either of two basic approaches. The history of change in a language or group of languages may be analyzed in terms of linguistic attributes, entirely separate from considerations of space and even time (although time is implicit in the concept of change). Alternatively, the actual space-time experience of a language may be traced; its probable speakers and containing culture or cultures may be identified and located in space at successive time levels. These basic approaches may of course be combined in the pursuit of special objectives yielding a third approach. Obviously the first and third methods of study require the skill of the professional linguist. The second method can be used by the archæologist who draws upon the contributions of the linguists, and in this chapter I shall discuss as fully as the evidence permits the location of certain far-western language groups in time and space. The study of linguistic prehistory provides some of the clearest evidence available of migrations and dispersals of human groups in ancient times, and demonstrates the occurrence of some important movements of peoples in the Far West that archæological methods alone would probably not have revealed. Maps 5 and 6 show the distribution, as presently understood, of language groups in far-western North America.

I am not a linguist, and for evidence of relationships between languages and estimates of time elapsed since related languages diverged from a common ancestral speech community, I shall rely on glottochronological studies offered by linguists. Glottochronology is a statistical method that measures the degree to which related languages differ in basic vocabulary, and, by a formula based on known rates of linguistic change, transforms this measurement into an estimate of the minimum number of years elapsed since the languages began to grow apart. For the purposes of this discussion, the validity of the glottochronological method is accepted; that it is not 100 percent accurate as chronological indicator is also accepted. Linguists working with glottochronology check their results against other sources of information for validation just as archæologists check C-14 dates against supporting evidence of stratigraphy and paleontology for validation.

When carefully used, glottochronology seems to be fairly accurate as an instrument for determining the degree of linguistic relationship within the last 5,000 years or 50 minimum centuries.* When applied to problems of relationship at the 10,000 year level, glottochronological results are at best speculative. Disciplined speculation, however, not only has nothing wrong with it, but is a fundamental part of the framework of science. Beyond 10,000 years in linguistic reconstruction even disciplined speculation is but an interesting intellectual exercise.

Important glottochronological studies have been made in three groups of languages in my area of interest: the Athapascan, Salish, and Uto-Aztecan stocks. Speculative discussions have also been devoted to the linguistic prehistory of two groups higher up in the classificatory hierarchy, the Penutian and Hokan linguistic phyla. I shall discuss the glottochronological evidence bearing on the three lower-order language stocks followed by brief references to the positions in space and time of the larger linguistic phyla.

THE ATHAPASCANS

Hoijer (1956) is my major source of information

---

* Voegelin (1958:57) expresses somewhat *acidly* a dissenting point of view: ". . . that absolute chronology will come to be regarded as an endearing predilection of Swadesh and others—at a time, in the middle of the 20th century, when social scientists were bowing in respect to statistical procedures in general, and anthropology in particular was going from one triumph in absolute chronology to another, from dendrochronology to radiocarbon."

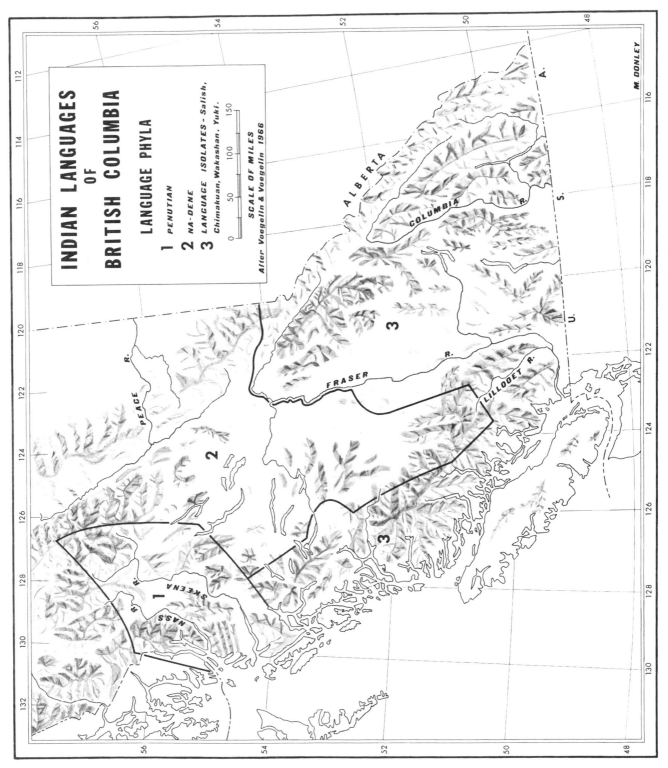

Map 5. Linguistic distribution in British Columbia.

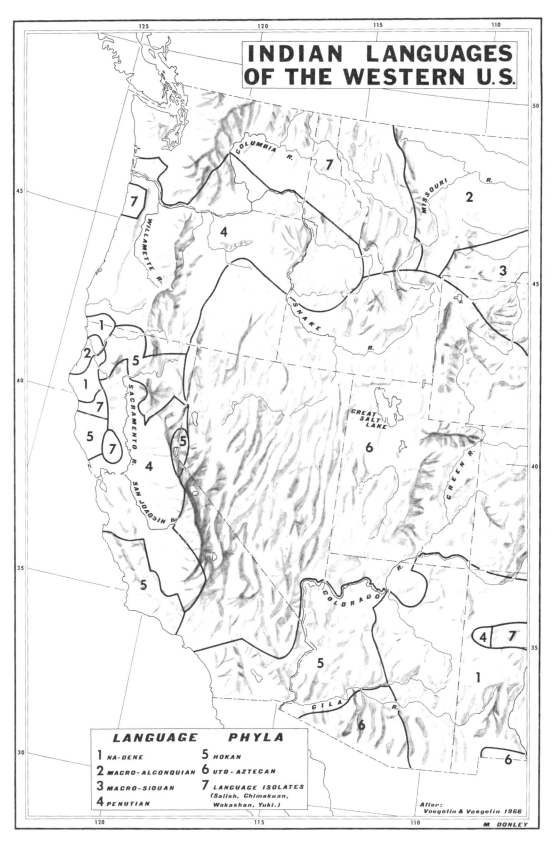

MAP 6. Linguistic distribution in the western United States.

on the group. Hymes (1957) studied the Athapascan problem with a slightly different approach than Hoijer, but his results supported the main conclusions of Hoijer. Hoijer identifies three linguistic groupings: Northern, Pacific Coast, and Apachean.

The original homeland of the Athapascan language is in the general area of the Northern groups; the Pacific Coast and Apachean groups diverged in that area at different times and eventually arrived by unknown routes at their present habitats. Glottochronological data show that the major breakup of the Athapascan language community is surprisingly recent, having started about 1,300 years ago. The three major groups had split apart by shortly after 1,000 years ago, and internal divergences within the groups continued to develop until as late as 600 years ago in the Apachean case and 500 years ago in the Northern case. The fifteen language groups and their general locations at the time of contact are:

Northern Languages—7

Beaver   Hare   Galice
Carrier   Kutchin   Chipewyan
Sarcee

Location: Spoken in various regions of the Canadian Northwest and Alaska. Galice in southwestern Oregon is listed with the Northern group but might equally well be placed with the California languages.

Northwestern California (Pacific Coast) Languages—3

Hupa   Mattole   Kato

Location: Spoken in coastal northwestern California.

Apachean Languages—5

Navaho   Jicarilla   Chircahua
Lipan   San Carlos

Location: Spoken in New Mexico and Arizona.

Divergence Dates—The Northern Groups

Table 6 summarizes Hoijer's data (1956: 224, Table III) giving the number of years ago at which divergence between pairs of Northern languages occurred.

Thus, within the Northern group, the breakup began approximately 1,000 years ago, and the divergence dates of eighteen of twenty-one pairs fall before 628 years ago, indicating that the period of major breakup was complete by that time.

Divergence Dates—The Pacific Coast Groups

The divergence dates between the Northern languages and three Pacific Coast languages, Kato, Hupa, and Mattole, are given in Table 7. Galice, which occurs in southwestern Oregon, is treated by Hoijer as a Northern language. Other Athapascan groups, the Klatskanie and the Kwalhioqua, also occur in the Puget-Willamette Trough at the Columbia River, but no glottochronological data are available for them. Comparison of the tabulations for the Pacific and Northern groups shows that 15 out of 21 of the divergence times between Pacific Coast and Northern languages are greater than 1,000 years, while among only two sets of languages in the Northern group are divergence times greater than 1,000 years. This would indicate that the separation of the Pacific Coast group was close to, and may have initiated, the great breakup of the Athapascan languages. It is not clear whether the progenitors of the Pacific languages started their move south as a group, to break up later, or whether three ancestral populations followed one another at short intervals. Since, however, there is scarcely a spread of 100 years between the internal divergence times for three of the four languages of the group (Mattole-Kato divergence, 858 years ago; Hupa-Kato, 963 years; Hupa-Mattole, 963 years), the question is not critical. It is clear that for most of its history the Pacific group has exhibited the subdivisions it exhibited in historic times, although Galice evidently emerged as a separate entity some two to three centuries later than Mattole-Hupa-Kato (Galice-Kato divergence time, 724 years ago).[*]

---

[*] The statement by Elsasser and Heizer (1966:2), "The Hupa are estimated, by lexicostatic method (Hoijer 1956; Hymes 1957) to have been resident on the Lower Trinity River for about 1,000 years . . . ," is a misinterpretation of glottochronological data. These say only that the divergence time of the Hupa and the Northern groups was about 1,000 years and give no information whatever on the arrival date of the Hupa on the Lower Trinity River.

TABLE 6

DIVERGENCE DATES BETWEEN PAIRS OF NORTHERN LANGUAGES

Divergence Dates	Pairs of Northern Languages
1. Less than 600 years ago (3 sets of languages)	Beaver—Chipewyan (477) Kutchin—Hare (506) Sarcee—Beaver (597)
2. Less than 628 to 724 years ago (7 sets of languages)	Chipewyan—Kutchin (628) Beaver—Hare (628) Carrier—Chipewyan (628) Galice—Beaver (628) Chipewyan—Hare (660) Sarcee—Chipewyan (660) Galice—Chipewyan (724)
3. Less than 755 to 858 years ago (7 sets of languages)	Beaver—Kutchin (755) Galice—Carrier (823) Carrier—Kutchin (858) Carrier—Hare (858) Galice—Sacree (823) Carrier—Beaver (755) Carrier—Sarcee (823)
4. Less than 928 to 1036 years ago (4 sets of languages)	Sarcee—Hare (928) Galice—Hare (963) Sarcee—Kutchin (1036) Galice—Kutchin (1036)

SOURCE. Adapted from Hoijer 1956;Table III.

Divergence Dates—The Apachean Groups

Hoijer's dates of divergence between Apachean and Northern and Pacific Coast languages appear in Table 8. This tabulation indicates that thirty-one of thirty-five divergence times between Apachean and Northern groups are under 1,000 years, while thirteen of fifteen divergence times between Apachean and Pacific groups exceed 1,000 years. These times, considered along with the great divergence times between Northern and Pacific groups, clearly indicate that the Apachean languages diverged from the main body of Athapascan speakers in the north only after the Pacific groups had already moved off.

The internal relationships of Apachean languages are shown in Table 9. Hoijer (1956:226) suggests the Apachean peoples moved off from the north "as a unit," noting that "These figures emphasize the extremely close relationships of the Apachean languages; it would appear that the earliest divergence occurred only a little more than 400 years ago."

The later histories of the Northern and Apachean speech communities are beyond the scope of this book, and these groups are not further considered, their introduction here having been only for the purpose of placing the Pacific Coast group in context.

There are three possible migration routes to be considered for the Pacific Athapascans: first, an intermontane route into southern Oregon, thence across the Cascade Mountains or down the Klamath River into northwestern California; second, a route across the Cascade Mountains from central Washington into the southern Puget Trough and then south through the Willamette Valley into southwestern Oregon and northwestern California; and, third, access at some point to the Pacific Coast and movement south following the coast.

I propose that of these three possibilities the second is the most probable. For the intermontane route there is simply no concrete evidence, positive or negative, from which to reason, and the rain forest

TABLE 7

DIVERGENCE DATES BETWEEN NORTHERN LANGUAGES
AND PACIFIC COAST LANGUAGES

Northern Languages	Pacific Coast Languages		
	Kato	Hupa	Mattole
Galice	724	858	1000
Beaver	724	928	1112
Chipewyan	823	963	1150
Carrier	1036	1036	1150
Hare	1036	1189	1150
Sarcee	1073	1150	1189
Kutchin	1036	1229	1311

SOURCE: Hoijer 1956: 231, Table V.

and rugged character of the Pacific Coast would have made coastal movement an extraordinarily hard task. The best spoor for trailing an Athapascan movement south through the Puget-Willamette lowlands is the enclaves of Athapascan speakers that occur along the proposed route—the Klatskanie on the lower Columbia River in Oregon and the Kwalhioqua across the river in Washington where these groups possibly lived one time as neighbors (Swanson 1952:458). Their southward movement would have passed through Chinook territory where resistance might have been encountered, and perhaps the "dropping off" of these two groups in an environment not too unlike that of their interior homeland represents a response to Chinook resistance. Farther south Athapascan was the language spoken in the upper Umpqua drainage and along the Oregon coast from the southern boundary of the Coos at the Coquille River to northwestern California, where lived the Mattole, Hupa, and Kato.

This north-south pattern of distribution constitutes the basis for my thesis of Pacific Athapascan migration via the Puget-Willamette corridor. Jacobs (1937) has argued that the presence of Athapascan languages in the upper Umpqua drainage is not due to Athapascan immigration but to adoption of the language from northwestern California groups. This is a possible interpretation, but it is clear that in historic times the Willamette Valley served as a major north-south avenue of movement and contact among Indian groups, and there is no reason to doubt that this usage had a reasonably long history.

THE SALISH

The Salish stock of languages at the time of contact, together with the related Wakashan and Chemaukan stocks, occupied a territory from the Rocky Mountains to the Pacific Ocean between roughly 45° and 55° north latitude. The Chemaukan occupied parts of the western and northern coastal strip of the Olympic Peninsula while the Wakashan were on Vancouver Island and along a strip of the northern British Columbia coast where they separated the Bella Coola, the most northerly Salish group, from other Salish speakers to the south.* East of the Salish were the Algonkian and Kutenai, to the southeast were Shoshoneans and Siouans, and on the south in the intermontane area were Penutian-speaking groups. At the mouth of the Columbia River an intrusive block of Penutian-speaking Chinook separated the Oregon group of Salish from the Salish of the Washington coast. The Salish languages thus present a continuous geo-

---

* The Salish, Wakashan, and Chemaukan stocks are grouped together by Swadesh (1953) as the Mosan linguistic phylum, which he suggests has an overall time depth of about 9,000 years. Glottochronological estimates indicate that Salish had become a separate language by at least 5,500 years ago, and that Wakashan and Chemaukan were discrete stocks beginning to show internal differentiation within themselves by about 2,900 and 2,100 years ago respectively.

TABLE 8

DIVERGENCE DATES BETWEEN APACHEAN, NORTHERN,
AND PACIFIC COAST LANGUAGES

| Northern and Pacific Coast Languages | Apachean Languages | | | | |
	Navaho	Chiricahua	San Carlos	Jicarilla	Lipan
Chipewyan	628	660	790	724	724
Beaver	660	660	823	790	823
Galice	790	755	790	858	892
Carrier	790	823	928	892	858
Hare	892	790	928	928	928
Kutchin	858	823	1000	963	1000
Sarcee	928	928	1036	928	1000
Kato	928	963	1000	1036	1073
Mattole	1036	1036	1112	1036	1150
Hupa	1073	1073	1189	1112	1229

SOURCE: Hoijer 1956: 230, Table IV.

graphic distribution over much of the Northwest, broken only along the Pacific Coast. Their speakers occupied both coastal and interior environments, and their cultures were adapted to the ecological conditions of two quite disparate environmental zones.

The classification of the Salish stock of languages has evolved from Boas's simple Interior Salish-Coast Salish division to the more complex proposals of Swadesh (1950, 1953), Dyen (1962), Suttles and Elmendorf (1963), and Elmendorf (1965). Swadesh's classification, reproduced here, is based on glottochronological measurements of relative distance between various Salishan languages. It presents a fourfold grouping, the major categories of which are the Bella Coola Division, the Coast Division, the Oregon Division, and the Interior Division.

I. Bella Coola Division

II. Coast Division

A. North Georgia Branch

1. Comox
2. Seshalt
3. Pentlatch

B. South Georgia Branch

1. Squamish
2. Nanaimo Group
   a. Fraser
   b. Nanaimo

3. Lkungen Group
   a. Lummi
   b. Lkungen
   c. Clallam
4. Nootsak

C. Puget Sound Branch
   a. Skagit–Snohomish
   b. Nisqualli

D. Hood Canal Branch
   a. Twana

E. Olympic Branch
   1. Satsop Group
      a. Cowlitz
      b. Chehalis–Satsop
   2. Lower Chehalis
   3. Quinault

III. Oregon Division
   a. Tillamook
   b. Siletz

IV. Interior Division
   1. Lillooet
   2. Thompson Group
      a. Thompson
      b. Shuswap
   3. Okanagon Group
      a. Okanagon–Colville–Sanpoil–Lake
      b. Spokane–Kalispel–Pend d'Oreille
   4. Columbia
   5. Coeur d'Alène

TABLE 9

Internal Relationships of Apachean Languages

	Navaho	Chiricahua	San Carlos	Jicarilla
Chiricahua	149			
San Carlos	279	227		
Jicarilla	279	200	335	
Lipan	335	227	419	227

Source: Hoijer 1956:226, Table I.

Dyen, accepting Swadesh's general construct, modified it by distinguishing several more refined subcategories within it. Suttles and Elmendorf, employing a modified version of Swadesh's linguistic method, altered Swadesh's scheme by proposing a concept of two north-south "chains" of closely related languages, one along the coast and one in the interior. The Coast chain they proposed consists of North Georgia, South Georgia, Puget Sound, Hood Canal, and Olympic "links." The Oregon Division of the Swadesh scheme is in their system "a detached southern member of the coast chain," while Swadesh's Bella Coola Division is "a detached northernmost member of this chain." Elmendorf (1965) considers the Interior chain to consist of seven coordinate speech communities—the Shuswap, Lillooet, Thompson, Okanagan, Wenatchi–Columbia, Coeur d'Alene, and Spokane–Kalispel–Flathead.

The center of dispersal for the Salish languages from early or proto-Salish has been suggested by Swadesh (1950:167) as being "probably north and somewhat west of the modern center of Salishan territory." Presumably this location would place the center on the east side of the Coast Mountains in the interior of British Columbia. Diebold (1960:9–10) suggests essentially the same location, as nearly as can be determined from his map. Suttles and Elmendorf (1963:49), after considering the ecological areas to which the Salish speakers have adjusted, suggest that "prior to three thousand years ago, we see the Salish occupying the less damp portions of the western Cascade slope, with perhaps an offshoot just east of the mountains." In a later paper Elmendorf (1965:73) suggests that the home of the eastern offshoot, the proto-Interior Salish speech community, "may have centered in the Lillooet Lake and Thomp-

son River areas of southwestern interior British Columbia." Obviously there is minor disagreement on the precise location of the early Salish homeland, but there are no major discrepancies between the viewpoints of the several authorities. In view of archæological evidence, which will be discussed in a later chapter, I find an interior center east of the Coast Mountains of British Columbia likely. Divergence and dispersal could have started east of the Coast Mountains with later spread of the westward-moving groups into the coastal area. Such a suggestion does not conflict with the evidence presented by Suttles and Elmendorf, but only moves the dynamics of change and contact along the coast into a different perspective.

The Bella Coola, representing the most northern of the Salish languages, occupied the upper reaches of Burke and Dean channels and the Bella Coola River. West of them along the coast and flanking them on the north and south were the Kwakiutl, a Wakashan-speaking group. The Kwakiutl at the time of white contact had closed off the Bella Coola from the sea. Kwakiutl divergence from the other Wakashan languages, which is generally assumed to have started on Vancouver Island, is calculated to have occurred 2,900 years ago (Swadesh 1959:24). Their expansion to the mainland would have been at some time subsequent to this date, and it is entirely likely that before this time there was coastal contact between the Bella Coola and the Coast Salish of the North Georgia Branch farther south.

I have proposed that the home of the Early Salish was probably east of the Coast Mountains in the interior; it was probably somewhat to the north and east of the present Lillooet territory, a country of mountains and river valley, coniferous forests and open prairies, of anadromous fish, land animals, and berries for food. I further suggest that when the differentiation of Salish language groups began at perhaps 6,500 to 7,000 years ago (date based on Elmendorf 1965:73, see below), the Early Bella Coola were in contact with the Early Lillooet, but to an ever-diminishing extent as time passed with the Bella Coola people gradually moving north. In the course of this movement they reached the pass across the Coast Mountains and moved down the river which now bears their name, eventually coming to the place which includes the Bella Coola River and the upper waters of the Burke and Dean inlets.

Since it is extremely unlikely that the Early Bella Coola would have severed all connections with their former homeland east of the mountains, it is reasonable to believe that these interior connections would have been exploited. In historic times the Bella Coola traded with the adjacent Athapascan-speaking Chilcotin of the interior along the "grease trail" or West Road over the Coast Mountains, as I pointed out in Chapter 2, and were perfectly at home as visitors in the interior country. The wedge-like distribution and position of the Chilcotin in the northwestern sector of the Interior Salish area in historic times suggests that the Chilcotin had thrust southward, displacing the Lillooet from this territory, which is immediately north of their present range. If these speculations are correct, then the well-established historical trade communication over the grease trail between the Bella Coola and the Chilcotin may be a carry-over of a much older relationship between the Bella Coola and Lillooet.

Farther to the south, Suttles and Elmendorf (1963) state that the closest Interior-Coast relationships are between the Lillooet and Thompson of the Interior chain and the South Georgia, North Georgia, and Puget Sound branches of the Coast chain. Swadesh's calculations on Salish internal relationships show essentially the same thing (Swadesh 1950:160, Table 2) with the closest Interior-Coast relationship being between the Lillooet and the Fraser-Nanaimo group. Since the Lillooet were in historic times middlemen in the trade between the lower Fraser River and the Interior, and since the Thompson, in contact with the Lillooet, apparently served as middlemen

between the Lillooet and groups farther to the east and south, this relationship between Coast Salish and the Interior Lillooet and Thompson languages is not unexpected. The probable time depth of this connection is suggested by Elmendorf's (1965:73–77) proposed historical model for the Interior Salish speech community, which places the separation of proto-IS (Interior Salish) from a basic proto-Salish linguistic community between 4900 B.C. and 4000 B.C. The Coast Salish-Thompson-Lillooet relationship must date from at least that time.

Elmendorf distinguishes five periods in the history of Interior Salish:

I. Period of IS linguistic unity; a single speech community whose language may be designated as proto-IS. . . . [It] probably remained for a long time thereafter without any marked internal divergence. The most probable location of this proto-IS community falls in the northwestern part of present IS territory; it may have centered in the Lillooet Lake and Thompson River areas. . . .

II. Period of a twofold dialect split, between western and eastern sections of the original proto-IS community. This divergence may have accompanied or followed an expansion of IS speakers into the Okanagan Valley.

III. Period in which internal divergence began within both the western and eastern dialects, which were perhaps still only dialectically separated from one another. . . .

IV. A subsequent period during which northward expansion of part of the western group brought about separation of Shu [Shuswap] and Thu [Thompson]. Slightly earlier, further eastward movement of both the pre-Oka-Kal [Okanagan-Kalispel] and pre-CA [Coeur d'Alene] communities took place in the eastern group, bringing the last community into northern Idaho. . . .

V. Further, and later, eastward movements of parts of the pre-Kal [Kalispel] dialect community, from the Spokane River region in eastern Washington. . . . (Elmendorf 1965: 73-74 passim).

By this last major movement the Interior Salish reached their maximum territorial expansion into Montana.

Suggested approximate dates for these periods are:

Period I — 4900 B.C. to 2500 B.C.

Period II — 2500 B.C. to 1000 B.C.

Period III — 1000 B.C. to A.D. 0

Periods IV and V — Post-Christian including last 1,000 years

The extensive territorial expansion and movement implied by this model comprises an important archæological problem for the interior Northwest which I return to in Chapter 9.

The most southerly of the Salish speakers, the Tillamook and their close relatives the Siletz, lived on the northern Oregon coast south of the Columbia River in historic times. The lower Chinook (Penutian speakers from the intermontane area), extending for some miles both north and south of the mouth of the Columbia River, separated the Oregon Salish from their linguistic relatives along the Washington coast to the north.

The closest linguistic relations of the Tillamook are with the Twana of the Hood Canal branch (Suttles and Elmendorf 1963:50, n. 4), and the Interior Okanagan and Thompson. The close relationship between the Tillamook and the Twana, and of both with the Okanagan and Thompson, suggests that originally the Early Tillamook and Twana were east of the Cascade Mountains, possibly in territory later occupied by Interior Salish speakers of the Columbia language. They may have moved either together or in close succession across the Cascade Mountains into the southern Puget Sound area where perhaps they remained in contact for some time (cf. Suttles and Elmendorf [1963:45, 47] for generally similar suggestions). Later the Tillamook moved on again, either south to the lower Columbia River and down it to the coast, or west to the Washington coast and then south. They were finally at the mouth of the Columbia, and probably at that time there was a continuous belt of Salish-speaking peoples along the Pacific Coast from the Columbia River in the south to the Bella Coola River in the north. Subsequently the Penutian-speaking Chinook of the upper Columbia moved downriver, eventually to the coast, and separated the Tillamook (and their close relatives the Siletz) from contact with the Salish of the Washington coast. Of course it is possible that the in-migrating Oregon Salish speakers leapfrogged long established Chinookan occupation.

Archæological evidence (Newman 1959) shows a fully developed Northwest Coast culture in existence on the Netarts sandspit in the historic Tillamook location on the Oregon coast by A.D. 1675±150 years (M-806). An earlier occupation at A.D. 1400 is also recorded, and while this does not represent as fully developed a culture as the later occupation, it seems to be a somewhat similar manifestation of the same sea-land adaptation. It must be recognized that the A.D. 1400 date may not represent the earliest occupation of the site since excavation could not proceed below the level of the freshwater table which bisected the occupation deposit. There may quite possibly have been earlier occupation representing the first efforts of an interior people to exploit the coastal environment.

THE UTO-AZTECANS

Writers since 1957 have tried with varying degrees of success to define the position of the Uto-Aztecan languages in time and space as they relate to far-western prehistory (Lamb 1958; Taylor 1961; Hopkins 1965; Miller 1964; Goss 1968; Swadesh 1964). Others have studied the position of a single language such as the Ute (Gunnerson 1962; Goss 1968). Goss (1968) has summarized each of these contributions, as well as some other papers, evaluated them, and presented an excellent "micro-study" of Yutish.

In early historic times, languages of the great Uto-Aztecan stock were spoken over interior western North America from near the Columbia River on the north to the Valley of Mexico on the south. The culturally simple Utes of the Great Basin-Plains and the mighty Aztecs of Mexico were members of the grouping. Linguists are generally agreed that the likely Uto-Aztecan homeland was in the general region of the Arizona-Sonora border, lands now occupied by the Pima. From this homeland, language communities spread both north and south. Since this book is concerned with the area north of the international border, I limit my treatment here to some of the languages of the Northern Uto-Aztecan subdivision. Goss (1968:25) gives the following classification of the Northern Uto-Aztecan languages and the glottochronological times defining the levels of subdivision.

The (Northern) Utaztekan Stock (35–50 m.c.*)

  I. *Numic Family* (25–35 m.c.)

    1. *Monish Genus* (5–25 m.c.)

---

* [m.c. = minimum centuries]

A. Mono Language (5 m.c.)

B. Paviotso Language (5 m.c.)

2. *Shoshonish Genus* (5–25 m.c.)

A. Shoshone Language (5 m.c.)

a. Shoshone Dialect (–5 m.c.)

b. Comanche Dialect (–5 m.c.)

3. *Yutish Genus* (5–25 m.c.)

A. Kawaiisu Language (5 m.c.)

B. Ute Language (5 m.c.)

a. Chemehuevi Dialect (–5 m.c.)

b. Kaibab Dialect (–5 m.c.)

c. Northern Ute Dialect (–5 m.c.)

d. Southern Ute Dialect (–5 m.c.)

II. *Tubatulabalic Family* (25–35 m.c.)

A. Tubatulabal Language (5 m.c.)

III. *Luisenic Family* (25 35 m.c.)

(no detail here)

IV. *Hopic Family* (25–35 m.c.)

A. Hopi Language (5 m.c.)

Sometime between 3,500 and 5,000 years ago, Northern Uto-Aztecan linguistic divergence had occurred to the point that there were then at least the beginnings of four families: the Tubatulabalic and Hopic by 3,300 years ago and the Luisenic and Numic by about 3,000 years ago. The Luisenic speakers gradually pushed across Southern California to the coast. The Tubatulabalic group is thought to have centered on the western slopes of the Sierra Nevada range in the upper Kern River valley region. The Numic were generally on the east in the area of Death Valley. Since my major concern is the Numic family, I shall confine my discussion to that group.

Numic and Tubatulabalic began to separate about 3,000 years ago and about 20 centuries ago Numic broke up with Monoish and Shoshonish separating first and Yutish following shortly later. "The evidence seems to indicate that dialects of these three Numic proto-languages occupied a relatively small area in the western edge of the Great Basin up until about 10 centuries ago, when a great and swift movement northward and eastward into the Basin began" (Goss 1968:8). Since the area of greatest linguistic diversity in the Northern Uto-Aztecan region is in the southern Sierras of California, it is concluded that this is the area of differentiation. The three Numic genera were already distinct at the time the expansion began, so each linguistic group must have acted independently, although it is not clear if the movements began about the same time or were separated by some intervals. Because the dialect variation is so small in each of the genera, it is concluded that the expansion in each case was rapid and "one can only with the greatest difficulty imagine that they could have occupied the vast area in which we find them for more than a few centuries" (Lamb 1958:99).

Mono and Paviotso (Northern Paiute) occupied areas differing greatly in size. The Mono language was centered in an area south of the "watershed divide between the headwaters of the Owens River and Mono Lake Basin" (Lamb 1958:96). The Paviotso branch was the one to engage in the great territorial expansion of the Monoish genus, and they extended across northern Nevada to the north and west of the Shoshoni and into southeastern Oregon and southwestern Idaho. Lewis and Clark report evidence that at the time of their journey down the Columbia in 1805, the Paiute (Paviotso) were exerting pressure on Columbia River peoples.

The Shoshonish expansion must have been equally rapid. It covered a greater distance than the Monoish, extending across Idaho into western Wyoming, with the Comanche dialect moving out into the southern High Plains after separation from its northern relatives.

The prehistory of the Ute language has been studied more intensively than that of any of the other divisions of the Numic group. A set of favorable circumstances has provided the opportunity: an excellent linguist, with some initial archæological training, in the person of James A. Goss; a very good archæological record for critical parts of the area concerned, in which nonagricultural culture succeeded agricultural, providing the opportunity for identification of cultural change with a clarity and crispness quite impossible in areas of only hunting-gathering cultures; a long historical record for the area of study; and an aboriginal experience that overlapped the period of historical documentation.

TABLE 10

Simplified Correlation of the Evidence
Of Yutish Expansion

Type of Evidence	Geographical Area					
	Cal.	Nev.	S. W. Utah	E. Utah	W. Col.	E. Col.
Linguistic	900	800	700	400	300	200
Oral-tradition (very tenuous)	—	—	—	400	—	200
Archæological	—	816	716	—	—	—
Direct historical	—	—	—	368	340	280

Note: Numbers represent approximate date in number of years ago.
Source: Goss 1968:37, Table 2.

Because of these sources of information and the capacity to exploit and bring all of them into focus, Goss has not only given us a record of Ute prehistory but a model for similar studies under favorable circumstances.

Goss (1965), in a contribution to the Wetherill Mesa project on Ute-Anasazi relations, agreed with Lamb in setting the time of separation of the Kawaiisu-Ute branches of the Yutish genus at between 500 and 1,000 years ago, probably somewhat nearer the larger figure. At 700 years ago, the period of Anasazi regression (Hopic language probably), the Utes and Chemehuevi were living "on the western boundary of the Great Basin in what is now southeastern California" (Goss 1965:81). Expansion from this homeland was slow, and the Utes did not arrive in the northernmost Anasazi area until approximately A.D. 1500 or probably about 200 years after it had been abandoned. They arrived in the Mesa Verde area somewhat later—not long before 1680.

In 1968 Goss reported further on a "microstudy" of the Ute designed to test the Lamb hypothesis and to show the effective use to which linguistics, archæology, oral tradition, and direct historical evidence could be put in prehistoric reconstruction. He was able to sketch a convincing narrative of Ute expansion into the High Plains. Goss's evidence is summarized in Table 10.

The linguistic prehistory of the Great Basin is aptly summarized by Lamb (1958:99–100):

Since these languages [Paviotso, Shoshoni, Ute] spread out from a southwestern corner, the most likely conclusion, from linguistic evidence, is that much of the northern and eastern part of the Great Basin was not occupied by speakers of the present Numic languages at the time Columbus discovered America. And, as of around 1,000 years ago and earlier, the major part of the Great Basin is unaccounted for linguistically. This area may have been occupied by speakers of languages which moved elsewhere, or the languages may have become extinct. Some of the languages which became extinct could, of course, have been Utaztekan, but they could just as well, or perhaps more likely, have been languages related to Hokan, Zuni, Keres, Algonkian, or even some stock now totally extinct. The people who inhabited this large unaccounted-for area may have moved out, or they may have remained, and adopted the new languages.

It is worthwhile to speculate briefly about that unknown time before the northward spread of Uto-Aztecan speakers into the Great Basin. Archæology presents convincing evidence, at least to many of us, that the intermontane area south of the Columbia River was occupied, perhaps very lightly, by at least 15,000 years ago. If one accepts the validity of the Santa Rosa Island finds, as I and some others do, then we may have man there in the West by 30,000 years ago. In either case, there is a vast extent of time unaccounted for linguistically. It seems to me, too, that we have to suppose that the sources of all the American Indian languages were on this continent by about 11,000 years ago, or very shortly thereafter, because at that time the Bering Land Bridge ceased to exist. Subsequent movements in either direction across Bering Strait would have been only episodic.

The location and distribution of early languages would initially have been related to the paths of inmigration, but as time passed linguistic boundaries would have been modified for a number of reasons. The area west of the Rocky Mountains could, because of the effects on human occupation of its diverse and changing environments, be expected to have exhibited greater linguistic diversity than any other major area of the continent.

For what the archæological evidence is worth, it would seem to indicate that there were two lines of cultural contact and perhaps population movement from the north toward the south starting in the Anathermal. Evidence from a later period appears to point to northward movement from the Great Basin into the Columbia Plateau in the earlier part of the Altithermal (Cressman et al. 1960), while the picture from the Columbia Plateau seems to record a variety of influences impinging on the area from outside sources not clearly identified. Far to the south the occupants of Ventana Cave in western Arizona were in contact at an early time level, either by trade or by collecting expeditions, with the Gulf of California. Later trade was well established across Southern California to the coast, and farther north the same kind of relations were established across the Sierra Nevada range. Contact across the Rocky Mountains with the western Plains, except in British Columbia, was late and discontinuous in space (the evidence for these assertions is presented in detail in Chapter 8).

I have argued elsewhere (Cressman 1964) that because of the stringency of the food resources in the Great Basin, the population had to be intellectually flexible, adaptive to securing and utilizing food where it could be found. The price of specialization and taboo was too high—starvation even in the best of times. This basic condition of life, I argued, would make for an intellectual orientation in which the individual was important; individual choice had a high value and social organization had to be simple and fluid. I believe that the evidence of the late Numic vast and rapid expansion with adaptation to the different environments and the methods of their exploitation is corroborative evidence. Could one safely deduce from the archæological evidence of shifting cultural relationships and these theoretical considerations a strong probability that during the long history of the Great Basin peoples the most likely situation was one of great linguistic fluidity, with no single linguistic group dominating the area, at least for any great length of time? The available linguistic evidence fits these deductions encouragingly well.

Some linguists (see Lamb 1964:123–25) have defined a very large grouping of related languages for the Far West which they have called the Macro-Penutian phylum. Swadesh (1956) included in this phylum languages as distant as the Tsimshian of the northern British Columbia coast and the Zuñi of Arizona-New Mexico, and proposed a probable time depth of divergence of about 10,000 years. He suggested the homeland or center of divergence might have been northern Oregon. Goss (1968) and apparently others have certain reservations about the definition of the Macro-Penutian grouping, but for the argument to be made here these reservations are not significant.

Of great interest in the present context is the scattered distribution of and linguistic distance between the Penutian languages, implying that the southward expansion of Penutian was not a largely simultaneous affair similar to the Numic expansion of late prehistory, but instead involved small groups wandering south from time to time, not all following the same route. The distribution of Penutian speakers makes it quite reasonable to suppose that some Penutian groups occupied the Great Basin prior to the time of the Numic expansion and that they were crowded out by Numic speakers. It is also reasonable to suggest that the Penutian speakers were not the original occupants of the Great Basin. The distribution of the Hokan in California, and far to the southwest in the Texas-Coahuila border region, suggests that they were much more widely spread at one time, and it is not unlikely that they too were in the Great Basin. Kroeber (1955) believes that the distribution of Hokan speech communities in scattered groups in the mountains and along the coast of California suggests that they were pushed into these refuge areas by pressure from the east. The pattern of distribution of Penutian groups in California lends support to the idea that Penutians did the pushing.

The Klamath Indians, a Penutian-speaking (Sahaptin) group of the Klamath Lake area in south-central Oregon, furnish a case where further speculation may be of some interest because good archæological data are available. Some years ago I argued, from the archæological evidence, that this area (treated here as a part of the Great Basin on physiographic grounds) had been occupied probably since 10,000 years ago; that occupation had been continuous; and that there were slow cultural accretions but no cultural discontinuity or sudden introduction of new traits (Cressman 1956b). These ideas gain some support also from the fact that the Klamath have no oral tradition of any other homeland. The Klamath speak Sahaptin, a Penutian language, and given the archæological evidence of cultural continuity, a strong argument can be made that this area of the Northern Great Basin and adjacent northern Oregon represents the Penutian center of divergence.

Traditions of Northern Paiute expansion at the expense of the Klamath offer tenuous evidence that until shortly after 1,000 years ago, speakers of the latter language extended much farther south and east into the Intermontane Region than they did at the time of white contact. Kelly (1932:72) quotes a Surprise Valley Paiute tradition that at one time "these Paiute were living east of Steens Mountain, in Oregon, but eventually they drove out the Klamath [the Klamath at that time were reported to have occupied the entire south-central Oregon country to Steens Mountain] and took possession." If the traditions are based on historical events, then they furnish evidence for the language spoken by at least some of the intermontane inhabitants previous to the arrival of the Northern Paiutes and provide an answer in part to the question raised by Lamb, quoted on p. 100. While anthropologists have tended not to place reliance on such tales, these legends may be the rumble of thunder of a distant storm, unseen, not experienced, but with a reality that is clear from the faintly audible sounds which reach us.

The linguistic prehistory of the Far West poses for the reflective person challenging problems far beyond the strictly historical ones. What were the motivations for the separation of groups of people? What causes motivated the separation and distant wanderings of two separate groups of Athapascans from their homeland within a relatively short interval of time? What impelled the Numic speakers, far to the south of the Athapascans, to move suddenly and rapidly into vast, unknown lands? Is it fortuitous that the first Athapascan and the Numic movements began at about the same time, about 1,000 years ago? Environmental explanations are inadequate; the movements were selective within groups in the same environment on the one hand, and involved populations in utterly different environments on the other. The student is forced to look to local psychological and social factors for adequate causes. Perhaps dissension for reasons unknown set group against group, and some, under dynamic leadership, were willing to attempt new adventures and experiences of the unknown to maintain their values. Whatever the reasons for the events, the fact of their occurrence and the activities of the people who underwent them are truly epic parts of the human experience; their full meaning awaits the attention of the appropriate artist.

The processes of subsistence and adaptation by which people managed to survive and make significant cultural achievements in this diversified and often harsh far-western environment are the subject of the next chapter.

Subsistence and Adaptation

A wanderer is man from his birth.
He was born in a ship
On the breast of the river of Time;
Brimming with wonder and joy
He spreads out his arms to the light,
Rivets his gaze on the banks of the stream.

As what he sees is, so have his thoughts been
Whether he wakes,
Where the snowy mountainous pass,
Echoing the screams of the eagles,
Hems in its gorges the bed
Of the new-born clear-flowing stream;
Whether he first sees light
Where the river in gleaming rings
Sluggishly winds through the plain;
Whether in sound of the swallowing sea—
As is the world on the banks,
So is the mind of man.

Matthew Arnold, The Future

THIS CHAPTER reflects the fundamental premise of biology that the overriding compulsion of life is survival of the species. The reproductive unit must have sufficient stability through time for its members or one of the reproducing pair to introduce the young to necessary survival techniques. When reproduction and adult survival and consequent reproduction exceed the loss by death, the species survives. All this takes place within the framework of particular environments, the familiar environmental niche.

Man, no less than the other animals, is a creature of this same compulsion. Man, among animals, is a uniquely social animal. He cannot live alone and there is no case on record of human life existing at only the family level without some form of friendly interaction with other families. Families compose societies, which are the media for the functioning of human life. The family, as Lévi-Strauss (1956) said, exists for the maintenance of society. Society then becomes the medium through which human life carries out its biological imperative. What the archæologist digs up is essentially the product of social action at some level of social integration, and the life he tries to reconstruct is that of the social group or groups that composed the society.

Man's chief difference from other animals is that he is a culture building animal. As such an animal, he uses his culture to exploit his environment—in other words, to adapt to it. In this way he has demonstrated his ability to adapt to any environment the earth has to offer. Culture is an adaptive mechanism and therefore can be expected to vary with the demands of the environment. Adaptation to environment also makes biological demands, but in the case of man, because of culture, these are of much less importance than in the nonhuman organisms.

The gaining of subsistence is the basic substratum requirement for species survival, whether it be of man or of any other animal, and the simpler the culture the more exclusively will the behavior patterns of a society be organized toward developing successful subsistence patterns. Similar ecologies will, therefore, be expected to produce generally similar means of exploitation. This does not mean that there will be similarities in all details, but the significance of these ideas for the prehistorian is that many of the same *kinds* of tools or other objects related to environmental exploitation must have been developed in separate but similar environments with no historical connection between them. This is, of course, the

103

old diffusion versus independent invention argument. It is obvious that I am inclined, as indicated by these statements, to be much more sympathetic to the proposition of much more independent invention than some of my colleagues. The people who successfully settled a new world in all its diversity certainly could not have lacked keen observational and innovative capacity.

Far-western North American prehistory, with the exception of the Southwest after it received agriculture from Mexico, is the record of hunters, fishers, fowlers, and gatherers for many thousands of years. This life was lived in diverse environments, which changed through time, as I discussed earlier. The remarkable thing is the successful lifeways that were developed. It seems to me that any reasonable understanding of this part of the human experience requires that it be approached in its dynamic aspects of man developing the techniques for exploiting the many diverse environments. The kinds of artifacts we dig up, their forms and functions, their historical relations in space and time, or the settlement patterns, or all other aspects of the long past life, find their significance in this frame of reference. Since my major interest here is process rather than artifacts, I shall discuss the processes by which people gained their subsistence and adapted to the different environments. It should be kept in mind that probably no single economic activity was exclusive. Certainly the record shows, where it is reasonably full, that hunters were also gatherers and fishermen were hunters and fowlers and probably gatherers. In each ecological area there was a predominant economic activity, which was made possible by the natural environment. When I speak of hunters, for example, I shall be discussing the society where this economic activity was the predominant, but not the only, subsistence support.

HUNTING

The Wanderers who first set foot in the New World were skillful hunters or they would never have survived. The methods used in the hunt depended to a great extent on the habits of the game animal, whether it was gregarious or solitary. Solitary animals, such as the bear, had to be stalked by a hunter with one or two companions or even by the hunter alone. Deer, elk, and mountain sheep could be moved by drivers past hunters lying in ambush. Swift animals, like the horse, and massive ones, like the mammoth, had to be taken by stealth. Either the hunters had to lie concealed at water holes to kill an unwary beast or, by some maneuver, startle the herd and drive one or more individuals into the mud and soft sand where their movements were impeded. All the evidence from kill sites of mammoth, horse, and camel is of this nature. We do not know how far in the past these methods of hunting were developed, but they must be as old as the history of man as hunter.

Early hunters learned to take advantage of the ease with which bison could be stampeded. The Plainview site is probably a record of stampeded animals mired down in a soft lake bed. The remains of the bogged-down bison near the Lindenmeier site may be the same kind of record. The clearest record was reported by Wheat (1967), and this was a cleverly organized stampede of a herd into an arroyo about 8,500 years ago.

Antelope, shy, curious, and extremely fast for short distances, had to be hunted by methods that capitalized on their peculiar characteristics. Although we do not know when it started, one method was used by which the animals were slowly edged into a large herd and the herd was gradually driven between wings of brush or rock toward a stone corral or enclosure. Hunters lay in wait around the outside of the corral, and, when the drivers closed in after the animals, the beasts were shot down. While the antelope was a longtime inhabitant of the western plains (Wisconsin and Recent time), there are only a few antelope remains in caves or open campsites to show he was an important article of food. I do not recall a single antelope bone ever having been found in all the sites I have excavated in the Northern Great Basin. Antelope were there, however, as shown by the antelope horn handle for a knife found in Catlow Cave No. 1 (Cressman et al. 1942). This was probably a shed horn sheath picked up and used by the person who left it in the cave. Jennings (1957: 224) reports for Danger Cave in the Eastern Great Basin that "The chief game resource appears to have been ungulates. Of these the most frequently encountered is the antelope." Mountain sheep were next in frequency while bison were scarce but did occur through levels D II to D V. It is difficult to determine from Jennings's figures the relative importance of these animals as food objects. The ungulates are not subdivided by genera, so the relative time of appearance of the different genera in the cave deposit cannot be given. The two top levels, V and IV, contain 78 percent of the ungulate bones, and the C-14 dates for these levels fall within the period of appoximately 2250 B.C. and A.D. 20.

It is quite possible that effective methods of taking antelope developed quite late. The antelope hunt among the later Great Basin people was a well-organized community affair under the leadership of a shaman. The element of supernatural involvement in behalf of the hunters suggests that normal hunting methods had never been very successful. The antelope drive was a feature of Great Basin life in historic times, but evidence when it began is lacking.

The earliest evidence of sea lion hunting is that from the basal stratum of Malaga Cove. Otoliths of these animals, along with those of others, have been found in this stratum (personal communication, J.R. Moriarity to L.S. Cressman). While no C-14 date exists for this occupation, typologically it appears to be a peripheral manifestation of the San Dieguito culture. If that is the case, it would probably date from the period between 8,000 and 10,000 years ago, and more likely closer to the latter than the former.

Sea lions have to be taken from rocky points of the coast, offshore rocky islands, or the open sea. The offshore islands are the most likely place. While it might be possible for a single hunter to stalk a herd of these beasts on the rocky shore and make a kill, it is very unlikely since the sea lion, in spite of his awkwardness out of water, is a very wary animal. Offshore island hunting offers the opportunity to approach a resting herd from two sides, with a land-based party coordinating its movements with hunters in a boat approaching from the opposite side toward the resting place of the herd. The diversionary approach by water could be coordinated with a rush by the land-based hunters, and, in this case, there would be a good chance of a kill as the animals lunged awkwardly to the rocky edge to plunge into the sea. Such a method of hunting would require seagoing transportation, and that such transportation existed

is demonstrated by the otoliths of deep-sea fish in the same stratum with the sea lion specimens. Of course the hunt could be carried out by boat alone, in which case a final rush would give the hunters a chance for spearing or harpooning their quarry. The Eskimo method of walrus hunting is similar to this. It is not likely, in my opinion, that deep-sea transportation and its use in hunting originated at Malaga Cove, but this site offers the first record of an adaptation to an environment different from any I previously discussed.

Evidence is lacking for the use of pits in game trails as a hunting device from the early period, although it is reported in some areas of the Northwest by ethnographers. The lack of evidence archæologically may be simply the result of natural processes, which would have filled up the pits with debris and thus obliterated the evidence. It seems reasonable that pit hunting would have been used, for it is not far removed psychologically from the method of taking large game in bogs or other sources, which limited the mobility of the quarry. The man-made pit would have been the counterpart of the natural trap. Obviously this is speculation, but it may not be too wide of the mark. The progression of weapons in the New World must have paralleled that in Europe, from thrusting and throwing spear to spear-thrower and then to the bow and arrow. The simple spear-thrower is known in Europe from the Upper Paleolithic, but we lack evidence for that period in Asia. The earliest archæological record of the spear-thrower or atlatl in the New World is from Oregon. An atlatl spur at Fort Rock Cave (Cressman et al. 1940), probably dating from approximately 8,500 years ago, and two spurs from the Five-Mile Rapids site east of The Dalles on the Columbia River (Cressman et al. 1960), with the older probably contemporary with the Fort Rock specimen, demonstrate the presence of the compound atlatl.* Two spurs very much like those

---

* New-World atlatls are of two basic types, which are distinguished according to the device used for articulating the atlatl with the spear or dart. In the simple type, the hook or spur, which engages the dart, is an integral part of the atlatl; in the compound type, the hook is a separate piece of bone, ivory, stone, or antler, which was lashed or set into the end of the atlatl.

from the Five-Mile Rapids were taken from Cougar Mountain Cave by Cowles and are probably contemporary with the Fort Rock specimen. No firm dates are available for the simple types excavated from other Oregon caves of the Northern Great Basin. The present information suggests that in the Northern Great Basin and adjacent Columbia Plateau the compound variety preceded the simple, but of course further evidence may change this apparent relationship. One may certainly infer from the evident mastery of the mechanical principles involved and the excellent workmanship that there had been a long experience with this weapon.

The compound atlatl appears to be distributed in the Arctic, along the Pacific Northwest Coast, into southeastern Washington, through Oregon in a corridor east of the Cascade Mountains, into Northern and Central California (Riddell 1960), and on the Channel Islands (Riddell and McGreein 1969; Eberhart 1957:156). The California occurrences are later than those in Oregon and Washington. No record exists for the Klamath Lakes area, which would connect with the Karlo region, or for a clear connection between the Karlo region and the Central California area, although the Washo may represent this continuity. The gaps may eventually be filled in.

A probable connection exists between the compound atlatl and the canoe or boat-shaped atlatl weight. This type of weight, although not found directly attached to the compound atlatl except in one instance I know of (Figure 25 C, D), has essentially the same distribution as the compound atlatl. The boat-shaped weight does not, however, occur in the Arctic, which is probably to be explained by the fact that the Eskimo throwing board is a heavy weapon which would not have been benefited by the addition of a weight; the Eskimos were too expert mechanically to have added anything functionally useless to an otherwise effective weapon.

The simple atlatl appears later in the archæological record than the compound (Figure 25 A, B). Its distribution seems to lie farther to the east, extending from the Columbia Plateau (Strong 1966), through the Lovelock Cave area of western Nevada, and into the southwestern Anasazi area. The evidence from Lovelock Cave on the variety of atlatls recovered there is not unequivocal, but they appear to be the simple variety. One specimen (Loud and Harrington 1929:99, Figure 16), which might be interpreted as a compound type, looks more like a repair job than original construction when one examines the different surfaces of the instrument.

The atlatl was eventually replaced by the bow and arrow, but not suddenly. The archæological record from Lovelock Cave and Roaring Springs Cave and Catlow Cave No. 1 in Oregon shows that there was a considerable period during which both weapons were used. In Lovelock Cave arrows and atlatl darts both appear in Level III, but before that there are only atlatl darts and after that only arrows. Level II has a C-14 date of 1686±220 B.P., and Level V is dated at 3172±260 B.P. (Cressman 1956a). Unfortunately, precise dates are lacking for the other levels. Riddell (1960) reports a C-14 date (LJ-76) of 2350±150 B.P. from charcoal at the nearby Karlo site which is associated with cultural material like that of Levels III and IV at Lovelock Cave. Atlatl spurs and arrow points are both found at Karlo. Apparently a date of around 2,300 years ago would not be far wrong for the time at which the bow displaced the atlatl in the western part of the Great Basin, and probably elsewhere in the West, although the instrument may have continued in use or as a symbol of some value from the past for much longer periods of time in various areas.

The atlatl reported by Strong (1966), Figure 25 A, B, is a case in point. This weapon was found, along with a portion of a similar one, by a collector in a pack rat's nest in a cave already worked over by a previous collector. The owner, through the efforts of Mr. Strong at my request, made available a portion of the broken specimen for C-14 dating. Mr. David L. Cole generously arranged for the dating. The date (GaK-1316) is 1470±140 B.P. The complete specimen is a beautiful weapon but so fragile that it hardly seems possible that it could have been used to hurl a dart.

In considering the problem of survival and adaptation, one cannot but be surprised at the length of time it apparently required for the more effective weapon, the bow and arrow, to be culturally accepted. The time interval separating Level II and Level V in Lovelock Cave is approximately 1,500 years. For the first half of this period only the atlatl

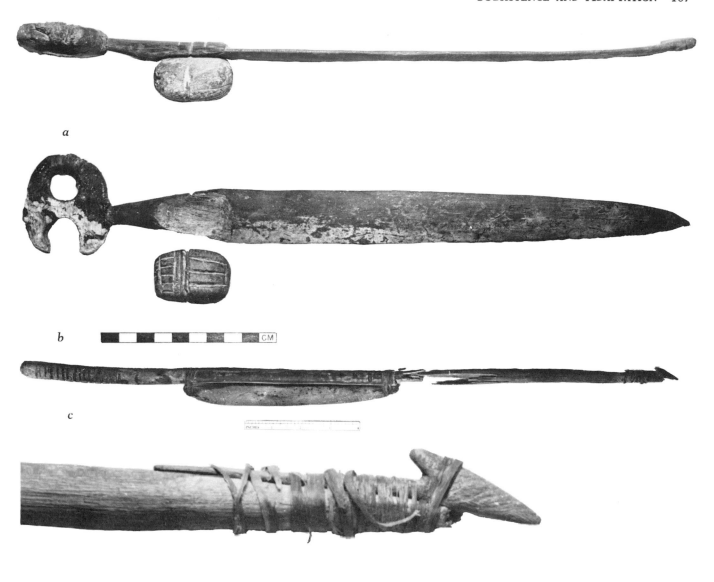

FIGURE 25. Atlatls. A. McClure atlatl; simple type; side view with weight in place as found; age 1470±140 B.P. (GaK-1316). B. Top view of A; weight removed, handle made of mountain sheep horn, one side damaged. C. Nicolarsen atlatl; compound type. D. Detail of spur and lashing on C. *Photographs by Emory Strong; publication authorized by Bill McClure and Jack Nicolarsen.*

is found, and during the second half both the atlatl and the bow occur. Thus, perhaps 750 years of synchronous use of both weapons is indicated by the archæological record.

What is the meaning?

This question, like so many others, is easier to ask than to answer. It is obvious that there was no rush to buy a more efficient mousetrap. The bow and arrow must have been at first almost shockingly new when compared with the old, highly esteemed atlatl (the decorative skill applied to some atlatls indicates this attitude), and they must have been relatively very inefficient. It is customary to think of the bow and arrow as having been diffused from Asia. This assumption, I think, is seriously open to question. If the weapon passed from group to group, one would have expected related knowledge about its manufacture and use to have passed with it. But in the New World, the long period of overlap with its predecessor seems to indicate that the pertinent knowledge required to produce and use a good bow and arrow was learned slowly by much trial and error. It required a long time for potential users to be "sold" on the idea. The principles involved in the bow and arrow are absolutely different from those in the atlatl. As Kroeber (1948:356-57) has pointed out, the bow has to have antecedents which incorporated some of the mechanical principles pertinent to it, such as a string under tension and its response when released. The requirements are met by various traps such as snares, the bow drill, and other objects. All these were in use in the Great Basin for a very long time before the first validated arrow appears. This leads me to the opinion that there is a very strong chance the bow was an independent invention in the New World and the background situation for it was particularly favorable in the Great Basin and its environs.

Once the bow and arrow were perfected, the people had a weapon far more useful in the pursuit of both large and small game, particularly the latter, than ever before. The adaptation of the bunt from atlatl usage, although in a new form for stunning small animals like rodents and birds, must have been a very effective cultural development even though the range was short. Three or four short crossed sticks were lashed over the distal end of the arrow in lieu of a stone point (Cressman et al. 1942). The widespread distribution of this item in the Far West, apparently in a short period, probably indicates its effectiveness. All demonstrations of the use of the atlatl show that, except for the Aleut-Eskimo, the user threw from a standing position either because of custom or assumed or real motor requirements. The bow, however, could have been used either in a standing or crouching position, thus giving the hunter much better cover. It is clear that as the bow and arrow increased in quality, the people had a better chance for a higher level of subsistence through more effective adaptive procedures.

Long before the bow and arrow came into use the archæological record shows that hunters were using other devices for taking small game. Various

kinds of traps—the snare, the deadfall, and others—were in use, together with nets which may have been used in a variety of ways. Obviously most of the evidence for this must come from the dry caves of the Great Basin, for the evidence we rely on consists of very fragile materials—pieces of string, sticks cut in certain ways, fragments of nets. It is surprising that so much does remain.

Using traps in the food quest represents a sharp psychological break with the method of killing the quarry with a weapon in that there is no longer direct involvement between the hunter and the hunted. What the steps were in this psychological reorientation we do not know. Speculatively we may suggest that the concealed pit in the game trail was an outgrowth of immobilizing the quarry in a bog. If game trails could be used this way, perhaps some reflective hunter came up with the idea of devices of other kinds to exploit the potentialities of the trails at times when the hunter was not there as was sometimes the case with the concealed pit. Whatever the developmental steps may have been, once the techniques of exploiting game trails were developed, man had in a way something entirely new, an investment in capital that he put to work for his benefit. The man with a trapline thus had a device for supplementing his food supply beyond that which his skill and luck as a hunter could possibly provide. The traps set along the game trails, whether those of rodents or large mammals, would work for him while he was engaged in some other activity or doing nothing at all.

Cordage was found in Danger Cave (Jennings 1957) in the earliest level with a date of approximately 10,000 years ago. Whether this was used for traps of any kind is problematical, but there is a good probability that it was since the archæological record from the Great Basin is clear that the preferred use for cordage was for nets used in trapping.

A fragmentary sandal from Fishbone Cave on the eastern shoreline of dry Lake Winnemucca in Nevada, with a C-14 date for the containing level of approximately 11,000 years ago (Orr 1956a), shows a date earlier than that from Danger Cave for the technique of making twisted strands from bark of tule(?), *Scirpus lacustris*. Fort Rock Cave in south-central Oregon has produced finely twined sandals made from sagebrush bark cordage and twined basketry fabricated from tule C-14 dated at 9,000 years ago. Since there must have been a reasonable time for the development of the technique of making cordage, the beginnings must well antedate the appearance of these finished products. Cross-dating the time of their appearance in the caves with the dates for the "big-game hunters," it is quite clear that they are contemporary. It is a reasonable inference that the hunters of large game were supplementing their food supply by the use of traps to work for them in the taking of small game.

Once the principle of the net was worked out, the net could be adapted to a variety of uses. Very long nets were used in rabbit drives in which the drivers forced the rabbits ahead into the stretched net where they could be clubbed to death. The Klamath also used the net to entangle waterfowl, usually at night. The net was strung between two canoes just above the surface of the water and other canoes startled the ducks, resting on the water, into flight toward the stretched net where they became entangled. The use of nets in both these ways is widespread throughout the world. It is not known with certainty when or where these methods first appeared, but the cordage from the dry caves of the Great Basin is the oldest of record in the New World.

The diversity of devices for taking small game shows the skills with which these inhabitants of the arid Great Basin exploited various ideas to a high degree to wring a subsistence out of their environment. To survive they had to take advantage of every opportunity that the environment provided, and the record shows an ingenuity and skill to this end that deserves high admiration.

The use of bone for projectile points in early horizons at inland, New-World sites is documented for some Clovis sites, for lower Klamath Lake, the upper Klamath Lake area, and Lind Coulee (Cotter 1937; Cressman et al. 1942; Cressman 1956b; Daugherty 1956a). These were long points with a beveled base to provide a tight lashing to the shaft. Portions of long bones of large mammals were used for these projectiles. They were generally ground to a cylindrical form, but not always, depending on the bone available.

Daugherty (1956a) reports for the Lind Coulee site a fragment of a serrated bone projectile that can hardly be anything but an incipient harpoon. It is unilaterally barbed with the last barb sloping toward the opposite direction from the others. Daugherty suggests, and I agree with him, that this was probably for attachment of a line. Clark (1952:30, Figure 9, No. 1) illustrates a European Late Paleolithic Hamburgian specimen with essentially the same kind of device for line attachment. Since the Lind Coulee specimen in its reconstructed length is just over 75 millimeters long and 11 millimeters thick at the butt, it would have been a formidable weapon. Bird bones and those of large and small mammals were found at the site but no fish bones were reported. The site is inferred to have been a recurrently used campsite along the shoreline of a shallow lake or a sluggish stream. This specimen has considerable importance in the discussion of subsistence and adaptation, for it represents a very early record of this kind of weapon at an inland site (C-14 date, average of two runs from charred bone, is 8,700±400 years ago: C-827), possibly for hunting land animals.

Various kinds of weapons, including presumably harpoons, were in use at The Dalles (Cressman et al. 1960:47, 87, Figures 20c, 40a, b, c) well before 9,000 years ago and perhaps at the Fraser Canyon site of comparable age near Hope, British Columbia. Both sites were used for taking salmon, and at The Dalles seals were also killed. Thus the concept of the harpoon, if my identification is correct, was known at The Dalles before 9,000 years ago. This is the earliest indication of its use so far in the New-World archæological record.

These fishermen of the Fraser and Columbia rivers were also hunters, as the bones of elk, deer, and bear in the Five-Mile Rapids site indicate. It is probable that at those times during the year when salmon were not running up the rivers to their spawning beds, the hunting of land mammals was the major subsistence activity of the population; this would have taken them into the land away from the river. The hunters of the Lind Coulee site may well have been fishermen on the Columbia River and its tributaries in season. If these speculations are valid, then it is reasonable to assume that knowledge of the harpoon was common property but that in general it was a specialized instrument. The Lind Coulee specimen may well represent an experiment in using the weapon in hunting land mammals or birds.

FOWLING

Fowling, hunting birds by projectiles in contrast to trapping, is best demonstrated at the Five-Mile Rapids site (Cressman et al. 1960). Bird bones, both land and aquatic varieties, have been reported for various far-western sites at different time horizons, but the methods by which the birds were taken is relatively unknown. It is known that at the Five-Mile Rapids site the bola was used, as it was at approximately the same time farther up the Columbia and on the lower Snake River.

The mineralization of bone and antler in the Five-Mile Rapids site fortunately preserved a great number of bird bones, especially from the Early Level. Over 1,000 bird bones were recovered and a minimum of 624 individuals was established. These bones were divided by percentage among the following kinds of birds: cormorant—18.9%; condor—10.2%; turkey vulture—2.1%; bald eagle—19.6%; gull—42.0%. Each of the remaining kinds was less than 2 percent; thus, 92.8 percent of all birds belonged to the raptorial and scavenging kinds. Fish are an important element in the diet of these birds. The fish may be taken from the water or their carcasses picked up on sandbars or beaches. Since, at the time of the enormous salmon runs, salmon die after spawning and their bodies float down with the current, there must have been great numbers of carcasses deposited on the shore.

Another characteristic of these birds is that when on the ground they usually have to run a few steps to get airborne. At this time, and in their slow initial flight, they are relatively easy prey for the hunter. Since a number of birds may be eating on a single carcass or on closely spaced carcasses, with attention focused on eating and protecting their food from competitors, the entangling bola would have been a very effective weapon with a good chance of securing a number of birds at a single throw. The bola may be hurled into closely grouped flying birds, but it is less effective against the single bird than the bird dart or similar weapons.

Cressman et al. (1960: Figure 21) show that a few birds, 5 to be exact, were found in Level 36 then none until Level 32 with 20, Level 31 with 33, and Level 30 with 122 birds. Now, the bola appears toward the end of Level 33, at about the same time or very slightly before the birds found in Level 32. There is a fairly close correspondence in the behavior of the two curves, bolas and birds, with both terminating at approximately Level 20. While the curve for the incidence of mammal bones behaves in much the same way and might be read to show a correlation with the use of the bola, the data itself does not permit such an inference to be drawn. There were but 87 individuals in the category "mammal bones," and percentages calculated on this base would be unduly affected by sampling error. If the bola was used for any of these mammals, it must have been frightfully ineffectual. The two most numerous animals are marmot (14) and cervid (11), followed by *Thomomys* (7), and beaver, seal, and canids (each with 6). Out of this series the only animal that might have been a target for a bola would have been deer or elk, but it is more likely that the atlatl would have been preferred. What these faunal curves indicate, in my opinion, is a gradual improvement in adaptation to a particular ecological niche, and then after a time a change in the character of the niche requiring a new adaptation which took a long time to develop. An important element in this adaptation was the bola, and it was used for taking large birds.

One naturally asks, "Was the bola invented here on the shore of the Columbia River more than 9,000 years ago, or was it brought in by some wandering band of hunters already familiar with its use in the hunting of land animals?" The record shows that the site had been occupied for a long time before the bola was first used. If we wish to bring it from elsewhere we have to conclude that the earlier occupants did not develop the bola themselves and that its appearance is due to the arrival of a new group familiar with its use. This inference is of course possible, but it would be strengthened if there was some known place from which the "bola users" could have come.

Three sites for possible bolas have been reported for North America (Wormington 1957). A round, girdled ball of chalk from the Frontier complex in

Nebraska and a round stone ball from Deadman Cave in Utah may be parts of bolas, but they occur as single specimens and leave the identification very much in doubt. Specimens from Manzano Cave in New Mexico are much more convincing as bolas. Five were found and three of these were together. The dates on all these specimens are equivocal, but none seems to be early enough, even if the identification is correct, to serve as the predecessor of those used at The Dalles.

Round stone balls have been found in considerable numbers in the bed of Fort Rock Lake in south-central Oregon and adjacent areas. These vary in size from perhaps 5 to 10 centimeters. Most are said to have a small area, perhaps 2 centimeters in diameter, ground flat. I doubt that these are bolas. I once saw a collection of these found as a cache in the Sycan Marsh, which lies on the Klamath Lake side of the Winter Rim, the western side of Summer Lake basin. I do not remember the exact number in the collection, but I believe it was around ten and each differed in size from the others, starting with a small one of about 5 centimeters in diameter and going up to the largest at about 15 centimeters. They were beautifully made, pecked but not polished, but at this time I cannot remember if they had the flattened surface. The variation in size of this series leads me to question their use as bola stones. Perhaps they were used in some forgotten game.

The curve for the stratigraphic distribution of bolas at Five-Mile Rapids could very well indicate a local invention and its rapid exploitation. The bola is a simple weapon compared with the bow. Further, the bola did not replace a weapon with a long tradition, as did the bow, but was an entirely new weapon. As a new weapon, it would not have had to overcome any psychological resistance, and its effectiveness would have been a convincing argument for its rapid adoption as indicated by the sudden rise of the curve. The technological skill that characterized these men, as shown by the varieties of artifacts and the skills employed in their manufacture, indicates that they had ingenuity and ability of a high order. I, on the basis of all the evidence, believe that their inventiveness and adaptiveness accounts for the appearance and use of the bola to take these large birds along the Columbia River. We do not need to look elsewhere for a source, although I certainly admit that eventually one may be found. Regardless of the origin of the bola at Five-Mile Rapids, its use more than 9,000 years ago represents an achievement of an extremely high level in the full adaptation to a particular ecological niche.

FISHING

Fish have provided an important article of diet in the subsistence patterns of far-western Indians. Marine fish, freshwater varieties, mollusks, and crustaceans all contributed at various times and places. The availability of the different varieties varies both in time of the year and environmentally. Halibut live in waters with cold temperatures and the albacore in warm. Red abalone require colder water—8°-18°—than the black who are at home from 10° to much above 18° centigrade (personal communication, J.R. Moriarty to L.S. Cressman, January 25, 1968). Salmon return from the ocean to spawn at certain seasons of the year and are available to fishermen only during the relatively short period of their upstream migration. Nonanadromous fish usually become more readily available as they prepare to spawn and congregate in shallow water or small streams. In some lakes and streams fish are available the year around. Through time in the Far West the changing environment has affected the distribution of fishery resources. The glacial ice of the Vashon Stade closed the Fraser River, and there is a suggestion that runs of salmon, or at least successful spawning, were also prevented in the Columbia River during the Sumas Stade (Cressman et al. 1960). The use of fish of any kind for food depended upon the desire to use them and the means for catching them. The development of the necessary skills, like all other technological developments, was progressive, but the archæological record of the development is extremely spotty. The nature of the instruments used and the hazards of preservation account for the lacunae in the record.

The following methods for taking fish were all used in various localities of the Far West at the time of contact (Rostlund 1952).

  1. Line with hook or hooks
     a. Single hook or gorge
     b. Trotline with multiple hooks

2. Net
   a. Dip; from bank, platform, or canoe
   b. Gill; set between anchoring posts or canoes
   c. Seine; pulled by two canoes
   d. Funnel-shaped; for herring or eulachon
3. Projectiles
   a. Spear; barbed or leister
   b. Harpoon; plain or toggling
   c. Bow and arrow
4. Snare or noose
5. Herring rake
6. Weirs and traps
7. Decoy; dark hut and leister
8. Torchlight fishing; spear or line used
9. Poisoning

Along the British Columbia coast exploitation of the natural resources of the sea reached its highest development, and a brief description of the methods used there at the time of white contact will afford a background for discussion of the archæological record. The offshore islands broke the violence of the surf for much of the area, and fiords provided long stretches of relatively quiet water. The anadromous fish passed through these waters on their way to their inland spawning grounds following customary routes. The cold water of the northern sea offered a favorable habitat for such fish as the halibut, and in the spring countless numbers of eulachen came in great schools driven by their spawning compulsion. Thus both pelagic and anadromous varieties of fish were available and methods of catching them were devised.

Halibut and cod were taken by angling with hook and line, for they are bottom feeders and will take bait at all times. The halibut hook was a composite device with a piece of bone (later iron) for a point attached to a large wooden shaft, which was usually carved with some characteristic symbolic design of the area bringing its talismanic power to the fisherman's aid.

The herring rake was used to take the eulachen. The rake was a plank or board with a series of sharp bone points inserted in one edge. The rake was then fastened to a handle 12 to 18 feet in length. The rake was pulled through the shoals of fish with a paddling motion by the operator in the bow of the canoe, snagging numbers of the small fish on the way. The operator continued his sweep, lifting the rake over the canoe behind him where the struggling fish were dropped.

A funnel-shaped, small mesh net was used by the Haida of the Queen Charlotte Islands, and later was adopted by neighbors, as a more effective device than the rake to catch eulachen. Nets were used as seines, gill nets, dip nets, and trawl nets (seines and gill nets may not be aboriginal). Trolling with hook and line was a method of catching salmon, for they will take bait in salt water. Fish traps were constructed that guided the salmon into long funnel-like baskets from which they could not escape. Other basketry traps were set on tidal flats to entrap fish during the high tide and the owner would gather his catch as the tide receded. Toggling harpoons were used for salmon swimming near the surface. One type, with two foreshafts of different lengths, was in general use for salmon and was also used for sturgeon fishing. The murky water of the Fraser River required the sturgeon fisherman using a harpoon to work entirely by "feel." As he probed the riverbed from his canoe for this bottom-feeding fish, his sense of touch had to tell him when the points were against a fish. He then gave a strong thrust with the harpoon.

Along with the fish, practically all other fauna and some flora of the sea were utilized for food or as an aid in getting food—for example, kelp was used for making fishing lines. One should not get the impression that all these riches were the common property of all peoples along the Northwest Coast. Availability of resources varied with the ecology, and, consequently, some places were more favorable for exploiting the salmon than others; the same was true for varieties of shellfish, sea lions, whales, and seals. The rich maritime resources of the Northwest Coast were exploited so fully that the hunting of land mammals occupied a minimum of the subsistence activities.

On the mainland some of the Salish groups, whose habitats were not particularly blessed by the riches of the sea, gave a more than average attention to hunting. Successful hunts provided them with supplies, which they traded with neighbors who relied more heavily on food from the sea (Barnett 1955).

Berries collected in season from the mountains in the hinterlands of both islands and mainland provided an additional article of diet. The emphasis, however, through the entire area was on the riches of the sea. Rostlund (1952) in his evaluation of the "importance of fish in annual food economy" lists fish as the most important staple for all the tribes of the Northwest Coast.

The development of fishing, like that of the bola discussed above, was an addition to methods of subsistence already in use and not a displacement of one method by another, as was the case of the bow and arrow and the atlatl; therefore, there was no competition between a new method and an old established one. One may reasonably expect then that the addition of fishing to the varieties of methods of securing food would have proceeded rapidly. It is also likely, though not demonstrated, that devices already in use in taking land animals involved all the mechanical principles necessary for application to fishing devices. Bones of grouse and hare occur in the Magdalenian sites of the Old World (Clark 1952), and it is quite possible, even probable as Clark suggests, that these bones are evidence of snares and traps. I have mentioned the cordage in the first level of Danger Cave, and there is a good possibility that it was used in a net to take small mammals or birds. The presence of both aquatic and land birds at the Paisley-Five-Mile Point Cave No. 3 suggests the use of snares and traps as in the Magdalenian sites.

The time when fishing began in either the Old or the new World can only be approximated. Paintings of fish occur in some of the caves of the Upper Paleolithic of Europe. Bones of salmon, trout, and other fish also occur in some Magdalenian sites. Probably one would be safe in putting a date of approximately 12,000 years ago on these bones. Salmon were being taken from the Columbia River somewhat more than 9,000 years ago. We are not sure in either instance that the record is the beginning of fishing. Nor is it certain that anadromous fish were the first taken; perhaps they came from lakes or streams and had no connection with the sea. The earliest date for fish bones, *Gila bicolor,* from the caves on the shore of pluvial Fort Rock Lake, is 9,670±180 C-14 years ago (GaK-2142). Did the first fisherman get the idea that, like other animals,

fish would make food as he saw them in the unpolluted waters? Or did he see the eagle or the osprey drop like a plummet into the water and rise with a fish flashing in its talons? Or perhaps he watched from concealment as bear stood in the rapids and, with great skill, hooked out fish with their paws as the fish swam upstream to the spawning grounds. Whatever the stimulus or stimuli may have been, men rapidly developed varieties of ways to take fish, and so effective were their efforts that in some areas like the Columbia and Fraser drainage systems the basic elements of the native economy and subsistence patterns were established by 9,000 years ago.

Rostlund (1952:117) states that the gorge was certainly "the most primitive of all hook-and-line devices and presumably the oldest." Clark (1952) reports the gorge was found in the Grimaldi caves in Europe, a location giving it an Upper Paleolithic date. The gorge occurred at the Kawumkan Midden on the Klamath Indian Reservation in Level III (Cressman 1956b). I estimated the period covered by the level to range from more than 7,500 to about 3,500 years ago. On the basis of information available since that study and by cross dating, I am inclined to believe both dates should be earlier. The gorge did not appear at the Five-Mile Rapids site at The Dalles although it is occasionally found later in other sites. The gorge has to be used from a canoe or a favorable spot along the shore. The whole Klamath Lake area was favorable to the use of the gorge and line, but the Columbia with its swift current was not.

The composite hook (a piece of wood with a sharply pointed piece of bone attached to the distal end and the bone pointing toward the other end forming a V with the piece of wood) has a wide distribution, but its relative position chronologically to the gorge is unknown. Rostlund (1952) suggests that both the gorge and the composite fishhook came from Asia. The latter he suspects is a device that reached the New World and became a part of the American Indian cultural inventory before Eskimos were exposed to it. It then diffused to the Eskimos from the American Indians. He bases his theory on the distinctive method of use, 'jigging," used by the Eskimo in contrast to the usual hook-and-line fishing of the Indians. I suggest that the Eskimo method of jigging was probably a function of fishing through a hole in the ice and is thus without chronological significance.

Composite fishhooks come from coastal sites (Berreman 1944) and from a site on the north side of Coquille River a short distance inside the bar. Neither of these sites is firmly dated other than as precontact. Lovelock Cave has also provided this type of fishhook, but unfortunately there is no record of the provenience so no date can be assigned to it. A variant kind comes from a rock-shelter on the Deschutes River, Oregon, site Je82, where six of these hooks were found (Ross 1963). They are carved from dense bone of some large animal. All are made to the same pattern and are approximately the same size—about 3 centimeters in overall length. They occur in association with a great number of large mussel shells (*Margaritifera*) (Roscoe 1967). The associated projectile points align the people who left this material with the mid-Columbia river area. A C-14 date of 2650±185 B.P. (I-1500) is derived from a hearth near which the hooks were found. If our identification of the artifacts is correct and our inference of cultural relationship is sound, then specimens of this type should be found along the mid-Columbia and its tributary streams, at least those coming in from the south. The Deschutes River is probably unfavorable to any kind of hook-and-line fishing except from the bank, although the fact that six hooks were found close together suggests the possibility of their use on a trotline.

The composite hook lends itself well to trolling and to use with a handline from a canoe or the shore. One would expect to find it in sites around lakes, along the coast, or along the lower stretches of tidal rivers. We may have failed to identify pointed bone barbs from these sites as parts of a composite hook, particularly if the base were missing.

The trotline or setline in fishing is the analogue of the trapline in hunting. The trotline is a long line with a number of hooks hung on short lines from it. The line may be suspended between two anchored canoes or between stakes. The fisherman is then free to do something else while the trotline works for him. Rostlund (1952) quotes various reports of the great effectiveness of the trotline. Ethnographically, the use is reported for the Shuswap of the interior of

British Columbia, the Northwest Coast, the Northern Paiute in the Lovelock area along the Humboldt River, the Klamath, Modoc, and tribes of the upper Sacramento drainage, as well as the Hupa and Tolowa of northwestern California and southwestern Oregon. An archæological example of such a line is illustrated in Loud and Harrington (1929:Plate 51) from Lovelock Cave, but no depth provenience information is available, and the specimen is thus undated.

Three kinds of projectiles have been used in fishing; the bow and arrow, the spear, and the harpoon. The use of the conventional form of any of these requires that the fish be at or near the surface. If the projectile is thrown rather than thrust, its course will quickly be diverted by the water and the lightness of the wooden shaft. The bow and arrow were most effective in shallow pools left in a stream during a period of low water flow or after fish were stupefied by poison. It is reported that use of the bow and arrow to shoot fish was tabooed along the Oregon coast, but it is reported for most of the rest of the Far West. However, but for the exceptions mentioned above, in shallow water and after poisoning, the use of the bow and arrow was mostly for sport or engaged in by boys for fun. Demonstration from archæological data of the use of this instrument for fishing is improbable; it was used for shooting at too many other kinds of targets as well.

A major problem in fishing with projectiles is the retrieval of the fish. The unilaterally barbed spear would have been very effective in retrieving if the barbs were long enough to embed themselves in the flesh. These fish spears were important in the Maglemosian of northern Europe (Clark 1952) and were used specially for pike. A barbed bone fragment from the Lind Coulee site (Daugherty 1956a) could conceivably have been used as a fish spear or even as a harpoon, for the notch at the base indicates a provision for attachment of a line for some purpose.

Nine unilaterally barbed bone and antler fish spear points have been reported from Pyramid Lake (Ting 1967), a little more than 30 miles north and east of Reno, Nevada. These are surface finds that come from the shoreline between the 3,785 and 3,805 feet levels. Four of the five specimens illustrated by Ting in his Figure 1 have barbs long enough to embed deeply into the flesh and help in retrieval. That these are fish spears is further indicated by the associated materials from the same shoreline level—leister prongs or tines, parts of three-part composite harpoons, gorges and bone barbs from composite fishhooks, along with various kinds of sinkers. All this is fishing gear. On the basis of projectile point types also found in the vicinity, it is suggested that the Early Lovelock culture period is represented. The range of equipment for taking fish at Pyramid Lake, probably around 3,000 years ago, shows a remarkable adaptive capacity in these Great Basin people, and it does not matter whether they developed these methods or secured some or all of them by diffusion. They knew well what to do with them.

Rostlund's "Map 35, Distribution of aboriginal fish spears" (1952) shows that the leister, a special two- or three-pronged fish spear, was in use at contact time from the Columbia River drainage north. The most frequent occurrence is in the intermontane area of the drainage of the Columbia and Fraser rivers; the frequency along the coast is much less. This distribution is to be expected, for the leister is a thrusting instrument and can be used effectively in deep water in only limited circumstances. Why it did not extend to California and most areas of the Great Basin (but does occur archæologically at Pyramid Lake) is not known. I suggest that the use of fish poisoning, which occurs in the area lacking the leister, blocked its introduction. The two methods are mutually exclusive. In the Northern California area weirs and traps in addition to poison probably provided adequate results in fishing.

It has been suggested that the leister is represented by some of the small pieces of bone and antler from the Early Level at the Five-Mile Rapids site at The Dalles. I had not originally interpreted them as such. I can, however, well see the possibility of the specimen illustrated in Cressman et al. (1960: Figures 20 C, 40 A, B, C) as being a part of a leister prong. It would have been the point of a lateral tine. The tine would have had to have been grooved at the end to permit the point to be set in the groove and fastened by some adhesive and a binding using the shallow grooves. The specimen occurs at about the time the first seal appears in the fill, and fish were also being taken. It obviously could have been

either a part of a leister or the point of a harpoon. The evidence for either is not clear. It gives a date of about 9,000 years ago and is about the same age as the unilaterally barbed bone fragment from Lind Coulee, which seems to have used the same method of hafting. I still prefer my original indentification of the specimen as a part of a harpoon.

There is no doubt that the harpoon succeeded, and in the main replaced, the fish spear. The harpoon with its retrieval line was much more efficient in holding the fish, and since the fish was what the fisherman was after, the harpoon in one form or another practically replaced the spear. It is well to keep in mind the basic difference between a spear and a harpoon: both may be hurled or thrust, but the spear has a head fixed to the shaft and it is not intended to come loose. The harpoon, on the other hand, is constructed so that the head will come loose and remain in the prey, and the retrieval line enables the harpooner, with luck, to land his fish. The major difference between the harpoons used for sea mammal hunting and fishing is largely a matter of size and arming. The principles are the same—detachable head held by a retrieving line. Fish spears might have a barbed point (Bennyhoff 1950) following the same principle as the leister. The harpoon, whether first developed for hunting on land or in water, represents a strikingly new invention in the disengaging head held by a retrieving line.

Another characteristic of the harpoon to increase its lethal capacity was added with the invention of the toggling head. The toggling harpoon head, after penetrating the target, turns at an angle as the line tightens and thus is set securely in the animal. The toggling harpoon appears late in the prehistoric sequence, but at contact time had a distribution practically throughout the whole Far West, probably as a result of its effectiveness. Bennyhoff (1950:305) quotes Kroeber as saying "the toggle harpoon was probably known to every group in California whose territory contained sufficient bodies of water. The Colorado River tribes provide the only known exception. . . ." Harpoons in the Great Basin are reported from Pyramid Lake, but it is not clear whether they were the toggling type or not. They probably were the three-piece toggling type, which occurs in archæological sites from northwestern California, along the Oregon Coast, along the Columbia River, and in the Columbia and Fraser plateaus. Its distribution may be extended with further archæological work.

The salmon harpoon may take a variety of forms such as a single, unbarbed, sharply pointed bone similar to a gorge or a three-part specimen with a central rounded piece ending in a point with two spurs or valves which form barbs or a single or two-pointed variety in which there are two foreshafts of equal or unequal lengths each having a detachable point held to the main shaft by the retrieval line. Each of these may be the toggling variety. It is possible that the smaller unilaterally or bilaterally barbed harpoons found along the coast, especially in the vicinity of rivers used by salmon, were used interchangeably for small sea mammals or salmon. In general, the distribution of the toggling fish harpoon follows that of the salmon. Cole (1966) reports a unilaterally barbed harpoon (three barbs) with a notch for line attachment from site 45KL5 on the Washington site of the Columbia River in the John Day Dam reservoir. It dates from about 2,500 years ago.

It is not possible to say at present where the toggling principle was invented. The wide distribution of the toggling salmon harpoon at contact time may belie its relative recency. The three-piece toggle point is found on the Columbia and Snake rivers in contexts indicating its use at somewhat more than 1,000 years ago, but at that time it was apparently a fully accepted cultural element. The specimen reported from Pyramid Lake is possibly close to the same time. While it was the most common salmon harpoon of ethnographic California, it "is known archæologically only along the northern coast" (Bennyhoff 1950:322). It is known along the Oregon coast (Berreman 1944; Newman 1959), but the dates appear to be somewhat later than those for the interior and in line with those from Northern California. There is of course the possibility that the toggling harpoon, or the principle of it, was introduced from the north, but it appears to me to be more likely that it represents a localized development by the fishermen of the interior plateaus whose economy depended to such a large extent on the salmon.

The simple gorge with a line attached in a medial groove, it seems to me, operated on the toggling principle; that is when the line was pulled after the fish swallowed the gorge the instrument tended to turn at right angles to the line of force exerted by the pull; otherwise the gorge would not have embedded itself in the fish. If the line had been fastened at or close to the end, the direction of pull by the fisherman would have brought the gorge out in the same manner it entered and there would have been little chance of hooking the fish. If this speculation is correct, the toggling principle may have been as old as the gorge, but it took an extremely long time for human ingenuity to apply it to another instrument on the basis of firm archæological evidence at the present time. Moriarity (personal communication, J.R. Moriarty to L.S. Cressman) reports a toggle bone fishhook with a 6000 B.P. date. (See my reference to the gorge at Kawumkan Springs, p. 113.) The spread of the toggling harpoon in some form over such a wide area with relatively little time depth, at least as presently indicated by archæology, is strong evidence of its relative efficiency and man's willingness to accept it.

The archæological record, if we abstract the data from the Far West as a whole, indicates that the development of projectiles for taking fish was from the simple bone or antler point, possibly having a unilateral row of low barbs, to the two-pronged spear without barbs, to two pronged spear with barbed prongs (probably the leister), to the simple harpoon, and, finally, to the toggling harpoon in a variety of forms. It is impossible to put this sequence in a chronological framework. It is clear that there was not a single center of development from which each new instrument and its use spread. Some areas failed to adopt some devices as human ingenuity developed novel regional forms to exploit more effectively the fish of their locale. Bennyhoff (1950) presents effectively information from California illustrating the irregularity of the historical record locally. Whatever the forms of weapons used, it is clear that relatively effective ones were in use during an early period at The Dalles, at the site near Hope on the Fraser River, and at the Kawumkan Springs site on the former Klamath Indian Reservation. At Kawumkan Springs (Cressman 1956b) the vertebra of a fish, identified by Carl Hubbs as probably a king or chinook salmon about four feet long, was found in Level IV, which can be equated with the two northern sites in time. A chinook salmon four feet long will weigh about fifty pounds and that is a big fish. A lethal weapon and a good fisherman, probably at the entrance to the spring from the Sprague River, are indicated by the testimony of the salmon bone.

Methods of taking fish, other than those just discussed, were in use and on the whole were far more effective if one measures the fish caught against human effort involved. These methods—the use of nets, weirs, traps, and poison—have, with the exception of poison, their analogies in the hunting of land animals. Weirs find their counterpart in the wings leading to the corral in the antelope drive or corresponding devices for directing the movement of bison or jack rabbits. As I pointed out above, the trapline was a kind of capitalistic investment in productive enterprise, so these methods of taking fish are of the same order. The use of a projectile requires one man, one weapon, and, with luck, produces one fish. There can be no doubt that these methods, where applicable, were far more effective in providing the large supplies of fish needed for these groups, which relied heavily upon that food source for their subsistence. Jenness (1932:63), writing of the Indians of British Columbia and the western Eskimos, says: "Despite their variety, all these methods fielded but a small toll of fish compared with the number caught with nets, traps, and weirs." Bennyhoff (1950:305) writes: "Most, if not all, of the ethnographic reports from California emphasize the importance of varied nets, weirs, dams, and poisons in the capture of large quantities of fish, particularly for storage. The toggle harpoons, fish spear, and fishhook were subsidiary implements, to be used more for supplying daily needs." Of these methods and the implements or structures involved in their use, the weirs are almost the sole source of archæological evidence. Sometimes traps will be preserved under unusually favorable circumstances, such as preservation by mud and sand in quiet tidal waters or stone traps, like those of the Kwakiutl, which were built within the intertidal zone.

Since the use of these methods depended on appropriate conditions presented by the particular environment, it is to be expected that the distribution of each will reflect the environmental conditions.

The weir and trap may be used together—the weir to guide fish into the trap from which they may be taken when the owner wishes. Either may be used alone under favorable circumstances. The weir may be used to direct fish through a small passage where they may be harpooned. The trap may be used where the nature of the channel directs the movement of fish into a single passage. Traps of a different kind were used by the Gulf of Georgia people and apparently along the Columbia up to where it is joined by the Willamette River. In this method, a basketry type of trap was made and set in the intertidal zone to catch fish at high tide. At low tide the fish that had been unable to escape from the trap would be gathered. I mentioned above the Kwakiutl stone trap, a horseshoe-shaped construction of stone, which operated in the intertidal zone. The weir and trap combination would have been more efficient than the simple weir and harpooner, for it operated without the presence of the human owner and depended only on the movements of fish. The trap alone would have been less effective than the weir and trap combination, for it was limited to special places where the channel was favorable to its use. The weir modified the stream channel to control or direct swimming fish.

Occasionally remains of weirs are reported, but for the most part they can hardly be expected to be preserved for any length of time. They may be large or small depending on the nature of the stream or river in which they are built and the labor available to help in the construction. They have been built of stones or logs and brush, the brush made thick enough to hinder the passage of fish. It is completely unreasonable to expect these structures to survive the fury of the rivers and streams coming from the mountains in flood during the winter and spring.

While swift flowing streams used by anadromous fish are the most likely places to find weirs and traps, the use of poison requires a different kind of water. A sluggishly flowing stream, a lake, or a mountain stream in the dry season when there is little current and many pools of quiet water, are the bodies of water in which poison can be effectively used. Poison was extensively used in Northern California and the Great Basin, where there was any water. Limited use is reported for the Columbia

Plateau in the area of tributary streams running to the Columbia River from the eastern flanks of the Cascade Mountains (Rostlund 1952:189, Map 39). It is absent in the rest of the Far West. No archæological evidence can be expected for the use of fish poison.

While fish poisoning has been reported for the Lake Baikal region, China, and Japan, the great gap between those areas and the Far West, and the nature of the intervening environment, argue against any historical connection. The distribution of fish poisoning shows that it spread pretty much to the limit of its practical use. The diversity of plants used for poisoning suggests a long experience of trial and error and a close knowledge of the plant cover. The evidence of the distribution and the nature of the knowledge required for the complex indicates to me that this is an independent development in the New World, probably with its origins in the Great Basin where the inhabitants, almost at the beginning of the archæological record, had a wide knowledge of plants, their different attributes, and the uses to which they could beneficially be put.

Nets may be operated by hand, as the dip net; set, as the gill-net; pulled by humans or canoes, like the seine; or pulled by canoes at near bottom depths, as the trawl net. The last is for deepwater fishing and was not in use in native North America. The seine is reported ethnographically from the Columbia River and the British Columbia coast, but in each case there is doubt that it was a native invention. The same skepticism is expressed about the gill net. The dip net was most useful in connection with anadromous fish in pools below falls, where they congregated before attempting the jump, and along rocky shores, where channels in the rocks directed the course of the ascending fish near where a favorably placed rock provided a spot for the fisherman to stand or where a fishing platform could be constructed upon which the holder of the dip net stood. The dip net was used effectively in both the Columbia and the Fraser plateaus. It was not a complicated instrument. It consisted of a pole—the length determined by the height of the fishing position above the water and the depth at which it was to be used—a ring of wood perhaps three feet in diameter fastened to one end of the pole, and a generally conical-shaped net attached to the ring. The dip net required considerable strength to operate and a sensitive feeling in the hands for any contact of a body against the net. It was this impact of the fish against the net, ever so slight, that told the fisherman to react.

Setnets or seines are the only kinds which would require weights. The top edge of the net must be kept at a fixed level and the bottom at the full width of the net below the top. Floats are required for the first and weights for the second purpose. Floats, like the nets, are perishable; weights are not since they are made from stone. The weights, therefore, are the only direct evidence of nets to be preserved in archæological sites. We usually look for a girdled, drilled, or notched stone as evidence of use of the net weight, but the simple attribute of girdling or notching on a stone is not definitive evidence of its use as a net weight or sinker. Hammerstones and club heads were also girdled for attachment to a handle. The hammerstone should show evidence of percussion in contrast to the net weight, but the stone club head would lack this attribute. The cultural and ecological contexts in which these objects are found often must be determining factors in identification.

A weight might have been enclosed in a net or bag and suspended from the net by a cord. Bolas used both these principles of attachment to the cord. A type of "weight" found at the Five-Mile Rapids site and again in the Aleutians (Cressman et al. 1960:58 Figures 48a) appears to have been used in this manner. The groove close to the top would appear to be too shallow to hold a cord intended to support the weight of the stone, but it would support a cord which tied the top of an enclosing bag which, in turn, was suspended from the bottom edge of the net. At the Five-Mile Rapids site these "weights" occur only before 7,000 to 7,500 years ago, except one which appeared to be entirely out of context.

If setnets were being used at The Dalles in the Early Period, then the users had to have some place to anchor the ends of the net stretched across a channel used by the migrating salmon or else had to have canoes that could have been used for the same purpose, either in a fixed position or in motion. Canoes might have been used above or below the rapids. At the rapids there were various breaks in the basalt extending in the same direction as the flow of the river. Salmon used these to some extent in preference to fighting the violence of the main part of the rapids. In the early days of commercial exploitation of salmon, a fish wheel was set up to work one of these channels and enormous numbers of salmon were taken. The construction of the canal around the rapids has destroyed the original character of the shoreline and the adjacent old rock bed of the river. I believe it is quite probable that nets were used across these channels in the basalt outside the main rapids and that the heavy, pear-shaped "weights" were used in that connection. Heavy weights would have been needed in the swift currents. Cressman et al. (1960:Map 3, Figures 29, 61) illustrate the geological features involved in the above discussion (see Figure 26). In Cressman et al. 1960, their Figure 61b of the river shows it in partial flood.

The curve for stratigraphic distribution of fish bones in the Five-Mile Rapids site (Cressman et al. 1960:Figure 21) indicates a steady and rather rapid rise in the number to a plateau, then a rather rapid drop-off. This could mean fluctuations in the number of fish available, or in the number of people catching fish, or improved methods of catching fish, or various combinations of these possibilities. I think the likelihood of an increase in the fishing population using the site is very slight for there was only so much room available both for living space and fishing sites. I am inclined to believe that the increased quantities of fish bone indicate an improvement in the methods of taking fish together, perhaps, with an increased supply. It is difficult to visualize how so many salmon could have been taken by spear or even harpoon in the water conditions existing in the area. Dip nets would have left no sign of their use, but nets of some kind must have been used, apparently to the exclusion of other fishing gear in view of the absence of clear-cut evidence of any kind after the very early occupation of the site.

There is no reason to believe that fishing with spears, harpoons, or nets originated on the Columbia River. The presence of cordage from the very early occupation of Danger Cave, which was contemporary with cordage at The Dalles, strongly suggests that the net was in use for some purpose in that area at that time, since cordage of the kind found was mostly used in the Great Basin for nets. The prin-

ciple of the net used in the taking of land animals could have been transferred very easily to catching fish in inland waters. This inference is certainly sound in view of the fact that the projectile type of weapon first used in fishing was apparently that already in use in hunting land animals. Adaptations of these weapons followed as experience demonstrated the need for special types to kill fish and retrieve them from the water. Bennyhoff (1950:305) suggests the antiquity of net fishing: "The development of two functional families of net and weir fishermen among the Patwin implies considerable antiquity of specialization in technique, as does the common insistence in the first-salmon ceremony that the first fish be caught with a net or some means other than the spear or harpoon."

The significance of the Five-Mile Rapids site and the site near Hope in Fraser Canyon is that they demonstrate that the population of the Fraser and Columbia plateaus had started their exploitation of the rich resources of the rivers and by 9,000 years ago had made a successful adaptation to this aspect of their environment. The people established the salmon as the basic element in their economy, a fact that was to have far-reaching effects on their whole subsequent development, both internally and in setting them off from their neighbors in the intermontane area to the south.

GATHERING

Gathering did not begin with the appearance in the archæological record of milling stones, manos and metates, or pestles and mortars. These stones indicate the *appearance of a new method of food preparation, nothing more.* These were, however, important. But there must have been methods of breaking up or smashing seeds before the appearance of the clearly recognized milling stone. Anyone who had the idea that a bone could be broken by hitting it with a rock to get at the contained marrow must certainly have tried the same method of making seeds more edible. The hunter was aware of grinding and scraping methods for he used them in the fabrication of weapons of wood, antler, and bone. The innate play tendency of man, random or purposeless activity expressed through the alliance of mind and

Figure 26. The Columbia River at the Long Narrows of Lewis and Clark, present Five-Mile Rapids east of The Dalles, Oregon. The small channels in the bedrock basalt were used by the salmon moving upstream and provided favored fishing sites; settlements on both sides of the river. *Cressman et al. 1960:Figure 29.*

hand, must have resulted many times in the use of stones for both pounding and grinding as men and their families clustered about a campfire. The im-portant thing was that someone recognized the possibilities in this random activity and applied it to grinding seeds. My guess is that it was a woman.

Throughout the Far West, milling was being practiced at a very early time. Milling was in use by the earliest occupants of Ventana Cave, the earliest occupants of Danger Cave, those at Kawumkan Springs, and those at the Five-Mile Rapids site, where two manos and metates were found in Level 28 and dated at approximately 9,000 years ago. A mano found on top of the basalar gravel at Fort Rock Cave is dated at 13,200±720 B.P. (GaK-1738). Milling stones are reported for La Jolla I, probably between 6,000 and 7,000 years ago, and eventually the date for Southern California will undoubtedly be pushed earlier.

Mortars and pestles are reported for Ventana Cave, although beginning slightly later than the mano-metate, and they occur in smaller numbers throughout. Block and bedrock mortars occur and Haury et al. (1950) suggest the possibility of the use of wooden mortars on the basis of the lack of rounding wear on the bottoms of some pestles. Only two pestles are reported for Danger Cave, one of unknown provenience and one from Level III. At Fort Rock Cave a crude mortar came from a deposit immediately overlying the basalar gravels. At Kawumkan Springs (Cressman 1956b) both the mano-metate and the mortar-pestle complexes existed from the beginning of occupation and maintained their ratios, one to the other, throughout the use of the site. A total of 472 specimens of both complexes were found and the ratio of mano-metate to mortar-pestle was 6 to 4. While the numbers of each vary from level to level, the ratio remains about the same (Cressman 1950:420). At The Dalles the mortar-pestle combination is limited to the late period, after approximately 7,000 years ago. No bedrock mortars were noted at this site, but above site WS-1 at the west end of the rapids one was seen by a spring. Ethnographically, wooden mortars made from the boles on oak trees were used in The Dalles area, and a few stone mortars, frequently sculptured, were found in the archæological deposits.

Farther up the Columbia River hopper-mortars are found. It is difficult to distinguish these from shallow metates. They were used with a basketry hopper to hold the material to be pounded and ground. The hopper-mortar combination was vastly easier to make than a stone mortar and probably served the purpose equally well.

The archæological record thus shows that the milling process of food preparation is almost as old as the oldest firmly validated sites. The mano-metate appears to have been the earlier of the two complexes, although the mortar-pestle occurs very shortly after. The mano-metate is the simpler of the two milling complexes and could reasonably be expected to have been developed first. Once adopted the instruments took different forms in various areas, presumably to provide better methods of accomplishing the work or to meet the habitual motor habits of the users. One of the most striking examples of the development of a specialized mano is that of the *wokas-*(*Nuphar polyespalum*) grinding "two horned mano," the development of which I have tried to illustrate elsewhere (Cressman 1956b:421, Chart 2).

In the Far West two striking examples of adaptation by the exploitation of seeds and nuts stand out. The *wokas* of the Klamath Indians and the acorn of the Northern California Indians both lent themselves to preparation and storage for future use and were extremely important subsistence items. Separate patterns of gathering and preparation evolved around each, and this is reflected in appropriate tools and movements of the population. The *wokas* was mostly available in the Klamath Marsh, where the people moved late in summer when the lily pods were ready to drop their seeds. The women gathered the seeds by knocking them into a dugout canoe similar to the regular canoe used by the men but smaller. The canoe was moved by means of a pole, split at one end with the parts separated by an inserted bracing stick. This pole, when pushed against the muddy bottom, did not sink into the mud and so the canoe could be moved slowly about in the gathering process. I mentioned above the special milling stone used for the *wokas*. After the harvest was completed, the preparation of the seeds could take place and then the groups could return to their winter houses.

The acorn gatherers had to move from grove to grove. The acorns were ground in basketry hopper-mortars. The large number of bedrock mortars in oak groves indicates quite clearly that acorns were also ground at a gathering site. The prepared meal had to be leached to remove the tannin before it was edible.

These two methods of exploiting the food resources of different kinds of environments, one a marsh and lake and the other a somewhat arid mountain and stream area, illustrate effectively the ingenuity of the human group in the adaptive process. The archæological record shows that the knowledge of milling as an aid in the process of food preparation was, in the Far West at least, a part of the cultural inventory of the people who were hunting the Pleistocene animals, which were later to become extinct. The record thereafter is one of increasing the effectiveness of early tool types. One would expect to find milling tools being more important in an area with heavy dependence on gathering, such as the Great Basin and the arid Southwest, and this is the case.

Along the middle Columbia River in Oregon and Washington the mortars, and pestles, too, in the late period provided a medium for sculpturing and some of the most beautiful pieces are small mortars. As I have suggested (Cressman et al. 1960), the use of stone as the medium for expression of æsthetic values may have given a stimulus to the development of the mortar-pestle complex quite apart from its utility in food preparation. A somewhat analogous situation may have taken place in the historic Diegueño culture in which mortars were made as a part of the puberty ceremonies but not used further as instruments of food preparation.

About the only other evidence of gathering activities found in archæological sites are sickles made from mountain sheep horns and basketry trays. The latter were used for parching seeds as indicated by the signs of burning by hot coals. The former have not been found in the Northern Great Basin but occur in the Nevada caves. Basketry parching trays are found in the south-central Oregon caves and have a wide distribution in the Great Basin.

ADAPTATION AND ENVIRONMENTAL CHANGE

When one considers the great time depth of far-western occupation and the changes in the natural environment over thousands of years, it is clear that the adaptive processes just discussed have at times functioned under conditions quite different from those of the present. The Pacific Coast during a glacial period presented a quite different habitat.

The lowering of sea level by 100 meters, where the continental shelf is wide, provided a coastal plain of varying miles in width; where rocky headlands and a narrow continental shelf defined the coast, there was but little difference from the conditions of the present. On the wide coastal plain of Southern California and Santa Rosa Island, huge deposits of alluvium were laid down (in turn to be cut away into the cliffs we now see) by the rise of sea level that accompanied deglaciation. These coastal plains with their embayments, lagoons, etc., would have been the habitats of the people of that time. It is in such places that the "hearths" of Santa Rosa Island and the San Diego area are found. In Northern California and Oregon and Washington no really comparable situation existed. There was no British Columbia coast during the Vashon Stade or any glacial period; it was probably under 5,000 feet or even more of ice.

Glacial stades affected the Columbia and Fraser plateaus. The Fraser Plateau was under ice to an elevation of 8,000 feet during the Vashon Stade. Lobes of ice reached the Columbia River, even crossing it in places. The Sumas Stade is not evident south of the Canadian border, with the exception of possibly a small manifestation in the eastern part of the state of Washington. British Columbia, however, under those conditions would not have provided a human habitat, but the Columbia Plateau to the south would have been an inviting one. At this same time, the Columbia River at the Five-Mile Rapids site was flowing at an elevation of slightly more than 150 feet above sea level, while in contrast the mean low water level at The Dalles in modern times (before the building of The Dalles Dam) was only 50 feet. The Columbia River at the 150 foot level was a different challenge to man than it was at its modern level.

Other suggestions of environmental change affecting the Columbia River area as human habitat are not supportable. Sanger (1967) has suggested that a dam formed in the Columbia by the great slide at Cascade Locks brought about a change in the level of the river, which permitted salmon to pass the "impassable" falls at Celilo. Previous to this time he assumes that salmon could not pass the Celilo Falls, and this accounts for the lack of salmon bones in sites along the middle course of the Columbia for a considerable period in contrast with the situation in British Columbia. That there was a temporary dam is clear. It is also clear that it was temporary, since a dam for any length of time would have caused the building of a delta at the point where the river would have deposited the large amount of sediment it carried. No such delta exists. Also, there would have been evidence of sedimentation in the sites in the area occupied by the dam had it been of any duration. Such evidence of sedimentation in archæological sites in the area does not exist. Sites excavated above Celilo Falls in the John Day Dam reservoir area dating during the time the dam was supposed to exist contain salmon bones, the occupation was not disrupted, and there is no evidence of sedimentation (personal communication, D.L. Cole to L.S. Cressman). The absence of salmon bones in the sites considered by Sanger must be due to some other cause than a supposed change in the ecology brought about by a gigantic landslide.

It has also been suggested that during the Altithermal the Columbia River was lowered for a long enough period to cut terraces and permit ventifacts (stones scarred by wind action) to be formed at a level below that of present low water (Richmond et al. 1965:240). If this were the case, it would indicate a tremendously arid condition in the Columbia and Fraser plateaus seriously affecting the region as a habitat, but conflicting evidence contradicts this inference. Sam Sargent, who was the geologist in charge of construction of the dam at The Dalles, had to make intensive studies of the geology and history of the river. He had the opportunity to examine the exposed bedrock of the river channel during the coffer dam construction and diversion of the river from the main channel. In conversations about the problem of the levels of the river he has told me that while the evidence of sandblasting—the kind of action necessary to produce ventifacts—is very clear on the bedrock at the present level of the river, there is absolutely none below water level that would indicate an earlier period of sandblasting. Therefore, in the permanent bedrock, which would provide the least controversial testimony to a condition applying to the whole river, the critical evidence does not exist.

The climatic conditions of the Late Pleistocene affected the Great Basin environment differently than they did the plateau areas. During the period of the full pluvial lakes, conditions were favorable for stable occupation because of the water supply. Not only were grasses and seeds more abundant than now, but so was game. When desiccation of the lakes occurred, the environment became less favorable and the unit of land necessary to support a human being increased. By the time of the Altithermal period, if not well before, the characteristic Great Basin pattern of seasonal migration developed to meet the challenge of the new environment.

It has been thought by some archæologists that the Great Basin was depopulated during the dry Altithermal period, even though convincing evidence has been available for more than twenty-five years that this was not the case. There is evidence for a reduction of population density, but not depopulation. There were four possible responses to the problems created by the arid Altithermal climate: (1) extinction, (2) out-migration, (3) survival around the few continuing water sources, and (4) occupation of areas of higher elevation along the flanks of the mountains. The first of these alternatives can be ruled out, but probably the other solutions were all used to some extent, and those who remained within the confines of the Great Basin probably survived by exploiting the opportunities of both (3) and (4).

ECOLOGICAL ADAPTATION AND SOCIAL ORGANIZATION

The variety of ecological conditions and adaptations to them throughout the Far West had different effects on the social organization of different areas. It is important to keep in mind that along with improvements in the technological means for more effective food collection, there must have been accompanying developments in social organization, the means of regulating group activity, by which the technology was put to use.

Steward (1938, 1955) described the economic and social life of historic Great Basin groups and the relation of their social behavior to the environment as mediated through their subsistence activities. The level of social organization was the nuclear family. He notes that

Owing to the cultural ecological processes—to the exploitation of their particular environment by means of the techniques available to them—families functioned independently in most cultural activities, and the few collective inter-familial pursuits did not serve to give permanent cohesion to extended families, bands, communities, or other higher levels of sociocultural integration in the Southwest (Steward 1955:119).

The "overwhelming importance" of the food quest characterizes other groups having a family level of integration, but the Great Basin peoples, Steward states, were unique because the peculiar nature of their environment and their methods of exploiting it brought about a distinctive array of activities and associations among families.

Rats, mice, gophers, lizards, snakes, rabbits, larvae of various kinds, crickets, grasshoppers, etc., contributed heavily to the meat supply, probably more than did larger game, according to Steward. In the rivers of the Columbia River drainage there were runs of anadromous fish in season, but the remnants of the runs in the high tributary streams reachable by Great Basin folk were so small that they were important only relatively. In the Humboldt River and in rivers flowing from the Sierra Mountains, native fish were taken. At least 100 varieties of plants and grasses provided seeds and roots. And in the piñon area, the nut of the piñon pine provided a food resource of the greatest importance. In the fall when these nuts had ripened the families gathered there and collected large quantities to store in caches in the earth with the hope that their efforts had provided enough to support them through the winter months. But all this activity was carried on by a single family or two or three related families. Spring nearly always found them close to starvation, waiting eagerly for the first roots or bulbs and any game, large or small, to relieve their hunger.

The only collective activities that involved groups larger than the family were antelope and rabbit drives. These were brief occasions, however, and once the hunt was over the groups broke up into the individual families composing them. After "feast" it was "famine" because the Great Basin groups had no means of preserving meat and so it had to be eaten before it had spoiled too badly. Life for those outside the piñon area was even harder.

More or less permanent villages were possible only in certain favorable areas such as the Owens Valley and a few localities elsewhere on the east side of the Sierras where streams from the mountains provided a fairly reliable water supply and better seed and related food sources. These were centers from which the occupants could move for short periods of time in the process of gathering food within a relatively close distance and to which they could return with their harvest. Most of the Great Basin offered no such opportunity.

The archæological evidence allows Steward's characterization of Great Basin social organization to be projected far back in time. The archæological record shows that the material culture and technology of the Great Basin peoples, the Desert culture, has changed little in at least 10,000 years. The changes were mostly in the field of improved devices for exploiting the environment, as I pointed out earlier in this chapter. Great Basin culture was essentially an indigenous growth, and its remarkable conservatism is perhaps unique in the field of culture history. This continuity in material culture and exploitative activity is presumptive evidence of continuity also in social organization. An apparent contradiction posed by the relatively recent arrival of the Shoshoneans in the Great Basin is easily resolved.

If the linguistic evidence for Shoshonean expansion presented in Chapter 6 is valid, then the Shoshoneans have occupied the greater part of the basin for only about 1,000 years. Yet, there is no convincing evidence in the archæological record by which the arrival of these people can be determined on the basis of any change in the cultural inventory. The reason is that the center of diffusion of the Shoshonean languages was is an environment quite like that of the Great Basin, in fact was in a part of it. The rapid spread of the Shoshoneans is indeed in part to be explained by the fact that they were already familiar with the necessary exploitative techniques required for the ecological area into which they moved. In fact, these techniques were already their lifeway. The Shoshoneans are simply the final actors on the stage in the Great Basin; the play is the same.

Theoretical and environmental considerations may be used to suggest that in very early times a somewhat higher level of sociocultural integration than that described above existed in the Great Basin. Steward considers the patrilineal band as representing a higher stage of social integration than the nuclear family, and, in this context, he writes (1955:124) that "Dispersed and small game herds are. . . .a condition of partilineal bands. . . ." Since such game herds were largely lacking in the Great Basin of the ethnographic period, the nuclear family was the highest level of social integration available to the inhabitants. The archæological record documents with considerable fullness, however, that in the Late Pleistocene and into the Anathermal there were more varieties of game and that apparently there was a greater emphasis on hunting at that time. Along with the hunting of large game there was also the hunting of small game and gathering. The types of larger game available were those described as a determining factor in the existence of the patrilineal band. One must therefore ask the question, "If there is a relation between the type of subsistence activity and the level of social integration, was the early population that exploited these resources organized into patrilineal bands?" It seems difficult to avoid an affirmative answer if Steward's assumption is correct. If such were the case, then the nuclear family level of social integration in the Great Basin must represent a regression to a simpler level as the food resources decreased after the end of the Pleistocene to those historically available.

The pattern of life in the Great Basin developed through a versatility of response to environmental challenge, a flexibility in other responses, in personality if you will, that was not to be expected in a people with a single great food resource like the bison of the Plains or the salmon of the Northwest Coast. As a result of the exigencies of the food quest, intergroup relations in the Great Basin were fundamentally peaceful. This was the price of survival. The migratory life of the different families led them into contact with other families, into the same valleys and hills where food was to be found. Such contact served to spread information where the crops of seeds or other foods were better than in some other places. They also provided social contacts to alleviate the tedium of loneliness and a source of marriage partners. None of this could have happened if a warlike pattern of culture existed. Predatory bands developed only after the introduction of the horse and the coming of the whites, and the latter were usually the objects of predation. Those Indians who lacked horses favored a friendly relation with the whites in an effort to continue the pattern of intergroup relations with which they were familiar.

The Columbia Plateau required a somewhat different kind of social interaction to meet the challenges of that area than was successful in the Great Basin. The determining factor here was the dependence on anadromous fish for so much of their food. The fish, more numerous larger game animals than in the Great Basin, and generous supplies of roots in this area of greater precipitation and water, set the scene. Even with a more favorable habitat, though, subsistence was frequently very little above the starvation level. Lewis and Clark describe how, on their return up the Columbia in the spring of 1806 in the stretch of the river from The Dalles to Celilo Falls, where in the previous October they had seen the great stores of pounded salmon for food and trade, they found the Indians near starvation apparently because of the unaccustomed lateness of the salmon run. Primarily, it was the nature of the salmon runs which exerted the determining influence on the groups' movements.

Salmon of different varieties run in the Columbia River from early spring into the fall. The runs do not represent a constant supply of fish, for different varieties arrive in the river at different times. The various confluents of the river draw off segments of each run and the farther up the river the fewer the fish. The spawning runs of the salmon require some to move upstream 200 to 300 miles. The longer the upstream movement, the poorer the condition of the fish both because of the drain on their strength and the approach of the spawning activity. Some salmon do not eat on their spawning flight. Then, too, not all stretches of the river provide equally good sites for fishing. Some human groups were, therefore, more favorably situated than others, either because of their occupation of the more favorable fishing sites or because they occupied a lower stretch of the river where the salmon were more plentiful and in prime condition. The most favorable stretch for salmon fishing was from The Dalles to Celilo Falls, the country of the Chinook-speaking Wishram and Wasco, and the Sahaptin Tenino. This unequal distribution of the major food resource might very well have resulted in a warlike form of group interaction. On the contrary, intergroup relations on the Columbia were peaceful, with the only major hostile activity directed outward toward the Northern Paiute on the south and the western Plains people on the east. Aggression within the area was largely an individual or family affair and was settled without wider involvements. Perhaps aggression toward the south and east served adequately to satisfy any aggressive tendencies which might have built internally.

Two studies, Anastasio (1955) and Walker (1967), provide the best ethnographic evidence bearing on the relation of the salmon runs to group interaction. Anastasio's study is concerned in general with cooperative activity carried out by "Task Groups." Walker, while he is concerned with the Columbia Plateau as a whole, uses Nez Percé fishing practices to illustrate the general condition. By the ethnographic period, Plains influence had made itself felt in the presence and use of the horse, the bison hunt, and in the appearance of a movement toward development of chiefs and political organization. These patterns can be dismissed from the earlier lifeway of the Columbia Plateau peoples, and they do not figure in the discussion to follow.

Ownership of fishing places within an area was essentially ownership of "rights" vested in families and transmitted along family lines. Since the distribution of favorable sites was quite uneven along the river, some form of socially approved access to fishing spots by outsiders had to be developed to prevent conflict. Intermarriage between groups through band or village exogamy, with bilateral kinship, and residence in the main patrilocal over a period of time set up a network of intergroup relationships. In addition, there grew up a system of "trading partnerships" between males throughout different bands. Intermarriage and trading relationships constituted devices which provided friendly relations between groups over a wide area. These relations were closer the less the distance between bands, but the interlocking network eventually provided a series of friendly associations throughout the Columbia Plateau.

Bands even from different linguistic groups joined to hunt bison across the Rocky Mountains, but the organization lasted only as long as the hunt required. Other bands combined in common labor under a "boss" to build fishweirs where a major human effort was required. Again, the association was limited to the period required by the labor. These activities are the analogies of the antelope and rabbit drives of their southern neighbors.

The Nez Percé, the most easterly of the Columbia Plateau groups, visited when the salmon runs were at their optimum at the falls of the Willamette River at present-day Oregon City, at The Dalles-Celilo Falls area, and at Kettle Falls far up the main stem of the Columbia, as well as at intervening places. Their movement to the upriver fishing sites was progressively later. While this group represents the most widely ranging one, nevertheless, it is typical of the pattern in the Columbia Plateau.

It is estimated that fish supplied from one-third to one-half the total diet of the Columbia Plateau people. Probably the amount varied from group to group according to their energy and the accessibility of fishing sites. Following fish in importance in the diet were roots and bulbs, with seeds of less importance. The different ecological areas of the Columbia Plateau provided different resources, and this condition stimulated trade by which imbalances were adjusted and intergroup relations stimulated.

As fishing brought large numbers of people together, so did root gathering in various areas where there was a great abundance. The "first root" ceremony signaled the beginning of the collecting, as did the "first salmon" ceremony for fishing. Thereafter the various families could go on with the gathering. But these associations of food gatherers and fishermen were also the media for trade, discussion of matters of mutual concern, probably preliminaries to intermarriage, and gossip of all kinds, along with gambling on a large scale. These same by-products of group interaction occurred as the groups moved to and settled in, for a time, at the different fishing grounds they visited.

In contrast to the nuclear family level of integration characteristic of the Great Basin, there developed probably very early in the Columbia Plateau, certainly several thousand years ago, a band or village level of integration, undoubtedly a result of the ecological situation with its abundant river resources. Permanent villages were established in a linear pattern along the banks of streams, though there was no formal internal structuring of placement of houses. While the villages were permanent, they were not occupied the year around, for the food quest took the occupants on customary wanderings according to the times and places where food was to be found. The approach of winter saw the people return to their villages and prepare for the hardships sure to be ahead for them.

The variety of projectile point types and the similarity of the housekeeping equipment in the different but closely-spaced archæological sites in the John Day Dam area of the Columbia River has led Cole to infer that there was a patrilocal, exogamous form of social organization (personal communication D.L. Cole to L.S. Cressman). Supporting explanation may lie in the intermarriage, trade, and fishing practices discussed above. Whatever the case may be, one thing is clear—the "cross-utilization of economic resources in the Plateau" described by Walker (1967) makes the reconstruction of detailed prehistory of the area extraordinarily difficult, unless it is viewed in its larger aspect of adaptation to the ecological challenges and opportunities.

Class structure developed in the British Columbia coastal and island populations and spread southward in ever-lessening strength. It extended south of the Columbia River only weakly and spread upriver to the Wishram-Wasco groups where it appears in an extremely attenuated form. This aspect of social structure is to be associated with the very abundant food resources of the coastal area, for class differences are a luxury which can only be developed and enjoyed where there is a substantial food supply and the means and will to exploit it. Emphasis on wealth and class structure appeared as far south as northwestern California, especially among the Yurok, and here too is related to the exploitation of marine resources, especially sea mammals. Other than in these places, class structured societies did not develop in the Far West. A wealth of natural resources does not mean that a class differentiated society must or will develop; but such a society cannot develop without an adequate economic basis.

Summarizing this chapter, using as my major theoretical orientation the thesis that the end activity of all organisms, including man, is survival of the species, I discussed the development of effective subsistence devices, both technological and social. Since the Recent generic fauna is relatively inpoverished (Hibbard et al. 1965), composed of remnants left by the extinction of certain large Pleistocene forms with no new generic forms evolving, the human population had a less generous food supply available than their ancestors, a condition directing their subsistence activities toward more efficient exploitation of potential food resources. Ingenuity and imaginative innovation guided their efforts toward effective solutions to their subsistence problems.

I discussed the various resources in the different environments, pointing out how through interaction of culture and environment the different populations made their adaptations to the available resources. Finally, I discussed the levels of social integration in the Great Basin and the Columbia Plateau by which effective adaptation was made to the respective areal environments. The respective levels must be considered, it seems to me, as both the means and the end product and as an expression of ecological adaptation at the level of aboriginal culture. A class structured society occurred among the peoples of the British Columbia coastal and island area and within their range of influence, and among the Yurok, where a sufficiently high level of food collection above subsistence requirements made such development possible. A high level of food collection does not necessarily result in a class structured society, as the evidence from Central California shows, but without it classes do not develop. The appearance of a class structured society in the Pacific Northwest Coast area must, therefore, have been the result of historical-cultural events, but what they were is a problem for future research. Finally, it is a reasonable inference from the ethnographic record, supported by the archæological record, that the far-western peoples had achieved, in general, within the limits of aboriginal technology, the fullest possible exploitation of their environments. Probably the only significant exception is Central California, which might have developed agriculture under influence from the Southwest, but did not.

Monuments to the Dead

For each age is a dream that is dying,
Or one that is coming to birth.

Arthur W. E. O'Shaughnessy, Ode

IN MANY AREAS of the Far West the archæology has not been reported on in print with any completeness, even where extensive work has been done, and consequently discussions in this chapter will not treat equally all areas. The Great Basin, through the *University of Utah Anthropological Papers,* monographs, and journal articles, is well reported on. Likewise, California, through the *Reports of the University of California Archaeological Survey,* the *Annual Reports of the Archaeological Survey* of the University of California at Los Angeles, reports of the Southwest Museum, Los Angeles, the San Diego Museum of Man, and journal articles, is fairly well reported in available literature. Much of the tremendous amount of "salvage archæology" done along the middle Columbia and lower Snake rivers still awaits publication.

By 1942 significant contributions to the study of Early Man in the Southwest and the Great Basin had been made. Sound information on the basic character of the Great Basin culture had been published and a conceptual foundation adumbrated. World War II obviously put an end to all archæological research. Following the war there was a tremendous interest in archæological research stimulated in part and made effective by adequate funding from the federal government, something completely lacking before the war. The work of the last twenty years has provided most of the information for the prehistory of much of the western United States.

It is, I think, useful to give initially a short statement of the history of archæological work in each area, for this shows the particular lines of development. In some areas the first work was done by museums intent on making collections; in others the work was problem oriented and usually directed by university departments. The different orientations of these two kinds of programs had a very definite influence on developments in the respective areas. The pragmatic character of the salvage archæology,

for example, gave little time for the development of a conceptual framework. Material had to be immediately saved from destruction. The results of salvage archæology and problem-oriented archæology, therefore, require different kinds of analysis and evaluation. The first requires an empirical approach while the second invites an added theoretical one, and my discussion will vary in its approach from area to area according to the nature of the available information. I have previously (Cressman 1966a) reviewed critically some of the theoretical approaches to far-western prehistory and shall not repeat that material.

THE PACIFIC NORTHWEST

The Jesup North Pacific Expedition, organized by Franz Boas at the turn of the century and taking the name of its benefactor, operated out of the American Museum of Natural History. Its purpose was the exploration of the relations between the cultures of the Northwest Coast and those of northeast Asia and the intercultural relations of the Northwest Coast tribes. Archæology was included in the field of study, and Harlan I. Smith (1909a, b) carried out work for the expedition along the coast of Washington and southern British Columbia. Smith's excavation of the Eburne shell mound near the city of Vancouver, British Columbia, provided, as I pointed out in Chapter 5, the basis for the theory of a migration from the interior to the coast resulting in the foundation of the Northwest Coast culture. Drucker (1943) in 1938 extended Smith's coverage by making an archæological survey of the northern British Columbia coast. His 1943 publication incorporates these results with related published accounts and museum collections. Harlan I. Smith extended his work into the interior at Lytton and Lillooet, British Columbia, and the Yakima River valley in west-central Washington, and he brought together a considerable amount of information on material in private collections. H. W. Krieger published very short reports (1927, 1928a, b) on excavations in the Priest Rapids area of the Columbia River in central Washington. No full report of these excavations has ever been published.

Strong, Schenck, and Steward (1930) reported on their excavations and examinations of private collections from The Dalles-Deschutes region of the Columbia River. Most of their excavations were on Miller's Island near the mouth of the Deschutes River, with limited examination of the Wakemap Mound on the Washington side of the river at the head of Five-Mile Rapids. A very limited check was also made on mounds along the Calapuya River in the Willamette Valley. Most of the material recovered in this work was late prehistoric. The publication has considerable value for the fine illustrations of artifacts in private collections from the area and from their excavations, although the collectors' material lacks time depth information.

In 1934 H. W. Krieger was sent by the Smithsonian Institution, after considerable urging from various sources, to excavate in the Bonneville Dam area. This dam was the first in the series of Columbia River dams to be built. In addition to excavated material, he secured a large amount of material from private collectors, which is now at the Smithsonian Institution. No report on this material has been made. Collier, Hudson, and Ford (1942) reported on the survey and excavation in the Grand Coulee Dam reservoir area on the Columbia River in central Washington. This project was carried out at first by student volunteers, without pay, from the University of Oregon with logistic support from the Bureau of Reclamation, the builder of the dam. The Eastern Washington Historical Society at Spokane provided limited financial support for food. Later Washington State College and the University of Washington also contributed support and eventually a Youth Work Project was established to carry on the work. Present-day archæologists used to generous funding for their programs cannot be blamed if they look back with disbelief on this Grand Coulee project. Alex Krieger and Arlo Ford were the first student volunteers, and at the close of my season of fieldwork elsewhere, they were joined by Robert L. Stephenson, Allen Murphy, and Kenneth Leather-

man from my field party. These students were devoted to archæology and deserve much credit, which they have not received, for the work they did. The Bonneville and Grand Coulee Dam projects were the first efforts at salvage archæology in the Pacific Northwest.

Ray (1939), working entirely from ethnographic data and using the age-area method to establish relative time depth of cultural phenomena, demonstrated at the ethnographic time level the integrity of the Plateau as a culture area as well as some of its external cultural relations. Ray's analysis presented certain results important for the archæologist. First, he showed that while the Plateau had a cultural integrity as a whole, it had significant subdivisions in both an east-west and north-south direction. The area bordering the Cascade Mountains on the west was characterized by a large number of cultural items derived from the coast, especially in areas adjacent to the Fraser and Columbia rivers. In the center of this north-south corridor, the coastal influences were much less marked, and this area was closely oriented toward the central region of the Plateau to the east. Along the eastern edge of the Plateau, bordering on the western flanks of the Rocky Mountains, was a north-south corridor of strong Plains influence. Between these two north-south corridors, and tying in with the middle portion of the western corridor, was an area least affected by diffusion of foreign influences, which was presumed to represent the part of the Plateau that preserved the core of early culture.

Ray also divided the Plateau from north to south into three subareas: (1) the Athapascans, (2) the people of the Fraser Plateau between the Athapascans and the international border, and (3) those on the American side of the border. He points out (1939:149) that the linguistic boundary between Salish and Sahaptin-speaking peoples lies about 180 miles south of the cultural boundary between the Canadian and American groups. Of particular importance to the archæologist is his statement concerning the process of diffusion of alien elements into the Plateau.

> On the west the coastal elements were received gradually over a long period. A process of amalgamation kept pace with the innovations. But on the east very nearly the whole pattern of Plains culture swept over the adja-

cent Plateau in one great wave. The result was not transformation, as on the west, but mere superimposition. . . . On the whole, the Plateau has been more receptive to detached elements of culture than to whole complexes (146).

Ray's statements on the historical processes that reach beyond the time of historical documentation or human memory must be considered as a series of hypotheses which challenge the archæologist. Archæological work during the last fifteen years has provided a large body of evidence bearing on some of Ray's hypotheses, and it is the result of this work which I shall report. Unfortunately, due to the pressure of fieldwork under the salvage program, much of the pertinent material is not adequately available in published form.

The Fraser Plateau

Sanger (1964, 1966, 1967) has continued the work initiated by Borden in interior British Columbia. This work has been concentrated in a relatively small but critical area on the Fraser and Thompson rivers. The results are not claimed to be representative of all localities, but they do suggest the probable sequence of events in the southern portion of the Interior Plateau. As Sanger (1967:188) notes, "The radiocarbon-dated components comprise the first regional cultural chronology with any time depth from the Interior Plateau of British Columbia." Sanger's periods and dates are:

> Late Period from A.D. 1 to A.D. 1800
> Middle Period from 3000 B.C. to A.D. 1
> Early Period from 5500 B.C. to 3000 B.C.

After this sequence was set up, a C-14 date of 4700 B.C.±110 (I-2367) for an early component of the Middle Period was received. This is 1,700 years earlier than the previous date, but whether it will force revision of the chronology is not yet clear. Diagnostic materials, as to be expected in open sites, consist mostly of stone artifacts, including projectile points, microblades, and microblade cores. Woodworking tools also have a long history, and evidence for housepits occurs in the Middle Period.

Sanger states that the projectile points "appear" to represent two "traditions." It is not clear to me exactly what the distinctive attributes of each tradition are, but apparently the discrimination is based

upon character of workmanship, fineness of manufacture, and form. Both leaf-shaped and stemmed points with side and corner notches occur as well as stemmed points without notching. Lateral and basal grinding of the stems is extensive until late in the Middle Period and to some degree continues into the Late. Finally, after A.D. 1000, the small Desert Side-Notched point becomes the dominant form.

The use of edge and basal grinding on stemmed and notched points is interesting. The use of this device on fluted points and other "early" varieties is generally assumed to have been for the purpose of protecting the seizing because the edges of the points projected beyond the sides of the shaft, and, unless dulled, would have cut through the haft wrapping. On the other hand, the development of stems and notching is considered to have provided a more efficient hafting method in which the sides of the shaft extended beyond the edges of the stem. It is certainly generally true that edge and basal grinding are not characteristic of notched-and-stemmed points. The persistence of the technique described by Sanger may be a striking example of the persistence of a cultural element long after it was functionally useful; or it might represent the adoption of a trait, the significance of which was unknown, but which for some reason achieved a high cultural value. In view of the situation elsewhere, it seems to me that this attribute of the projectile points may be one of considerable significance both historically and psychologically. The most important information derived from the projectile points, however, is the fact that their form and technique indicate an orientation of their users primarily toward the Alberta Plains rather than toward the Columbia Plateau to the south, although in the Late Period similarity with the Columbia Plateau appears.

Microblades occur in large numbers, especially in the Middle Period, although they also occur in limited numbers in both the Early and Late Periods. A single Early-Period microblade from the Drynoch Slide site is dated at 5580 B.C.±270 (GSC-530). Both tongue-shaped and polyhedral cores are found, but the former are more numerous. The tongue-shaped cores definitely indicate a historical connection with Alaska and the southwestern Yukon, "approximating the antiquity of some of the oldest microblades radiocarbon-dated in western North America" (Sanger 1967:191). Microblades occur elsewhere in the Fraser Plateau, but their recorded appearance is equivalent to the late-Middle period of Sanger's sequence. Borden reports microblades from near the head of the Fraser Canyon, and farther north in the Interior Plateau at Natalkuz Lake he has excavated microblades dated at 461 B.C. (Borden 1962b:17).

Woodworking, as inferred from the presence of antler wedges and ground beaver incisors, begins in the Early Period and continues throughout. In the later Middle Period, nephrite celts and pecked stone mauls appear in the inventory together with houses of semisubterranean type.

The sites indicate a settlement pattern along the rivers and lakes, and probably seasonal use of different sites according to the availability of fish and other game, a pattern characteristic of the area at the ethnographic horizon.

The Columbia Plateau

The archæological salvage program along the Columbia River in the series of reservoir areas there has produced a tremendous amount of information on the prehistory of the area from The Dalles, where the river begins its course through the gorge of the Cascades, to a point well above the Vantage area on the middle Columbia. Unfortunately, little of the results of this work has been published; reports to the sponsoring authority have generally been available, but these give but a limited record of the results of the work. Until this mass of material is published and synthesized, no really firm picture of the localized developments and their significance in the larger framework of the area is possible. The only major archæological study directed toward interpretation of the developments of Plateau culture is that by Swanson (1962d). The more important site reports, in which some limited attempt is made to evaluate the significance of results in the wider framework of the Plateau, are Cressmen et al. (1960), Osborne (1957a), and Shiner (1961). I shall use, too, information personally supplied by archæologists working in the middle Columbia and lower Snake river areas.

Swanson (1962d:iii) attempted to present "a pioneer sequence for the Columbia Plateau in Washing-

ton." Briefly, he infers the basic pattern of Plateau culture to have been established by about A.D. 1200–1300 in the middle Columbia area, although he states that some earlier manifestations are found both to the north and south of the area of his work at Vantage. Riverside villages appear to have been established, and the presence of marine shells indicates an active trade with the coast. This interaction is inferred to have been a stimulating factor in the development of larger communities.

Previous to A.D. 1200, the occupation sites are away from the Columbia River, and on the basis of the artifacts and their distribution he (Swanson 1962: 83) postulates a "forest-hunting culture . . . spread along the foothills and in the valleys on both sides of the Cascade Range." This culture he believes was "probably established not later than 1500 B.C." He sees the structure of Plateau culture emerging "from that of this Northern Forest Culture, [and] it seems likely that the same would be true for the historic pattern of the Coast Salish." Antecedents of his Northern Forest culture he sees as possibly related to the Lind Coulee manifestation (cf. Chapter 4).

Swanson (1962:38) sets up a sequence of three phases "based upon composite characteristics drawn from a number of archæological sites. . . . The phases are intended to distinguish minor, but probably significant, changes which took place in time." Efforts were made to establish a chronology largely from geological depositional sequences, which reflected inferred climatic changes, volcanic ash deposits, and cultural cross dating with other sites in the Columbia Plateau. Swanson's series, in order from earliest to latest, is: Vantage I-II, Frenchman Springs I-III, Cayuse I-III. Vantage I is assigned to the Anathermal; Vantage II to the Altithermal; Frenchman Springs I appears at or near the end of the Altithermal. The temporal position of Cayuse I is not suggested directly, but since that phase is marked by the movement of settlements to the riverbank and the appearance of fishing gear, it must be dated about A.D. 1300, the time at which Swanson fixes the establishment of the Plateau culture.

Two studies, Osborne (1957a) and Shiner (1961), based on excavations and surveys in the McNary Dam reservoir area during the period 1947 to 1952, were the first of many projects carried out by the

River Basin Survey's salvage program and are pioneer work for modern scientific excavation for the Columbia Plateau. Osborne's sites, however, lacked appreciable time depth, and he was not able to add significantly to the record of cultural development in the Columbia Plateau.

Shiner's conclusions are that

> The local sequence in the McNary region, even though dates are not available, shows a gradual development from simple to complex. Although there seemed to be two horizons in which a number of new artifacts appeared, at Cold Springs and again at the beginning of the late prehistoric period, there is no reason to believe that culture changes of a revolutionary nature took place. There is no evidence of a migration or of a new culture appearing on the scene. The persistence of old artifact types and the gradual acquisition of new ones tend to confirm a local development of culture (Shiner 1961:260).

Butler (1961b:70) proposed the concept of an Old Cordilleran culture as a "working hypothesis, an historical construct subject to logical analysis." This hypothesis, in part, runs as follows:

> That there is a cultural tradition which is represented by one of the early components or a series of components at sites along the Pacific Ranges of the cordilleras of the New World as far south as southern California, and in northeastern Mexico and on down into South America, and as far north as the Columbia Valley and perhaps further into the Frazer [sic] Valley. That it is a tradition characterized by a leaf-shaped point and blade complex, along with a generalized assortment of cutting, chopping and scraping implements. That its carriers pursued a generalized hunting-fishing-gathering economy. That during the Altithermal, the outward-pushing Desert Culture tradition soon modified and eventually dominated this tradition but in those areas far removed from Desert Culture influence, the tradition developed along independent lines, becoming a maritime tradition in the Northwest Coast area. That in its earliest arrival in the Pacific Northwest, the tradition occurs in sites more to the interior than the coast, but that it rapidly penetrated to the fall line of the major rivers draining the interior and subsequently spread out from there. That it arrived in the Pacific Northwest probably no earlier than 12,000 years ago, or near the end of the Pleistocene and was established in South America by at least 8,000 years ago. And finally, that it was contemporaneous with such Early Lithic traditions as Clovis, Folsom, Scottsbluff, etc....

The diagnostic attribute of this tradition is the Cascade point, originally defined as follows: "generally long, narrow, leaf-shaped or bi-pointed items which tend to be quite thick in proportion to their width . . . and are usually thickest above the butt end; none shows evidence of basal thinning. Most of the points are diamond-shaped in cross-section, particularly above the butt end" (Butler 1961b:28).

More recent work has not borne out Butler's proposed early dates, nor his suggestion of a two-continent distribution, but has shown quite clearly that a generalized hunting-fishing-gathering culture such as he described occurred widely in the Columbia Plateau region between approximately 8,000 and 5,000 years ago (Leonhardy and Rice 1970). It is equally clear, however, that the Old Cordilleran culture was not the basal culture of the Northwest, and that a well-defined cultural complex several thousand years older must be considered for this position.

If any single unifying concept serves to explain the development of the culture of the Columbia and Fraser plateaus it is to be found in the processes by which the early people learned to exploit the fisheries of the great Columbia and Fraser river systems; salmon became the basic economic element in the subsistence culture in both areas.

Extensive archæological work on both sides of the Columbia River from The Dalles upriver to its confluence with the Snake River and along the lower reaches of the Snake clearly demonstrate the truth of the proposition just stated. Work in the area is still underway both in the field and in the preparation of reports. The University of Oregon carried out the fieldwork from The Dalles to the head of slack water below the McNary Dam, while Washington State University has been responsible for work on the lower Snake River and its tributaries. The University of Washington carried out the excavation of Wakemap Mound, apparently a Late-Period site, on the Washington shore at the head of the Five-Mile Rapids during the building of The Dalles Dam.

Information generously supplied by the archæologists who have worked in the area and reports furnished to the funding organizations make it clear that a fairly uniform or common adaptation to the problems of riverine exploitation was developed between 11,000 and 10,000 years ago. Of course expectable local variations in artifact assemblages occur.

The Dalles site at Five-Mile Rapids provided the finest fishing locality in this entire stretch of the Columbia River, and it is only reasonable to expect the evidence for that activity to be prominently displayed there. The exceptional preservation by mineralization of all bone and antler material in the early levels laid down before approximately 8,000 years ago provided a full inventory of the artifacts and animals used for food and perhaps even other purposes. I shall briefly summarize the record drawing mostly from that for the Five-Mile Rapids site (Cressman and Cole 1962).

The earliest evidence of man on the middle Columbia River is from the glacial Lake Missoula flood (previously called the Spokane Flood) gravels on the John Day River high above its confluence with the Columbia River (Cressman et al. 1960). I discussed the basalt knife artifact and its provenience briefly in Chapter 4. As I pointed out then, the presence of this knife in these gravels is clear proof of the presence of man in the area before the flood, which occurred at approximately 20,000 years ago. It also indicates his presence before the Vashon Stade of 25,000 years ago closed the ice-free corridor. The earliest artifacts in a cultural setting or context occur between 10,000 to 11,000 years ago in a series of sites between The Dalles and the lower Snake River.

I (Cressman et al. 1960) presented the archæological record at The Dalles in terms of a chronological sequence using the segments Early, Transitional, and Late. The Early Period dates from about 11,000 to 7,500 years ago; the time between 10,000 and 8,500 years ago was apparently the period of maximum cultural activity. C-14 dates are: 9,785± 220 (Y-340); 7,675±100 (Y-341); 7,875±100 (Y-342); 6,090±80 (Y-343); 2,395±80 (Y345a).

Apparently the earliest use of the site, and this is probably true for the whole stretch of the river, was not for fishing but for hunting. The animals hunted were fox, a member of the cat family, muskrat, beaver, marmot, cervid (elk or deer), a canid (probably coyote), and seal. A cormorant, a bald eagle, and three gulls also belong to this stage. No fish bones appear. The limited number of these animals, only a single specimen or two or three, suggests sporadic use of the area by small hunting parties. (Note: all bones of one species are counted as those of an individual unless there is more than one specimen of the same bone.)

About 10,000 years ago a sudden and significant change in the culture occurred, both in the range of artifact types and the numbers of specimens for a given period of time. In addition, and this was of the greatest importance, salmon bones appeared for the first time. Bird bones began to increase in the deposit at the same time, for the three species mentioned above, and others as well, appear in Level 32, the point at which the sudden change appears. In contrast, the terrestrial animals occur in small numbers and the rate of occurrence is essentially constant. Salmon bones and bird bones increase in numbers slowly for a short period of time then very rapidly, as though methods of taking this prey had been perfected. The record of change in incidence for the birds, fish, and cultural activity is the same, all showing a slow increase, a rapid rise to a high point or plateau, then a slow decline to the end of the Early Period, over a segment of time of some 1,500 to 2,000 years. The nature of the sediments at the site indicates a high water level in the Columbia throughout most of this period.

The Early Period is characterized by a rich bone and antler industry, burins, bolas, the core-and-blade technology, unifacial and bifacial blades made both by percussion and pressure, great numbers of salmon vertebrae, bones of large raptorial birds and a few of other kinds, mammal bones, red ochre in all stages of preparation from the raw material to the finished pigment, and projectile points, most of which are nonstemmed or have a stem tapering to a pointed or slightly rounded base. There are girdled weights we called plumb bobs, probably used with fishnets, for nets must have been used to take the greater number of salmon. Burins were used to manufacture products from elk antler, and the nibbling method was used to make circular cuts to separate pieces into smaller segments. Antler wedges, much like splitting wedges, were used to soften and polish skins (perhaps bird as well as mammal). Antler cylinders were used for stone flaking. The compound atlatl and the boat-shaped atlatl weight were in use. The use of red ochre suggests ceremonial activity. Lithic products were uniformly of a very high quality of craftsmanship, and the use of heat to reduce the refractory quality of stone in the production of points was practiced. The period is one of a significantly high level of cultural development; it represents a culture that was based on full exploitation of riverine resources. In handling the material one gets the impression that there were values placed on high quality workmanship, that the people were innovative, not only in technology but in the development of ceremonial and æsthetic values.

By 8,000 years ago the vigor of this culture was sharply declining, and by 7,500 years ago the hallmarks of the Early Period had largely disappeared. The girdled bola, the raptorial birds, and the burin and related bone and antler tools no longer appear in the deposit. They trickle out, as it were. Other basic artifact types occur; there is change but not a sudden break. A climatic change is in process as shown by the beginning of cross-bedding in wind-blown sand in the site deposits.

The Transitional Period extends from 7,500 to 5,000 years ago (all dates are approximations extrapolated from C-14 determinations for the Early and Late Periods and character of fill). The artifacts are like those found in the Early, but, except for a few pieces, the really distinctive Early types disappear. Choppers, cutting tools, and projectile points and knives make up the bulk of the deposits, and with about the same incidence as in the late Early Period. Some chemical property of the fill evidently leached out bone and any antler material, which may have been left by the occupants of the site; none appears after a few specimens in the early part of the period until sometime after 1820. Human skeletons of that date appear as patterns of dust, completely decalcified. Evidence indicates that fishing continued by use of nets, for the plumb bob type of weight continues in use. On the other hand, the girdled bolas associated in the Early Period with the large raptorial birds no longer occur. Burins drop out of the inventory suggesting that the cervids, with which they may have been associated, were, like the raptorial birds, no longer available. Marked cross-bedding characterizes the site fill indicating strong winds, probably erosion which exposed sand surfaces, higher temperatures than previously, and a lower level of the river; all conditions are characteristic of those that are thought to have obtained during the Altithermal climatic period.

One cutting tool, a peripherally flaked cobble, begins to gain favor at this time at the expense of blades. This tool is made from a flat stone found on the exposed gravel bars and is given a cutting edge by knocking off flakes around the edge. It was much easier to make than the flaked blades and, while much less attractive, probably served almost as well. Its greatest popularity is in the Late Period.

The Late Period begins at approximately 6,000 years ago. It is well marked by an increased intensity in the use of the site; a C-14 date of 6090±80 B.P. (Y-343) fixes the time of the beginning. Aeolian derived sand and a heavy concentration of cultural material comprises the fill. While some artifacts of a generalized use continue from the Early through the Transitional into the Late Period, this last period is characterized by an exuberant development of stone sculpture, of carving and incising of bone, and of a range in varieties and quality of fabrication of projectile points probably unequaled in the Far West. Many of these artifacts were ceremonial; others were objects for everyday use. There were carved mortars and pestles, bone carved with representative and abstract designs, animals sculptured in stone, elaborate petroglyph designs, nipple-ended mauls, pipes, beads, and so on. Since there is the continuation of certain artifact types from the very beginning of occupation to the end, it is difficult to avoid the conclusion that rejuvenation of the culture about 6,000 years ago, with the appearance of a few new traits and the subsequent elaboration of the total inventory into a distinctive cultural expression, was due to the introduction of novel traits carried by migrants from elsewhere, probably the Great Basin. Along with this cultural stimulus there occurred an improvement in the climate about 4,500 years ago, which would have improved the total environment as habitat. The production of ceremonial and art objects in the Late Period beyond those things needed for subsistence parallels the situation in the Early Period and indicates that the economy in these periods was sufficient to provide a social surplus.

Leonhardy and Rice (1970) have more finely divided and detailed the sequence for the area in their "A Proposed Culture Typology for the Lower

Snake River Region," based on data mostly accumulated since the publication of the work at The Dalles. Rice (1972) has since described more fully the Windust phase, first in the sequence. The list of phases and their distinguishing characteristics follows.

*Windust Phase: 10,500±8000 B.P.** The artifact inventory consists of projectile point forms having "relatively short blades, shoulders of varying prominence, principally straight or contracting stems and straight or slightly concave bases" (Rice 1972:4). Rarely lanceolate points occur; large end scrapers, single and multiple faceted burins, bolas, large scraping planes, uniface and biface choppers, together with the points, compose most of the lithic materials. The lithic technology was well developed producing tabular and prismatic flakes, the latter from polyhedral cores. Bone artifacts include needles, atlatl spurs, and unidentifiable fragments.

The faunal remains are all Recent with a variety of elk (*Cervus canadensis*) larger than the type now found in the area.

Cremation of the dead is apparently indicated at the Marmes Rockshelter.

The Windust Phase shares many artifact varieties with the middle Columbia sites: Wildcat Canyon in the John Day Dam reservoir (not yet reported on) and the Five-Mile Rapids site at The Dalles. Leonhardy has expressed the opinion that the Northern Great Basin is the source of this middle Columbia and lower Snake River culture (personal communication, F.C. Leonhardy to L.S. Cressman).

Cascade Phase: 8000 B.P.-5000 B.P. This manifestation is essentially that earlier referred to by Butler (1961a) as the Old Cordilleran culture. Two subphases are recognized, but the only difference between them is the presence of the side-notched point in the later as a subphase indicator.

The Cascade point is now dominant and in some components exclusive. The lithic inventory is essentially the same as that for the Windust phase except for Cascade and side-notched point types and the

edge-ground cobble,† which, along with the Casade point, is spoken of as a hallmark of the phase. The bone tool inventory has not changed from the Windust series. The addition of salmon as an important item to the food resources appears; otherwise the same foods continued to be exploited. Both flexed and extended burials occur. *Olivella* shell beads with the grave goods indicate trade with the coast.

A hiatus in the chronology and the cultural tradition follows the Cascade Phase. The chronological hiatus may be as much as 2,000 years or considerably less. In view of the uncertainty, the next phase is dated immediately after the ending of the Cascade Phase.

Tucannon Phase: 5000 B.P.-2500 B.P. The cultural inventory indicates a clear break with the earlier tradition. Two new types of projectile points replace the earlier varieties, one kind having a short blade with shoulders of varying prominence and contracting stem, and a second kind notched low on the side or corners to produce an expanding stem with short barbs. Added to the usual utility tools are sinkers, hopper mortar bases, and pestles. An antler wedge and a bone shuttle for net weaving occur. Atlatls appear to be lacking. Lithic technology is crude and improverished when compared with that of the preceding and succeeding phases. A single flexed burial occurs. Fish and the usual land mammals of the area comprise the food inventory. River mussels appear to be a major part of the diet rather than casual additions as earlier.

Harder Phase: 2500 B.P.-700 B.P. Two subphases are distinguished based upon differences in settlement patterns and stratigraphy: an early period with scattered house pits and a later with a village clustering The village house seems to have been a shallow, circular excavation covered by a conical framework of split poles in turn covered by mats or thatch. The artifact inventories of the subphases are essentially identical although variation in the relative proportions occur. The points are mostly corner and basal notched. Lanceolate and pentagonal knives occur in

---

* I have changed the authors' dates from those of the common calendar to a close approximation of the customary radiocarbon use, i.e., to years B.P., Before the Present, with 1950 as the base referent.

† The edge-ground cobble is the same artifact as the side-polisher found at The Dalles where it occurs at least 1,000 years earlier. Likewise, salmon at The Dalles were being used as an important food resource 1,000 or more years before their use appears in the Cascade Phase.

both subphases. Bone awls, needles, beads, and incised gaming pieces are present. The fauna, with the exception of the domesticated dog, approximates that of the preceding phase.

Piqúnin Phase: 700 years B.P.-300 years B.P. Information on this phase is derived from scattered campsites with no depth and one stratified village site, Wexpúsnime (45GA61), which consists of circular house pits, each about 6 meters in diameter and 50 centimeters deep, with a superstructure similar to that described for the Harder Phase. Multiple floors indicate reuse of the same pit over the years.

The delicate corner-notched and base-notched projectile points characteristic of late times on the middle Columbia now predominate. A concave bitted scraper suggests a woodworking tool; lanceolate and pentagonal knives continue. Decorated pestles are added to the previous lithic inventory. Composite harpoon parts, matting needles, bone awls, and twined basketry all occur.

The Numipu Phase is "a putative phase intended to represent the archæological manifestations of Ethnographic Indian Culture . . ." and is outside my frame of reference. No discussion will be given.

It should be possible by careful analysis, when full reports are available from the sites along this stretch of the Columbia and lower Snake rivers, to determine with reasonable confidence when the socio-economic-kinship patterns related to the fisheries, described in the last chapter, occurred. These patterns were certainly instrumental in the rapid diffusion of many cultural traits.

It is now possible to say that the appearance of true Plateau culture is relatively late, occurring certainly after 4,000 years ago. The Fraser Plateau culture, with northern and eastern affinities, provided the base for the regional development of the Fraser Plateau beginning some 7,500 years ago. A regional development starting by at least 10,000 years ago on the middle Columbia and lower Snake rivers had passed through its climax by 7,500 years ago. The rejuvenation of the culture along the Columbia River after 6,000 years ago evidently resulted in expansion and diffusion of culture northward along the Okanagan River into the Fraser Plateau; diffusion in the opposite direction also occurred. Diffusion to

and from the coast also occurred in both areas. In the Late Period (or Tucannon phase of Leonhardy and Rice) the Plateau culture area, with expectable minor variations, was firmly established.

THE FRASER LOWLAND AND ADJACENT ISLANDS

I include under this rather awkward heading the lower Fraser Canyon from north of Yale, the lowland valley of the Fraser from the canyon to the sea, the islands lying between the mainland and Vancouver Island, Vancouver Island, and a part of Washington south to 48° north latitude, or about the northern limit of Puget Sound. Archæologically, at least during the last four millennia, this area seems to have been characterized by essentially related cultural developments. Borden (various) has provided the source of information for the Fraser Canyon and the valley of the Fraser. Kidd (1964) has synthesized the material from the available sources on the islands and the Washington mainland. My material is drawn from these two sources. Data on Vancouver Island is provided by Capes (1964), on the Gulf Islands by Mitchell (1968b).

The Fraser Canyon

Borden's site, DjRi 3, in the Fraser Canyon is the earliest firmly-documented record of occupation. It is questionable if it should be discussed as a part of the record of this area or of the interior. Typologically it seems to reflect more an interior orientation than a westerly one. It has been interpreted as a seasonal fishing site, quite correctly in my opinion, and as such it had to draw its users from an area where there was an available population. There was such in the interior, at any rate to the south, and there is none documented for the immediate west. The typology suggests the same line of argument. However, given the location on the western side of Cascade divide, and in view of Borden's cogent remark that because of isostatic depression of the Fraser Lowland in the early post-Pleistocene, the Indians who first fished here "were little more than 20 miles from the mouth of the river and salt water" (Borden 1962b:11), I am including it here.

The date of the earliest occupation of this site is 9000±150 B.P. (S-113) followed by a later deposit at 8150±310 B.P. (S-47). Another culture-bearing stratum is dated at 7350±150 B.P. (S-61) and this closes the early use of this site. Borden designates the culture represented by these three dates as the Milliken phase. This is followed by the Mt. Mazama phase, dated only indirectly by the presence of volcanic ash. The Mt. Mazama phase appears to be a hypothetical construct for while it is associated with Zone D, this zone is described as "Sterile gravel and coarse sands laid down by a small stream now extinct" (Borden 1961a:6, Table 1). There is, then, a hiatus in the occupation of DjRi 3 until the Baldwin phase, which extended from 2800±130 (M-1513) to 2360±60 B.P. (S-112). Another gap in the sequence is followed by the Emery phase, estimated to have begun shortly after A.D. 500, and this is followed by the Esilao phase starting at 570±100 years ago, or approximately A.D. 1280 (M-1511).

The Esilao Village site, DjRi 5, contributes a somewhat shorter cultural record to the canyon sequence. It begins with the Eayem phase extending from 5490±500 (M-1547) to 4420±160 B.P. (M-1544). A break in the sequence extends to 2000±120 B.P. (M-1543), a date marking the beginning of the Skamel phase. This short phase is followed by the Emery and Esilao phases, as at Site DjRi 3. The Eayem phase overlaps the upper part of the Mt. Mazama phase and apparently fills in part of the subsequent hiatus noted above for Site DjRi 3.

The two sites discussed are separated by only a few miles with DjRi 3 being the more westerly. The cultural record prior to about A.D. 500 seems to consist of a series of components distinctive for each site; thereafter the record is common and the same phases are represented in both sites. Exactly what the significance of this fact is is not clear. It may represent different social groups, different opportunities in the use of the canyon for taking fish depending on the availability of suitable fishing sites, or some other reason. Because of the turbulent history of the river in this early post-glacial period, it is likely that there was considerable modification of the banks and consequently changes in the availability of good fishing sites.

The artifact inventory of the canyon sequence may be roughly stated as follows:

Milliken Phase: 9000±150–7350±150 B.P. Heavy choppers, flake choppers, scrapers, etc., occur throughout the phase, and in the later part are small bi-points, constricted-base bi-points, large bi-points, scrapers, and burins. This inventory is strongly suggestive of that of the Early Period at Five-Mile Rapids on the Columbia River, although it lacks bone and antler and fish bones, a condition probably due to chemical action of the containing earth. Bolas are also lacking, but the subsistence activities at the two sites are apparently alike.

The Mt. Mazama Phase: est. 6300 B.P. Heavy choppers, bi-points, leaf-shaped points with a straight base, large flake scrapers, etc., mark this phase, which appears to be a rather weak representation of the previous one. There is no clear break between them. Both in time and in the poverty of the inventory compared with that of the preceding phase, this phase is comparable to the Transitional Period at Five-Mile Rapids. This observation raises the question: What situation or condition of general applicability could be the cause of a decline in occupational intensity on both the Columbia and the Fraser at this time? The Altithermal is too easy an answer, for the pollen record shows that while this period of aridity is recorded for British Columbia, it was of shorter duration and evidently less severe than south of the Columbia Plateau.

The Eayem Phase: 5490±500–4420±160 B.P. Here are flake scrapers, large, flat pebble choppers and large flake knives, points like those from the Early Period at Five-Mile Rapids, as well as shouldered and straight-stemmed points, ground slate knife fragments, drills, and ornaments. The ground slate knife fragments and the stemmed and shouldered points are significant additions to the inventory.

The Baldwin Phase: 2800–2360 B.P. The mortar, metate, and mano appear for the first time suggesting a southern interior relation. Choppers and the general type of cutting and scraping tools occur. A few Cascade points appear and a variety of stemmed and shouldered points, but no notched of any kind. Microblades and polyhedral cores, labrets, saws, ground bit adzes, ground splitting stone wedges, pestle-like hammers for driving wedges, and beads are now present. This range of artifacts clearly indicates the approach to the full-scale ethnographic culture. The tools necessary for a heavy woodworking industry are now present.

A puzzling problem is the lack of any obvious close connection with the interior culture reported by Sanger in the Lytton area a hundred miles up-river. Micro-blades first appear in the canyon sites more than 4,000 years later than in the Lytton area, but even then the tongue-shaped cores found at Lytton do not occur in the canyon nor do the micro-blades occur in the canyon in such large proportions as at the interior sites. It hardly seems probable that fishing parties from the Lytton area would come to the canyon when equally good sites were available much closer, and if such were the case, that they would not have left some of the diagnostic traits of their culture other than generalized implements and fishing gear needed for a special and short-lived activity. Certainly from the Baldwin phase on there is evidence of greater social mobility and perhaps coincident population increase if the greater number of traits held in common between Canyon and Interior can be used as an index.

Since the remaining phases represent merely an extension of the Baldwin phase pattern into the ethnographic period, there is no necessity to discuss them here.

Borden (1968b) described the Pasika complex (Pasika phase), a strictly pebble tool industry, which he interprets to be earlier than the Milliken phase. The site (DjRi 7) is at South Yale on the south side of the Fraser River about 2½ miles downstream from the Milliken locality. The materials are found on the surface and embedded in the five terraces above the present level of the river. Borden infers that those in the lowest terrace, which was being cut at the time of the Milliken phase, are intrusive from the upper terraces. No living floors or hearths or any organic material has been found at the locality. Dating, therefore, has to be done by reference to geological features.

There seems to be no doubt that most of these "Pebble Tools," although possibly not all, are artifacts. They are unifacially flaked by percussion by which one or more large flakes were detached from the rock. In some cases smaller flakes were removed to resharpen or modify the edge. The cutting edge is formed by the contact of the cortex with the edge of the flake scar.

The chronological position of the terraces at South Yale is in debate. Borden takes the position that the terraces date from the Everson Interstadial, about 10,000 B.C. to 7500 B.C. Geologists, however, disagree, and it is the opinion of this group that the Fraser terraces are post-Pleistocene, that is post-Sumas (Mitchell 1965). Obviously, in view of the conflicting opinions on the geological position of the terraces, evaluation of the significance of the South Yale site will have to wait until the geological problem is solved.

I have referred to this site out of order in the Fraser Canyon sequence because of its present, in my judgment, equivocal status.

The Fraser Lowlands

Borden (1962b:12) wrote: "A time span of some 4,000 years intervenes between the last of the early occupational horizon of the Fraser Canyon site and sites investigated to date one hundred miles to the west near the present mouth of the river. A tremendous cultural development, of which we know nothing as yet, had taken place meanwhile. . . . " It does not seem improbable to me, given the Pleistocene depression by glacial ice and subsequent gradual isostatic rebound and emergence from the sea of the Fraser Lowland, that sites will eventually be found, with the younger ones progressively down-river, that will help to fill the gap in the cultural record of the area. All the sites upon which the present record of lowland prehistory is based are in the delta, either close to the present shoreline or a few miles removed, but at the time of occupation they were on the shoreline.

Borden has proposed two phases for the lowland, the Marpole phase and the Locarno Beach phase. These appear to overlap in time with the Marpole beginning earlier and persisting later than the Locarno. He speaks of the Locarno Beach phase as being a cultural variant whose main centers may have been on the Gulf Islands. At the time of his writing the only two known Locarno Beach sites were on the "outermost fringe of the delta region" (Borden 1962b:12). Since that time, work has been carried out on Vancouver Island that assists in clarifying the relation of the two phases. This material is unpublished but the results will be mentioned later.

The Locarno Beach Phase: 493 B.C.–476 B.C. The two components of this phase are the Locarno Beach site, now about four miles from the shoreline and within Vancouver, and Whalen Farm I, the early level of a site at the southwestern part of the delta on the Point Roberts peninsula on the Washington side of the international boundary. The most conspicuous features of this phase are the ground slate industry and the minor role of chipped stone. In the trait inventory are one-piece toggling harpoons, composite toggling harpoon heads, antler foreshafts for toggling harpoon heads, slate grinding tools, ulos and other knives, a medial labret, and a small human head carved in bone. The character of this culture is distinctly oriented toward the exploitation of marine resources with a technological emphasis different from that of the interior.

The Marpole Phase: 943 B.C.–A.D. 179. Components of this phase are found at the famous Eburne shell mound and the Point Grey site (Borden 1950: 14). Emphasis on heavy woodworking is inferred from the presence of celts, splitting wedges of antler, and hands mauls. Celts are made from both nephrite and serpentine, and there is one from a giant mussel shell. Stone vessels, pecked and incised "to produce representative forms," along with carved bone and stone objects, are also present. Chipped stone points are much more numerous than ground slate. Barbed harpoons with tang and fixed bone points occur. This complex of features is clearly distinct from that of the Locarno Beach phase. The emphasis on chipped stone, stone containers, and nephrite and serpentine celts gives the assemblage a distinct interior orientation.

Whalen II: A.D. 377±140. Whalen II is represented by the upper level at the Whalen Farm site. It is characterized by the appearance of microblades, chipped stone points, and woodworking tools. Whalen II demonstrates continuity between the Marpole phase and the full ethnographic Salish culture, which is dated by Borden (1950, 1951) from the Stelax Village, Musqueam, at A.D. 1297±30.

Washington Coast and Islands

The coastal area includes the stretch from the delta of the Skagit River south to approximately 48° north latitude, and the San Juan Islands comprise the insular portion of this area of discussion. Kidd (1964) provides the best source of information for the area, and I have relied on him for my comments. He uses a fourfold division of Early, Middle, Late, and Historic periods. I shall discuss the first three in summary fashion and relate them to the sequence established by Borden for the Fraser Lowland.

Early Period. The sites of this period are all located in the vicinity of the south fork of the Stillaguamish River. The south and north forks join at the village of Arlington. The sites with the exception of the Olcott site, are all surface manifestations completely lacking depth, and at all of them, including the Olcott site, there was a total absence of organic remains or firehearths. The sites occur on what are probably terraces of the south fork or its feeder streams. Kidd, quoting geological sources, suggests that when the retreating ice was somewhat north of the Stillaguamish but over the drainage of the Skagit, that river was diverted into the Stillaguamish.

The cultural criteria of the Early Period, in addition to the location of the sites on stream terraces, are: large choppers and scrapers (some of which may be conical cores), large, thick willow- or laurel-leaf shaped points and knives, few or no stemmed and notched points, and use of basalt and argillite for tools. These tools are said to show a patina and usually an oxidized, reddish-brown weathering crust on the worked surfaces, which is "*apparently* as thick as the one on unworked pebbles found in the near-local fill" (Kidd 1964:26). This observation may be taken to indicate a considerable age for the artifacts, though it is difficult to understand how the weathering depth could be as thick on worked or flaked surfaces from which the original weathered cortex had been removed as on completely unworked pebbles that still retain the original cortex.

The problem of dating these sites is extremely difficult. There are no C-14 dates, so geological information provides the only possible basis. The location of the sites on terraces from 100 to 200 feet above sea level and the fact that some of the terraces are not now associated with streams indicate that, at the time of use, the environment was quite different from the present. The glacial history of the Fraser Lowland makes it clear that the sites *cannot be more than 13,000 years old,* and a reasonable date is probably closer to 10,000 to 10,500 years ago since the cultural inventory seems to have close affinities with the Early Period of the Fraser Canyon and some aspects of the Five-Mile Rapids site at The Dalles, which date in this time range.

Middle Period. The criteria of the Middle Period abstracted from Kidd are: the occurrence of sites generally on islands on or near open water or on major rivers at a relatively low elevation above sea level; the appearance of shell mounds; the appearance of stone grinding, especially of nephrite, soapstone, and slate; increased varieties of projectile points as triangular, stemmed, and notched points are added to the laurel-leaf, single-tipped kind and the bi-points; the use of a greater proportion of crypto-crystalline rocks than basalt as the raw material for stone chipping; the "virtual" disappearance of the heavy chopping and scraper assemblage; a marked increase of bone and antler in the middens; and the appearance of sculpture in stone, bone, and antler.

The island occupation clearly indicates a well-developed system of deepwater transport.

The materials from the Middle Period are clearly related to and contemporaneous with the Locarno Beach and Marpole phases and the Whalen II component of the Fraser Lowland. Some of the Washington components resemble the Locarno Beach phase while others resemble the Marpole phase. These two phases appear to have been shared throughout northern coastal Washington and the Fraser Lowland, and it appears to me that this period presents for the first time the emergence of a clearly defined culture. Of course there are variations, but what culture lacks them?

Late Period. This period in western Washington corresponds to Borden's "Full Salish" of the Fraser delta represented by Stelax Village at Musqueam. By this time stone chipping has nearly disappeared from the technology, and thin ground slate knives and points and bone points, some of which are barbed and others flat or plano-convex in cross-section without barbs, have replaced stone-chipped knives and points. Pointed poll adz blades are abundant in contrast with the earlier parallel sided variety, and flanged and nipple-top hand mauls occur. The beaver-tooth chisel, antler splitting wedges, and adz hafts are found. Composite harpoons are numerous.

The Late Period represents simply a development from the Middle with a somewhat more efficient exploitation of the environmental resources and some limited influences from the interior such as the nipple-top maul. This tool appears at the Five-Mile Rapids site in Level 3 with a date of approximately 4,000 years ago. While this tool may have been one to catch the fancy of the woodworker, I cannot see how it could in any way be more efficient than a simple, undecorated maul which was already available to them. Obviously trade and water transport were effectively developed. Trade with the interior is apparent.

In western Washington the same kind of a hiatus of several thousand years between the Early and Middle Periods occurred as existed farther north between the early Fraser Canyon and the later Fraser Lowland occupations. The significance of this common historical experience would seem to be that the cultural-historical processes for this region were essentially the same. The development of deepwater transport could have been a determining factor in this history through the effective and rapid diffusion of traits between islands and island and mainland. Borden (1962b) has suggested the possibility of the Gulf Islands as the source of the insular and coastline culture represented by the Locarno Beach phase. The San Juan Islands at present do not provide it, but do share in the subsequent development. Evidence suggests Vancouver Island is a possible source.

Vancouver Island. Capes (1964) has reported a series of sites and C-14 dates from the eastern side of Vancouver Island that may have considerable import for further research on the problem of cultural origins in the Gulf Islands. All sites are middens containing mammal and fish bones, usually in limited amounts, and shells of a variety of mollusks.

The earliest site is Millard's Creek, DkSf-2A, with a C-14 date of 8300±200 B.P. (S-142). Shellfish gathering supplemented hunting of land animals to provide food. One slender leaf-shaped point, rounded at the base, is reminiscent of some of the Stillaguamish River specimens from Washington. It also resembles those illustrated from the early Fraser Canyon series, but appears to be much more poorly made. Large numbers of obsidian (found only on the mainland)

and quartz crystal flakes were found, and one possible microblade made from a quartz crystal is reported.

This site, although having very few artifacts, is of great significance in the early prehistory of Vancouver Island and has implications for the mainland and the intervening islands. Since the date does not represent the very beginning of the occupation of the midden, perhaps people were living in the area even earlier. These people did not originate on Vancouver Island so they had to come by boat from the mainland or from the islands to the south. The whole Gulf of Georgia, the Fraser River, and the waters leading to Puget Sound were open to them. Also at this time they were exploiting both the land and sea for food. Perhaps it would not be wide of the mark to say that the canoe laid the base for the development of the distinctive culture of this area as did the domestication of the camel for the arid lands and the horse for the steppes, and this occurred more than 8,000 years ago.

The shell-midden site, EeSu-1, at Fort Rupert near the north end of Vancouver Island has a C-14 date of 5275±110 B.P. (no lab. no. given) for Layer 3, from which comes the main concentration of artifacts. Shell debris continues to a somewhat greater depth, but no artifacts were recovered below Layer 7. Excavation extended down through Layer 11, but the bottom of the midden was not reached. Capes reports that "thirteen small bone points, three bone awls, two barbed bone points, one bevelled edged sandstone fish knife (?), one [jadeite] celt, whetstone fragments, and two pieces of obsidian, were predominantly from the shell and earth deposit, mostly from Layer 3. The charcoal submitted for dating came from this stratum" (Capes 1964:72). This site, like Millard's Creek, is considerably older than any other presently dated site in the Fraser Lowland.

Other sites reported by Capes are intermediate in age between the Fort Rupert site and the Sandwick site, DkSg-2. The Sandwick site is dated at 400±60 B.P. (S-104) and is thought to represent the ethnographic Pentlatch Salish (Capes 1964:78). The artifact inventory for each of these sites is too small to permit any attempt to assign them to specific phases as presently formulated, and they do not allow an adequate assessment of the possibility mentioned

above that the Locarno Beach phase originated on Vancouver Island. The sites are, however, of great importance as part of a body of evidence showing that Vancouver Island was occupied equally as early as the Fraser Canyon and Washington Lowland, and that this occupation continued down to the ethnographic present.

Mitchell (1968b) has reported on excavations carried out on the Gulf Islands and has reformulated the cultural sequence on the basis of new evidence. He proposes the name Early Lithic for the previously used Early and terminates it about 6,000 to 7,000 years ago. Then follows the Locarno Beach phase, after a lengthy hiatus in the record, with dates covering a period from 1210±130 B.C. (GSC-437) to 250±120 B.C. (M-1515). The Marpole phase follows with the earliest C-14 date for a Marpole phase site at 950±170 B.C. (S-17b) and the latest at A.D. 406±130 (UW43). Mitchell includes the Whalen II component in the Marpole phase and suggests a termination date of A.D. 700 or 800. Developed Coast Salish follows Marpole. Mitchell's date, placing the Locarno Beach phase some 700 years earlier in the Gulf Islands than on the mainlands, supports Borden's hypothesized Locarno Beach origins in the islands.

Whatever final refinements and corrections are eventually made in the prehistory of the Fraser Canyon–Fraser Lowland–and archipelago area, at present it is clear that the area was occupied from approximately 9,000 years ago, and that the development of sea transportation provided the key for exploitation of the environmental opportunities. A way of life was built up for the area both by independent local development of similar tools for exploitation of similar resources and by contact, which resulted in the borrowing of traits. There is cultural continuity until historic times, but this does not rule out intrusions of outside groups since such groups would have had to adjust to the way of life necessary for this environment in order to survive. Massive migrations seem unlikely in view of the linguistic record reviewed in Chapter 4, but it appears equally evident that some displacements occurred.

The Great Basin

The development of the archæology of the Great Basin has been largely, at least in its early stages, a result of historical accident, though it eventually became highly problem oriented. It was for the most part outside the area of the archæological salvage program since there is scarcely enough water in most of the streams to dam up. The University of Oregon has carried out most of the work in the Northern Great Basin. The University of California at Berkeley has worked the Lahontan area and the University of Utah the Lake Bonneville area. The southwestern area has been studied by parties from the Southwest Museum, the Museum of Man at San Diego, and the University of California at Los Angeles and at Berkeley. The Nevada State Museum at Carson City and the University of Nevada have been active in the Lahontan area.

Lovelock Cave, about 22 miles southwest of Lovelock, Nevada, provided the first significant archæological collection from the Great Basin in 1912 (Loud and Harrington 1929), but because of Loud's method of excavation to secure a "collection," as Kroeber had suggested, and the limitations under which he worked, the material was almost worthless for archæological purposes. Harrington, with Loud, returned in 1924 under the auspices of the Museum of the American Indian, Heye Foundation of New York, to attempt to find an undisturbed area and conduct stratigraphic excavation. One such area was found and excavated and this furnished the only stratigraphic record we have for that important cave. The rich collection from Lovelock Cave stood without recognizable referents in Great Basin prehistory. The general opinion was that it probably represented the hypothetical Basket Maker I of the Southwest sequence as then proposed.

Important work of the 1930s included the excavation of Gypsum Cave (Harrington 1933) in southern Nevada a few miles from Las Vegas, Zingg's (1933) formulation of an ancient Uto-Aztecan culture in the Great Basin, founded upon ethnographic and extremely limited archæologic data, and Steward's (1937) and Elmer Smith's (1952) excavations in caves of the Great Salt Lake area in northern Utah.

It was a common tendency then to interpret anything bearing similarity to the southwestern Anasazi area as derived from it, and the work of Smith and Steward in the caves of the Great Salt Lake area was colored by this orientation. External sources for the

Great Basin culture were sought elsewhere as well, and Steward (1940) formulated the theory of a variety of divergent origins from the neighboring peoples. He concluded that *"the total Intermontane culture was the product of diverse borrowing from different sources at different periods and of a certain measure of internal development"* (51) (emphasis added).

My students and I, assisted with specialists from geology, volcanology, paleontology, botany, biology, and palynology, under the leadership and with the support of Dr. John C. Merriam, President-Emeritus, Carnegie Institution of Washington, D.C., carried out in the Northern Great Basin a problem-oriented program of excavation from 1932 to 1940 (with the exception of the year 1936). The program was extended from 1947 through 1949, and again in 1951, to the upper Klamath Lake area, the most westerly of the series of southern Oregon lakes (Cressman et al. 1942; Cressman 1956b and various). This program, carried out before the development of radiocarbon dating, had demonstrated that the Northern Great Basin had been occupied by man at the same time as *Equus,* the camel, and a variety of bison; that occupation had been continuous to the time of the white man's arrival, but that the intensity of occupation varied with climatically induced changes in the environment as habitat; that the climatic changes defined by Antevs (1948) could be used as a working chronological device; that palynology in conjunction with the climatic change model could provide a relative chronology; that volcanism, in particular the Mt. Mazama eruption, could provide a valuable horizon marker and dating device; and that the regional technology was highly developed in lithic manufacture and textile fabrication of twined basketry and sandals. All dating, however, was relative and derived from the sources just mentioned.

As a result of this systematic program of research I advanced the following opinion.

There is no escaping the conclusion that the cave culture of south-central Oregon fits into the larger pattern of the Basin-Southwest (and perhaps we should add the Plateau) area of sagebrush-juniper cover. However, here as in other parts of this area, specializations and enrichments of the culture developed, giving a localized character to the product as distinctive in its way as that of the Big Bend, the Coahuilla, or the Four Corners (Cressman et al. 1942:140).

This was the first thesis derived from archæological data of a basic, indigenous culture for the whole of the Great Basin. Jennings (1957:285) wrote:

> Danger Cave provides further validation for the general ideas Cressman has expressed for the past 15 years. Beginning in 1940 Cressman has steadfastly maintained that there was an ancient gathering complex throughout the entire Basin and that *it likely was the base for most of the cultures of the Basin* [emphasis added]. He has never wavered from this position and must be credited with having correctly assessed the scanty archæological, geological and cultural evidence at his command.

My conclusion was in direct conflict with that of Steward's, but it became the accepted position on Great Basin prehistory as Jennings generously states.

Following the development of C-14 dating, which in general substantiated the chronological position taken in the 1942 publication, I briefly suggested the process of adaptation to various more favorable habitats within the Great Basin as a means of surviving during the climatic changes to which the area was subjected (Cressman 1951:309–10). The 1947 program of excavation in the Klamath Lake basin of Oregon had two purposes. First, since the Klamath Lake area was structurally a Great Basin feature (but because of its distinctive environmental features it had not gone through the climatic changes which apparently had disrupted occupation of more arid areas), it was hoped that a continuum of cultural development from the early Great Basin manifestations to the historic Klamath could be secured. I speculated that such a continuum, if it existed, would be the result of successful adaptation to a lacustrine and marsh environment. The corollary aim was to test the theory of out-migration from the Great Basin, as a result of unfavorable climatic change, by seeking a continuous archæological record that would provide a referent for comparison with arid-zone sites at different time levels. The Klamath Lake area program was concluded in 1951 (Cressman 1956b). The archæological record of the Klamath Lake area showed an increasingly successful adaptation to the riverine, marsh, and lake environment from a generalized Great Basin base. In addition, it showed that the process by which this adaptation took place was one of internal development, which was aided by limited selective borrowing of foreign culture elements at different times and from different sources. These borrowed elements, however, were always incorporated into the general conservative scheme of the Klamath pattern without being disruptive. Perhaps one exception was the borrowing of a completely alien concept of class based upon wealth, but even this opinion is arguable.

In 1954 at the organizational meeting of the Great Basin Archæological Conference at Globe, Arizona, I presented a paper, which J.D. Jennings kindly read for me in my absence, in which I suggested that the name Great Basin culture should be used for the overall culture of the Great Basin to indicate its general similarity and to indicate that as a significant area of study it should be set off from the wider area outside of the Great Basin, even though at certain periods of development cultural variations existed within the area. To indicate that in the Great Basin there were localized areas of specialization within the general pattern in response to special ecological conditions, I suggested that the word "facies" might well be used.

Jennings and Norbeck (1955:3) presented the concept of the Desert culture, "a desert way of life fundamentally like that of historic times. . . . The Desert culture was not restricted to the Great Basin but was a pattern found, following the disappearance of large game, throughout a wide area of the west surrounding the Basin." They also made clear that there were areas of specialized cultures within the Great Basin, in particular around the shores of fresh-water lakes, for which the name Desert culture might be inappropriate. I would agree that since there are areas of specialized manifestations within the larger pattern to which the name does not apply, it seems to be a rather infelicitous expression to define the Great Basin culture. The expression is in the literature, but its applicability is undergoing scrutiny (Cressman 1964; Irwin-Williams 1967a). In my judgment its usage should be discarded, for the important ideas that Jennings and Norbeck brought together would be more meaningful if a more apt name were chosen.

Jennings (1957), from 1949 through 1953, was excavating Danger, Raven, and Juke Box caves. Danger Cave was far and away the most important for it gave what was lacking in Great Basin archæology up to that time, a continuous sequence of occupation from 10,000 and 11,000 years ago until nearly historic times. The latest C-14 date at Danger Cave is A.D. 20, and it was long thought that this represented the termination of occupation there. A recent reanalysis of Danger Cave artifacts, and comparison of them with the dated sequence from nearby Hogup Cave, indicates, however, that occupation continued long after the beginning of the Christian era (Aikens 1970). Danger Cave probably did not represent a place of continuous occupation but was used for short periods of time by gathering and hunting parties moving in the continuous search for food through that inhospitable country.

Jennings used the Danger Cave report to give a firm statement, based on the excavations and comparative Great Basin studies, on this "desert lifeway," that is, the Great Basin lifeway. Two comments stand out. First, "There were regional differences in the Desert culture, of course, and there was slight change in—or additions to—some of their tool forms or techniques of fabrication" (Jennings 1957:8). Second, "One of the most interesting aspects of the Desert culture is its stability. In the Basin proper it never showed significant change" (Jennings 1957:8). Thus it is quite clear that Jennings and I, as well as others, have insisted on these two characteristics of the Great Basin culture: a basic similarity in the culture throughout the area founded on the adaptive processes for survival, and regional variation on the basic pattern in different ecological areas. The idea one often hears expressed—that the Great Basin culture was a monotonously uniform expression of human activity—has no basis in responsible literature on the subject.

Great Basin archæology thus has proceeded from scattered cave excavations to a well-formed conceptual framework organized in cultural-ecological terms. Research at present appears to be concerned with two major types of problems. One is the description of local variations in terms of cultural ecology, the other is the isolation of major components in the development of Great Basin prehistory, especially at early time levels.

The Northern Great Basin

The Pluvial Fort Rock Lake basin, which contains the longest well-validated record of human occupation in the area, serves well as the type situation for the whole Northern Great Basin. The Fort Rock basin is formed by a depressed fault block lying between 120°20′ and 121°10′ west longitude and 43°03′ and 43°30′ north latitude. The axis of the basin runs approximately east-west. It is bilobed with a constriction just east of its center; the axes of the lobes run north 30° west. The overall length of the lake bed is about 40 miles; its width varies from 6 miles at the constriction to 35 miles across the lobes. It is the most northerly extension of the Great Basin. The name Fort Rock was given to a dominating feature of the lake bed, the massive remains of a volcano about 1 mile northwest of the village of Fort Rock. The name, by extension, now applies to the whole area.

Four well-defined terraces cut into the volcano occur at 4,430, 4,419, 4,406, and 4,386 feet above sea level. The lowest of these is dated at 13,380±230 radiocarbon years ago from a shell sample after correction for fractionation (GaK-1752). When the lake level stood at each of the three older terraces, three islands were above the water level in Fort Rock Lake: (1) Beggarheel Butte, in which the Fort Rock cave lies, is 1 mile due west of Fort Rock; (2) Cougar Mountain is 9 miles east and slightly north of Fort Rock; and (3) the Connley Hills are about 12 miles south of Fort Rock. As the lake level subsided toward the lowest terrace sometime but probably not long before 13,000 years ago, a connection with the shore to the west of Fort Rock cave was established across a bar. It is not known when connections were made for the other islands, but probably not very long afterward. The slow but continued desiccation of the lake and the enlarging shoreline connections offered choice occupation sites close to the water's edge and close to the ponds and small lakes found in the lake's later stages.

Fort Rock Cave, a shelter on Cougar Mountain, six shelters closely spaced on the south side of the Connley Hills, and a burial and a shelter at Table Rock, a nearby feature of the Connley Hills, provide a complex of sites occupied concurrently for 11,000 years, except for a 2,000-year hiatus between 7,000 and 5,000 years ago during the Altithermal. Fort Rock Cave was occupied first at slightly more than 13,000 years ago. This number of closely spaced sites, occupied concurrently for so long in the same ecosystem in which climatic change was marked, is unique in far-western prehistory.

Unfortunately, the Connley caves had been damaged in the rear and on the surface by collectors, and our excavations were confined to the fill at the mouth of the shelters, thus limiting our recovery material essentially to lithic products. At Fort Rock Cave, originally excavated in 1938, a massive roof fall of huge rocks was blasted and removed in the hope of finding undisturbed material, but the tremendous weight of the rocks had crushed everything beneath them. A large flat rock on the opposite side of the cave entrance had also fallen from the roof, and this was removed with a bulldozer without damage to the underlying fill. It was under this rock close to the gravel on the cave floor where a hearth was found that dated at 13,200 radiocarbon years ago. A C-14 date from close under this rock showed that it had fallen shortly after 4,000 years ago.

Each cave in the basin contained a layer of Mt. Mazama pumice, which provided an excellent stratigraphic control. Twenty-eight radiocarbon dates from hearth charcoal gave an outstanding series with each cave or shelter being represented. By means of the pumice stratum and the radiocarbon dates, it was possible to construct a chronological column representative of the whole basin. No pollen was found in any of the soil samples, but chunks of charcoal from the source samples used for radiocarbon dating were identified to provide evidence of the flora. Bird, mammal, and fish bones contributed to our information on the environmental sequences and the order and times of their appearances, for all were closely tied to the series of radiocarbon dates. A profile of phytoliths recorded from a column immediately outside of Connley Cave No. 4, and calibrated stratigraphically with the cave fill, provided a record of the relative amount of grasses in the area through the time represented by the column, and thus a record of climatic change. The availability of this range of information made it possible to construct a cultural-geological column that recorded the cultural activities in the lake basin and correlated them rather closely with the evidence of climatic change and its effect on the lake basin and its immediate environs as a habitat.

The cultural column is divided into four periods: Period 1—14,000 to 11,000 years ago; Period 2—11,000 to 8,000 years ago; Period 3—8,000 to 7,000 years ago; and Period 4—5,000 to 3,000 years ago. The 2,000 year interval between 7,000 and 5,000 years ago is not identified as a cultural period because evidence of occupation during that time was lacking. The sequence does not extend upward in time beyond 3,000 years ago because the most recent archæological deposits had been destroyed by artifact collectors prior to the initiation of the research. Intensity of occupation of the caves was determined by calculating the percentage of total lithic debris, total artifacts, and bone by site and level. The curves for this indicator for each cave were remarkably similar, and this record could thus serve as an indicator of the quality of the area as a habitat. In the detailed monographic report of the site, Bedwell (1969) defined four periods of occupational intensity in a separate sequence parallel to the cultural periodization just given, but for the sake of simplicity, I use a single set of periods to control both kinds of data.

Subjective examination of the cultural material suggested the four periods, and to verify this ordering Bedwell carried out extensive statistical analysis of both quantitative and qualitative attributes of various categories of artifacts. The statistical analysis indicated that the assemblages of each period differed from those of adjoining periods, and that the resemblance between Periods 3 and 4 was closer than between 3 and 2, or Periods 2 and 1. The characteristics of each period follow. (Cf. Figure 27 A, B)

Period 1 Assemblage: 14,000–11,000 B.P. The assemblage from a hearth at Fort Rock Cave dated at 13,200±720 B.P. (GaK1738) includes a point similar to the lozenge-shaped Lake Mohave type and a small unnotched point with slight fluting from a concave base. The slight fluting appears to be simply a thinning technique. Both points are made of obsidian and show rather poor workmanship. In addition, there are several scrapers, gravers, reworked flakes, and, surprisingly enough, a mano. Bedwell supervised the excavation and is certain of the mano's association. The core-and-blade technique is apparently present in the assemblage, as well as the true burin. There is one specimen, made on a blade-

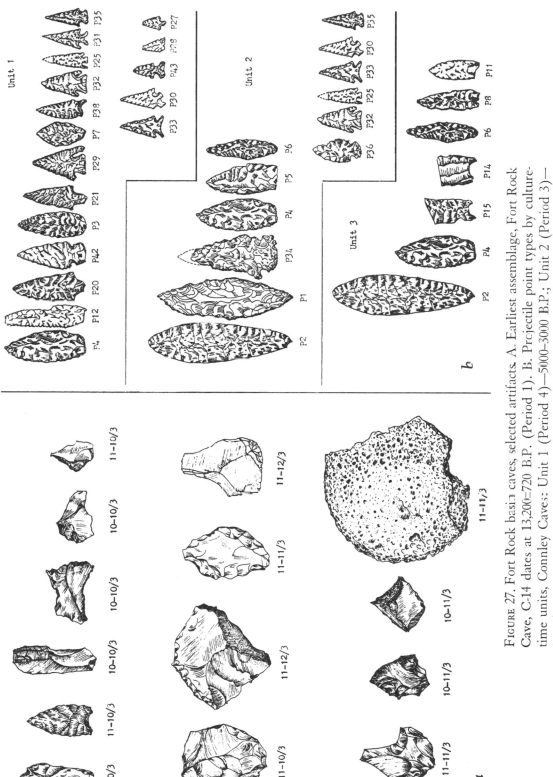

FIGURE 27. Fort Rock basin caves, selected artifacts. A. Earliest assemblage, Fort Rock Cave, C-14 dates at 13,200±720 B.P. (Period 1). B. Projectile point types by culture-time units, Connley Caves: Unit 1 (Period 4)—5000–3000 B.P.; Unit 2 (Period 3)—8000–7000 B.P.; Unit 3 (Period 2)—11,000–8000 B.P. Unit 4 (Period 1), 14,000–11,000 B.P., is represented by A. The period between 7000 and 5000 B.P. is not represented since the caves were unoccupied because of the effects of the Altithermal climate and the Mt. Mazama eruption. The sequence ends at 3000 B.P. because of vandalism in the upper portion of the cave fill. *Bedwell and Cressman 1971:Figures 8, 9.*

like piece, which may be an incipient crescent. Stone-working technique emphasizes flaking at right angles to the long axis of the artifact. Cougar Mountain Cave No. 2 yielded only use-reworked flakes at the level dated 11,950±350 B.P. (GaK1751). This site was apparently a workshop where large "clamshell"-like flakes were first struck off from quarried Cougar Mountain obsidian preparatory to further fabrication.

Period 2 Assemblage: 11,000–8000 B.P. Six closely spaced C-14 dates falling between 10,200 and 9,500 years ago give on the whole a usable reference for dating this period of maximum cultural activity (Bedwell 1969:55, 56). All points are unnotched. The large-shouldered, lanceolate-like Haskett point first reported from Idaho by Butler (1967); the small, unnotched, concave-base point with slight fluting, comparable to the non-Lake Mohave type from the Period 1 assemblage but better made; the rear portion of a point thinned by fairly long multiple fluting in the Clovis manner; a rather straight-edged, narrow, concave-base point; a leaf-shaped point with a straight base; a bi-point and the large-stemmed, concave-base Lind Coulee and Windust point types all appear in this period. Edges are typically ground. Manos, gravers, knives, scrapers, and anvil stones also occur in this period, and from Fort Rock Cave come the famous well-made sandals woven of sagebrush bark (cf. frontispiece) and a fragment of fine-twined basketry with false embroidery.

The Haskett point is also found in surface collections from south-central Oregon and the high Lake Lahontan beach in the Fallon area of western Nevada. The fluted specimen has analogues with those in the Tonopah and Borax Lake collections. The presence of the core-and-blade technique in this assemblage is clearly shown by a large fragment of a long chert projectile point and a classical (personal communication, D.E. Crabtree to L.S. Cressman) end-of-blade scraper made from basalt. Crescents from Fort Rock Cave are also a part of the assemblage. Flaking, as in Period 1, appears to be mostly by percussion.

The picture this period presents is one of continued development of flaking techniques with the same specimens found as in the earlier period. There is improvement in workmanship and modification of point types, apparently in the interest of improved hafting, as though the manufacturers were experimenting with solutions to this problem. Successful adaptation to a favorable habitat is clear, and changes that occur appear to be internal and developmental.

Period 3 Assemblage: 8000–7000 B.P. This period, which terminates with the Mt. Mazama eruption, is one of decreasing use of the caves with a high degree of probability that the decline is a response to the worsening habitat as implied by climatic indicators. A significant change in the lithic assemblage occurs with the appearance of the corner-notching projectile point. This point type does not appear in sufficient numbers to suggest a population movement, but instead there are at first only one or two such points, then a gradual increase in numbers. The Haskett point continues, as do several others of the general leaf-shaped variety, but fluting is lacking. For the period as a whole, some 50 percent of all points are corner-notched and two are side-notched. The corner-notched points appear as additions to the inventory and do not suddenly displace earlier types. The tempo of appearance and increase in number of these points suggests that they represent local internal development in response to the problem of hafting, and that because of their effective solution of this problem, they gained rapidly in popularity. The same evidence, however, could be used to argue for diffusion and then local adoption, but we know of no earlier occurrence of corner-notched points at present that might serve as a source for diffusion.

Two manos and one mortar occur in the Period 3 assemblage. Use-reworked flakes make up 51 percent of the inventory of knives and scrapers in the preceding Period 2, but 73 percent in this one, and 79 percent in the following Period 4. A significant change also occurs in the lithic source material. In the preceding period, basalt comprised 37 percent and obsidian 53 percent of the lithic source material. In this period, basalt drops to 8 percent and obsidian rises to 89 percent, a condition carrying into the final period.

Another change during this period is in stone flaking technology. While the previous method of flaking at right angles to the long axis of the artifact continues, the technique of flaking at oblique angles appears, with the flake scar sloping toward the base of the artifact. Bedwell's detailed analysis of flake scars indicates that this change signifies the appearance of pressure flaking. The points generally decrease in size. A bone flaking tool, commonly used in pressure flaking, also appears at this time.

Period 4 Assemblage: 5000–3000 B.P. Eleven C-14 dates fall in this period with one cluster between 4700 and 4300 B.P. and another between 3700 and 3000 B.P. (Bedwell 1969:55, 56). This period clearly represents a further development of the trends seen in Period 3. Since the time between the end of Period 3 at 7000 B.P. and the beginning of Period 4 at 5000 B.P. is not represented by significant deposits in the caves, the developmental continuity from Period 3 and Period 4 in the caves must mean that during the hiatus in cave occupation people carrying on the traditions of Period 3 occupied the surrounding area where habitats were favorable. This conclusion is also supported by an infant burial from Table Rock Site No. 2 dated at 5220±210 years B.P. (GaK1748). For the 2,000 years intervening between Period 3 and Period 4, the desiccated lake bed was avoided as a habitat, but in the meantime improved methods of adaptation were worked out in the surrounding area to be brought back into the lake bed area as it improved as a habitat under the more favorable climatic conditions of the Medithermal.

A slender, corner-notched projectile point makes up 70 percent of all points in Period 4, while 89 percent of all the studied specimens of the corner-notched type appear in this unit. (The remaining 11 percent all occur in the preceding Period 3.) Pressure flaking is now dominant with oblique flake scars now occurring on 56 percent of all points, while in the preceding Period 3 they were present on 29 percent, and in Period 2 on 12 percent. Basketry and matting occur as grave goods with the Table Rock burial; their absence in the Connley Caves is probably due to deterioration from moisture. The rest of the lithic inventory is that common to the Great Basin at this time period. The study concludes at 3000 B.P.

In summary, Fort Rock basin was used as an aboriginal human habitat from before 13,000 years ago until the coming of the white man, although the caves and shelters of the lake bed were used but

little between 7,000 and 5,000 years ago. Intensity of occupation was definitely a function of the quality of the habitat for human life. The earliest assemblage, dated at 13,200 years ago, shows sophisticated methods of fabrication of stone tools and weapons. The climax of the early occupation occurs between 10,200 and 9,500 years ago, although the same way of life, as reflected in the material culture, continues with diminishing intensity until 8,000 years ago. During the climax period, a far-flung similarity of artifacts and fabricating techniques occurs across southeastern Washington, the lower Snake River, the middle Columbia River in Oregon, south-central Idaho, the Fort Rock area, the Western Great Basin, southeastern California, and the San Diego County area. Both ends of the Central Valley of California are presently included. Obviously, early historical connections down the eastern flanks of the Cascade-Sierra Nevada mountains are indicated by this distribution. The nature of these relationships is not at present understood, and the problem provides opportunities for future research.

The culture continuum in the Fort Rock basin confirms the interpretation, made many times by various writers, that Great Basin culture developed largely on its own terms, mostly by internal innovation, and was a culture remarkable for its capacity to exploit even the harshest environment, even though survival was often at or close to the subsistence level.

The earliest Northern and Western Great Basin culture appears to have been somewhat different from that of the Eastern Great Basin before 8,000 years ago, a situation that Bedwell (1973) believes might be reasonably used to date the appearance of the Desert culture in the Northern Great Basin. Because of the strong similarities between the Fort Rock area assemblages and assemblages as far south as Lake Mohave in Southern California, Bedwell has suggested the name "Western Pluvial Lakes Tradition" for the pre-Desert culture appearing in this vast area between about 11,000 and 8,000 years ago. This cultural similarity is due, in Bedwell's opinion, to the fact that a similar lake-grassland environment extended throughout this area along the eastern edge of the Cascade-Sierra Nevada mountains.

Basketry, twined ware, woven wicker, and coiled basketry are hallmarks of the Great Basin culture.

Twined ware (Catlow Twine, Cressman et al. 1942) was the predominant type in the Northern Great Basin, and the collection from the south-central Oregon caves is the finest collection of its kind in the Far West from the prehistoric period. One of the oldest dated specimens is associated with a sandal from Fort Rock Cave dated at 9053±350 B.P. (C-428). This is a fragment of fine twined ware decorated with false embroidery. This fine work bespeaks a long tradition, as do the finely twined sandals with which it was associated, and it is an excellent example of the exploitation in a culture of a special aspect of that culture beyond all practical needs of the people to achieve a product of significant beauty.

Grosscup (1960:46-47), for reasons not clear to me, questioned the 9,000-year age ascription for the Catlow Twine from Fort Rock Cave and suggested that perhaps its occurrence in Lovelock Cave, after approximately 4,000 years ago, marked its earliest appearance. There is, however, no reason to doubt the evidence on which the original date was based, and other independent evidence confirms and extends the age of Catlow Twine back beyond 9000 B.P. Orr (1956a) excavated a fragment of basket from Fishbone Cave on the northeastern shore of Lake Winnemucca, Nevada. This specimen, fragments from possibly the same basket, are clearly Catlow Twine ware. They are attributed to Level IV, which has been dated at approximately 11,000 years ago. It is not impossible that the Lahontan basin may have been the place where Catlow Twine developed, with the people of the Oregon caves exploiting the potential of the ware to such a high degree and maintaining the technique down to, and perhaps beyond, the time of Christ.

In concluding this section, an important potential source of further information from the Fort Rock area may be brought to the reader's attention. In the eastern part of the Fort Rock basin is Fossil Lake, famous for the tremendous number of specimens of fossil fauna taken from that area (Allison 1966b). Bones of *Equus* were found at Fort Rock Cave in 1966, and they establish the contemporaneity of man and Pleistocene fauna in the basin. Early collectors of specimens from Fossil Lake reported the presence of projectile points among the fossil bones there. Some thought that an association was implied while others denied it, for the intellectual climate of the time made such an association unacceptable. Obviously, the artifacts, as we now know, might very well have been associated with the animals they were used to kill and butcher and may have been dropped along with the bones. Apparently Fossil Lake was a shallow remnant of the larger body of water around which animals congregated for food and water. They mired down in the muck, some to die as their struggles carried them more firmly into the soft mass, others to be killed by animal predators, and still others probably to have been killed by human predators. The horse recovered from Fort Rock Cave might have been taken in such a fashion.

The area remains an important potential Early Man site, although professional paleontologists and collectors have combed the Fossil Lake bed so thoroughly that it is a lucky day on which a good specimen may be found. In 1966 I found several choppers close to the back dirt of excavations from which fossil elephant and Equus remains had been excavated, but, of course, no association could be demonstrated. It is possible that some other place may yet be found in the basin where associations between tools and Pleistocene fauna may be demonstrated, if by some lucky chance the wind removes the covering of sand and pumice from the right area.

The Eastern Great Basin

The Eastern Great Basin corresponds roughly to the western half of the present-day state of Utah. It is bounded on the east by the Wasatch Mountains and dominated in the north by the Great Salt Lake, a remnant of Pleistocene Lake Bonneville. Danger Cave (Jennings 1957) and Hogup Cave (Aikens et al. 1970) are the best sources of information on the prehistory of the area. Morss (1931) described the enigmatic, horticulturally-based Fremont culture, located generally in the Fremont River drainage of eastern Utah, confluent to the Colorado River. Elmer Smith (1952) and Julian Steward (1937) had carried out excavations for the University of Utah in the caves of the Great Salt Lake region. Steward had found in the caves material that certainly duplicated some of that characteristic of the Fremont culture; there were, however, other traits similar to the generalized Great Basin type. Steward proposed the name Promontory culture for the manifestations found in the Promontory Point caves northwest of Salt Lake City and considered the source of this culture to be generally in the northern Plains. Both Danger and Hogup caves contained evidence of the Fremont culture at appropriate points in their history, while the total picture provided by these caves was that of the Great Basin lifeway.

Danger Cave, a few miles north of Wendover, Nevada, on the Nevada-Utah line, is situated on the western shoreline of Lake Bonneville. The earliest of four closely clustered C-14 dates for the first brief use of the cave was at 9500±600 B.C. (C-609). After a short interruption, occupation continued down to nearly historic time. The exact time of the final occupation of the cave is unclear because the apparently latest deposits, at the extreme front of the cave, had been removed by excavations carried out before the advent of radiocarbon dating. The cave was not occupied constantly as a dwelling place, but was used from time to time for short periods by bands of hunters operating in its vicinity. Danger Cave was very dry, and practically everything that had ever been dropped by the occupants had been preserved.

Danger Cave's great importance derived from the fact that it provided for the first time a rich, dry cave record in the Great Basin continuing through a very long period, and it had available radiocarbon dating to provide a firm chronology. Man's association with extinct Pleistocene fauna in the Great Basin had been demonstrated more than ten years before the excavation of Danger Cave, and rich collections had been excavated from the Northern and Western Great Basin caves. This work, however, had all been done before the development of radiocarbon dating and therefore lacked a precise chronology; furthermore, the record was a composite one made from the results obtained from numerous shelters and caves occupied for relatively short but overlapping periods of time. Though it was but one cave, and with all that implies for sample bias, Danger Cave corrected both these deficiencies.

Criticism of the Danger Cave record generally followed two lines: first, that the deposits were confused and the stratigraphic record, therefore, was unreliable; second, that the cave record was not typical of Great Basin cultural development. I shall hold comment on the first criticism until after discussion of Hogup Cave but comment now on the second.

Warren and Ranere (1968) criticized Jennings's use of Danger Cave as a typical example of Great Basin cultural developments, pointing out that there were various components, especially at an early time level, making up the totality of Great Basin culture. As far as I can judge from Jennings's writings (Jennings and Norbeck 1955; Jennings 1957), he would not be in disagreement with his critics. I have pointed out above that Jennings recognized variations in the pattern of the total culture, especially in relation to different ecological opportunities. He did not assert that Danger Cave gave a complete manifestation of all aspects of Great Basin culture, only the core; and I think that is a fair estimate of the record's significance. Corroborative evidence for Jennings's position came from Hogup Cave, not far distant, with a cultural record corresponding to the last three-quarters of occupation of Danger Cave, and that the most significant part for cultural reconstruction. Aikens, who excavated Hogup Cave, had the advantage of having all the Danger Cave material at the University of Utah available for comparison and further study. He was thus able to bring these two studies together and provide an excellent account of the prehistory of the northern part of the Eastern Great Basin.

Hogup Cave (Aikens et al. 1970) is located approximately 75 airline miles northwest of Salt Lake City, 65 miles northeast of Danger Cave, and 35 miles south of the Idaho border on the southwestern flank of low Hogup Mountain. On the west and south it faces the salt flats of the Great Salt Lake Desert and behind it on the east is the Great Salt Lake. It does not record as long an occupation as Danger Cave, starting at 6400±160 B.C. (GaK1569), but it is of great value because it was a seasonal habitation site instead of a place of temporary use by passing hunting parties. It is well stratified in terms of cave fill with sixteen major natural strata isolated as provenience controls. Twenty-three C-14 dates were evaluated and used as checks on the natural (geological) stratigraphy to provide the chronological control for the cultural stratigraphy.

The following résumé of regional prehistory, organized around the record at Hogup and Danger caves, is extracted from two brief unpublished summary papers by Aikens, who excavated the cave and prepared the final report (Aikens, Harper, and Fry 1970).

The Hogup Cave data, and comparisons with Danger Cave and other nearby sites, allow the construction of a five-period sequence from ca. 9500 B.C. to A.D. 1850 in the Great Salt Lake region and adjacent areas. The periods are, from earliest to latest, Bonneville, 9500 to 8000 B.C.; Wendover, 8000 to 1250 B.C.; Black Rock, 1250 B.C. to A.D. 500; Fremont, A.D. 500 to 1350; and Shoshoni, A.D. 1350 to 1850. The artifacts chosen as period diagnostics are merely those which tend to cluster into relatively restricted stratigraphic distributions at Hogup Cave; they form complexes of traits limited to relatively discrete segments of time. Each period possesses many other attributes as well that are important to understanding the total cultural pattern, but they are not useful as diagnostics per se because most of them are shared by all or at least most of the periods.

Bonneville Period: 9500–8000 B.C. The period is named after Pleistocene Lake Bonneville, the now dry basin that comprises the greater part of the Eastern Great Basin. The Bonneville period is described on the basis of the earliest cultural material at Danger Cave, which consisted of six small fire hearths, a few fragments of animal bone, several milling stones, and a projectile point that resembles some Plano forms from the Great Plains. The age ascription is based on four radiocarbon dates from Cultural Zone I that span the time range indicated. The period dates to a time at which, in other parts of North America, wide-ranging hunters were preying on such herd species as mammoth, bison, camel, and horse. In view of this, it is postulated that the hunting of large game may also have been a significant emphasis in the Bonneville lifeway. The scanty evidence currently available does not warrant additional speculation.

Wendover Period: 8000–1250 B.C. This period is named after the town of Wendover on the Utah-Nevada boundary west of the Great Salt Lake. Danger Cave, less than a mile northeast of the town, is the type locality for the period. Diagnostic artifacts include the projectile point types Elko eared, Elko split-stem, Elko side notched, Bitterroot side notched

the Little Lake or Pinto Basin series, Humboldt concave base, and Black Rock concave base. Other diagnostic attributes include the preferred use of obsidian for manufacture of projectile points; large asymmetrical ovate biface blades; small and large domed scrapers; high frequency of slab milling stones; L-shaped scapula awls; predominance of Z-twist over S-twist cordage; considerable variety in form and technique of the basketry complex; and the atlatl and dart.

The Wendover period is the representative *par excellence* of the Desert culture as it was originally defined by Jennings and Norbeck (1955) and described in detail by Jennings (1957:7). A conspicuous characteristic of the Wendover period is its very high degree of internal diversity when contrasted with later periods. This diversity is particularly evident in the projectile point inventory, in the basketry complex, and in the faunal collections. The indicators suggest a rather highly adapted way of life based on seed gathering and diversified small game hunting, and it is intriguing, but not convincing, to correlate the diversity of faunal species represented in the Wendover period with the diversity of projectile point types, suggesting that there may have been a degree of specialization of hunting projectiles to hunting tasks (Figures 28-29).

Black Rock Period: 1250 B.C.–A.D. 500. The period is named after Black Rock Cave at the southern end of the Great Salt Lake. Diagnostic attributes include the projectile point types Rose Spring corner notched, Eastgate expanding stem, and Elko corner notched. Other traits include preferential use of non-obsidian cryptocrystalline rock for projectile-point manufacture; sheep horn wrench; the distinctive Hogup Moccasin; predominance of S-twist over Z-twist cordage; sharp decline in variety of form and technique in the basketry complex, with one-rod and bundle, noninterlocking stitch becoming the dominant type; and concurrent use during the period of both the atlatl and dart and the bow and arrow.

The transition from the Wendover to the Black Rock period at Hogup Cave marks the most dramatic cultural shift noted in the entire sequence. Variety of projectile points and basketry types decreases markedly; milling stones become scarce; many small animals drop completely out of the faunal complex;

FIGURE 28. Projectile points from a single bison kill, Chubbuck Site, Colorado. Different types of points used by this hunting group show that social group and point type are not necessarily correlated. *Photograph courtesy of Joe Ben Wheat, University of Colorado Museum.*

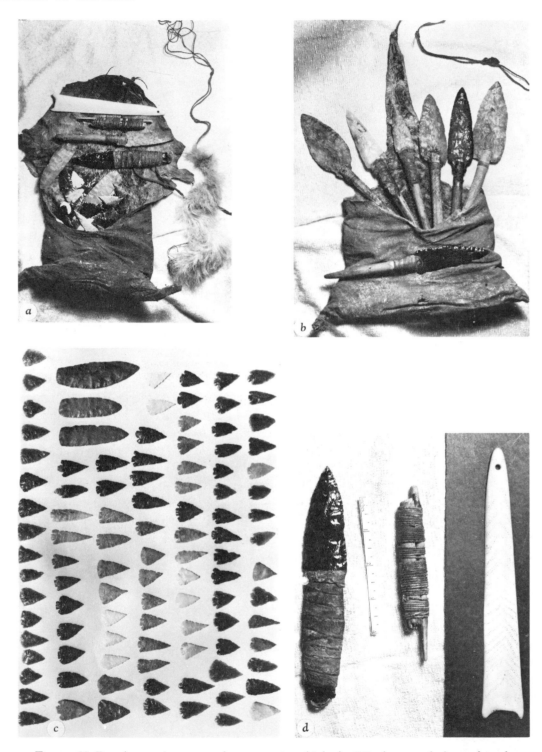

Figure 29. Pouches and contents from cave in which the Nicolarsen atlatl was found: A. Pouch opened; B. Pouch and contained atlatl foreshafts; C. Projectile points, etc., from pouch shown in A. Note different kinds of points used by one man as shown in A and B. Compare with Figure 28. The triangularly-shaped specimens may be pre-forms for making corner-notched points. Was the owner perhaps an itinerant knapper? D. Dagger, flaker, and pendant (?). *Photograph by Emory Strong; publication authorized by Jack Nicolarsen.*

and there is a shift toward emphasis on large game. The bow and arrow, small projectile points, and leather moccasins are the major new elements that appear during this time. The disjunctiveness of this cultural shift must not be overemphasized, however. Many elements that were present in the Wendover period remain a part of the inventory of the Black Rock period, and a clear thread of continuity between the two phases is evident. At sites other than Hogup Cave, a major shift in economic orientation during this period has not been noted, and it appears that this aspect of cultural change during the Black Rock period is not representative of a general trend for the region as a whole, but must be attributed to changes in the local environment of Hogup Cave.

Fremont Period: A.D. 500–1350. The horticulturally-based Fremont culture, originally recognized in the Fremont River drainage of east-central Utah by Morss (1931), is widespread in the Eastern Great Basin and adjacent Colorado Plateau region of Utah in this period. Diagnostic traits include most prominently house pits and above-ground jacal and adobe structures, maize-beans-squash horticulture, and a range of plain and painted pottery types. Projectile point types are the same as for the Black Rock period, with the addition of Desert side notched and Rose Spring side notched. Nonobsidian cryptocrystalline rock is preferred for the manufacture of projectile points as in the Black Rock period. Incised stones, tabular bone counters, painted bone splinters, bone disc beads, Olivella shell pendants, one-piece moccasins, Fremont moccasins and anthropomorphic figures made of plant fiber all become prominent in the cultural inventory of this time, although many have earlier antecedents. The dominant basketry type remains a one-rod and bundle, noninterlocking stitch ware, as in the Black Rock period, and the bow and arrow persists also from the earlier period.

In Hogup Cave, which provides the most detailed record for the period of transition, the Fremont culture emerges from the Black Rock period without marked discontinuity as the result of increments to the Black Rock cultural inventory. Like the preceding period, the Fremont period there exhibits more emphasis on the hunting of larger game animals than on the collection of small game and wild seeds, though these activities are still attested to to a degree.

Small amounts of maize found in the Fremont levels at Hogup suggest that the hunters who utilized the cave at this period were sent out from settled horticultural villages elsewhere in the region.

Shoshoni Period: A.D. 1350–1850. The ethnographic Shoshoni and their linguistic relatives supplanted the Fremont culture and occurred throughout its former range in historic times.

The Shoshoni period is very poorly defined archæologically. The deposits containing it are thin, and the cultural inventory of the phase is correspondingly thin. Other than by Shoshoni ware pottery and small Desert side-notched points, the archæological inventory is characterized mainly by its improverished nature. There is a loss of the diagnostic elements of the Fremont period, but evidently a continuation of the hunting-gathering aspect of its economic pattern, emphasizing the hunting of buffalo, antelope, and jackrabbits, along with some evidence of seed gathering.

To close out the discussion of the Eastern Great Basin the following brief observations are in order.

1. The criticism mentioned above that the reported stratigraphy of Danger Cave was invalid because of mixture of the fill is not borne out. Aikens made a stratigraphic reanalysis of the projectile points from Danger Cave after classifying them according to the method used for Hogup Cave. The result showed that the only place where significant mixture had occurred was in the top cultural level, D V, where apparently a stratigraphic difference was unnoticed in Danger Cave and there should have been a D VI cultural level.

2. The earliest date for human occupation in Danger Cave at 9500 B.C. is 2,000 years later than that at Fort Rock in the Northern Great Basin and 3,000 years later than at Wilson Butte Cave in the Snake River plain of southern Idaho. In the Western Great Basin there is a date of 11,000 years ago for Fishbone Cave on the shoreline of pluvial Lake Winnemucca.

3. There was a very long phase represented by the Wendover period of approximately 6,500 years of very efficient exploitation of the local economic resources. While changes in technology occurred during this period, nevertheless, it was essentially a period of a culture extraordinarily well adapted

to total exploitation of the environment. The bow and arrow appeared late in the period. Elko corner-notched points lasted through a span of 5,000 to 6,000 years; Elko-eared points were used for 2,000 years; and the Bitterroot side notched paralleled this time span. This record closely approximates that for the Northern Great Basin, and had the Fort Rock record not been interrupted by the eruption of the Mt. Mazama pumice for a period of 2,000 years, the cultural–ecological record in that area would probably have closely approximated that of the Eastern Great Basin. After a gradual decline, interrupted by the eruption, a cultural resurgence began about 5,000 years ago, and this would indicate a period of about 6,000 years of cultural stability with minor gradual change quite like that for the Wendover period.

4. The Fremont culture, which appeared as northwestern frontier settlements in the Salt Lake area in both Danger and Hogup caves after A.D. 500, cannot (as was once suggested by Steward 1937 and Aikens 1967) be derived from Athapascan sources, who were supposed to be migrants from the interior of British Columbia moving toward the American Southwest, because the culture predates the earliest date of divergence of the southern Athapascans from their northern neighbors at about A.D. 950. The Fremont culture is now thought to be a localized development centering on the Fremont River and to have been the recipient of influences from both the Southwest and the Northern Plains. The Promontory culture is but a localized derivative of the Fremont.

5. While there are differences between the cultural achievements in the Northern and the Eastern Great Basin, there is a strong core of similar methods of exploitation of the natural environment over extraordinarily long periods of time.

The Snake River Plain

The Snake River Plain, approximately 350 miles long and 50 to 75 miles wide, curves in a great southward-bending arc across southern Idaho like a protuberance of the adjacent western plateau. The plain, ranging in elevation from a little more than 2,000 feet in the west to over 7,000 in the east, is an incongruous physiographic feature among the rugged highlands of the northern Rocky Mountains (Malde 1965). More than thirty years ago some individuals (Kirk Bryan, the Harvard geologist; Ernst Antevs, the climatologist at Gila Pueblo; and the writer) called attention to the possibility that the ice-free passage provided by the Snake River Plain across the Rocky Mountains from the High Plains into the Great Basin could be of great significance in the study of the interrelations of the cultures of the two regions, which appeared to be of about the same age. Each of us, busy elsewhere with his own work, never had the opportunity to test this hypothesis.

Earl H. Swanson, Jr., came to Idaho State College, now Idaho State University, at Pocatello in 1957 and began a systematic archæological program of surveys and excavations in the Snake River Plain and the adjacent highlands. Swanson had enjoyed two years of postdoctoral study under the distinguished Frederick E. Zeuner, professor of Environmental Archæology, at the University of London, and brought to the study of the prehistory of the plain the environmental orientation of Zeuner, who was always trying to describe the culture and its changes in terms of its environmental context. It is to Swanson and his students that we are indebted for our knowledge of the Snake River Plain, and Swanson has graciously given me permission to draw upon an unpublished summary of the prehistory of the plain as he conceives it at this time.

The Snake River rises in Shoshone Lake in Yellowstone National Park at 8,000 feet elevation, and from there to about 7,000 feet the plain is forested and then parkland and wet meadows take over. Gradually this land cover is replaced, as one moves westward, by sagebrush–grassland. Below 6,000 feet occasional juniper forest occurs. Below 5,000 feet discontinuous sagebrush-grassland is characteristic. The megafauna has consisted of *Equus,* camel, mammoth, jaguar, dire wolf, deer, moose, antelope, mountain sheep, caribou, elk, and bison. Bison were rare below 5,000 feet altitude, and the principal big game herds were most numerous above that elevation on the Snake River Plain and in the many large valleys opening onto the plain from the north and south.

Swanson reports a series of three environmental fluctuations or epicycles for the plain dated as follows: (1) 12,400–7,150, (2) 7,150–3,400, (3) 3,400–100 radiocarbon years ago. Soil studies show that each cycle followed the same sequence: beginning dry, turning moist-cool, then warm. The beginning of the second cycle appears to have been drier than its predecessor or successor. This short period of extreme aridity falls between radiocarbon dates 7,150 and 5,800 year ago and marks the Altithermal period. These dates closely approximate those for the Northern Great Basin given above. There is no evidence during the Altithermal of wind deflation above the 6,000 foot altitude, while below 5,000 feet the evidence is extensive. The indirect evidence for the difference in ground cover at the two elevations shows the variation in the effects of a climatic episode.

It is within this environmental frame of reference that the human achievements are recorded and interpreted. Swanson states that the prehistory of the Snake River Plain and its hinterlands can be considered in two ways: (1) regional culture patterns, and (2) transitions in culture coincident with changes in the environment. These methods are complementary and both are used.

Birch Creek Phase: 8000–7150 B.P. There is first an Early Man period that has but one phase, the Birch Creek, but this is divided into Early and Late Periods. The Early portion is that before 8,000 or 8,500 years ago and the Late dates from 8,500 to 7,150 years ago. The time of earliest occupation (at Wilson Butte Cave, discussed in Chapter 4) was Pinedale II, and the environment would have been that of a grassy plain under the influence of its periglacial position. Mammals found associated with human occupation include sloth, camel, *Equus,* bison, and mountain sheep, not all, of course, found in a single site. The Late Period represents the time of transition from the generalized Early Man utilization of the Plain to the development of regional culture patterns. The date, 7,150 radiocarbon years ago, marks the beginning of the Altithermal in the plain, and at Wilson Butte Cave the indication is that the modern flora was established on the valley floor at that time.

Artifacts fall into two categories according to their provenience: those from surface sites without depth and those from stratified occupation sites. The former come mostly from the valley floor while the others are derived, with the exception of Wilson Butte Cave and the Wasden Site on the Snake River Plain itself, from shelters and sites within the valleys and canyons issuing from the bordering mountains. There is a significant difference between the two categories of artifacts. Points from the unstratified sites on the valley floor are closely related to those found on the High Plains across the Rocky Mountains: Clovis, Folsom, and others resembling Agate Basin, Hell Gap, Milnesand, Eden, Plainview, and Scottsbluff types. These undoubtedly are evidence of wide-ranging hunting parties from beyond the mountains. The Early part of the Birch Creek phase is marked by the large size of the points, with many from the surface finds having a length of 7 to 8 inches. The large size of these points suggests to me that they were used on thrusting or throwing spears.

In addition to the projectile points, the inventory of this period consists of small, steep end-scrapers, perforators, blades, and biface blanks.

The Late part of the Early Man phase, from about 8,500 to 7,100 years ago, is the period of transition to the appearance of regional culture patterns. It is the period of increasing desiccation terminating with the appearance of the Altithermal in the plain, although that episode occurs later above the 6,000 foot elevation in the surrounding mountains and to the east. The most striking cultural change during this period is the appearance of notched and stemmed points, which are smaller than those previously in use. These appear, as at Fort Rock, not as replacements, but as additions to the point inventory.

Swanson suggests that the appearance of the notched and stemmed points may be associated with an important technological change, the introduction of the bow and arrow. I do not think this can be the case, for reliable evidence from the Great Basin indicates the bow and arrow appeared probably at least 3,000 years later than would be required to support Swanson's suggestion. I suggest that the change in point types and size is due to: (1) separation of the Snake River Plain from the High Plains influence with the occupants of the later area now concentrating on the bison as a major food object; (2) increasing Great Basin influence; (3) change in the available game from the larger herbivorous varieties to the kinds characteristic of the modern environment.

The Bitterroot Culture Pattern: 7150–100 B.P. Two regional culture patterns are proposed, the Bitterroot pattern in the eastern part of the plain and the South Hills pattern in the west. The Bitterroot pattern appears to be limited on the west by the 5,000 foot contour of the western plain and to extend from the Salmon River canyon on the north to the rim of the Great Basin in southeastern Idaho. Swanson reports that comparable artifact types and patterns occur in Wyoming, possibly eastern Montana, and Alberta. The South Hills pattern reaches westward from the 5,000 foot contour in the plain, occurring in the mountains south of the plain and in the Owyhee uplands to the southwest.

The Bitterroot culture pattern is divided into four phases:

Bitterroot phase	7150–3400 B.P.
Beaverhead phase	3400–2900 B.P.
Blue Dome phase	2900–700 B.P.
Lemhi phase	700–100 B.P.

The phases are discriminated from one another primarily by changing proportions of point type. There is, however, a continuity of artifacts, of animal remains, and of activities which can be inferred from this evidence. The artifacts consist of conical cores, blades, knives, scrapers, steep end-scrapers, fleshers, and side-notched, corner-notched, and stemmed points, which occur from the beginning to the end of the Bitterroot sequence but in changing proportions. Metates and manos occur along with earth ovens. The ovens, bifacial blanks, and steep end-scrapers found in the Birch Creek phase continue through the Bitterroot pattern to the historic period. Natural seed beads continue from 8,000 years ago to historic times, when they are replaced by blue trade beads.

South Hills Culture Pattern: 7100–100 B.P. This pattern has not been divided into phases. Apparently settlement was continuous around springs above 5,000 feet elevation but discontinuous below that. This corresponds to the situation in the Bitterroot culture pattern area. The most striking difference between the two culture patterns is in the proportional difference between the projectile point types. Lanceolate points (Humboldt) and a stemmed (Pinto) variety appear through approximately a 7,000-year period and form a constant proportion of the point types present. This culture pattern also includes the deep bowl-shaped mortar and deer hoof rattles, contrasting with the mano-metate of the Bitterroot and its mountain sheep horn core, modified possibly for ceremonial use. With one or two exceptions, all the sites so far examined indicate light, intermittent occupation, and the smaller number of artifacts indicates a smaller population than in the Bitterroot pattern area. Some 50 miles north of the Boise Basin along the Weiser River occurs what may be an area of southeastern Columbia Plateau culture, or it may be an overlapping area of that culture and that of the South Hills.

Swanson sees the two culture patterns as variants of a common one, and the base apparently was the generalized Early Man ecosystem of the early part of the Birch Creek phase, which was modified during the transitional later portion of the phase in response to changing environmental conditions. He then carries the development of the two patterns down to historic times, arguing that the Bitterroot culture pattern is the archæological expression of Northern Shoshoni prehistory, and that the South Hills pattern may stand in a similar relation to the Western Shoshoni. The Bitterroot culture certainly had affinities across the Continental Divide, while the South Hills culture may have had affinities with the Northern Great Basin. Certainly both had relations with the Eastern Great Basin as demonstrated by the basketry. The Weiser Valley manifestations are suggested as archæological records of the Nez Percé.

A very brief statement by Swanson in support of his argument for the proposed relation between the Bitterroot culture and the northern Shoshoni follows:

the [Bitterroot] phases are distinguished from one another primarily by changing proportion of point types. Since this pattern extends into the historic period where natural seed beads are replaced by blue glass specimens, and gun flints occur side by side with side-notched projectile points, steep end scrapers, and fleshers which are still made and used at Fort Hall, it seems a reasonable inference that the Bitterroot culture is the archæological expression of Northern Shoshoni prehistory. The evidence and the interpretation challenge the linguistic hypothesis that Shoshoni were late migrants in this region arriving after A.D. 1300-1500. . . (personal communication, E.H. Swanson, Jr., to L.S. Cressman; Swanson 1972).

In summary, Swanson's studies have shown that a generally common environment was shared by the

Snake River Plain, the Northern Great Basin, and the southern Columbia River Plateau in the terminal Pleistocene and the Anathermal. A sparse human population with a relatively homogenous culture was dispersed through this area from mid-Pinedale time on. Intrusive bands from the High Plains crossed the Rocky Mountains to the east for several centuries leaving their artifacts in the plain, always in open sites; these occur now as surface finds. The intruders may have been summer hunting and/or exploring groups to this area so well stocked with game, who, after a reasonable period, returned across the mountains before the winter snows began. These bands apparently shared the area with the indigenous people whose contemporaneous remains are found in the caves on the valley floor and in caves in valleys opening from the mountains, but they left no permanent impression on the local culture.

About 8,500 years ago the Birch Creek phase, the common Early Man culture of the plain, began to differentiate into two variant regional patterns, the Bitterroot and the South Hills. The change was fully accomplished by approximately 7,100 years ago and is associated with the establishment of the modern flora, especially below 5,000 feet elevation. The Bitterroot pattern eventually shared many common lithic traits with neighbors across the Continental Divide indicating direct or indirect contact; the South Hills pattern shared lithic traits with the Northern Great Basin; both received their basketry from the Eastern Great Basin. The Snake River Plains people thus borrowed selectively, but the reason for this is not obvious. Eventually the Snake River Plain became a cultural cul-de-sac with the inhabitants becoming more recipients of novel ideas and things from their neighbors than dispensers to them. In historic times, the entire plain was occupied by Shoshoni-speaking people, who, on the basis of linguistic studies, were a part of the Numic expansion from the southwestern Great Basin starting about 1,000 years ago, but who, according to Swanson, are indigenous to the area with a history beginning in the Bitterroot phase if not earlier.

The Western Great Basin

This region is essentially coterminous with the limits of pluvial Lake Lahontan. On the west is the high escarpment of the Sierra Nevada range, while the eastern boundary is the divide between the Lake Lahontan and Lake Bonneville drainages. Along the Sierra escarpment a series of residual lakes draw their water from mountain sources and deep aquifers exposed by the Sierra fault; from north to south they are Honey, Pyramid, and Walker lakes. While these lakes were undoubtedly diminished during the Altithermal, it is doubtful if they ever dried completely. Farther to the south Mono and Owens lakes are part of the pluvial lake system but not part of the Lahontan basin.

The presence of these lakes and their shoreline areas at or near the escarpment, along with other fresh water supplied by mountain sources, provided a habitable corridor adjacent to the escarpment through which men and other animals could move with ease. In addition, hunting parties in the mountains became familiar with that terrain and could and did discover passes into the Central Valley of California. Lake Tahoe at the Sierra Nevada divide at approximately 39° north latitude and 120° west longitude furnished a considerable source of water for the lowland at the base of the mountains, flowing ultimately into Pyramid Lake.

Some 60 miles east of the Sierras are the Humboldt and Carson sinks where the Humboldt River, which heads in northeastern Nevada, and the Carson River, which flows out of the Sierra Nevadas, empty into adjacent desert basins. Because these basins lack outlets, the water is brackish but potable in the absence of anything better. The area was a haven for water birds of many kinds; small suckers and chubs occurred in large numbers; land mammals, of course, found both water and forage along the shorelines; along the shore and out into the shallow water tule stretched for miles, green in summer and brown in autumn. The tule provided food, material for cordage, basketry, sandals, other articles of clothing, the foundation for duck decoys, and other things.

The Humboldt Lake and Carson Sink area was an oasis and, as one would expect, a richer inventory of artifacts characterizes the adaptive activities of the inhabitants than in the less favorable habitats of the Great Basin. Lovelock Cave (Loud and Harrington 1929) and Humboldt Cave (Heizer and Krieger

1956), because they were so dry and were used to a large extent for caching valuable objects used in daily activities, have preserved better samples of the culture of the inhabitants than probably any other caves in the Great Basin. Both caves show most impressively how fully the people exploited the local resources of plants, especially tule, and fish, small game, and water fowl. The culture represented is basically that of the Great Basin and is an outstanding example of the richness made possible by an oasis environment. The culture, therefore, is an enriched variant of the Great Basin type. In the previous chapter I have discussed some of the adaptive aspects of the Great Basin culture as demonstrated by the Lovelock Cave record.

Lovelock Cave illustrates the richness achievable within the Great Basin culture pattern given a productive oasis environment. The cave was in use throughout the last 4,500 years as a place for caching important materials, and it was also used at various times as a place of occupation. Since "The entire Humboldt Cave archæological collection is clearly assignable to the Lovelock culture" (Heizer and Krieger 1956:76), I shall confine my discussion to Lovelock Cave.

In their 1924 excavations, Loud and Harrington set up a stratigraphic sequence based on their excavations at the southwest end of the cave. They recognized six major levels, which they combined into three developmental periods: Early, Transitional, and Late. Harrington, in Section IV, Probable History of the Cave (Loud and Harrington 1929:119-23), attempted to suggest a chronology for the periods based upon cross dating with the hypothetical Basket Maker I horizon of the Southwest. Later dates were suggested based upon an assumed steady rate of deposition of fill. He suggested that the date of the lowest level was about 1000 B.C. and the beginning of the "Later Period" about "1000 A.D." (Loud and Harrington 1929:122). He then says, "But of course this is mere speculation and may be far from the truth." As it turned out, Harrington was not too far from the truth.

Heizer, to secure firm dates for Lovelock Cave, many years later submitted samples for C-14 dating consisting of both burned and unburned bat guano from the "preoccupation level" (Libby 1952:86).

The burned guano gave a date of 4448±250 B.P. (C-277), and the unburned sample 6004±250 B.P. (C-278). The vegetal material was dated at 2482±260 B.P. (C-276).

The date, 2,482 years ago, seemed too late to some of us for the beginning of occupation of the cave. In order to get less equivocal dates, I arranged to have a series of *artifacts* from the stratigraphic section, Lot 15, dated (Cressman 1956a).* Sample C-735, dated at 3,172±260 years ago, came from Level 5, the next to the earliest level. The date for Level 2 is 1,686±220 (average of three dates; C-728-730). Levels 1, 3, 4, and 6 remain undated. Dates for these levels are estimated by extrapolation. It is generally thought that the earliest occupation was not before 4,500 years ago, corresponding to the approach of the Medithermal. Terminal use is estimated at A.D. 922. Grosscup (1960:11), on the assumption that the dates for Levels 2 and 5 represent mean dates for the levels and that the rate of deposition was constant, offered a series of dates for the six stratigraphic levels. Grosscup notes that the assumptions are open to question, but feels they are justified because "they do enable us to acquire working dates for interpretative purposes." His proposed dates are:

Level I:	565–922 A.D.
Level II:	29 B.C.–565 A.D.
Level III:	505–29 B.C.
Level IV:	980–505 B.C.
Level V:	1456–980 B.C.
Level VI:	2010–1456 B.C.

(Use of Roman numerals to order levels follows Grosscup.)

Another series of two C-14 dates from Lovelock Cave should be mentioned, both from human coprolites (Cowan 1967:25). Sample UCLA-1071F from an interior location, evidently a latrine, is dated at 1210±60 B.P., A.D. 740, while UCLA-1071E from a collection in a crevice outside the entrance is dated at 145±80 B.P., A.D. 1805. The first sample comes from Level I, according to Grosscup's chronology,

---

* Through the courtesy of the Museum of the American Indian, Heye Foundation, in 1940 I examined the materials from Lot 15 excavated by Loud and Harrington. I was particularly interested in the basketry and its stratigraphic distribution (Cressman et al. 1942:42, Figure 82 h, i).

although there appears to be no stratigraphic provenience. The latter must be associated with modern Paiute inhabitants who may or may not have used the cave for temporary shelter. The undigested food remains from the two samples are almost identical, but this fact does not indicate any cultural continuity linking the people who were responsible for the coprolites, only that both ate the available food, which remained constant in the Humboldt Lake vicinity.

For all practical purposes, Grosscup's period chronology may be accepted for the cave's use and for cross dating distinctive traits within the larger Humboldt-Carson Sink area. The majority of the traits, however, are general throughout the Great Basin and lack diagnostic value for cross dating.

Grosscup (1960) studied the Lovelock Cave collections from the 1924 excavation, which are housed in the Museum of the American Indian, Heye Foundation, and at the University of California, Berkeley, in an attempt to order chronologically the rich material. His study is the only attempt to give a complete description of the collections and to order them stratigraphically, aided by the C-14 dates then available. His Figure 10 represents his results. This chart contains 61 artifact type entries. For the Early Level 15 traits are indicated, but only 4 are firmly placed; 6 traits are Transitional only and 6 are Late only. The Early and Transitional shared 10 traits only and only 6 are shared by Transitional and Late (Grosscup 1960 passim). Grosscup notes several gaps in the Lovelock Cave record, but what we know from other sources clearly indicates that many of the lacunae must be the result of sampling error in excavation and not the absence of that trait among the inhabitants of Lovelock Cave. For example, twined tule bags, widely distributed in the Great Basin, are recorded for the Transitional Lovelock and the historic Paiute of the area, but not for the intervening Late Lovelock Period. Slings, reported as probably present in the Early Period at Lovelock Cave but lacking in later periods, were found in Humboldt Cave and, among the Lovelock-area Paiute, were used as toys. A full description of the culture of the inhabitants of the Humboldt Lake area will finally be possible when a large number of samples from other sites are coordinated

and a composite pattern described. Grosscup's analysis and summary provides a sound working basis on which to build.

I pointed out above that within the general framework of the stable Great Basin culture there were both internal changes and influences from other areas. Internal change at Lovelock is well illustrated by the development of wicker-ware burden baskets, which appear to have replaced coiled burden baskets in the Transitional. Wicker ware of the Lovelock variety has a distribution largely limited to the Humboldt Lake and Carson Sink area, where it is practically a hallmark of the Lovelock Transitional and Late Periods. Trade with the Pacific Coast people is indicated by the *Haliotis* and *Olivella* shell beads of the Early Period. What ideas may have accompanied the beads we do not know, but surely there must have been some imaginative response. What kind of gossip and question and answer must have marked the meetings of the intermediaries? It is hard to imagine that a people so sensitive to and observant of every item in their environment would not be curious about the country and perhaps the people from whom the iridescent *Haliotis* came.

The bow and arrow appear in excavation Level III, dated approximately 500 B.C.–A.D. 0, while the atlatl remained in use through that level. Assuming that the bow and arrow were first in use at the beginning of the level and the atlatl continued until the end, there is a period of 500 years when the two weapons were both used. The bow and arrow had to be either an alien introduction or a local (New-World) invention and the chances, in my opinion, favor the latter interpretation. Most notable, whatever the origin, is the length of time required for the bow and arrow, presumably a more efficient weapon, to find full cultural acceptance. I think this is a striking example of the conservatism of the Great Basin culture.

Grosscup estimates the date of abandonment of Lovelock Cave at A.D. 922 (Grosscup 1960:12). This date corresponds closely to the time calculated by Lamb and others (see Chapter 4) for the expansion of the Northern Paiute and may well be related to it. The most readily discernible trait differences between the Late Lovelock culture and that of the

Northern Paiutes is in basketry, the latter using twined ware in contrast to the coiled basketry and wicker ware of the Late Lovelock people. The difference on a more general cultural level is less than that between the Late and the Transitional Periods. It is difficult to see how it could be otherwise, for if the Northern Paiute were to survive in the same kind of environment, essentially the same kinds of devices would have been needed, and most of these would have been in the cultural inventory of the Northern Paiute before starting out on their dispersion. Their original environment was essentially the same, but perhaps not quite as good as that of the Humboldt Lake district.

Earlier cultural materials come from the Humboldt Lake area and the Carson Sink vicinity (Heizer 1951b, 1956; Grosscup 1956). The Leonard Rockshelter produced a very limited amount of cultural material, but its character and stratigraphic position give it importance. In the Carson Sink area, Hidden Cave and the 3,950 foot terrace of Lake Lahontan near the pass to Walker Lake are significant. Caves and terraces along the shoreline of Lake Winnemucca have also contributed earlier materials. Sites from Lake Winnemucca on the west to Danger Cave in Utah, from the Columbia River to Ventana Cave, and from the San Dieguito of Southern California, with firm dates of human presence more than 10,000 years ago, all suggest that the central area, that of the Humboldt River, should have been a human habitat at the same time.

The Leonard Rockshelter (Heizer 1951b) so far provides the earliest reasonably firm date for the Humboldt River area. Two dates from the layer of bat guano in the lowest level of the shelter, but derived from different samples, are somewhat confusing. Sample C-281 consisted of unburned guano. An average date based on two assays of the sample is 8,660±300 years ago. Sample C-298, run on atlatl foreshafts of greasewood from the same layer, gave a date of 7,038±350 years ago. Since wood is a better source material for C-14 dating than bat guano, the preferred date for the earliest component at the Leonard Rockshelter would seem to be that derived from the artifacts themselves. This date falls in the very earliest part of the Altithermal.

The artifacts comprising the earliest component at the Leonard Rockshelter were atlatl shaft fragments, a couple of obsidian flake scrapers, a "flint blade," and *Olivella* shell beads. Heizer (1951b) proposed calling this limited assemblage the "Humboldt Culture." A collection of "basalt core and heavy flake tools from the local 3,950 foot strand line" he calls the "Granite Point Culture" and assigns it to the Anathermal along with the early component from Leonard Rockshelter. Roust (1966:54-55), in his archæology of Granite Point, reports only 27 lithic specimens of which 22 were waste flakes, and the balance consisted of a small side-notched point, a drill, and three scrapers.

At a slightly higher elevation in a stratum consisting mostly of wind-blown dust at Leonard Rockshelter was an infant burial with fragments of a stiff-twined basket, possibly a parching tray, but nothing else. This material is called the "Leonard Culture" and is dated at 5,737±250 (C-554) years ago. It is obviously from the full Altithermal. Above the "Leonard Culture" is the "Lovelock Culture."

Heizer, in giving each of these manifestations rankings as independent cultures rather than as subdivisions of a single Great Basin culture, would seem to be deviating from what I described as a major development in the study of Great Basin prehistory, the development of a conceptual approach that visualized the Great Basin culture as a basically uniform adaptation to a generalized arid environment. Heizer's approach has been criticized but he maintains its validity (Heizer 1956:53). Grosscup (1956), discussing the Carson Sink area, uses the word "phase" as the taxonomic unit to which Heizer applies the word "Culture," so that we have Humboldt phase, Granite Point phase (?), Lovelock phase, a usage much more in keeping with the evidence. I have extended this discussion because I think the use of these names, "Humboldt Culture," etc., in view of the commonly understood meaning of the word culture by anthropologists, is misleading for any reader who neither controls the original data nor goes to the original sources. An infant burial and fragments of a basket are hardly sufficient evidence of the "lifeway" of a people to represent a culture.

Two points of great importance for Great Basin prehistory derive from the Leonard Rockshelter and closely related sites, First, as Heizer (1951b:94) points out, the presence of *Olivella* shells in the "Humboldt Culture" indicates contact with the Pacific Coast, either directly or through intermediaries. These people either traveled and secured these shells or, as is more likely, they passed in trade. Whichever way they came, it is clear these people in the hot and dusty valley of the Humboldt River were aware of another country, and they must have heard much, both fanciful and realistic, about it from those with whom they came in contact. The second point is that the hot and dry Altithermal must have nearly depopulated the Humboldt Lake area. The "Lovelock Culture" dates probably from the beginning of the Medithermal with a cooler and moister climate by which the landscape was rejuvenated as a habitat, eventually as an oasis. The "Leonard Culture" is the only evidence of full Altithermal occupation, and it appears to be the pathetic testimony of a family or two searching for water in a land where there was none. If the near depopulation hypothesis has value, then the origins or the earlier expression of the culture represented in the Early Lovelock Period must be sought elsewhere.

At Hathaway Beach in the Fallon area south of Carson Sink and at Hidden Cave in the same general area were found specimens considered to be of late Anathermal age on the basis of their geological associations. Grosscup (1956:62) says of these artifacts: "There are typological resemblances between Fallon material and that of Lake Mohave (Campbell et al. 1937) and Lind Coulee, but the closest resemblances are to specimens found by Dr. Cressman near Big Springs [Spring*] in Guano Valley, southeastern Oregon (Cressman 1936)." The Hathaway Beach material is not otherwise described, but apparently projectile points and crescents are the diagnostic elements for the relations suggested by Grosscup. This assemblage, an andesitic quarry close by from which materials were secured, and similar

materials from a site on the same terrace but some distance from the Hathaway Beach site, Grosscup calls the Fallon phase. He assigns the earliest Hidden Cave specimens to a Hidden Cave phase and places two projectile points found in Altithermal silts in Hidden Cave in a "tentative" Carson phase. The upper levels of Hidden Cave contained Lovelock Cave-type artifacts and are assigned to a Lovelock phase, with the most recent material probably representing prehistoric Paiute. The Fallon and Hidden Cave phases are dated from the Anathermal, and apparently the former is the earlier; the Carson phase is from the Altithermal and the Lovelock from the Medithermal. On the basis of the evidence available, meaningful correlations with the previously mentioned Humboldt and Leonard "Cultures" is impossible; only the Lovelock finds clear-cut similarities.

Sites on the Lake Lahontan 3,950 foot terrace, the Anathermal level of the lake, have recently begun to be studied and have added important information on the early occupation of western Nevada. The Sadmat Complex, from the Fallon area south of the Carson Sink, was named by combining the first three letters in the names of the two persons who collected the material, Mrs. Sadler and Mrs. Mateucci. The two collections come from an area of about 2 square miles. Only the Sadler collection was studied, but both collections are essentially the same. The Sadler collection consists of more than 500 specimens. There are 165 projectile points, 72 spokeshaves, 185 gravers and drills, 9 crescents, and numerous scrapers including the keeled and domed varieties (Warren and Ranere 1968).

The projectile points are classified as follows:

Haskett	74
Lake Mohave	24
Bi-pointed leaf shaped	25
Bi-pointed round base	32
Stemmed	6
Concave base triangular	2
Asymmetrical, broad based leaf shaped	2

The Haskett point (see p. 158, above; P2 in Figure 27B) was first recognized and named by Butler (1965) from finds made in Idaho. Warren and Ranere (1968) quote a personal communication from

---

* Big Spring is just south of the Nevada line, about 20 miles east of Guano Valley and as many south over the most wretched trail I have ever been on in a Model A pickup truck or any other.

Donald Crabtree, the well-known expert flint knapper, describing the flaking technique used for points of the same type identified from Lake Mohave, California. Crabtree notes the following attributes of the Haskett point technology:

(a) straight lateral margins
(b) collateral flaking at right angle to the margin
(c) diffuse bulb of force, resulting in shallow flake scars
(d) flakes terminate without margins, that is, they feather out at mid section of the blade
(e) point of pressure not applied directly in line with a ridge, therefore flakes expand
(f) first step in manufacture appears to have been done initially by well controlled direct percussion, then pressure flaking with ridge at margin of bulbar scars removed by very delicate pressure flaking
(g) thin lenticular cross-section (Warren and Ranere 1968:14).

Butler described two Haskett point types. Type 1 is broadest and thickest toward the point from the midline. The projectile tapers gradually and symmetrically to a rounded base. The edges are ground from the base forward for a distance of slightly less than one third of the total length. Size varies from about 7.3 to 12.5 centimeters. Type 2 is symmetrical being widest at the midpoint. Otherwise the types are alike except for size; type 2 tends to be longer with one specimen 22 centimeters long. The very broad distribution of this type is significant for the culture history of the Western Great Basin and will be discussed further in later pages.

The Coleman Site is located on the west side of Lake Winnemucca near the north end on and above the 3,950 feet Lake Lahontan Terrace. The site is quite close to the Falcon Hill cave excavated by Shutler but not yet described in publication. An andesitic volcanic plug a short distance up a draw coming into the lake bed from the hills to the west provided the raw materials for the Coleman site artifacts, as is shown by a quarry. Two workshops, a probable campsite, and the quarry have been located. Between 600 and 700 classifiable artifacts and nearly 2,000 waste flakes have been recovered. Crabtree has studied the material and reports that the cylinder flaking technique was the dominant one in use.

The Haskett point and the crescent appear to be lacking in the Coleman assemblage. There are stemmed projectile points, end and side scrapers, domed scrapers or planes made on flakes, and engraving tools. Warren and Ranere state, "However, this assemblage duplicates every major San Dieguito artifact type described by Warren and True (1961) except crescents and also exhibits a similar stone working technique" (1968:12). The Coleman Site assemblage thus shares some traits with the Sadmat but lacks the northern flavor of the latter.

The Sadmat and Coleman assemblages are clearly quite early and are probably related in some way to the Fallon phase materials mentioned by Grosscup. The relationship of these three complexes to the San Dieguito complex of Southern California and Nevada is also important and will be explored further below.

The Karlo Site (LAS-7; California Site Code) is an open site in northeastern California in Secret Valley about 15 miles north of Honey Lake in Lassen County. Honey Lake is a remnant of Lake Lahontan and at present is a playa some 15 miles wide that receives water from the Susan River. The lake in periods of good runoff from the Sierras may be as much as 12 feet deep, but during dry periods it is only a dry lake bed, the source of the familiar "dust devils."

The Karlo Site was excavated in 1955 under the direction of Francis A. Riddell (Riddell 1960). It is a midden generally 3 to 4 feet deep, geologically unstratified, and with apparently little or no cultural stratigraphy. Practically no textile materials were preserved in the midden undoubtedly due to dampness. Shell, stone, and bone artifacts comprise the cultural inventory. The partial skeletons of over thirty individuals were recovered of which thirteen crania have been described (Riddell 1960: Appendix A by Grover Krantz).

The shell material consists mostly of beads and ornaments. There are spire ground *Olivella,* square abalone (*Haliotis*), and mussel shell beads, miscellaneous varieties, and abalone shell ornaments.

In the stone inventory are projectile points, large chipped stone blades, and two fragments of "crescents" (but a number of objects called "crescents" [Ridell 1960: Figure 10 b, c] are surely something different from the characteristic crescent from early assemblages I have discussed and from the two fragments illustrated in Ridell's Figure 10 e, f). Cores and core tools, manos, metates, hopper-mortars, pestles, pipes, scoria rubbing stones, perforated stone discoidals, probable atlatl weights, and atlatl spurs make up the additional significant elements of the stone artifacts. There are human figurines of clay, baked clay objects bearing imprint of probable fine twined basketry, and pigment.

Bone awls, flaking tools, scapula saws, spatulate implements, tubular beads, bone and antler dice, etc., comprise the bone inventory.

This site was probably used repeatedly throughout the year by a group or groups who returned here to a home base from their hunting and collecting activities. A spring close to the site indicates the desirability of the location in this generally arid area.

The initial use of the site dates probably from around 4,000 years ago. A C-14 date, LJ-76, from the 24 to 36 inch level, but not at the bottom of the midden, is 2,350±150 years ago. Riddell suggests that the earlier material equates with Early and Transitional Lovelock. This time span he calls the Karlo period, and the remainder is termed the Late Period. Comparison with Central California equates the Karlo site occupation in time with the terminal Early and the Middle Horizon (Riddell 1960:91). This equivalence is based on cross dating by shell bead types and by comparison of the stone atlatl spurs found at Karlo with one from a site (SJO-112) near Stockton, California, containing burials and artifacts belonging to the late Early Horizon. Three atlatl spurs, two stone and one bone, were found at Karlo, but their stratigraphic positions are not clear. A fragment of a boatstone type of atlatl weight similar to those from the Martis complex and the Central California Middle Horizon was also found at Karlo. I have discussed the distribution of this artifact and the inserted atlatl spur in the previous chapter.

It has been suggested that the Karlo Site is probably a manifestation of the "Lovelock Culture" (Grosscup 1960). I believe that this suggestion is undesirable and really confuses the real situation. Perishable materials, which make up so much of the Lovelock Cave inventory, are practically lacking at Karlo, probably because of disintegration, but we cannot restore them. My guess is that many of the artifact types, basketry, etc., would have been com-

mon to the two sites for they are widespread, but that is only a guess. Bone awls are used in making coiled basketry, but since they are used for many other purposes (Osgood 1940), it is not safe to assume the fabrication and use of coiled basketry from their presence alone. Equation in time is one thing; equation in culture is another. The main significance of the Karlo Site, it seems to me, lies in the evidence it provides for communication between the Great Basin and the trans-Sierra region, and between the northern and southern reaches of the Basin. North-south communication along the base of the Sierras is, as I have emphasized earlier in this chapter, exhibited on a very early time level. Karlo appears to be one of the stations along this corridor.

Lake Tahoe lies about 100 miles south of Honey Lake just east of the crest of the Sierra Nevada Mountains. On both sides of the divide, but mostly on the east, are a large number of sites extending for about 40 miles from Lake Tahoe north. Two cultural manifestations are represented, the Martis complex and the Kings Beach complex. The first is named "from its location in Martis Valley along Martis Creek and [we] select Pla-5 as the type site. The latter culture we have designated 'Kings Beach Complex', and name Pla-9 as the type site" (Heizer and Elsasser 1953:19). Additional mapping has extended the distribution of "Martis-affiliated sites" almost to Honey Lake in Lassen County and added considerably to the number reported in 1953 (Elsasser 1960a:Map 10). Most of these lie north of Lake Tahoe. The Kings Beach complex sites have a more limited distribution within the general area just described. "[I]f there is any which could properly be referred to as the characteristic 'Martis area,' this would fall largely into the Transition Zone (cf. Maps 2 and 10), on the eastern and western sides of the range" (Elsasser 1960a:67). The preferred altitude is between 2,500 and 6,000 feet depending on which side of the range the site is located. Some sites occur as high as 8,000 feet, probably summer camps.

The Martis complex is characterized by a preference for basalt for chipped tools with obsidian and chert very rarely used; large, heavy projectile points roughly made and variable in kind; mano and metate for seed grinding; cylindrical pestle and bowl mortar (?); boatstones and, therefore, atlatl inferred;

economic emphasis on hunting and seed using; abundant flake scrapers with pressure-retouched edges; and expanded-base, finger-held flake drills or punches are common.

The Kings Beach complex has a preference for obsidian and siliceous chert for chipped stone implements and basalt is rarely used. Bedrock mortars for seed grinding are present; projectile points are small and side notched; economic emphasis is on fishing and seed using; bow and arrow are present; and scrapers are rare and drills absent (adapted from Heizer and Elsasser 1953).

The majority of sites are purely surface with a few showing unimpressive depth. Clear stratification cannot be said to occur. It is clear, however, that the Kings Beach is later than the Martis complex as demonstrated by cross dating. A tentative chronology (Elsasser 1960a:Table 15) terminates the Martis Complex at somewhere around A.D. 800, or even later, with no definite beginning but suggested around 4,000 years ago. The Kings Beach complex dates from A.D. 1100 to ethnographic time. Both complexes are in the territory held by the Washo.

The Washo are a Hokan-speaking people, the most easterly representatives in California of that once widely spread linguistic stock. Heizer and Elsasser (1953:2) write, "This linguistic affiliation [Hokan] indicates their ultimate origin [Washo] to the west in California." Kroeber (1925:569) says, "It is tempting to conjecture . . . that they are an ancient California tribe, which has gradually drifted, or been pressed, over the Sierra. But there are no concrete grounds other than speech to support such an assumption." As I pointed out in Chapter 6, the Hokan were at an early time in all likelihood in the Great Basin from which they were pushed, perhaps by Penutians, and Kroeber (1955) states that the Hokan distribution in California suggests that they represent displaced populations and that the pressure probably came from the east, which would be the Great Basin.

The problem of the Martis complex, both as to its origin and its relation to historic Washo, is of more than local interest. It is not clear at present that Martis develops through Kings Beach to Washo; nor is the origin of Martis known. Are the Washo a remnant, holding stubbornly to an ancient home, of the once widely spread Hokans or does the Martis complex

represent an amalgam of influences from both the Great Basin and Central California as people from these areas exploited the higher reaches of the Sierras in their seasonal food quests? The location of the majority of the sites on the east of the Sierra crest suggests a major orientation toward the Great Basin, that is, a greater use of the area by people from there. The answer to these questions will eventually be found in the excavation of stratified sites, if such exist. Work on both sides of the Sierras will be required. Price (in d'Azevedo, ed. 1963:92) tends to see a sequential development from Martis through Kings Beach to Washo. He says,

> The Washo, the earlier Kings Beach complex people, and the still older Martis complex people solved the problems of survival in quite similar ways. We suspect that they are the same people at different periods of time. Still, caution must be exercised in attempting to correlate archæological manifestations with ethnographic groups in the area.

The present writer tested the hypothesis that the Washo of the ethnographic present were closer to the archæologically known Lovelock culture than the Northern Paiute or Achomawi. This was done by comparing a list of 64 traits of Lovelock culture prepared by Grosscup (1954, 22-23) with the ethnographic trait lists by Stewart (1941) for Washo, Achomawi, and Tasiget Northern Paiute. This comparison showed that the three ethnographically known cultures were almost exactly equal in their similarity to Lovelock culture. It also showed that the material culture for the west central Great Basin was so similar that considerable caution is necessary in assigning a complex, a site, or a component to any particular historic tribe. In view of these facts it appears that extensive excavation, particularly of known Washo sites, will be necessary to confidently ascribe the Kings Beach complex to the prehistoric Washo.

It is obvious that there is no clear-cut answer either to the question of origin of the Martis complex or to that of cultural continuity in the area. The problem becomes more confused by the evidence of widespread trade north and south along the eastern flank of the Sierra Nevada, as well as trans-Sierran, as long as 4,000 years ago and even as much as 7,500 years ago, as shown by the Leonard Rockshelter with its *Olivella* shell beads from the Pacific Coast. If future work should succeed in identifying the Martis complex as a Great Basin derivative and as a stage leading to historic Washo, it would indicate that the Washo are a Hokan remnant who have held fast to an ancient territory, or to a refuge area at least, and survived by the development of appropriate adaptive techniques for the new environment.

In closing out the Great Basin discussion a few remarks are in order concerning regional similarities and differences. Adovasio (1970), in his study of the origin, development, and distribution of western archaic textiles, examined over 5,000 specimens of twined, coiled, and plaited baskets. His study indicated the existence of three divisions, which he calls "complexes," according to the regions of location: the Oregon complex, the Western Nevada complex, and the Eastern Great Basin complex. The preferred basketry types by regions are: Northern Great Basin (Oregon complex)—twining, coiling; Western Great Basin (Western Nevada complex)–wicker ware, coiling, twining; Eastern Great Basin complex —coiling, twining. I have presented the types in order of preference according to the percentage each composes in the total number of specimens recovered in each area.

Adovasio believes that twining started in the Northern Great Basin approximately 10,000 years ago and spread after a few centuries to the other two areas, but the date of 11,195 radiocarbon years ago for a twined specimen from Fishbone Cave on the shoreline of pluvial Lake Winnemucca in western Nevada places the technique in the western Nevada region at an even earlier time. Assessing the relationship between the three regional complexes, Adovasio concludes that

> most important, there is a marked trend toward regional specialization and technical divergence in each of the complexes through time, though at no period is evidence for mutual influence entirely lacking. . . . [T]he technical relationship throughout the sequence between the Oregon and Western Nevada complexes—with one notable exception, Stage III [4500-2000 b.c.] seems to be more pronounced than those relationships maintained by either area with the Eastern Basin. In retrospect, the Eastern Basin and the Oregon complexes show the least affinities, while the Western Nevada complex, because of its geographical position, shares to some extent the attributes of both (Adovasio 1970:14).

Cressman (Cressman et al. 1942:140), on the basis of the limited evidence available at that time, suggested a developmental sequence for the Great Basin culture, proposing a stream of cultural influences flowing from the Plateau and Northern Great Basin south into Nevada where it divided into two streams, one of which followed the western corridor along the Sierra escarpment to Southern and Central California and the other followed an eastern route (the Eastern Great Basin) eventually into the Anasazi area of the American Southwest. Adovasio's study gives strong support to this suggestion. Warren and Ranere (1968), using lithic material, indicated the evidence for connection between southern Idaho, the Northern Great Basin, the Western Great Basin, and Southern California at an early time level. Bedwell (1969) presented the evidence for cultural connection at different time levels between the Columbia Plateau, the Northern Great Basin, the Western Great Basin, Southern California, and the Central Valley of California. The divergence of this western line of influence in its cultural expression from that of the Eastern Great Basin was also made clear. All these points will be explored further in the section to follow.

CALIFORNIA

Southeastern California

Owens Lake lies some 200 miles south of Lake Tahoe along the escarpment forming the eastern boundary of the Sierra Nevada Mountains. Owens Lake is a part of a pluvial lake system beginning with Mono Lake (pluvial Lake Russel), about 120 miles to the north, and terminating in Death Valley (pluvial Lake Manly). This system was continuous probably only in the Early Wisconsin (Tahoe Glaciation). In Late Wisconsin (Tioga Glaciation) the chain was interrupted and neither Mono Lake nor Searles Lake overflowed although Owens Lake apparently did. In addition to this drainage system, lying just to the south was the drainage system of the Mohave River, which flowed generally easterly into Mohave Lake and then north to Lake Manly. These lakes were formed in the basins between the characteristic north-south trending mountains of the Great Basin, a feature I described in Chapter 2. What has been said above about the fluctuation of water resources in the Great Basin during the climatic fluctuations of the Pleistocene and post-Pleistocene applies here and probably to a greater degree because of the more southerly latitude, roughly between 35° and 38° north latitude. Evaporation would have been more rapid because of the higher temperatures and precipitation probably less. Mono and Owens lakes, however, received water from the Sierras with Pleistocene glaciers extending to Mono Lake. During the time of human occupation there occurred, thus, quite different environments, and during the early Medithermal the opportunities for human existence were superior to those at present.

Steward (1938:50) describes the Owens Valley as a habitat:

> On the west it is sharply bounded by the lofty Sierra Nevada range . . . and on the east by the Inyo and White Mountains. The crest of the former is nowhere under 10,000 feet altitude, with many peaks surpassing 14,000 feet. Heavy rain and snowfall in these summits is preserved in lakes, springs, snow fields, and even glaciers, from which streams flow out into the otherwise arid valley at intervals of 2 to 15 miles and finally seep out into swamps in the lowlands where they are drained off by Owens River. Deer and mountain sheep could be had in the high mountains; various seeds in the foothills; seeds, roots, antelope, and rabbits in the valley. The arid Inyo and White Mountains on the east give rise to no streams, but support extensive pine-nut groves and formerly had many mountain sheep and deer.
>
> This extraordinarily varied environment afforded all essential food resources within 20 miles of the villages, which were situated on the various streams.

The whole length of this long corridor provided access westward to the San Joaquin Valley, northward along the Sierra escarpment, and southward, especially in times of a more genial climate, to the Colorado River drainage and Southern and Baja California. The prehistory of this area then would be expected to show a variety of component influences, and this is what the record indicates.

Harrington (1957), during the years 1948 through 1951, excavated the Stahl Site south of Owens Lake, named after the lake's discoverer but generally referred to as Little Lake. The site represents the remains of a village with houses occupied by early "Pinto people" and with Shoshonean remains near and at the surface. The site, like that of historic Owens Valley villages, is "on the lower edge of a great alluvial fan emanating from several canyons in the high Sierra to the west—a gradual slope terminating at a low terrace adjoining the now dry stream-bed running down to Little Lake, the north shore of which is about three-quarters of a mile

distant" (Harrington 1957:10). The site is about 500 feet in diameter. Nearby, and possibly a part of the same settlement, at least during the earlier period, is a small cave in a huge lava mass. The contents of the cave, while not numerous, overlap those from the early Stahl site and then parallel those from Rose Spring and other later sites.

The date of the Stahl Site has been determined by geological means and typological cross dating. According to Harrington, the root holes of large trees extending well below the earliest level of occupation indicate a moister climate existed at the time of site occupation than now. This could have been either during the Anathermal or Medithermal. The occupation is associated with the latter through cross dating with the Early Horizon of Central California by bead imports. Harrington (1957:72) reports that a cave or rock shelter near Moapa, Nevada, contained a "deeply buried stratum yielding points similar to the shoulderless Pinto Basin type. . . . Charcoal from the hearth 54" below the surface yielded a date of $3,870\pm 250$ years, and that from the 78" hearth a date of $4,050\pm300$ years (no lab. no. given)." On this basis, Harrington estimated the age of the Pinto deposits at Little Lake at between 3,000 and 4,000 years ago.

In addition to the lithic assemblage there was discovered at the Stahl Site a series of house pits generally roughly oval in shape and averaging about 9 by 12 feet. Posts about 4 inches in diameter had been sunk into the ground to a depth of about 10 inches. Some of these postholes were slanting indicating that the posts sloped toward the center at the top. Probably this framework of posts was covered by mats or even bunches of grass and brush, but nothing remains. Some had small, shallow basin depressions that were interpreted as hearths. One with straight postholes suggests a straight-sided, flat-top roof type.

The lithic inventory, in addition to three varieties of Pinto Basin points, consisted of Lake Mohave-Silver Lake and willow-leaf-shaped specimens. In addition there was a Gypsum Cave type point found in a crevice in the cave. Many kinds of scrapers, knives, drills, scraper planes, choppers, and manos and metates compose the assemblage. *Olivella* shell spire beads indicate trade with California.

The Lake Mohave–Silver Lake points number 90, of which 17 are made from other than obsidian. There are 497 Pinto points, of which only 28 are not made from obsidian. The leaf-shaped points number 38 and 8 are not obsidian. The Pinto points are found at all levels but one, increasing in numbers from the 42 inch level to the surface. The Lake Mohave-Silver Lake points are found throughout except in the 37 to 42 inch level. There is one in each of the two lower levels, then 0, and 2, 20, 33, 12, and 17 in each succeeding higher level respectively. All leaf-shaped points come from above 30 inches. The preference for obsidian in all types and all levels is striking.

This distribution of points through time suggests, to me at least, that Harrington's proposal that the Lake Mohave-Silver Lake points were picked up from the surface of older sites for reuse by the later Pinto people is hardly tenable. Instead, it seems evident to me that the Stahl Site provides a record of the development of the Pinto-type point at a time when the Lake Mohave-Silver Lake types were still in use by the same people.

The Rose Spring Site (INY-372) is in Rose Valley, "a shallow declivity" approximately 10 miles north of Little Lake. The site, in a sagebrush covered, sandy deposit of several acres, lies at the foot of a cliff, and about 50 yards southwest is Rose Spring, still semiactive. The site was discovered and test pitted in 1951 by Harry Riddell. Because of the depth of the site and the possibility of a good stratigraphic sequence, the decision to excavate the site was carried out in 1956 under the direction of Francis A. Riddell. Lanning (1963) prepared the report.

Lanning sets up a sequence starting with a "hypothetical phase" based on one lanceolate point and a fragment, both from the surface, that he equates with points from the Hidden Cave phase and Angostura points, which they resemble. This is Owens Lake I of his chronology. A "tentative phase" based on the Lake Mohave-Silver Lake-type points at Little Lake (Stahl Site) is his Owens Lake II. Unless one firmly assumes that the Lake Mohave-Silver Lake points found in the Pinto assemblage were picked up from the surface of older sites and reused by the Pinto people, the chronology for Owens Lake II cannot be defended, and the suggested Owens Lake I rests on a very unsubstantial foundation. His third stage is Little Lake, represented by the Stahl Site, and from

here on he is on firmer ground. Early, Middle, and Late Rose Spring follow with Early and Late Cottonwood completing the sequence. His description of the well-documented stages follows:

III. *Little Lake.* Represented by the whole of the Pinto assemblage at the Little Lake site, excluding the later materials from the Stahl Site cave and from the upper levels of the open deposit. Pinto points, chipped stone discs, and stone saws are diagnostic. Limited numbers of Lake Mohave and Silver Lake points occur, as well as large choppers, core scrapers, scraper-planes, and leaf-shaped knives. Broad Leaf and Willow Leaf points, and drill type-1 are also found. The metate occurs, together with shaped and unshaped manos (types 1 and 3). House floors and post hole patterns at Little Lake give evidence that permanent or semi-permanent villages existed at this time.

IV. *Early Rose Spring.* Stratum 3 at Iny-372. There is a marked continuity of types from the Little Lake Complex, including leaf-shaped knives (types 1 and 2), Willow Leaf points, rare Pinto points, and type-1 drills. Only shaped manos are known in this phase, and core tools and shaped scrapers are now very rare. Humboldt Concave-base points seem to be limited to Early Rose Spring. New projectile point types include the Elko Series, Gypsum Cave, and large triangular forms. The occupation of the Fossil Falls site (Harrington 1952) apparently began at this time.

V. *Middle Rose Spring.* The Elko, Gypsum Cave, and large triangular point types continue into this phase, together with type-1 manos and rare core tools and shaped scrapers. The phase is characterized by the occurrence of Middle Horizon shell bead types, pumice shaft smoothers, and slate tablets, and by the introduction of small projectile points of the Rose Spring Series, notched-base and asymmetric knives (types 3 and 4), fine expanding-base drills (type 3), and chipped ovals. The occurrence of Rose Spring point types almost certainly signals the introduction of the bow. Middle Rose Spring probably covers a good deal of time during which typological change occurred in the artifacts, but the artifact sample is so small that it must be treated as a single phase for the present. It is represented by the whole of stratum 2 at the Rose Spring site.

VI. *Late Rose Spring.* This phase is defined by the large sample from lower stratum 1, 24-36", at Iny-372. Dart points no longer occur. The projectile points are almost all of the Rose Spring Series, but include the first few Cottonwood Triangular points and a couple of Eastgate Expanding-stem points as trade pieces. Knife types 2 and 4 continue, as do drill type 3, chipped ovals, and mano type 1. Split, punched *Olivella* 3b1 beads occur. Cobble pestles and steatite disc beads are introduced and, of the Rose Spring Series points, the Contracting-stem and aberrant types make their first appearance. Core tools and shaped scrapers are no longer found.

VII. *Early Cottonwood*. Represented by upper stratum 1 (0-24") at Iny-372 and by part of the Cottonwood Creek (Iny-2) collection. A number of new artifact types, diagnostic of the two Cottonwood phases, are first introduced. These include Owens Valley Brown Ware, clay and pumice pipes, thin-lipped *Olivella* 3a1 beads, and Desert Side-notched points. Drill type 2 seems to be limited to this phase. The phase is distinguished from the historic Late Cottonwood phase by the presence or continuation of stemmed projectile points (Rose Spring Series), knife type 2, drill type 3, chipped ovals, and mano type 1, none of which are found in Late Cottonwood.

VIII. *Late Cottonwood*. Represented by part of the collection from Iny-2. Though not yet isolated in excavation, there is clear evidence that this phase existed as a distinct archæological unit. Traits are assigned to it according to the following criteria:

1. Traits present at Iny-2 but not found in the midden at Iny-372 are assumed to be limited to Late Cottonwood.

2. Traits common at Iny-2 and found in upper stratum 1 at Iny-372 are taken as shared by Early and Late Cottonwood.

3. Traits common at Iny-372 but rare at Iny-2 are assumed to belong only to Early Cottonwood.

4. Traits mentioned or illustrated ethnographically are attributed to Late Cottonwood. Steward (1938) is the primary source. Perishable items, such as wooden mortars, are not discussed, because they cannot be compared to the nonperishable artifacts from the archæological sites (Lanning 1963:268-69).

The importance of Lanning's study lies in the establishment of a cultural and chronological sequence for Owens Lake and correlations with California and the Western Great Basin. His "Tentative Correlation" is reproduced in Table 11. While there will be differences of opinion in details until firm dates are provided by reliable C-14 dating, for more of the areas included the scheme provides a working chronology for the Western Great Basin.

Pluvial Lake Mohave (Campbell et al. 1937), some 60 miles east of Barstow, California, has been for decades a focal point for Early Man studies in Southern California. The Lake Mohave–Silver Lake projectile point types mentioned repeatedly above are named for the locality, and, in the opinion of Warren and Ranere (1968), the area is crucial to the definition and understanding of the early San Dieguito complex that occurs throughout the Southern California deserts.

The lake bed is bilobed; the lower or southern part is called Soda Lake and the northern Silver Lake. The combined area is pluvial Lake Mohave. At the north end is an outlet cut 11 feet deep into solid granite, which permitted the lake to overflow into the Amarogosa River and then into Death Valley (Lake Manly). Terraces occur at 937, 943, and 946 feet. Because of erosion the two higher terraces cannot always be definitely identified but the lower can. Below the 937 foot terrace there are a number of less well-defined beachlines marking later, short-lived lake stands. The character of the 937-foot beachline indicates a long period of lake level, and the sudden change in the terrace record indicates that after the water dropped below the level of the bottom of the outlet channel, 937 feet, the level of the lake dropped fairly rapidly, with temporary stands, but none long enough to cut significant beaches. This decline in the size of the lake is interpreted as suggesting the onset of a more arid climate.

Mr. and Mrs. Campbell, with colleagues from the Southwest Museum, Dr. Ernst Antevs as the consultant on climatic history, members of the staff of the California Institute of Technology, and others, made the initial study of the area in 1934 and 1935. The artifacts all came from the surface of the high beaches, that is between the 937- and 946-foot levels, with the exception of a few exposed in the beach materials where trenches had been cut during construction work. The limitation of the artifacts to the upper beaches and the evidence of those exposed in these trench walls provided the basis for associating the human occupancy with the period of the high-water level of the lake.

Subsequently, the correctness of the location of the artifacts and the accuracy of the geological observations and interpretations presented in the 1937 report were called into question. There followed a number of careful instrumental checks of the levels by Brainerd, and later by Warren, and of the association of the artifacts with the terraces reported by the Campbells. Warren and Ranere (1968:13) state:

TABLE 11
Tentative Correlation of Western Great Basin and California Sequences

Climatic Stage	Date	Central California	Owens Lake	Mohave Desert	Death Valley	Yosemite Valley	Lake Tahoe	Lassen County	Western Nevada
		Late Horizon 2	Cotton-wood	"Desert Mohave"	DV IV	Mariposa	Kings Beach	Amedee	Dune Springs
	AD 1000	Late Horizon 1	Late Rose Spring		DV III	Tamarack		Tommy Tucker	Late Lovelock
		Middle Horizon	Middle Rose Spring	Amargosa	Late DV II		Martis		Trans. Lovelock
	BC-AD								
Medithermal	BC 1000	Early Horizon	Early Rose Spring		Early DV II	Crane Flat		Karlo	Early Lovelock
	2000		Little Lake	Pinto					
	3000								Carson
Altithermal	4000								Leonard
	5000		(Owens Lake II)*	Lake Mohave	DV I				Fallon
Anathermal	6000	Farmington							Humboldt
	7000		(Owens Lake I)*						Hidden Cave

* tentative archæological complex.
Source: Lanning 1963:278.

After an archæological reconnaissance of the Lake Mohave Basin and surveying a large part of Silver Playa with transit and stadia rod, assisted by Dr. H. T. Ore, Department of Geology, Idaho State University, it is possible . . . to make the following remarks: (1) Campbell's description of site locations is essentially correct. (2) The exact elevations of the artifacts between 937 and 946 feet are probably not significant, because the so-called 'three beach levels,' if they exist, are so irregular due to erosion or other factors that they cannot be consistently recognized. (3) The beach lines above the level of the outlet channel could have been formed at widely separated times, so that the higher terraces could have been formed long before man arrived on the scene and therefore may not be significant to the interpretation of the surface collection.

They further state,

on the basis of more than a dozen radiocarbon dates from nine different geological strata associated with lake or shore features below the level of the outlet channel, a strong argument can be presented at this point that the lake level receded for the last time between 6,000 and 7,000 years B.C. These dates, therefore, are applicable to the artifacts associated with beach formation (Warren and Ranere 1968:14).

The Lake Mohave collection was never studied according to site provenience, only as a total collection. It consists of projectile points, blades, knives, varieties of scrapers, gravers made on a flake, domed scraper planes, crescents, etc. Milling stones are absent. There are several varieties of projectile points among which is one, consisting of seventeen specimens, identified as the Haskett type. Warren believes that the Lake Mohave collection is in the main attributable to the San Dieguito culture of Southern and Baja California, but evidence of a relationship to the Hascomat complex of the Western and Northern Great Basin is also strong.

I quoted above Donald Crabtree's description of Haskett points from Lake Mohave. Crabtree also described for Warren the technological attributes of San Dieguito artifacts from Lake Mohave as follows:

(a) irregular edges

(b) random percussion flaking with direction of force into body of the artifact, causing many step fractures

(c) often predominantly unifacial, approaching plano-convex

(d) made of fairly thick tabular flakes

(e) deep bulbs of percussion and step fractures cause irregular surface

(f) edges exhibit flat, crushed surfaces as if supported on an anvil

(g) workmanship more variable than on Haskett points (Warren and Ranere 1968:14).

It is clear from contrasting Crabtree's analysis and from Warren's and Ranere's comments that the Lake Mohave collection consists of artifacts produced by more than one technological tradition, but the significance of this complexity is not clear. The crescents and the domed scraper planes, often considered diagnostic of the San Dieguito complex, have a continuous distribution from the Pacific Northwest along the eastern flank of the Sierra Nevada Mountains through Southern California into Baja California. (I am not sure of crescents in Baja California.) The crescents occur very early in Fort Rock Cave, the earliest, an "incipient" crescent, at 13,200, others at approximately 12,000 years ago or slightly less, and elsewhere in sites reasonably soundly dated at more than 9,000 years ago. These crescents are so distinctive that it is difficult to explain their continuous distribution except on the grounds of historical connection. The domed scraper plane is perhaps different. Most of the occurrences are along rivers or old lake beaches where a supply of generally rounded, water-worn gravels occurs. In sites where these artifacts occur there is usually a supply of these gravels close at hand. They were generally made by splitting a single cobble and then steeply flaking it partly or entirely along the fractured edge. The simplicity of the techniques used and the similarity of source material suggests to me that parallel, independent invention could account for the multiple appearance of the domed scraper plane, but perhaps not. Their appearance at a much later date in the Little Lake stage of Owens Lake lends credence to the suggestion of repeated independent development.

The preponderance of San Dieguito-type flaked instruments (except crescents) at the Coleman Site at the north end of Lake Winnemucca, and the mixture of San Dieguito and Hascomat types at the Sadmat Site near Fallon, suggests an overlap of two major traditions of lithic manufacture in the Western Great Basin. I see no reason, however, not to believe that a population, even a small one, might not maintain two traditions of lithic technology, just as it has been demonstrated (Adovasio 1970) that given populations in the West maintained two or more traditions of basketry manufacture side by side over long periods. In fact, an analysis of nine stone projectile points from Connley Hills Cave No. 5 in the Fort Rock Lake basin of south-central Oregon by Donald Crabtree in 1968 revealed the presence of four different flaking traditions even within this tiny sample at about 9,500 B.P. (cf. Figures 28-29).

Despite my willingness to entertain the possibility that the Haskett and San Dieguito technological traditions are contemporary, I must emphasize, however, that firm evidence that would establish their chronological relationship is lacking. Until the dating problem can be cleared up, the chief interest of these traditions lies in their distribution, linking a continuous area from the Snake River Plain of southern Idaho to the Northern Great Basin of south-central Oregon to Lake Mohave via a corridor along the eastern flank of the Sierra Nevada Mountains. The historical significance of this distribution remains to be clarified.

Any attempt to understand the prehistory of this area at a time level more than 10,000 years ago requires one to make a very difficult intellectual and emotional orientation. We speak of pluvial conditions and arid conditions and too often they are simply words. When one has worked for many seasons in the desert and near-desert, it is extraordinarily difficult to visualize what the environment was like under the more favorable pluvial conditions. Yet one must do just that, for it was in such an environment that these early people lived and moved about. Anyone who has visited the Ventana Cave area in western Arizona, now in the Sonoran Desert zone, finds it difficult to visualize the nature of that environment at the time of the early occupation of that cave. Colbert (Haury 1950:148), after describing the fossil fauna, wrote: "In those days, the climate was seemingly moister than it is now, so that the environment for the fauna was one of a savannah or plains, *with persistent, shaded streams* [emphasis added], rather than desert, with intermittent drainage, which characterizes the region at the present time."

Wells and Berger (1967) have added significantly to our knowledge of the nature of the pluvial environment of the Mohave Desert by means of a study of fossil pack rat nests in the Mohave and Chihuahua deserts. The contents of the nests and the fecal remains of the rats provide a valuable record of the kinds of vegetation, and the nests have been radiocarbon dated. While the lowering of woodlands below the present elevation was not uniform for the Mohave Desert as a whole, the evidence suggests a downward shift of approximately 600 meters of the woodland zones. Juniper and piñon pine and seed-bearing plants were far more readily available than at present. "It is sufficient to note that, when relatively low arid ranges such as Turtle Mountains formerly supported piñon-juniper woodland, most of the other low arid mountains or drainage divides, not situated in especially intense rain shadow cast by the more massive mountain ranges, were probably also wooded" (Wells and Berger 1967:1645).

Warren and Ranere (1968), in the paper from which I have drawn some of the above material, were interested in exploring the hypothesis that the Great Basin culture was not a generally uniform lifeway as supposedly stated by Jennings and others, but that there were several components, especially at an early time level. I think they misinterpret Jennings and overstate the "uniformity" theory, but their data do support the theory of local variability in a generally uniform adaptive culture. It would be odd if there were not distinctive components. Throughout the whole Western and Northern Great Basin a series of sites, both open and cave, show disparate elements either developed within the area or derived from exterior sources and integrated to meet the *particular* challenges of the *particular* variations within the Great Basin environment. Cordage probably for nets appears about 11,000 years ago at Danger Cave and textiles and cordage at Fishbone Cave at about the same time level. The first is in the Lake Bonneville basin and the latter in the Lahontan basin. It is quite probable that the basins of Lake Bonneville and Lake Lahontan and those of the Northern Great Basin, with their different relations to the mountains against which they abut, may have had some kind of cultural variation on a generally similar base such as I have described for the Great Basin at a later period—the oasis kind of enrichment varying with the different resources provided, for example, tule (*Scirpus lacustris*) or piñon pine nut (*Pinus monophylla*).

Given the general similarity of the Great Basin environment and adjacent arid areas and their differences from others in North America, one would expect in terms of cultural ecology a generally similar system of exploitative techniques. This is what I think the record really shows when one looks at it in its integrative aspects. The climate of the Great Basin and related areas, such as western Arizona and Southern California, was much more favorable for human habitation in the last pluvial period. The early bands of hunters and, yes, gatherers, must have moved with considerable ease back and forth for great distances, meeting other groups both in friendship and hostility, with consequent exchange of ideas and information. This seems to be what the records of Ventana Cave, the San Dieguito culture, Lake Mohave, western Nevada, and the Northern Great Basin show.

I shall now turn my attention to trans-Sierran California.

Trans-Sierran California

Meighan (1959a) divides California into eight "Archæological Regions" (Figure 30). I have included the area of the Sierras east of the divide in my Great Basin discussion, for on the whole the closest cultural ties reflecting their orientation lie in that direction. Meighan's regions are essentially ecological, and the character and extent of some of them has changed through the time of human habitation. To the extent that culture reflects adaptation to the ecological potentials of a habitat, one would, therefore, expect that the cultural manifestations would correlate with the ecological potentials and change when they changed. So it must be kept in mind that within a region, for example, the Desert, the cultural evidence will reflect through time ecological potentials ranging from the pluvial climate to the present desert environment.

The earliest archæological investigations of any significance in California were those of the 1870s. These were by the United States Geographical Survey West of the 100th Meridian and the Pinart–de Cessac scientific expedition. The latter expedition was a part of a very ambitious project that visualized a kind of natural history survey of the whole West Coast of the New World. The two years de Cessac spent on the Channel Islands and the Santa Barbara mainland were devoted to anthropological investigations and were really made possible by the collapse of the major project (Reichlen and Heizer 1964). Collecting expeditions were also made for the Smithsonian Institution and the Peabody Museum of Harvard University. As late as 1901 Mrs. Phoebe Appleton Hearst, that "angel" of California anthropology, sent Jones to Santa Rosa Island to make a collection for the fledgling Museum of Anthropology at the University of California at Berkeley (Jones 1956). The net results of these "expeditions," not really "investigations," were the amassing of extensive collections for the interested museums. While the rich archæological potential of the Channel Islands and adjacent coast was demonstrated by these expeditions, almost forty years elapsed before really scientific work was undertaken. In the meantime, the scientific potential of the islands, in particular Santa Cruz and San Miguel, had been greatly reduced by the introduction of sheep, overgrazing with subsequent erosion, and the ever-present private collector.

The first systematic archæological investigations in California were those by the University of California in the shell mounds of the San Francisco Bay region when Professor John C. Merriam, paleontologist, took the initiative in the early years of the century in starting the work later carried out by archæologists (Uhle 1907; Nelson 1909, 1910). While a limited number of projects were carried out by the University of California (Schenck 1926; Gifford and Schenck 1926; Schenck and Dawson 1929; Olson 1930), its archæological program was essentially sporadic until after World War II.

In the southern deserts and along the South Coast local museums sponsored the work that in general laid the foundation for the cultural sequences that have in recent years been made more explicit. Malcolm Rogers (1939, various) of the Museum of Man at San Diego was responsible for recognizing the San Dieguito culture and outlining the basic character of the early culture of the Desert Region. He also included the South Coast in his studies and identified the La Jolla culture.

The Southwest Museum at Los Angeles carried out a program of study of Lake Mohave and related

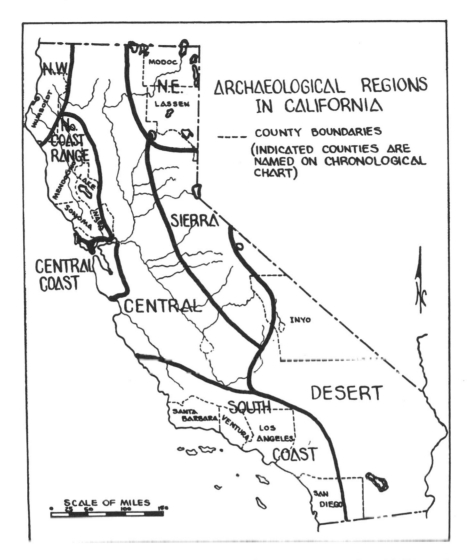

FIGURE 30. Archæological regions in California. *Meighan 1959a:296, Figure 5.*

pluvial lake basins (Campbell and Campbell 1935; Campbell et al. 1937) as well as other projects, and on the South Coast the Museum of Natural History, Santa Barbara, provided the lead, establishing the cultural sequence now accepted (Rogers, D. B. 1929). It continued work along the coast and on the Channel Islands, especially Santa Rosa Island where work still is in progress (Orr 1968).

The Sacramento Junior College for some years after the mid-thirties carried out excavations in the mounds in the Central Region at the lower Sacramento and upper San Joaquin valleys, work that laid the foundation for the well-known cultural sequences of Central California (Lillard, Heizer, and Fenenga 1939). This was the situation, for all practical pur-

poses, in California until after World War II. By 1939, for the Desert, South Coast, and Central regions, the prehistory had to some extent been adumbrated. In contrast to the Great Basin, a great deal was known. The programs of museums and the University of California paralleled the kind of programs responsible for the development of the archæology of the United States Southwest.

Following World War II, a new pattern of archæological research activity began, and while some of the museums are still active, especially when a federal contract can be secured for archæological salvage projects, the focus of work now is in the large universities in all regions of the state. The excellent series of papers in the archæological survey reports and the archæological survey annual report by the University of California at Berkeley and Los Angeles, respectively, provides the major source to which one must turn now for the study of California archæology.

The tremendous surge in archæological activity during the last twenty-five years has produced an extremely complex—even confusing—situation because of the great diversity of cultural manifestations described and the names assigned to them. Beardsley (1948, 1954) and Heizer (1949a) proposed a developmental sequence for Central California and suggested interrelationships between Central California and the San Francisco Bay area. D. B. Rogers (1929) had proposed his three-stage development for the Santa Barbara coast. Wallace (1955) published a "suggested chronology" and correlation of localities for Southern California. Within the last few years there have been efforts to revise previously proposed regional sequences (Warren and True 1961; Ezell and Moriarty in progress on the San Dieguito; Moriarity 1967). Meighan (1959a, 1965) considered the state as a whole and published brief summaries of its prehistory, emphasizing in particular adaptation to diverse environments. In his 1959 paper he used fruitfully the concept of ecological adaptation as the integrative and explanatory device to bring order out of the mass of data.

There appears now to be a healthy skepticism and conflict of opinion among California specialists on the justification for some of the taxonomic subdivisions in common use. Even the validity of some of the long accepted sequences of development and of concepts of interareal relations are being questioned. I shall summarize what, in my opinion, appears to be the present state of knowledge in the three major regions—the Desert, the South Coast, and Central California.

The Desert Region

The San Dieguito culture characterizes this region, outlined in Figure 30, but only at an early time period. I referred anticipatorily to this culture earlier in my discussion of the Lake Mohave manifestations. Rogers (1939) first described the manifestations, now subsumed under the name San Dieguito, that occur throughout an area extending from Baja California to Lake Mohave and the Colorado desert.

He worked entirely from surface collections with the exception of one from the Harris Site on the San Dieguito River, a stratified site that came to be the type site for the culture. The artifact inventory of the sites consisted of bifacially flaked knives or points, choppers, scraper planes, varieties of scrapers, gravers, and "crescents," etc., the tool and weapon kit of hunters. Wood, antler, and bone were absent, probably because of the destructive effect of the elements on open sites.

Rogers, using the typological method, attempted to order his materials from the surface collections of the interior. This resulted in a rather complex proposal starting with a basic Malpais industry, which developed into two lines, the Playa and the San Dieguito. The San Dieguito line developed through a series of steps, I-IV, with the last limited to Baja California. The Playa, found in the Eastern Area and Nevada, also went through a development, but a more complex one, with a Yuman complex diverging into the Western Area of the San Dieguito after San Dieguito III. He conjectured that the Great Basin was the source of the San Dieguito culture.

Rogers conceived in 1939 of this entire development taking place within a time span from about 2000 B.C. to historic times. The appearance, however, of San Dieguito materials in the early level of Ventana Cave and C-14 dates for the Harris Site, before Rogers's unfortunate death in a traffic accident, provided the information to demonstrate that his estimate of the chronology of the San Dieguito culture was woefully short. Even though he had stoutly maintained his position on the chronology, in the face of the new evidence he readjusted his thinking to accept the early date indicated by cross dating with Ventana Cave.

Rogers (Pourade 1966:24) threw his net over a vast area for the San Dieguito culture and divided it into a Southwestern Aspect, mostly in Baja California, a Southeastern Aspect, in the Colorado River drainage, a Central Aspect, including the pluvial lakes of California and extending north along the eastern flank of the Sierras and probably into Oregon, and a Western Aspect, indicated by the Borax Lake assemblage. As a working hypothesis such a division has something to be said for it. As a scheme based upon firm evidence of similarities in internal relations and demonstrable differences from other areas, the proposed distribution and coherence into a single culture does not hold up. There are puzzling evidences of possible relations throughout the area; at present the significance of this is not clear.

There is no convincing evidence, either from stratigraphic studies or seriation of surface sites, that the San Dieguito of the California Desert Region can be divided into San Dieguito I, II, and III. It is apparently a single culture with slight but not significant local variations, some of which may be due to sample limitation.

No "pure" San Dieguito sites are known from the immediate Pacific Coast. The usual sites, apart from the strandlines of the pluvial lakes, are found on hilltops and have little or no depth because of erosion. In addition, even if there had once been some depth with cultural differentiation, the erosional processes, which removed the supporting earth, would have mingled the artifacts inseparably. The Harris Site, oddly enough used as the "type" site, is in the bed of the San Dieguito River, not on a hilltop, although the hill above apparently had a site. The Harris Site was apparently a transient campsite and a quarry used through a long period of time.

Sites do occur along the coast that appear to reflect San Dieguito influence, if not peripheral evidence of the culture itself. The lowest or basal stratum of Malaga Cove, along the coast, but not on a hilltop, seems to represent San Dieguito. The early Topanga manifestations, Figure 31, near Los Angeles, which are on hilltops, certainly seem to be related to the San Dieguito. Moriarty (1967:555) suggests that the reason no pre-Desert (San Dieguito) sites have been found along the coast is that they have been inundated by the rising sea level. "It seems very probable that the first arrivals ranged and camped along a shoreline that is now 18 to 38 m below sea level." I find myself in sympathy with this suggestion both on the grounds of the evidence of taking sea mammals and deep-sea fish at Malaga Cove IV and on theoretical grounds. I cannot believe that people who wandered so widely on their food quest, and perhaps to satisfy curiosity, would have avoided the sea.

The South Coast

The South Coast includes the coastal area and western slopes of the Coast Range from Avila in San Luis Obispo County south to include about the northern half of the western coast of Baja California and the Channel Islands. On the mainland, the areas best known are Santa Barbara, Ventura, Los Angeles, and San Diego counties. While much material has been taken from the islands, especially Santa Cruz, relatively little scientific excavation has been done with the exception of Santa Rosa Island (Orr 1968). San Diego County represents the cultural focus of the southern part of this coastal strip, the other counties represent the northern part with Santa Barbara the focal area.

The La Jolla culture of the southern part of the area was recognized by Malcolm Rogers as the successor of the San Dieguito in San Diego County, but its developmental relation, if any, was unknown. D. B. Rogers (1929) proposed a three-stage cultural development for the northern part of the South Coast centered in the Santa Barbara region. His stages were: (1) The Oak Grove People, (2) The Hunting People, and (3) The Canaliño Culture, with the Chumash linguistic group representing the protohistoric and historic people of the region. In this whole region subsistence activity was the exploitation of the food resources of the coast with its rocks, estuaries, and the open sea, and the land with its seeds, fruits, and animals, large and small; use of terrestrial resources varied in importance according to the differences in habitat and season of the year. The marine-based economy became more important with the development of more effective techniques through time. In the north acorns were a vital part of the food supply. In the north and on the islands the villagers buried their dead in cemeteries, usually with rich offerings of grave goods. Consequently, since cemeteries provided richer inventories of artifacts, most of our information comes from that source. One is impressed in reading the literature by the efforts to find the cemetery at a site with relatively little interest in what the actual living areas might show. Work in recent years has changed this focus of interest, probably because there are fewer unexploited cemeteries remaining and because of emphasis on different types of archæological research.

The La Jolla culture, dating from about 7,500 to 3,000 years ago, is characterized by its subsistence pattern, its location along the coast, with the settle-

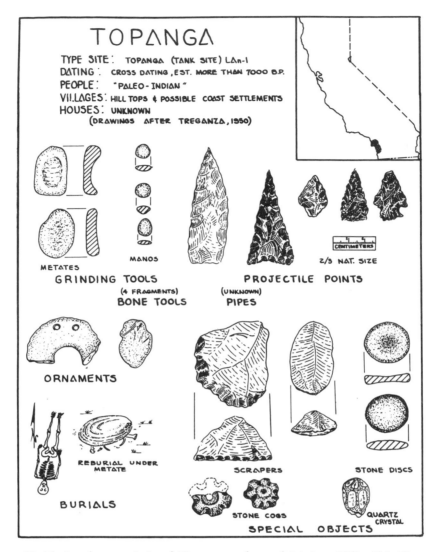

TOPANGA

TYPE SITE: TOPANGA (TANK SITE) LAn-1
DATING: CROSS DATING, EST. MORE THAN 7000 B.P.
PEOPLE: "PALEO-INDIAN"
VILLAGES: HILL TOPS & POSSIBLE COAST SETTLEMENTS
HOUSES: UNKNOWN
(DRAWINGS AFTER TREGANZA, 1950)

METATES
MANOS
GRINDING TOOLS

(4 FRAGMENTS)
BONE TOOLS

(UNKNOWN)
PIPES

PROJECTILE POINTS

2/3 NAT. SIZE
CENTIMETERS

ORNAMENTS

REBURIAL UNDER METATE

BURIALS

SCRAPERS

STONE COGS

STONE DISCS

QUARTZ CRYSTAL

SPECIAL OBJECTS

Figure 31. Traits characteristic of Topanga culture. *Meighan 1959a:291, Figure 1.*

ments marked by shell mounds of food debris, and a rather meager lithic industry but heavy use of milling stones. The presence of the milling stone is the diagnostic taxonomic element separating the La Jolla and the San Dieguito. Since the San Dieguito lacked the milling stone, any site in the area possessing it by definition cannot be San Dieguito. Regardless of whether this taxonomic device is historically justified, it is established in use by archæologists who perceive a developmental change in the appearance of the "Milling Stone Horizon" (Wallace 1955). From personal experience over many years and from having examined more milling stones than I like to think of, I am not convinced that a milling stone can always be so easily recognized. This is

specially true in sites along a river where gravels were used as a source for tools, on beaches of lakes now dry, or in middens along the coast where gravels are abundant. Be that as it may, the La Jollans had the milling stone, but the San Dieguitans lacked it according to present theory. Malcolm Rogers in 1924 at the Escondido Creek Slough site (SDM-W-9) in San Diego County observed the stratigraphic superposition of La Jolla material over San Dieguito (Pourade 1966:88). The later sequential position of La Jollan to San Dieguito has been confirmed stratigraphically and by many C-14 dates.

In 1929 Malcolm Rogers, with a grant-in-aid from the Smithsonian Institution, made a systematic study of the shell mounds of San Diego County and Baja

California as far south as San Quentin by test trenching. As a result of this study he suggested two phases, La Jolla I and II, based on both cultural and geographical factors. The cultural distinction was simply a somewhat richer lithic inventory in La Jolla II and a different settlement pattern. The latter he attributed to land-form and sea-level changes as effective causes. He was strongly impressed by the similarities between the San Dieguito and his La Jolla I. "In fact, a chief difference between the contrasted patterns lies in the absence of the metate in the San Dieguito I pattern and its presence in the La Jolla I pattern" (Pourade 1966:38-39). This observation and further evidence, which I shall discuss later, supports the view of a very close historical-developmental relationship between the San Dieguito and La Jolla cultures.

Wallace (1955:Table I) gives the following La Jolla I cultural inventory: shellfish and seed collecting, mullers-milling stones, few large and crude stone projectile points, retouched flakes, beach cobble choppers, few spire-lopped *Olivella* beads, flexed burial with covering rock cairns and few grave offerings, but the house type is unknown.

La Jolla II, according to Wallace, is the San Diego County manifestation of a long developmental stage intervening between the "Milling Stone Horizon" and the Late Prehistoric Cultures. There was little change in the La Jolla adaptive culture. The bow and arrow is thought to have made its appearance at this time. The flaked tools were better made and there was an increase in variety over the preceding period. The mortar and pestle complex appears to have been lacking or at any rate has not been reported. The La Jolla is "assumed to have merged with Diegueño, the last prehistoric phase" (Wallace 1955:222).

Moriarty (1966) proposed three "phases" for the La Jolla culture. Phases I and II correspond to those of Rogers and Wallace. Phase III represents the final stage in the development that eventually merged with the Yuman Diegueño, who apparently moved into the coastal area over a long period of time. He proposed the following phase chronology on the basis of a large number of C-14 dates: La Jolla I 7,500-5,460, La Jolla II 4,970-4,520, La Jolla III 4,100-3,240 C-14 years ago. The major defining characteristic of Phase III was a shift in occupation pattern.

"It [La Jolla III] is marked by a distinct change in the geographic locale of sites. There is good evidence that the coastal dwelling La Jolla people were forced to move their sites to lower elevations and along the edges of a series of coastal lagoons in San Diego County" (Moriarty 1966:22). Moriarity postulates that gradual climatic desiccation lowered the water table and reduced the supplies of freshwater forcing a change in the settlement pattern. The lagoons in their upper portions provided a freshwater supply from the inflowing streams and thus offered a new locale for settlement. Sea level was 30 to 40 feet lower at that time. As sea level rose it built up a series of barrier beaches fronting the lagoons and the inhabitants settled on or at least lived on or near these beaches. The rising sea level forced the progressive abandonment of these sites and in each case left a "sheet of artifact material on the near-shore sea bottom, extending offshore from the present beach to the 30 or 40 feet curve" (22). Skin diving archæologists have explored these sites and recovered numerous artifacts, Figures 19 and 20 (Marshall and Moriarty 1964). Figure 32 shows the number of selected artifacts and the depths from which they were recovered. The artifacts continue the La Jolla series with slight diversification increasing with age. The only artifact difference of any significance from La Jolla II is the mortar, which Wallace (1955) reported as lacking, but the presence or absence of the mortar in late Phase II sites may be a result of sampling vagaries.

The practice of subdividing the La Jolla culture into a series of phases seems to me to be of dubious value. The culture is primarily found along the coast and recorded by the shell middens left by the people. It is known that the people did go into the interior to hunt, but it is not known if the shell mound areas were completely abandoned for periods of time by the entire group moving to the interior. Along the northern Pacific Coast parties, usually men, went into the mountains for short periods of time to hunt and women went to gather berries at appropriate times, but the settlements were never completely abandoned—certainly not in late prehistoric time—and there is no reason to believe that the practice had ever been different. Change in La Jolla culture seems to be gradual with nothing indicating any signifi-

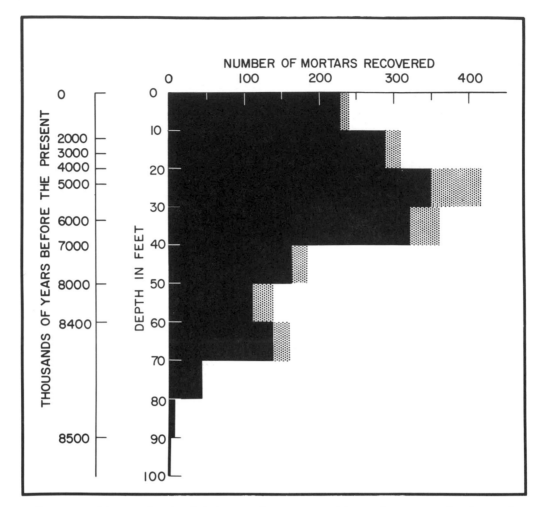

Figure 32. Mortars, by depth below surface, recovered by underwater archæology off the La Jolla, California, coast. Age before present determined by correlating position with curve for rise of sea level. *Photograph courtesy of James R. Moriarty.*

cant alteration in adaptive patterns, and under these circumstances I do not see what is gained by making any subdivisions in the culture. To do so appears to me to be a form of the venial sin of taxonomic over-scrupulousness of which so many of us are guilty.

Moriarty (1967), on the basis of the excavation of site U.C.L.J.-M-15 at Agua Hedionda Lagoon in Southern California, has proposed a "Transitional" phase between San Dieguito and La Jolla. The site is a midden 170 centimeters deep with no break in the profile. La Jolla material, including milling stones, extends to a depth of 140 centimeters.

> The artifact assemblage from 13 to 17 dm. showed a distinct change in part of its mineralogical content, as well as in typology. Fairly large amounts of small felsite flakes began to appear, and the base of a large projectile point or biface was recovered. The technique and pattern appeared similar to those of San Dieguito material, a resemblance confirmed by laboratory comparison with these artifacts were choppers, scrapers, and hammerstones typical of La Jolla I (Moriarty 1967:555).

This level is pre-"Milling Stone," or San Dieguito, yet the presence here of the flaked stone tools also found in La Jolla I culture provides the tie-in between the two levels. Two C-14 dates (no lab. nos. given), one from the earliest level at which milling stones occurred and the other from the bottom of the midden, give dates of 7420 B.P. and 9020 B.P. respectively. This site shows, then, that there was a continuity of development from San Dieguito into La Jolla along the coast and that the "Transition" was underway about 9,000 years ago. This is the earliest date from the mainland at present for the subsistence pattern indicated by the shell mounds built from the debris of saltwater mollusks used for food.

The Agua Hediondo site indicates, I believe, the line to be taken in dealing with the question of the relationship of the San Dieguito culture to the La Jolla culture. This site is unique along the San Diego coastline because it has not suffered from erosion by the rising sea level. Only the remotest chance will provide another site under similar conditions for corroborative material. As Moriarty indicates, the shoreline at 9,000 years ago would have been .5 miles seaward from its present location. It would have been still more distant 10,000 to 12,000 years ago. In the light of present evidence, it is not unreasonable to assume that still earlier records of the San Dieguito-La Jolla relations lie beneath the sea. The La Jolla is a southern manifestation of the exploitation of the marine resources characteristic of the whole South Coast and Channel Islands region.

The Santa Barbara area near the north end of the South Coast region, occupied by the historic Chumash, provides the record of the prehistoric culture of the northern counties. D. B. Rogers (1929) proposed three cultural stages, the Oak Grove People ("Milling Stone Horizon" of Wallace), the Hunting People, and the Canaliño. D. B. Rogers described different population types as carriers of the three different cultures, but it is not clear if he thought that the respective successor groups arrived in a country already abandoned or took it over by conquest. The various possibilities he suggests indicate that there was no certainty in his mind.

Synonymous and overlapping terminological systems complicate and confuse the archæological picture (summarized by Harrison and Harrison 1966:62-63). For the sake of simplicity, I use Rogers's original terminology. The *earliest manifestation* of the Oak Grove people is that of a simple culture exploiting the resources of the seashore with emphasis on the resources of the lagoons and sloughs. There were small population groups usually occupying hilltop sites, but not always. Frequently these sites were in groves of oaks. Food resources were derived from both sea and land, although large land mammals played a minor role in the diet. Burial was customarily in the fully extended position. Houses were small,

circular structures 12 to 15 feet in diameter set some 20 to 30 inches in the ground. A supporting frame of saplings probably was covered with a number of mats. Body decoration consisted of a rather meager variety of shell beads, mostly the spire-ground *Olivella*. Clothing is unknown. Particularly characteristic was the large number of manos and metates. Burials were covered by cairns of boulders and metates, either broken or unbroken. Red ochre stain is frequently found in the graves but its manner of use is unknown.

Following this lifeway is one showing certain new features as well as features appearing to be simply developmental in origin. The basket-mortar appears for the first time, a utensil where a basket was fastened by melted asphaltum into a groove worked in a flat rock around a slight concavity. This is the first appearance of this well-known instrument and is interpreted to mean a new way of preparing acorns for food. Flaked stone objects increase in number and quality. Some of these may be atlatl points, spear points, or knives. The quality of workmanship has improved. Small sandstone bowls also occur but their use is uncertain. Their small size suggests that they were used for seed grinding or for holding food. The lack of recognizable house pits suggests that any form of shelter was temporary. Small villages were close to the sea, on headlands, or along estuaries or sloughs, as was the case earlier. Burials were customarily flexed and cemeteries were within the village, but burials also occurred scattered about the midden of the village site. Occasionally a platform, as had been done previously, had been built over the grave. Food was derived from the sea and the land. There appears to have been a greater proportion of large land mammals in the diet than previously. This lifeway Rogers assigns to his Hunting People. Whatever its origin, it represents a more efficient exploitation of the environment.

The final stage, the Canaliño, Figure 33, leading to the historic Chumash, represents the full exploitation of the environment. Large villages occupied favorable spaces close to the sea and the adjacent lagoons and sloughs, while temporary campsites in the open and in dry caves are found in the adjacent interior mountains. Houses were circular, 12 to 20 feet in diameter, with the supporting framework

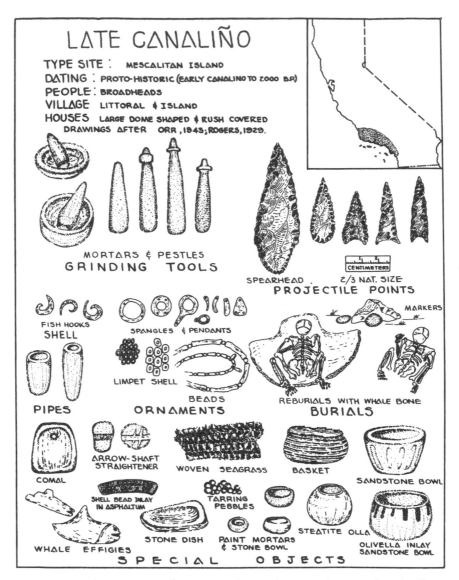

FIGURE 33. Traits characteristic of Late Canaliño culture. *Meighan 1959a:292, Figure 2.*

consisting of willows set into the ground and then curved in and fastened at the top giving a hemispherical shape. A square opening for a smoke hole was left at the top. Horizontally around this vertical framework poles were lashed except at one point at ground level and for some distance up from it to provide entrance and exit. The frame was then covered by a thatching of mats sewed together. The fireplace was in the center. Burial was customarily in cemeteries located in the center of the village but also took place randomly in the village midden. The use of burial goods was extensive and consisted predominantly of ceremonial objects and items of body adornment in the form of shell beads and pendants of great variety and exquisite workmanship. Projectile points were smaller and more finely made than in the preceding period. The basket hopper now was made by attaching the basket with asphaltum to the rim of a well-made mortar. The mano and metate continued in use. Full exploitation of the resources of the sea was developed with the well-known plank canoe, harpoons, fish-hooks, both circular and composite, and the gorge, etc. Artistic work reached an extremely high level utilizing the available shell for decorative material and asphaltum for fixing the decorative form to the object. The tiny blades, "bladelets," burins, and drills were developed to achieve the production of the lovely art forms in shell (Heizer and Kelley 1962).

Olson (1930) suggested three stages of development for the Canaliño. The picture is one of continuing more efficient exploitation of the total resources of the area with the addition of trade items, steatite from Catalina Island, and trade with the Channel Islands as well as with the population of the interior Central Valley. The full exploitation of the natural resources permitted these people to have large sedentary villages and a population density the equivalent of that of the agricultural Pueblo peoples (Kroeber 1939).

Orr (1968) provides the only report of systematic archæology on any of the Channel Islands—Santa Rosa Island. I have discussed earlier the evidence relative to Pleistocene man on Santa Rosa Island and shall limit myself now to the post-Pleistocene occupation. It will be recalled that the shoreline of Santa Rosa Island extended some miles beyond its present limit during the period of eustatic lowering of sea level. Outside of the dwarf mammoth and seeds and roots, the only food supply was that provided by the sea. Any occupation would be expected to have been related to the location of the shoreline. With the rising sea level, the habitable area was gradually reduced and any occupation sites would have been covered by the rising water. Sea cliffs characterize much of the present shoreline, and the presence of middens exposed in the cliff walls are proof of the relation of occupation and the earlier configuration of the land and sea I have explained (Orr 1968:135, Figure 44, p. 137). The Channel Islands have only a limited terrestrial fauna, in addition to the dwarf or pygmy mammoth, which became extinct at the end of the Pleistocene, a dwarf fox and a species, or perhaps two, of mice. Any population to survive, therefore, had to depend on the resources of the sea and on seeds and roots from land plants.

Orr has divided the recent occupation into three time periods, Dune Dweller, Highland, and Canaliño, from earliest to last. The differentiation is based on settlement pattern, artifact inventory, and C-14 dates.

The earliest shell middens precede the Dune Dweller period and appear to be intermediate between Orr's "Mammoth Eaters" and the well-developed shell mounds of the Dune Dwellers. "These early shell mounds are represented in the several buried 'black lines' of the Tecolote, Survey, and Garanon sites. . . " (Orr 1968:96). These small shell middens at Survey Point, dated at 12,620 C-14 years ago and at Tecolote Point at 11,900 years ago, Orr puts in the Pleistocene, which he terminates between 10,000 and 11,000 years ago. The next dated site is 7,400 C-14 years ago, but there are several small sites that may fall in the period between these dates. At about 10,000 years ago there was a rapid rise in sea level; it is quite possible that there were sites now covered by the marine transgression. The island must have maintained a relatively large population for there are "about 200 villages known on the present land mass of Santa Rosa Island which, for the most part, were occupied between 7,400 and about 150 years ago. . ." (Orr 1968:93). More than 100 of these represent the Highland stage occupation (cf. below).

The Dune Dwellers take their name from the location of their villages, many of which date from around 7,500 years ago, on and among the sand dunes. Midden refuse varies in thickness from a thin band to more than 2 feet. Seventeen sites are definitely known to belong to this stage and perhaps others may eventually be assigned to it. While these large sand dunes are now mostly along the sea cliffs, at the time of the original occupation they were several hundred yards inland from the sea. The dunes are composed of clean, white sand and contrast sharply with the black organic matter of the midden. Once the grass cover, which binds the surface is broken, erosion of the dune and midden is rapid in the high winds on the island, and a site can be quickly destroyed.

Burials were made in the dune sand adjacent to the midden area, and at first the corpse was flexed and buried in a sitting position (Tecolote Point, 7,000 years ago), but at a later time flexed and on-the-side burial occurs at Survey Point, site 131.5, and a brilliant but fugitive red paint, the identity of which has proved impossible to discover, was applied to the skulls. Grave goods consist mostly of beads. In order of numbers found they are the barrel-shaped *Olivella* (that is both spire and base ground off), the spire-ground and the rectangular *Olivella*. This inventory is greatly increased through time by the use of other varieties of shells and different kinds of beads.

Food was of course largely derived from the sea and consisted in the earlier period of red abalone (*Haliotis refescens*), fish, with some specimens up to 10 feet in length, and marine mammals. The red abalone requires a somewhat colder water than the black and is thus considered a sign of cooler water temperature and appropriate climatic conditions. In the later period, while red abalone is still found in limited quantities, the leading shellfish foods were the black abalone and the California mussel (*Mytilus californianus*). Whales, too, became important in the diet in this period.

While very few stone artifacts occur in the early part of the period, and none that are "diagnostic," the presence of obsidian and quartz crystals indicates trade with the mainland. The use of asphaltum was known and "well-made donut stones" are found. The earliest mainland data I know of for this last type of artifact is about 4,830 radiocarbon years ago (Harrison and Harrison 1966:29, 34).

In site 131.5 at Survey Point, near the Tecolote Point site dated at 7,000 years ago but considered somewhat later than that, appear "deer bone whistles and beads, bone pendants, and steatite from Santa Catalina Island as trade goods" (Orr 1968:98). It is unfortunate that no firm dates are available for the appearance of these items, for the deer bone had to be imported from the mainland either raw or in finished form and steatite, which was later to achieve such an important position in the Canaliño culture, had to be imported directly from Santa Catalina or through middlemen. At this date, whatever it is, a wide-flung trade system was in operation.

Shelters must have been on the surface and made of perishable materials for no evidence of house pits exists.

Orr reports an apparent hiatus in the occupation of the sand dune area from probably about 6,000 to 4,300 years ago when it was reoccupied until approximately 3,000 years ago. This latter period is somewhat different culturally from the earlier but apparently not significantly enough to classify it otherwise than as a late phase of the Dune Dwellers. One wonders if the hiatus may not eventually be filled by excavation of other sites in the area, for how otherwise can one explain a hiatus of 2,000 years and then the reappearance of what is simply a later development of the culture in the same place when there is no evidence of the missing culture elsewhere?

"The highlands of the Island are a series of grassy wave-cut terraces bisected by deep canyons, resulting in a series of long and wide flat-topped ridges between the canyons which are devoid of trees or bushes" (Orr 1968:178). Occupation sites are on small knolls 3 to 4 feet high, but some much higher, found on these terraces. More than half of the 182 sites belonging to this stage that are known on the island are found "between 300 and 1,000 feet elevation, the greatest number occurring between 400 and 500 feet" (Orr 1968:179). Most of the sites are marked by shallow pits, the remains of former houses that were randomly placed but in one case were arranged in two rows facing each other across a "street." At the time of occupation of this area, ranging on both sides of 5,000 years ago, the climate was moister and cooler than at present and "the highlands were covered with a forest of oak, Catalina cherry, elderberry, and probably other trees and bushes, which would provide food, fuel, wood for construction, and protection from wind or sun" (Orr 1968:99). Then there would have been water in the canyons and the pans, which collected the runoff. The people who lived in this environment inhabited sites ranging from 100 to 600 feet in length but typically sites are 150 to 300 feet long. Orr has called the occupants of the highlands "Highlanders" as a convenient designation until their cultural position is clearly fixed. The name is in keeping with the "Dune Dwellers."

The culture of the Highlanders appears to differ from that of the Dune Dwellers and the later Canaliño more quantitatively than qualitatively although certain traits appear here for the first time on the island. Burial practice differs from that of the Dune Dwellers, being flexed and on-the-side, while in the Dune Dwellers flexed in a sitting position was customary (cf. statement of later practice at Survey Point above). The amount of shell in the middens is proportionately less than that of the middens of their predecessors or successors. Mostly the shell is broken, "comminuted," Orr calls it.

The circular shell fishhook, "well-made, medium-sized," occurs for the first time on Santa Rosa in site

131.43 Fox, and this is the earliest C-14 date for this artifact, which occurs abundantly in the later Canaliño sites on the mainland. A C-14 date (UCLA-105) of 4,800±100 years ago was calculated for a lens of "relatively unbroken shells of *Mytilus* and *Haliotis*" at a depth of 9 to 12 inches with which the abalone shell fishhooks were associated. Another sample, a large *Haliotis rufescens* shell from 6 inches lower in the pit, gave a date of 5370±150 B.P. (L-446B).

Other new kinds of artifacts come from the same site apparently with the same association and dates. These are the very small gravers, perforators, drills, etc., which have been conjecturally described as "scarifiers," "tattoing needles," or something else. Heizer and Kelley (1962) have called this assemblage of tools "burins and bladelets," and it is clear that they were specialized tools developed for fabrication of the excellent shell products of the Canaliño stage. They occur on both the mainland and the islands, and a large number were brought back from Santa Cruz Island by de Cessac, and it was this collection described by Heizer and Kelley. This Santa Rosa date is the earliest at present for this tool assemblage.

Other than the micro-instruments for working shell, the stone inventory is limited. Mortars and pestles predominate. Pestles occur in three forms: well-made, tapered sandstone about 8 inches by 2 inches and worked all over; a very short, 2 to 2½ inches long, stubby specimen made on a natural beach cobble and shaped only on the base; a third form, large and crude, shaped only at the distal or pounding end. The "donuts" occur both as flattened and rounded forms and range in size from 2 to 5 inches. The projectile points are of particular interest for they resemble the Canaliño in skill of workmanship and form and occur rounded to pointed with a straight or a concave base. All these specimens come from the same site as the circular fishhooks and the same dates apply to them.

Orr suggests that the Highland culture existed during a period of moister and cooler climate than that which marked the subsequent Canaliño found along the coast in the same area as the Early Dune Dwellers. The cooler and moister climate of the period would have provided forest cover in the Highland zone. The trees and shrubs would have provided

protection from the cold, strong winds off the sea and from the sun in summer. Close to the sea cliffs in the dune areas there would have been no protection from the elements. It is conceivable, therefore, that the apparent hiatus in Dune Dweller occupation may represent no more than a shift in occupation area from shore to upland. One must remember that excavation in the known 182 Highland sites has been negligible, and it may be expected that further excavation will throw light on this question.

The Canaliño culture, which follows the Highland and lasts until the historic period, is generally similar to that of the mainland. The major exception is in the subsistence pattern, which was determined by the island habitat. The islanders subsisted almost wholly on a marine diet with evidently some slight reliance on a few seeds available on the island and varieties of tubers. The mainlanders added to their marine food supply seeds in much greater amounts, acorns, and terrestrial mammals. Mortars, pestles, manos and metates, steatite ollas, projectile points, knives and scrapers, the concomitants of this subsistence pattern, are common on the mainland but rare on Santa Rosa Island. The Canaliño village sites are found along the coast. Orr interprets the change in habitat as related to the milder climate beginning about 4,000 years ago. About 2,500 years ago he estimates that the full Canaliño culture appears in recognizable form on the island. Sites, however, appear on the sea cliffs in the same area as the early Dune Dwellers and in some instances superimposed on the Dune Dwellers and dated from about 4,300 years ago (UCLA-140, 4260±80 B.P.) until the abandonment of the island by the Indians. The culture of these sites certainly strongly suggests early Canaliño.

I find it very difficult to organize this mass of material from the South Coast Region mainland and Channel Islands in any meaningful way. The taxonomic exuberance of the area's archæologists implies a diversity in time and to some degree in space that is not convincing to me. There is certainly change through time and local variations occur in the cultural record, but the question, which keeps hammering away, is "What of it?" One point of view certainly is that there were separate populations associated with or that were the carriers of each of the three major taxonomic stages usually indicated. D. B. Rogers laid the foundation for this line of thinking. I do not think the evidence from the skeletal information is adequate to substantiate such a position. This does not mean that there was no infiltration of new blood into the area. Sometime during the period of 3,000 to 4,000 years ago population shifts occurred. The Penutian thrusts into California and Hokan displacements occurred apparently about this time. But the cultural changes are not as definite and sharp as Rogers suggested when one considers the evidence from recent excavations (Owens, Curtis, and Miller 1964; Harrison and Harrison 1966; Orr 1968).

One gets the impression from these reports, at least I do, of a continuously developing cultural adaptation to a particular environment showing more successful adaptation with the passage of time. Local variations, as Meighan (1959a) suggests, could very well represent the differential effect of ecological variations. This situation is strikingly illustrated in the limitations imposed by the Santa Rosa environment on the Canaliño culture when compared with the mainland development.

A chronology produced by C-14 dates associated with skeletons in a cemetery, which contained great numbers of burials and was used over a long period of time, does not give us a very "representative" record. Unless dates covering the period of use of the cemetery are available, it is not known to what period of use a single or even two or three dates apply. In a stratified site, dates covering the use of the site control that situation. Probably some of the lacunae in chronology for the area are due to this method of securing dates from cemeteries and the reliance on a date from a single skeleton or even two or three.

Kroeber (1939) and others have been puzzled by the high cultural development of the Chumash-speaking area. The diffusion of foreign cultural stimulation from the Northwest Coast of North America and Oceania have been called on to explain this puzzling phenomenon, but such introduction of alien elements has never been demonstrated. Some similarities of tools and instruments to those of the Northwest Coast and Oceania do occur, but all three of these cultures were developing in a maritime and coastal environment. What would be odd would be the lack of any similarities in the instruments needed to exploit the similar environments. As these adaptive

skills improved in efficiency the standard of living rose with time for activities other than those necessary to feed the body. Outside contacts, developed by both maritime and mainland trade, provided new ideas. Perhaps the infiltration of outlanders gave impetus to the development of new ways of life.

A major problem of the prehistory of the South Coast Region is the question of the priority of cultural development and relations between the mainland and the islands at various periods of time. Three possibilities exist: (1) the earliest cultural developments were on the islands and diffused to the mainland; (2) the earliest developments were on the mainland and diffused to the islands; (3) the cultural achievements of both grew out of a common early base and the end product represents the result of parallel development influenced, of course, by inter-area trade. Briefly, what is to be said for each of these?

Possibility 1: I know of no one who seriously argues for this position.

Possibility 2: Olson (1930:Figure 3) can only be interpreted as arguing for this possibility, mainland priority, and it is certainly the point of view tacitly or openly held by most archæologists. Olson has a "Hypothetical Archaic Period" preceding his "Early Mainland" while the "Early Island" sites lack ancestry and are equated with the latter half of his "Early Mainland" and the first part of his "Late Mainland." However, it must be kept in mind that in fact the shell middens on Santa Rosa Island at Survey Point and Tecolote Point, dated at 12,600 and 11,900 years ago respectively, are older than any comparable mainland sites. Unless earlier dates are found for mainland sites, the island culture cannot be derived from the mainland culture. Such dates at present do not exist.

Possibility 3: The Agua Hedionda site (U.C.L.J.-M-15), discussed above, bears on the problem of a common early mainland-channel coastal adaptation with subsequent parallel development. This site has provided the earliest record of a shell midden on the coast of the mainland, dated at 9,080 C-14 years ago (Moriarty 1967). The basal portion of the site from which the dated sample came is interpreted as "transitional" between the San Dieguito and the La Jolla. This date points toward the earliest midden dates for Santa Rosa Island, 10,000-12,000 years ago. I am not trying to derive the mainland culture from the islands; rather, what this site indicates to me is that on the mainland at approximately the same time as on Santa Rosa Island there was a way of life exploiting the marine resources. There must have been sites both on Santa Rosa and off the present Southern California coast representing this way of life, but these sites are now submerged by the higher sea level. The evidence of human occupation at both ends of the Central Valley, apparently at about the same time level as the Agua Hedionda site, makes it very unlikely that the coast of the Santa Barbara area and farther south was unoccupied at the same time.

The picture I see, as I reflect on this situation, is that of an early occupation of the islands and mainland, derived from the probably much earlier occupation, the evidence for which I have discussed in Chapter 4. This early culture, which I would place at 10,000 years ago and earlier, was already experimenting with exploitation of the marine resources as a food source as the shell middens indicate. Within this area as time passed adaptation became more successful with common needs producing common solutions and somewhat different ecological niches bringing about variations in adaptation. Trade by land and sea diffused traits and ideas throughout the area, and such trade started early. Masses of red abalone, *Haliotis rufescens,* shells are found in various places in the Early Sand Dune sites of Santa Rosa Island, and such storage must surely have been for export. There is a date for one such dump of 7,440 C-14 years ago. For these reasons it is my opinion that Possibility 3 has the highest probability of being correct.

Meighan (1965:713) provides a brief summary of the coastal development in its dynamic aspects in the exploitation of the environment:

> By about 7,500 years ago, at least part of the coastal region was widely settled, and a shift took place to a more varied and diversified kind of economy, with close adaptation to the resources of the numerous ecological niches of the western coastline. . . . Adaptation to the Pacific Ocean also began then and included the gathering of shellfish, hunting of sea mammals (probably largely on the beaches and thus with the same weapons and techniques as were used for land animals), and a limited amount of ocean fishing. The latter implies the development of some sort of boat. Compared to later peoples, however, they exploited the sea much less, and the ocean provided only supplemental food until about 4,000 to 5,000 years ago. [The Channel Islands lacked land animals almost completely.] From 4,000 years ago to the disappearance of Indian culture, all areas of the West Coast have had some peoples who were primarily dependent on ocean resources. The general picture is one of increasing familiarity with the ocean and increasing skill at exploiting it.

Finally, for what it is worth, after working with this material from the South Coast Region, it seems to me that it would make sense for ease of handling and comprehension, and would not be in conflict with the record, to organize it in terms of three cultural phases arranged on the basis of internal coherence and consistency. These would be the La Jolla, the Santa Barbara, and the Channel Island phases. Anyone wishing to do so could further subdivide any phase if he were convinced by the evidence that it was desirable. La Jolla, etc., appear as distinct cultures in the literature, yet, as I have pointed out, there is a basic similarity along the coast and in the whole region really a single culture. Differences and similarities, as well as temporal differentials, would be indicated by this phase categorization.

The Central Region

The Central Region of California occupies the Central Valley, a portion of the Central Coast between Monterey Bay and Avila, and extends across the mountains of the north to the Oregon country. It lies between the Sierra Nevada and Coast ranges, with the exception of that portion on the Central Coast.

Lillard, Heizer, and Fenenga (1939) proposed a developmental sequence of Early, Transitional, and Late periods on the evidence excavated from mounds in the delta of the Sacramento River. Later other sites on the delta of the San Joaquin River were incorporated into the sequence, and the sequence came to be referred to as Early, Middle, and Late "Horizons" (Beardsley 1948:5-6). Heizer (1949a) and Beardsley (1954) have provided detailed studies and attempted to place the evidence in a wider frame of reference, even on a continental scale. The proposed sequence has been a favorite reference for cross dating cultural manifestations outside California and has held a kind of prestige status in comparative studies.

It is now clear that the proposed sequence applies only to the delta area of the Central Region. C-14 dates have provided a pretty firm foundation for chronological definition of the various horizons there approximately as follows: Early, Figure 34, from 6,000 to 4,000 years ago, Middle, from 4,000 to 1,000 years ago, and Late, Figure 35, from 1,000 years ago to the arrival of the Spaniards near the end of the sixteenth century. The Early Horizon is based on four archæological components known collectively as the Windmiller facies.

The delta area provided an extraordinarily favorable habitat. The sites were usually on mounds along the sloughs or on the banks of feeder rivers. The marshes and sloughs provided nesting and feeding grounds for innumerable birds. Small animals were numerous. Tules (*Scirpus lacustris*), cattail (*Typha latifolia*), and other marsh grasses must have covered miles of the land surface providing in some cases food, in others material for mats and basketry and even articles of clothing and shelter. Acorns abounded. Larger mammals were to be found in the valley and into the mountains. Fresh water was available. Mollusks were to be had from the tidal flats and fish from the rivers. The climate was genial. In this area there developed large sedentary villages thanks to the riches of the natural environment.

One would expect a continuum of culture in such an environment in the absence of natural disaster or social catastrophe. In the Middle Horizon there appears to have been some kind of social unease as indicated by not uncommon finds of skeletons with projectile points embedded in them. Yet there seems to be no clear evidence of invasion. If there were an infiltration of alien groups, it does not show in the cultural record. Perhaps, if there were, their culture was close enough to that of the local people to make it impossible for us to discover the event. At any rate, it is possible that this time of unrest is related to that which appears to have occurred in the Santa Barbara area; it occurs about the same time and may be related to the same social–historical cause or causes.

The distinction between the different "Horizons" has to be made on the basis of the "total configura-

tion of the artifacts." Beardsley (1948:5) writes: "Many Early Horizon traits gradually become extinct in the Middle Horizon, while new traits are introduced which finally flower in the Late Horizon. Yet the cultural configurations of each horizon are essentially distinctive." Figure 36 illustrates the occurrence and history of twenty-seven traits, which he chose as those most accurately representing the cultural development of the Sacramento Valley area. Of these traits not one is limited to either the Early or Middle Horizon. Three are limited to the Early and Middle Horizons: extended burials, *Haliotis* beads, and metates. Two are limited to the Middle, Late, and Historic: cremation and stone beads. One is limited to the Late and Historic Horizons: clamshell beads. There is obviously change in the emphasis from horizon to horizon.

The chart clearly indicates an increasingly successful exploitation of the local environment and expanded trade relations, or at least a greater amount of trade, with the coastal areas. Fishing increases in importance; hunting decreases slightly after the Early Horizon then remains steady; mortars increase in importance and displace the metate, probably indicating the successful exploitation of the oak groves. The presence of *Haliotis* and *Olivella* and clamshells for beads and ornaments is indicative of trade with maritime sources, and the increase in the use of these materials through time reflects the trading activities.

Some recently published information should be referred to because it gives a perspective on the occupation of the Central Valley previously unaccepted. Harrington (1948) reported on discoveries at Borax Lake approximately 100 miles north of San Francisco on the east flank of the Coast Range. He interpreted the "fluted" points and certain other artifacts found there as indication of a contemporaneity with the Folsom fluted of the High Plains. Considerable skepticism marked the response of archæologists, including myself in a review, to the proposed relation to the Folsom or to the suggested date. Meighan and Haynes (1968) have recently examined new material secured by excavation and reexamined some of the specimens secured by Harrington, mainly fluted points and crescents like those from the Great Basin and the Southern California deserts. They applied obsidian hydration rate studies to a large number of

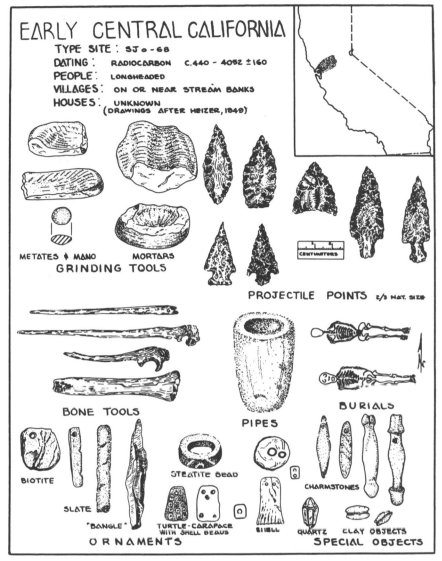

FIGURE 34. Traits characteristic of Early Central California culture. *Meighan 1959a: 292, Figure 3.*

fluted-point specimens and secured an average of 9 microns of thickness of hydration. Since there is no standardized hydration rate for the ecological area from which these specimens come, any conclusions as to indicated age are inferential and must be based on the rate for a closely similar area. On this latter basis the age is suggested as approximately 9,000 years ago. The assemblage from which the artifacts were taken for hydration studies, on the basis of illustrations, is strikingly like the Tonopah, Nevada, site (Campbell and Campbell 1940), and the Fort Rock Lake basin material excavated by my party in 1967 and dated more than 9,000 years ago.

Near the southern end of the Central Valley two pieces of evidence, one firm and the other tenuous, indicate man was there more than 8,000 years ago. The firm date, unpublished, derived from charcoal from a deeply buried site in the southern San Joaquin Valley, is over 8,000 years ago. The other evidence comes from the Tranquility Site near Fresno, to which I referred in Chapter 4, where there is strong suggestive evidence of association between human skeletal material and the fossilized bones of *Equus, Camelops,* and *Bison* (Angel 1966). Because the association cannot be tied down beyond any doubt, the site report has been held from publication, but

FIGURE 35. Traits characteristic of Late Central California culture (Phase II). *Meighan 1959a:294, Figure 4.*

Angel has published on the skeletal remains, for he is strongly impressed by the evidence that the association is valid.

Given this situation at both ends of the Central Valley it is difficult to believe that there was no contemporary occupation predating the Early Horizon in the intervening favorable area. Tantalizing bits of evidence exist but their significance is not clear. Capay Man and Stanford Man may be indications of early habitation. The Farmington Gravels site, once attributed an age of approximately 9,000 years, has recently been dated to the post-Christian era by two C-14 determinations (Heizer 1964). At present one cannot profitably speculate further.

Other Regions

The Central Coast, which includes San Francisco Bay, is obviously related to the cultural developments of the interior delta region, but the exact nature is unclear. Heizer (1949a) and Beardsley (1954) present the view that the earliest culture of the San Francisco Bay Region correlates with the Middle Horizon of the delta area. There is certainly the implication in their work that the bay area culture is derivative from the interior. The earliest coastal

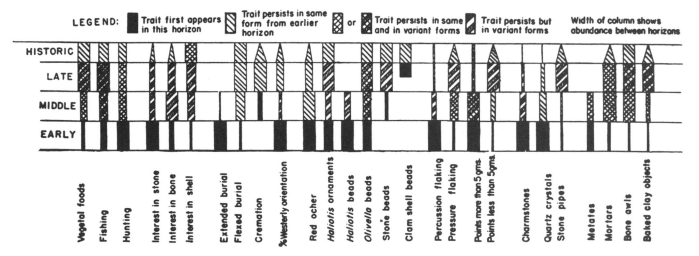

FIGURE 36. Culture development in Central California. *Beardsley 1948:5, Figure 2.*

manifestation is assumed to be that of the Emeryville Shell Mound, and that is dated by various means, but not C-14, at about 4,000 years ago. Sites along the coast proper and the shore of the bay have undoubtedly been affected by the rising sea level.

Gerow (1968), on the basis of careful analysis of the University Village Site near Stanford University on the southerly reaches of the bay, questions the interpretation of the development of the culture of the bay area as expressed by Beardsley and others. He also questions the age of the Windmiller facies (Early Horizon). The University Village Site is equated with the Early Horizon, which he dates at no older than 2000 B.C. He writes: "In the final analysis, the present data do not support the Central California Taxonomic System which portrays the Bay Region as an ecologic variant of a single development or succession of culture types and peoples within Central California. Rather, the data seem to be more compatible with a model of convergence" (Gerow 1968:126).

In the North Coast Range, Meighan (personal communication, C.W. Meighan to L.S. Cressman) has suggested a chronology for the region centering on the Borax Lake area, which includes Sonoma, Lake, and Mendocino counties. The Borax Lake period with fluted points and crescents he suggests is older than 6000 B.C., as I indicated above. This is followed by a second period marked by the presence of metates from 5000 B.C. to 2000 B.C. The first period dating is based on obsidian hydration dating, geology,

and typology. The second also uses hydration dating and artifact comparisons and a C-14 date for a metate-bearing site from this region. The Mendocino period follows, occupying the span from 1000 B.C. to A.D. 0.

The North West Coast Region at the present time appears to have no dates earlier than about 1,000 years ago. I cannot believe this is a true reflection of the time of occupation of that area, especially in view of a C-14 date of more than 3,000 years ago for the Pistol River site along the southwestern Oregon Coast not many miles north of the North West Coast Region. The question of the relation of the rising sea level to coastal sites again intrudes. The earliest records show a culture well adjusted to exploitation of the marine resources, the rivers, and the mountains, making use of fish, game, seeds, and fruits, especially the acorn.

Meighan (1959a:303–4) has given, for the student who is interested in understanding the cultural developments of aboriginal California without getting lost in a taxonomic chaos, the best statement:

California prehistory shows a continuous search for more efficient adaptation to the environment, and later cultures may be quite different from the early ones in the efficiency of their subsistence techniques. The difference between California and most other parts of North America is that the Californians devoted their interests to improving their lot while maintaining cultures that belong in the Archaic pattern rather than substituting agricultural techniques. That they succeeded is shown by a population that increased through time, by greater numbers and more kinds of artifacts. In addition, there is an increased elaboration of artifacts, with more attention being paid to artistic embellishment and the production of ornaments and other nonfunctional objects. . . .

Another reflection of improved 'Archaic' economy is seen in the shift in reliance from one resource to another. The early cultures of southern California were essentially land-oriented, basing their living upon seeds and land animals. When they did use the resources of the sea, they collected the obvious and easy-to-get shellfish, such as mussels and abalones. Through time there appears a shift to marine resources, the culmination being the fishing economy of the Canaliño. Such a change permitted greatly increased population, centers of population housing over 1,000 people, and greatly increased leisure time for the production of art objects and ceremonial paraphernalia. In terms of population increase, the southern Californians developed as fast and as far as the Southwestern agriculturists. Other segments of the California population did not experience as great an increase, probably largely because their local environments did not permit as greatly enriched exploitation. However, the general picture is one of experimentation and cultural change with recent culture somewhat better adapted to the environment.

Figure 37 provides a summary of the "Correlations in California Archæology" simply as an organizing device and is reproduced here with Meighan's permission (1959a, Figure 6). The chart is not meant to be a final statement. I have changed dates in my discussion in accordance with Meighan's suggestions. Dates for the San Dieguito are changed in the text and Meighan agrees in general with them.

Western Oregon

Oregon west of the Cascade Mountains is little known archæologically. It may be thought of as the Oregon Coast and the Willamette Valley, although south of the valley the mountains are continuous from the Cascade range to the coast, and this geographic feature throws that area into the Northern California-Siskiyou Mountains developmental area (at least on the basis of present information that appears to be the case). It is essential to present the limited information available to close the gap between northwestern California and western Washington.

The Oregon Coast

The Oregon Coast, approximately 350 miles in length, is rugged and spectacularly beautiful with the Coast Range mountains dropping off to the sea with little or no coastal plain (Figure 38). Rivers rising on the west slope of the Coast Range flow, with the exception of the Siuslaw, Umpqua, and Rogue rivers, by short courses to the sea. Starting from the Coquille River, approximately 250 miles south of the Columbia River, all rivers northward are "drowned" as a result of the rising sea level and crustal deformation, and tidewater extends in each case from ten to fifteen miles upriver. Between these rivers are the rain forest and rugged mountains. The coast is not protected from the fury of the Pacific storms by offshore islands, and so this rugged coast experiences extremely high and violent surf.

Only four published sources provide information on the prehistory of the Oregon Coast: Schumacher (1874), Berreman (1944), Newman (1959), and Heflin (1966). Only the Berreman and Newman reports are the result of scientific excavation. Various projects are in progress under the sponsorship of Oregon universities, and these may be expected to provide further information.

In the absence of archæological information of significant antiquity, linguistic evidence has been used as a basis for inference. Chinookan (Penutian) speakers are found on both sides of the mouth of the Columbia River for some distance north and south. Eastward they extend continuously, with the exception of two small Athapascan enclaves (see above, pp. 93–94), to The Dalles to include the Wishram and Wasco. South of the Chinook are Penutian groups in the Willamette Valley, but on the coast are the Salish-speaking Tillamook and the Siletz. North along the Washington Coast beyond the Chinookan groups are Coast Salish, linguistic relatives of the Tillamook and Siletz. A series of separate linguistic enclaves, but belonging to the Penutian group, extend from the Siletz south to the Coquille River where they meet the Athapascan speakers extending northward from northwestern California. Since both the Athapascans and the Tillamook are late arrivals (after 1,000 years ago; see Chapter 6) in a vast area of Penutian speakers extending from the coast eastward through the intermontane region, it is inferred that there must have been originally a coastal occupation by representatives of this group.

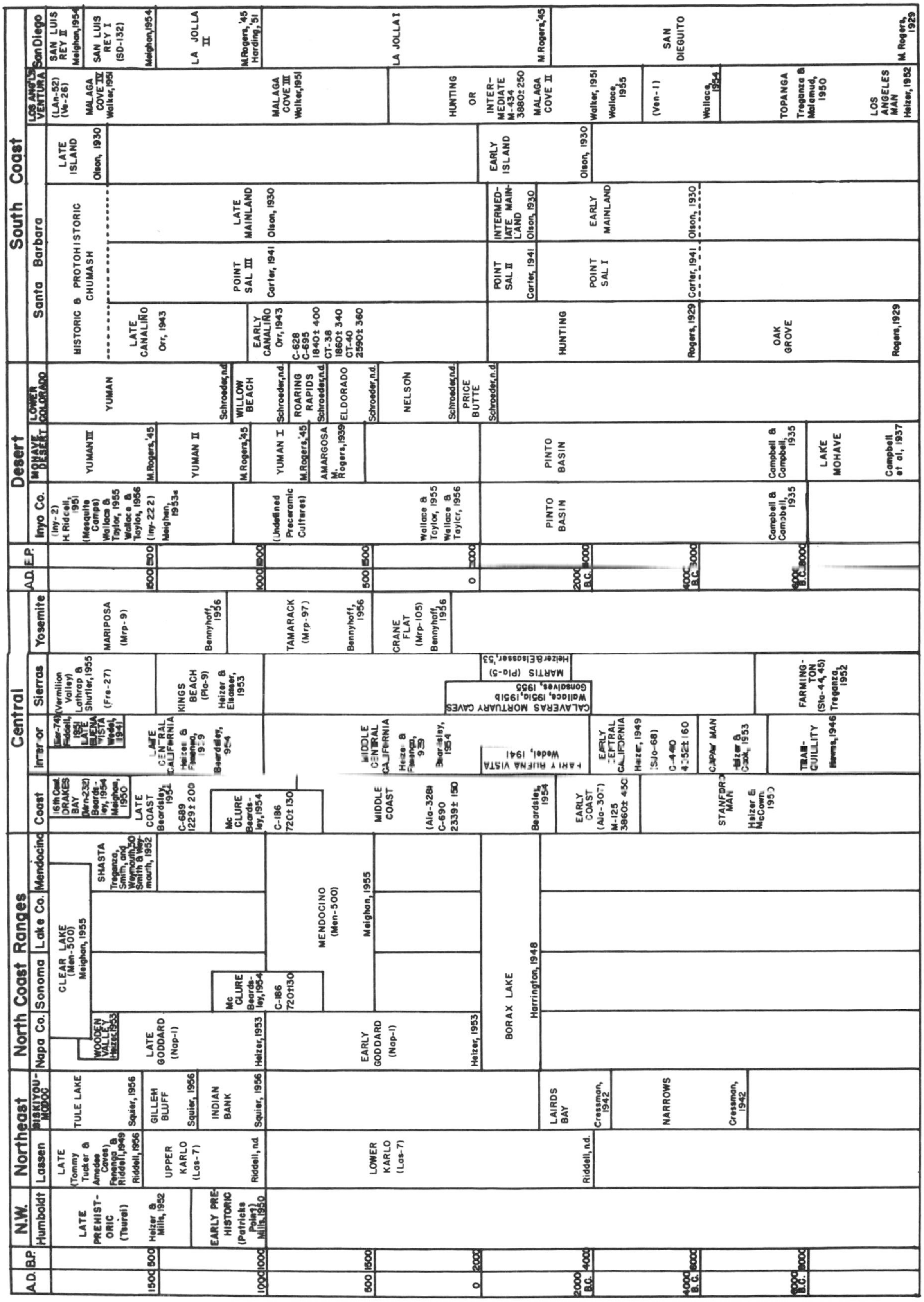

FIGURE 37. Correlations in California archaeology. In use this figure should be modified as suggested by Meighan and the author in the text. *Meighan 1959a:298–99, Figure 6.*

FIGURE 38. Oregon coast looking south from Cape Perpetua, Lane County. The rocky coast provided a rich supply of seafood as shown by the numerous shell middens; villages with few exceptions were along the rivers. *Photograph by author.*

Displacement at either end could have taken place by any of a number of means. I suggested in Chapter 6 the presence of Salish at the mouth of the Columbia River before a downriver movement of Chinook speakers divided them; I think, however, that probably as good a case could be made for Tillamook leapfrogging the Chinook holdings or even peaceful acceptance by the Chinooks of the migrating Salish. Contacts between the Chinook and their Salish neighbors appear to have been friendly, a relationship hardly suggestive of a history of conquest. The lack of evidence of occupation as much as 1,000 years ago, a condition seeming to controvert the inference of early occupation, is explained by the hypothesis that the rising sea level has inundated the earlier sites (see Chapter 3, pp. 47–50).

The Chetco site (Figure 39), Lone Ranch (Berreman 1944) on the south coast, the Tillamook village site on the Netarts Sandpit (Figure 40) (Newman 1959), and the Pistol River site, CU 61 (Heflin 1966), all show a full adaptation to the coastal habitat; the record of the process of adaptation is lacking.

Site CU-62, close to CU-61, throws light both on the antiquity of coastal settlement and the adaptive process. CU-62 is the remains of a structure (house?) nearly destroyed during highway construction. A partially burned beam is dated at 3000±90 years B.P. (GAK-1317); this is the earliest date for the long stretch of coast from Northern California (San Francisco Bay) to western Washington. The only artifacts recovered are large, heavy points with edge projections suggesting serration. Berreman has reported finding the same kind of points at Whale

FIGURE 39. Lone Ranch Site, Curry County, Oregon, a Chetco site of the southwest coast, now a state park. The parked cars are on the upper boundary of the site. A crescent beach with the surf broken by the offshore rocks (stacks), a freshwater stream, easy access inland, high cliffs at each horn of the crescent to break the winds, and a rich supply of both marine and land resources made this an ideal settlement site. Whale's Head, three miles north, is almost a duplicate of this site and is probably larger. *Photograph by author.*

Head Cove a short distance away. (I am indebted to Mr. D. L. Cole for the unpublished information on CU-62.)

Excavations and collectors' material indicate heavier occupation and richer deposits of artifacts in both the north and the south, a situation that probably reflects superior ecological opportunities and their exploitation, greater freedom of coastwise movement by canoe transport, and, in the north, the stimulation received from British Columbia and the interior, and, in the south, the reception of enriching influences from northwestern California. The **central Oregon Coast of the Penutian enclaves was**

an isolated cultural segment. Meighan's interpretation of the development of coastal California culture applies equally to the Oregon Coast.

The Willamette Valley

The Willamette Valley is the Oregon portion of the Willamette-Puget Trough extending southward some 125 miles from the Columbia River between the Cascade Mountains and the Coast Range. It varies in width from perhaps twenty to forty miles and is terminated on the south by the northern outliers of the Siskiyou Mountains. The Willamette River drains the valley, receiving the confluents from both adjacent mountain ranges on its course to the

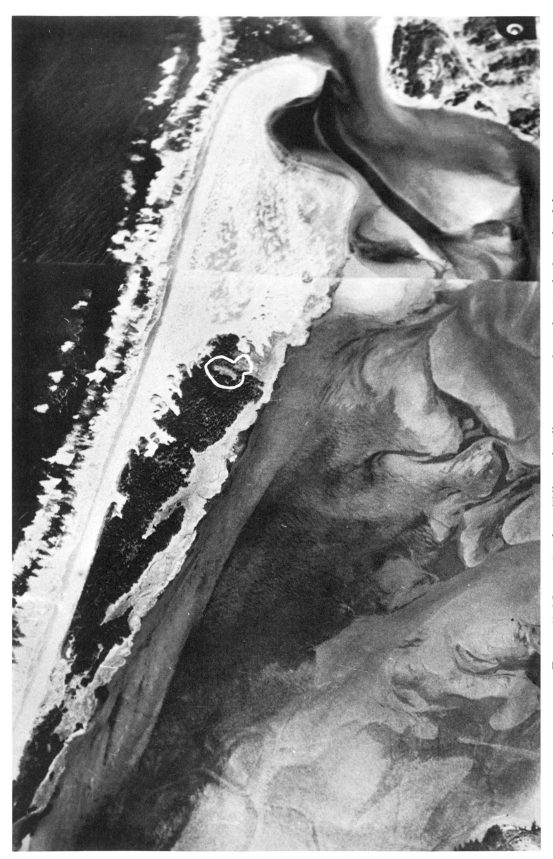

FIGURE 40. Netarts Sandspit, Tillamook village site inside circle. On the lee side of the forest- and brush-covered dune ridge, it was protected from the winds. A bayshore locality such as this provided clams, crustaceans, other mollusks, fish, and sea and land mammals. Mussels had to be brought from rock outcrops at a distance. *Aerial photograph, U.S. Coast and Geodetic Survey, 854, 10/15/55.*

Columbia River (Map 3). Passes crossed both ranges and travel south was easy (Chapter 2, p. 22).

Tenuous evidence suggests the presence of man with the mammoth in the valley (Cressman and Laughlin 1941; Cressman 1947). Occupation dating from 8000 B.P. has been firmly established at the Cascadia Cave site in the foothills of the Cascade Mountains in the Santiam River drainage (Newman 1966). In the southern portion of the valley, recent work by University of Oregon parties has established a firm chronology from about 4000 B.P.

Chinook-speaking peoples extended up the Willamette River to the falls of the Willamette, and for all practical purposes this stretch of the river was an extension of the Columbia and reflected the culture of the Columbia River people. The falls was a very important fishing site and people congregated there during the fish runs (see Chapter 7). Trade took place here and artifacts and associated behavior, at home up the Columbia River, also found a home in the Willamette Valley (Laughlin 1941, 1943). Trade took place across the Coast Range, probably mostly from the northern valley to the Tillamook Bay area of the coast; it also passed southward to the Umpqua and Rogue River areas (Collins 1951).

Present evidence fails to show that the Willamette Valley inhabitants made any significant contribution to Pacific Northwest cultural development; they were recipients, not innovators, of culture.

Summary

I have attempted in this chapter to present a review of the development and present status of archæological research in the Far West. In doing so I have, as an archæologist should, brought in the history of work in the different areas of discussion, the people concerned, the institutions involved, and the objectives. It has not been a full discussion and such was not intended. I have been interested in trying to present the review as a dynamic record of research activity, to emphasize what seems to me of most importance, that is, the study of cultural dynamics as that has emerged. Without doubt ten years from now some of the points of view that appear clear will have been shown to be in error and others at present equivocal will no longer be so. The great environmental diversity of the areas of discussion created diverse problems of adjustment. The interior Columbia-Fraser plateaus with their coastal orientation; the Great Basin possessing a basically similar environment throughout but with ecological variations, oases, and varied relationships to mountain masses; and California with its great ecological diversity all have many different problems. The northern plateaus, specially in later time, were exposed to influences from the Plains. The Great Basin both gave to and received from adjacent areas. California, while it received influences from the Southwest to a limited degree, was buffered by the Great Basin and, like its northwestern neighbors, had only the sea on the west. In attempting to review the results of archæological work in this wide an area, I have tried to present and evaluate conflicting views as far as it is possible for me to do so. My own views have been in conflict at times with those of others. I have tried to report the evidence and evaluate it with the intention of focusing attention on the questions of "what" and "how" and sometimes "why," the last in science, always a difficult, dangerous procedure.

Résumé and Observations

*It is true that none of us will know very much; and most
of us will see the end of our days without understanding
in all its detail and beauty the wonders uncovered even in
a single branch of a single science. Most of us will not
even know, as a member of any intimate circle, anyone
who has such knowledge; but it is also true that, although
we are sure not to know everything and rather likely not
to know very much, we can know anything that is known
to man, and may, with luck and sweat, even find out
some things that have not before been known to him.*

J. Robert Oppenheimer, Science and the Common Understanding

I DO NOT INTEND this chapter to be a full résumé; it
is in part an effort at a partial synthesis and some
observations I believe important for my concluding
statement. No documentation will be used for statements since it has been given in detail previously.

ARRIVAL AND DISPERSION

Sometime during the Pleistocene the Eurasiatic
animal, Man, cast in his lot with the other animals
wandering about on and crossing back and forth on
the land connection, which from time to time joined
northeast Asia and northwest North America. This
fateful action eventually resulted in the populating
of the New World and provided a remarkably significant segment of the human experience. When man
took this step, under what conditions, the nature of
his coming, and his subsequent achievements in the
Far West have been the concern of this study. To
attempt to answer these questions requires the use
of information from biology, geology, anthropology,
and even from humanists whose concern is the human
condition.

In the third interglacial period in the northeast
portion of Asia, basically China, there was a population of *Homo sapiens,* and from that time on they
formed an available population source for those who
wandered out onto the land connection in their hunting activities or to gratify sheer curiosity or both.
During the periods of glaciation, with which the land
connections were associated, the Yukon drainage,
shut off from the rest of North America by the vast
ice fields, was an ice-free cul-de-sac that has to be
considered an extension of the Asiatic land mass.
Movement back and forth across this land mass was
possible for many thousands of years, and the land
connection itself at the time of maximum glaciation
was a low-relief tundra 1,000 miles wide. North
American fauna beyond the peripheries of the ice
were excluded from participation in these movements. Then with deglaciation the land connection
was sumberged by the rising sea level and the Yukon
area was separated from the Asiatic continent to become a part of the North American habitat. Now
movement between Asia and North America was
interrupted for thousands of years and all movement
was intracontinental. Thus the times of the land
connections, the deglaciations, and the availability of
land as human habitat are critical questions that must
be answered in the effort to reconstruct the human
prehistory of the Far West.

There is no way of knowing how many years of
wandering passed before the first man set foot, without being aware of the momentous occasion, on the
soil of the North American continent. During all the
time of the land connection his mental orientation
must have been directed toward Asia, the land from
which he had come. Deglaciation produced an effect
that is difficult to fully appreciate. Instead of tundra
as far as the eye could see there was now the stormy
sea separating the continents. There was but one way
to go—ahead. Now there was a continent to conquer,
and the history of that continent would never be the
same, nor that of the conquerors to be. These climatic

episodes cast the future of a great population, the American Indians, and its land.

Movement into the continent was probably initiated by small bands of intrepid men and women from the southern and eastern peripheries of the Yukon refugium slowly testing the land ahead as a habitat. Until they had passed beyond the limits of the glacial wastage area their progress must have been circuitous and heartbreakingly slow; the toll in lives, especially of the very young, must have been appalling. Yet there was no turning back.

Whether these firstcomers moved south through the Intermontane Region or along the eastern slope of the Rocky Mountains or both is uncertain. It is certain that whatever way they came the obstacles, especially for the northern part of the journey, were forbidding. Rivers, large and small, had to be crossed by ingenuity and sheer daring; obstacles of enormous bogs had to be overcome; and there was always the threat of savage animals with only hostile men lacking. From southwestern Alberta southward natural obstacles faded in importance to the Wanderers, and in the Intermontane Region, once the Columbia River was behind them, there were no significant barriers. After reaching the southern boundary of the Great Basin some made their way west to the genial environment of the Southern California coast where the shoreline extended some miles westward because of the lowered sea level; others pushed on south into Mexico; and others probably explored the vast Plains toward the Mississippi River.

These were the first comers. How long this slow infiltration into several thousand miles of the continent required is beyond our present knowledge. What moved these people on and on and on? Surely they passed through many inviting environments, and the population pressure was not sufficient to reduce significantly the food supply. Something more than mere predation was the motive sending them into unexplored lands. This occupation of the New World by these Wanderers is one of Man's greatest achievements, yet the human aspects escape our knowledge.

BIOLOGICAL EVIDENCE

To know what these men and women who were to conquer a continent looked like is a natural concern of all interested people, yet that curiosity must go unsatisfied, at least in terms of what we know at present. Illustrators for books and periodical articles present drawings and paintings of what they think on the matter. Their works are the products of their own fancies and provide the reader with no reliable information on the subject. There are simply no skeletal remains of these earliest pioneers to provide the basic information about a physical type.

Comparisons at very general levels of discrimination between the fragmentary fossil specimens of the Upper Pleistocene of China and the earliest specimens from the New World indicate certain similarities of a gross nature. Lack of close likeness is expectable in view of the thousands of years separating the groups. The American Indians lack the blood-group B characteristic of the fully evolved Mongoloid type, and, therefore, their separation from the Asiatic pool must have preceded the appearance of the blood-group B. The fossil specimens from the Upper Pleistocene of China are inferred to be proto-Mongoloid. The American Indians belong to the O blood group with a percentage of type A. Where type B occurs mixture is inferred. The Eskimos, relative latecomers to the aboriginal population of the continent, are carriers of type B.

Even though there were available adequate samples of skeletal populations from the earliest occupants of the continent and their followers, the conventional methods of traditional anthropometry would not be of much help in unraveling the tangled threads of prehistory. Descriptions of populations could be provided, but explanations of their development could not; the ever-present argument between heredity and environment as causes did not lend itself to answer by the older methods. Efforts to apply the genetics of blood type to skeletal material, once held with high hopes as a fruitful method of population discrimination, has, as I pointed out, been called into question.

Genetic studies of skeletal material are possible, are being undertaken, and give some promise of determining relationships between population groups. The distribution of discontinuous traits, studies of certain aspects of cranial bones rather than the total cranium, these and other discriminating traits appear to be genetic in origin and free from normal influence by any element of the environment. Laboratory research, however, indicates the likely possibility of the development of reliable techniques for blood typing recovered skeletal material.

Living populations are the end product of thousands of years of evolution. Unless there is strong evidence of population shifts in a given area, it is reasonable to infer that the population is representative of the ancestral population for a past of unknown duration of time. This does not mean there has been no change, for such would have occurred as the result of biological, social, and natural causes, such as extreme changes in climate. The fact such changes occur makes it a hazardous procedure to use skeletal material described by rather gross anthropometric norms as a test of similarity or difference between population groups with the intent of indicating historical connection or the lack of it.

There is no one American Indian type in the Far West nor in the hemisphere—there are many types. In Chapter 5 I pointed out the diversity of types of living populations in the Far West as reported by Boas. It is tempting to use this information as a crutch to support one's uncertain way in the course of historical reconstruction. It is, however, a very weak support. While stature, the trait most heavily relied on, has a genetic base, it is, nevertheless, one of the most sensitive physical characteristics to respond to social and natural environmental influences.

Certain patterns of distribution appear, but the meaning is certainly not clear. Tallness characterizes the northernmost coastal tribes, Tlingit, Haida, and Tsimshian, but stature decreases as one moves south, then to increase as one approaches the Columbia River. Here the stature is tall, corresponding to that of the up-river Sahaptin speakers to whom the lower Columbia people were related linguistically. Going south, stature decreases and does not again reach the height found at the mouth of the Columbia River or in the northernmost stretch of the coast. The shortest of all the people along the northern coast (i.e., west of the Cascade Mountains) are those living along Harrison Lake, on the north side of the Fraser River, and on the flanks of the mountain range. The diversity in stature in the same general coastal environment, with roughly the same kind of food resources utilized, strongly suggests some biological,

genetic, factors as the cause. In the Intermontane Region south of the Athapascan boundary in British Columbia to the Colorado River in the south the stature is uniformly tall. Archæological evidence shows that this area at 10,000 years ago had much in common culturally, so much so that there must have been either an expansion of a single population or a considerable movement of groups who met and shared much of their cultural experience. These hypothetical conditions are not necessarily alternatives; perhaps they are different stages of the history of the basin-range environment. Certainly the environment for much of its history after 8,000 years ago provided only a subsistence economy, not the kind to stimulate growth potential. The situation strongly suggests a genetically tall population that persisted down to the time of white contact. Perhaps, also, the nature of social life and marriage stimulated the hybridization of genetic lines.

Along the coast south of the Columbia River, the population types were varied, in part according to the degree of isolation, both environmentally and socially.

Hopefully, an important contribution may be made, not only to our knowledge of far-western prehistory but to basic knowledge in general, by studies of skeletal material for evidence of pathological conditions. Skeletal material from the last three or four thousand years from different environments should provide evidence of nutritional deficiencies, interference with normal growth patterns, and other conditions that affect the bony skeleton. For example, Oregon, Washington, and neighboring eastern states were notorious for the high incidence of thyroid disorder in the white population until iodine was added to the diet or made available medicinally. Was the aboriginal population similarly affected? Hypothyroidism, the kind formerly endemic in the Northwest, produces a generally lower level of performance than is normal. There are various ramifications of this problem, which the thoughtful and informed person can explore; it is worth doing so.

Linguistic Evidence

Information on the distribution of languages is of importance to the prehistorian. One reason is that since a group speaking a common language usually shares a common culture, it is this group which has been the study of the traditional ethnographer. The archæologist usually tries to reconstruct the past of the group he is studying by starting with the "known" culture, that recorded by the ethnographer, and proceeding backward in time to reconstruct the past history of that culture. Until evidence to the contrary is discovered, it is assumed that all the sites within the boundary of the linguistic group belong to it. The problem of identification arises when the archæologist, as his excavations carry him earlier in time or to new sites within the common linguistic area, discovers some break in the continuity of the cultural development or its commonality; such a discontinuity indicates "something happened here," a break in the historical continuity of the linguistic group in the area and change in the area of land occupied. A second reason for the prehistorians' interest in language distribution through time and space is that language is probably man's most important invention, and any prehistory that lacks relevant linguistic information fails to account for a significant element of the human experience.

It is a tempting procedure for the archæologist, when he has a linguistic distribution map and a list of physical types on the same scale for the same area, to superimpose them and draw conclusions of causal relations when certain areas correspond. Since no causal connection between physical type and language spoken has ever been demonstrated, the correlation indicated by the maps is only that and is not a cause and effect relationship. Therefore, the cause for the correspondence indicated by the maps must be due to historical causes, and it is the job of the archæologist to discover them, if it can be done.

At a relatively shallow time depth the archæologist may be helped by the linguist through the use of vocabularies that record words for artifacts and features, such as house types or the lack of them. Even the oral literature is a possible source of information. All this, of course, refers to people with an unwritten language; a written language inscribed on durable material, once it can be read, changes the dimensions of the problem.

It is recognized by linguists that various groups of people with a common language or mutually understandable dialects spread through an area, large or small, will likely share in a common culture,

unless the area comprises widely different ecological regions. If this is true, then archæologists may reasonably infer that where a generally common culture exists there must have been a common means of verbal communication.*

Using this argument, one may legitimately infer from the remarkable number of common elements found in the cultural inventory between 9,000 and 10,000 years ago from southeastern Washington, along the Columbia River, through the Northern and Western Great Basin, and into Southern California that a mutually intelligible language existed. What the language was is purely speculative. Swadesh, however, suggests that the center of Penutian divergence could have been north-central Oregon at about 10,000 years ago. If he is correct then some language of that phylum would have existed in the Pacific Northwest where there is now evidence of human occupation earlier than 10,000 years ago, and it would have characterized the area of common culture that Bedwell has called Western Pluvial Lake tradition. Within this area starting about 9,000 years ago the culture began to organize into a series of regional foci, a process that would have intensified dialectical differences eventually producing different languages. Along the peripheries, however, would have been bilingual individuals who facilitated trade and perhaps provided the medium for loan words in the different languages. The various languages would have belonged to the Penutian phylum.

British Columbia's linguistic prehistory provides a number of very complex problems. Jenness (1932: 18) wrote: "British Columbia, therefore, like the Pacific coast of the United States, was a babel of conflicting tongues, suggesting that it had been a cul-de-sac from which neither invaded nor invader could escape." By 1940 the point of view was that of an orderly series of major languages from north to south: Athapascan, Algonquian (=Salish), Penutian

---

* In various parts of the world where trade was important but hindered by linguistic barriers, the difficulty was overcome by the development of a lingua franca. In the Pacific Northwest there was the "Chinook Jargon" used by Indians and whites alike, a common language that made possible communication across linguistic barriers. The presence of a manufactured language such as this has a different historical significance than the spread of a "natural" language.

(=Sahaptin). This orderly arrangement provided a "horizontal stratigraphy" and a good working model for the archæologist who would be working there in the future—no significant work had been done by that time. With the discovery, however, that the Salish and their neighbors on Vancouver Island and northeastern Washington were not related to the Algonquians, the whole theory of linguistic and archæological relationships was thrown into confusion.

It now appears that if the theory of prior Penutian occupation of the Northwest is sound, it is reasonable to expect that the fisherman on the Fraser River at 9,000 years ago belonged to that linguistic group, in view of the cultural similarity with southern sources either in the Intermontane Region or the Puget Lowland.

Later in the interior, as shown by Sanger's work, the earliest occupation is on the order of 7,500 years ago. His Early Period apparently consists of two traditions, one derived from Alaska and a second from Alberta across the Rocky Mountains. A long period of regional development occurred in southern interior British Columbia concurrent with that bordering on the middle Columbia River in the southern part of the plateau. Only late in prehistory did these two subregions come to share a substantially common culture—the Plateau culture area—and this culture area comprised the Salish, Sahaptin, and probably two smaller linguistic components.

One of the important problems of Northwest prehistory is that of the cultural and linguistic origins of the Salish. No satisfactory answer is presently available. All that can be said is that the Salish speakers, on the basis of limited but significant archæological information, probably represent a population originally derived from east of the Rocky Mountains in Alberta about 7,000 years ago. If this is true, their linguistic affiliation must be sought in that area, which is now Algonquian. It is not known what language was spoken in Alberta at the time postulated for the westward movement of the proto-Salish speakers.

A few remarks are in order concerning the Penutian expansion into California beginning, at least, about 4,000 years ago. This intrusion of Penutians is thought to have caused the dispersion of Hokan speakers into the peripheral environments of California. As far as I can see at present there is nothing in the culture–ecology relation to account for this expansion. The Penutian speakers had to come from the intermontane area. Environmental rejuvenation of the Intermontane Region had been underway, after the arid Altithermal, for several centuries, and this was accompanied by a cultural florescence. Perhaps some Penutians saw the Interior Valley of California as a more desirable habitat than even the improved Great Basin offered. No one knows. Was there a population "explosion" in the Great Basin with the climatic improvement that pushed the more daring west over the Sierra range? The question may be asked but it cannot at present be answered. Speculatively one might suggest that the renewed vitality of the culture of the Great Basin fostered a general expansionist psychology and this in turn was, at least, a strong, motivating force.

Among the problems facing the archæologist who attempts to account for the movements and/or presence of different linguistic groups is the nature of language itself. Some languages are very tenacious of their identity; others are much less so. Some languages are spread by "language capture," as Jacobs suspected for the Athapascans in northwestern California and southwestern Oregon. In this case the "captured" language disappears. In other cases the languages die out as the speakers die or are killed off. Archæology alone cannot document these occurrences; perhaps the linguist and archæologist in cooperation may do so, or the undocumented occurrences may remain part of the unknowns of prehistory.

CULTURAL EVIDENCE

Origin and Development of Lithic Technology

I presented in my discussion two contrasting theories of the origin and development of the sophisticated stone-working techniques in the New World: that the origin and development was autochthonous or that it was derived from Asia. I supported the autochthonous argument, but this does not mean that there were no Asiatic influences. When these arrived depends of course on the time of entry into the New World. If that occurred before 35,000 years ago, then the artifacts must have been those, on the basis of present knowledge of northeastern Asiatic prehistory, in use along the Pacific Coast of that area. These would have been chopping and cutting tools, hammering stones of various kinds, and probably perforating tools. Rude clothing of hides might have been in use and, perhaps, heavy tools of bone and wood, but these would not appear in the archæological record. The knowledge of stone flaking by percussion was known as shown by Old-World tools. This meager inventory, then, provided the basic tool kit of these new arrivals; on this they had to build.

Sometime between 35,000 and 25,000 years ago these people could have moved into the continent. In the course of their wanderings they would have been faced with numerous challenges to produce more effective tools for sheer survival in the new environments through which they passed. New kinds of stone became available and were certainly experimented with and used. These people had to be innovative to adapt to the numerous challenges of new environments. Whatever improvements in the technology or in the range of artifacts developed had to be internal. Here was a period of 10,000 years when they were on their own, so to speak.

The reestablishment of land connections again from 25,000 to perhaps 13,500 years ago reopened the way for the introduction of developed technologies from northeastern Asia, but these were limited in their distribution to the Yukon cul-de-sac until the way into the interior became open again 11,000 to 10,000 years ago. None of these new technologies were available to those who entered before 35,000 years ago, so there was a time span of 20,000 years for this original artifact inventory to be developed on its own terms. If this model of land connections, time, and population movements is valid, then one must conclude that the cultural inventory of the New World found south of the ice margin and dating from 10,000 years ago, at a conservative estimate, must have developed out of the very limited base brought by the earliest arrivals. Tlapacoya and other sites provide confirming evidence.

Subsistence, Adaptation, and Regional Specialization

The first tools and weapons brought into the New World, the rather generalized tools for defense and food acquisition and preparation, were carried by their possessors throughout the area of their occupation. During the long time of their expansion, additions to their inventory as well as improvements in specialized instruments were made. Projectile points, knives, and scrapers were made and the macroblade-and-core technique was invented and widely used. Since for many thousands of years the basic food was that of the wild animal supplemented, of course, by vegetal foods, the range of weapons followed a general pattern of development to produce increased efficiency in provision of animal foods. Because the basic culture was much the same, it is likely that similar innovations occurred frequently. An ovoid, elongate, biface could be produced by more than one method of flaking, but once it was produced in a given way at some place, it is likely that the method would be adopted locally. The movement of these groups in the food quest would bring them into contact with others, and through social interaction novelties would be exchanged and spread.

Individual variations among humans—curiosity and the "play function" itself, especially with the hands—are bound to produce innovation and variability in the products. In far-western prehistory, this development continued for many thousands of years and produced an efficient set of tools, but, as the record shows, there was little or no regional variation at very early times. Recall the cultural similarity reflected in the far-flung Western Pluvial Lake tradition.

When the inhabitants of an area became more aware of the particular resources of the environment, for example, the anadromous fish of the northwestern rivers, exploitation of that resource challenged the more alert and they began to devise methods to make use of it. The production of instruments to exploit this resource, lacking in other areas, together with the new dimension in the transhumance patterns such exploitation required, brought a new focus to the subsistence activities of the area's population. A *regional* way of life began to develop out of the widespread, basic hunting pattern. Environmental deterioration in the Great Basin by 8,000 years ago had forced the inhabitants to focus more sharply on the seeds and plant foods offered in that environment. The Great Basin culture became regionally the gathering area par excellence. Regional cultures, characterized by exploitation of the particular resources of the region, began in the Far West about 9,000 years ago and were well developed by 8,000 years ago. Within these larger regions subregions appeared as variations in ecological opportunities required different methods of exploitation. Examples are the subregions of the Great Basin, those centering on the Columbia River and the Fraser River in the plateau area, as well as others. Regional environmental opportunities were the motivating force in the Far West for the *initiation* of regional cultural diversity; personal initiative and cultural efficiency in exploitation became the means of achievement. There is no known way at present to relate this process causally to either physical type or linguistic achievement.

Developmental Theory and Relative Chronology

In Chapter 7, Subsistence and Adaptation, I had, to a very large extent, to start with the ethnographic record and extrapolate backward in time through the broken archæological record. When there are no actual chronological data available, the archæologist has resource to the "Developmental Theory" of cultural development to order his material temporally. Once he does this to his satisfaction he then tries to relate data from other parts of his area to this scheme.

This method of ordering cultural development, the whole and/or the component parts, has a high level of utility, but it must be used with caution since it is essentially drawn from the nineteenth-century theory of progress and has all the strengths and weaknesses of its intellectual parent. Unless one has a complete record of the history of an artifact, simple or complex, it is almost, if not quite, impossible to determine with assurance that a certain stage of the artifact's history represented in the fragmentary record is from the "developmental" or "deteriorating" stage. Further, the archæologist, a product of a sophisticated culture, attempts to reconstruct the aboriginal inventor's thought processes and their observable expression. This is an extraordinarily difficult thing to do; I doubt that it can be fully done, especially in view of the difficulty of seeing the "other fellow's point of view" in even our own rather small social circles. I do not mean that there is any difference between the neurophysiological mental processes of the aboriginal inventor

and the archæologist, but there is a vast difference in their respective apperceptive environments. Another question has to be raised: if one is considering an artifact type, pottery or basketry, which consists of both structure and decoration, the latter being of no significance in the utility of the object, is one to apply the developmental theory to the total object or to structure and to decoration as separate products? If the object class has a history, even a short one, without decoration, then it seems to me that structure and decoration are separate products and should be studied as such.

I discussed earlier the question of priority of types of basketry in the Great Basin and especially of certain types of twining in the Northern Great Basin. Various students have attempted to place the different types of basketry in a developmental order. This basketry needs to be considered in terms of basic structure *and* decorative techniques, but separately at first, then the two may be considered as they were combined. I am inclined to see the origin of twined basketry in the mental atmosphere that was associated with cordage production: the twisting of fibers together to make a cord. If Northern Great Basin twining is the earliest in the Far West, its antecedents must be local. All this basketry was made out of flexible materials that had to be twisted to form a "cord" that could be used to twist other cords into a flat relation a mat, or a receptacle with a rounded or pointed bottom, a basket. Only two structural kinds developed: a "plain twine" and an "open-diagonal twine"; the second was only a pleasing variation on the first. I think there can be no doubt that the plain preceded in time the open-diagonal variety. The decoration, which occurred in a considerable variety, is a quite different problem. Plain, undecorated basketry was certainly the earliest. I have spent a great deal of time in thoughtful analysis of this basketry and, particularly, its decoration and have even experimented somewhat to reproduce it. Yet I cannot say with any assurance that a certain type was the earliest nor can I put them in any developmental order. No one can say for certain why decoration was considered desirable in the first place. It is a remarkable achievement that these people living at such a low economic level and in dusty caves found some motivation to enhance the attractiveness of this ordinary household ware when it in no way improved the utility of the basket. Most of the best preserved samples of basketry come from cache deposits, and, since they were excavated before radiocarbon dating became available and were treated with preservative material, they cannot be precisely dated. Several well-controlled stratigraphic series, radiocarbon dated, will be required to order finally the development of the decorative techniques of Northern Great Basin twined basketry; the "Developmental Theory" I am sure will not suffice, and conclusions based on it are of dubious value.

Interior-Coastal Cultural Relations

I began this study in 1964 with a modest objective: a study of the relation of the prehistoric culture of the intermontane area (the interior) to that of the Pacific Coast. I soon had to redirect the program because the initial problem could be answered only in the frame of reference of the wider subject, far-western North American prehistory. At appropriate places in this study the subject has been discussed in detail, but some additional summary comments can be made.

Two questions need to be asked: was the coast occupied initially by a population that moved gradually southward along the coast from the Yukon refugium working out its adaptation to the maritime ecology as it progressed; or did the earliest population move into the interior by an inland route, and then, by slowly supplying pioneering groups, gradually populate the coast and develop varying degrees of effective adaptation?

Consider the first question. On the basis of present evidence the answer must be "No."

The second question must be answered "Yes," both on the basis of evidence and default by the first question.

What was the nature of this coastward movement of population? I see no evidence of any large or sudden movement; quite the contrary is true. The earliest evidence of coastal occupation is that of the Southern California coastal area and probably Santa Rosa Island. The major food concern of the Santa Rosa islanders seems to have been pygmy elephants, but this evidence may be a result of the excavation methods. At any rate, the evidence indicates these people were hunters. At the Scripps Campus site at La Jolla, the evidence of shell fragments about the probable hearth indicate that by about 25,000 years ago there was an awareness that the sea could be a supplier of food and that in some manner the awareness was being applied to the subsistence problem. In the same general area (Southern California coast) by approximately 10,000 years ago at Malaga Cove, there is evidence of deepwater fishing implying some methods of seagoing transportation. Therefore, by this time, as the evidence from the shell mounds of the coast and Santa Rosa Island shows, considerable success had been achieved in developing an adaptive culture along many miles of the coast. The later aboriginal history of this coast from well north of Santa Barbara south to Baja California, culminating in the Canaliño Culture with its most striking expression in that of the Chumash-speaking people of the Santa Barbara region, is to be understood as a continuing improvement of the ecological adaptation to the maritime environment.

A different type of movement and adaptation to the shoreline environment is represented along the central Oregon coast. Here a series of separate linguistic groups occupied a considerable stretch of the rocky coast. Settlements were mostly on each side of the mouth of short rivers flowing from the Coast Range; they were pretty effectively isolated from one another by the rain forest and rugged terrain between the rivers. Movement from the villages was generally for short distances along the coast and on the rivers, most of which were tidal for about 15 to 20 miles. Those groups that had the good fortune to hold large estuarine areas such as Yaquina and Tillamook bays were in the more favorable situation, for the readily available mud flats provided a richer supply of food than did the rocky headlands. These people were exploiters of the resources of the land for animals, the rivers for fish, and the shoreline for various crustaceans and mollusks, and occasional sea lions and seals.

Now these people spoke languages all classified in the Penutian phylum, that of the interior of Oregon. The rising sea level has drowned any evidence of shoreline occupation more than approximately 500 to 600 years ago, so when the initial occupation occurred is unknown. This coast is separated from the Intermontane Region by the Coast Range, the Willamette Valley, and the Cascade Range, in that order. The language of the Willamette Valley people was also of the Penutian stock, and regular trade was carried on between the coast and the valley in ethnographic times. Movement into the valley across the Cascade Range also occurred. In view of this evidence, one may infer cautiously that the movement to the coast was from central Oregon across the Cascade Range into the Willamette Valley and eventually to the coast. There is no evidence when such movements took place.

Farther north on the Oregon coast were the Salish-speaking Tillamook separated from their Coast Salish-speaking neighbors along the Washington coast by the Chinookan-speaking Clatsop. The latter must have moved down the Columbia River from The Dalles area by pushing through to the coast to separate the Tillamook, probably already settled at the mouth of the Columbia.

The southern Washington coast was similar in many respects to that of northern Oregon with bays, sandy beaches, and rocky headlands. The population spoke Coast Salish. The economy generally corresponded to that of the northern Oregon coast. Here, too, the time of initial occupation is unknown; there is no evidence of anything preceding the Salish-speaking movement, eventually from the interior of British Columbia.

From the Puget Lowlands north through British Columbia and the islands of the Gulf of Georgia, the problem of coastal occupation is very complex. The limited evidence available leads me to believe that the Puget Lowland was occupied, although sparsely, as much as 9,000 or even 10,000 years ago. Mitchell proposed an early "Lithic" period for the Gulf Islands ending about 7,000 to 8,000 years ago. Obsidian found in sites on Vancouver Island from this period indicates contact with the mainland. This evidence of coast-mainland contact is of particular importance because it demonstrates the development in the Gulf Islands of a system of deepwater transportation. In other words, a major element in the cultural inventory for adapting to the full maritime ecology was now available. If the people who achieved this adaptation came from an early population first found in the Puget Lowland, then it is likely that

they belonged linguistically to the Penutian phylum. The Locarno Beach period, which follows the Lithic on the Gulf Islands, shows a progressive improvement in its adaptive economy. It should be recalled that Borden first described and named the Locarno Beach phase from a site that, when occupied, was a beach site, but is now 4 miles inland because of the building up of the Fraser River delta. The Locarno Beach phase on the Gulf Islands, where Borden speculated it might have begun 1,000 years earlier than recorded on the mainland, shows a highly developed maritime culture. The following Marpole phase lacks the maritime color, being essentially a mainland culture with some slight coastal orientation. Fully developed Coast Salish culture appears between 400 and 600 years ago on the coastal mainland.

This record strongly suggests to me that there were two lines of culture contributing to the development of the culture of the Northwest Coast proper: an earlier one originating in the Puget Lowland extending to the San Juan Islands and then to the Gulf Islands; on the mainland a later source from the interior represented by the Marpole phase eventually reaching the coast and gradually making an adaptation to the maritime environment. If the Salish speakers who were to comprise the Coast Salish began coastward movement shortly after the divergence between Coast and Interior Salish languages, then evidence of such movement should be found in sites approaching the coast but is so far undiscovered. The final development of the Northwest Coast culture is in terms of the dynamics of maritime resource exploitation.

Trade in various goods, mostly what might be called luxury items, occurred between the coast and interior, extending as far as the Northern Plains. Food in the form of fish oil was traded by the Tsimshian and Bella Coola with the Athapascans of the interior for mountain sheep horn, furs, and other objects. The horn provided a raw material for coastal carvers. Pounded dried salmon was traded to the coast and elsewhere by the Wishram at The Dalles. *Olivella, Dentalium,* and other shells found their way from the coast to the interior. Nevada provided obsidian in trade to Central California, mostly by the Owens Valley route, and received shell beads in return. None of the trade involved population movements into new habitats, and its effect on the culture was marginal.

The Far West as a Distinctive Region In North American Prehistory

The prehistory of the Far West differs from that of the rest of the North American continent because it developed on its own terms. What major outside influences affected it were derived from Asia, and these did not reach below the most northerly areas. The diffusion of agriculture into the Southwest-Anasazi area and the great portion of the central and eastern regions of the continent brought those areas into the Mesoamerican orbit to a greater or lesser extent. This never happened to the Far West. The far-western record is one of an early adaptation to a vast area rich in game and other food resources. Within the larger region, cultural specialization developed to exploit more effectively the ecological opportunities offered by the subregions. The diverse environments of the Far West with their different resources provided the "challenge" and the "response" is represented in the regional cultures that were adapted to their exploitation. The prehistory of the Far West is to be seen as a chronicle of the development of more and more effective exploitation of the ecological opportunities offered by diverse environments as these were affected by climatic changes over time; it is essentially a closed system.

The prehistory I have tried to present is that based on what the archæologist recovers and what he may reasonably infer from it. It is of course primarily eco-cultural and at the economic and material culture level. The cultural anthropologist working with informant-derived material would undoubtedly provide emphases different from those I have found, but he would be working with living populations and at an entirely different time level. That such would be the case in no way minimizes the interest of the archæological record. My overview or synthesis of far-western North American prehistory brings into focus a host of problems, both large and small, that will stimulate the perceptive reader's interest. By bringing them into focus for the archæologists of the future to study and solve, I shall hopefully have made some contribution to an understanding of the human condition.

L'Envoi

I stated at the beginning of this study that it was to be considered as a progress report, a statement of the situation as permitted by the evidence presently available. It is the nature of all science that it develops through a process by which new evidence is discovered and made available. New evidence, as Robert Oppenheimer wrote, transcends the old. New conclusions are drawn. This study has amply illustrated this principle. The men who 30 years ago argued against the antiquity of man in the New World, as long as they were logically using the evidence available to them, were not wrong. Those who then and those who now steadfastly refuse to examine new evidence can be said to be unreasonable. Certainly new evidence will be discovered that transcends that available to me and conclusions different from mine will, therefore, be drawn. I hope some of my students will aid the process. An ideal has pervaded my teaching and research and I have held it up to my students to emulate, and it is to be found in this study. The ideal can best be expressed by the lines from the Irish poet, "A.E.," who some 50 years ago wrote in his poem, "On Behalf of Some Irishmen not Followers of Tradition":

No blazoned banner we unfold-
One charge alone we give to youth,
Against the sceptred myth to hold
The golden heresy of truth.

Bibliography

I originally used 1969 as the cutoff date for my bibliography, but, during subsequent work on the manuscript, publications became available giving information on areas that I had written about from personal information. These limited references have been included.

A

ACKERMAN, ROBERT E.
1968 The Archæology of the Glacier Bay Region, Southeastern Alaska. *Washington State University Laboratory of Anthropology, Report of Investigations,* no. 44. Pullman.

ADOVASIO, JAMES M.
1970 The Origin, Development and Distribution of Western Archaic Textiles. *Tebiwa,* vol. 13, no. 2, pp. 1-25. Pocatello.

AIKENS, C. MELVIN
1967 Plains Relationships of the Fremont Culture: A Hypothesis. *American Antiquity* 32:198-209. Washington, D.C.

1969 Hogup Cave: Chronology and Archæology. *Abstracts of Papers, 34th Annual Meeting of the Society for American Archaeology,* pp. 1-2. Milwaukee.

1970 Hogup Cave. *University of Utah Anthropological Papers,* no. 93. Salt Lake City.

AIKENS, C. MELVIN; KIMBALL T. HARPER; AND GARY F. FRY
1970 Hogup Cave: Interim Report. Paper read at the Annual Meeting of the Society for American Archæology, Santa Fe, 1968. Ditto.

ALLISON, IRA S.
1945 Pumice Beds at Summer Lake, Oregon. *Geological Society of America Bulletin* 56:789-808. New York.

1946 Pluvial Lakes and Pumice. *Scientific Monthly* 62:63-65. Washington, D.C.

1966a Pumice at Summer Lake, Oregon—A Correction. *Geological Society of America Bulletin* 77:329. New York.

1966b Fossil Lake, Oregon, Its Geology and Fossil Faunas. *Oregon State Monograph, Studies in Geology,* no. 9. Corvallis.

AMSDEN, CHARLES A.
1937 The Lake Mohave Artifacts. *In* "The Archæology of Pleistocene Lake Mohave: A Symposium." *Southwest Museum Papers,* no. 11, pp. 51-97. Los Angeles.

AMERICAN COMMISSION ON STRATIGRAPHIC NOMENCLATURE
1961 Code of Stratigraphic Nomenclature. *Bulletin of the American Association of Petroleum Geologists* 45:645-65. Tulsa.

ANASTASIO, ANGELO
1955 "Intergroup Relations in the Southern Plateau." Ph.D. dissertation, Faculty of the Division of Social Sciences, University of Chicago.

ANGEL, J. LAWRENCE
1966 Early Skeletons from Tranquility, California. *Smithsonian Contributions to Anthropology,* vol. 2, no. 1. Washington, D.C.

ANTEVS, ERNST
1948 Climatic Changes and Pre-White Man. *In* "The Great Basin, with Emphasis on Glacial and Postglacial Times." *Bulletin of the University of Utah,* vol. 38, no. 20. *Biological Series,* vol. 10, no. 7, pp. 168-91. Salt Lake City.

1952 Climatic History and the Antiquity of Man in California. *Reports of the University of California Archaeological Survey,* no. 16, pp. 23-31. Berkeley.

1953a On Division of the Last 20,000 Years. *Reports of the University of California Archaeological Survey,* no. 20, pp. 5-8. Berkeley.

1953b The Postpluvial or Neothermal. *Reports of the University of California Archaeological Survey,* no. 22, pp. 9-23. Berkeley.

1962 Late Quaternary Climates in Arizona. *American Antiquity* 28:193-98. Washington, D.C.

ARMSTRONG, JOHN E.; D. CRANDELL; D. EASTERBROOK; AND J. NOBLE
1965 Late Pleistocene Stratigraphy and Chronology in Southwestern British Columbia and Northwestern Washington. *Geological Society of America Bulletin* 76:321-30. New York.

ARMSTRONG, JOHN E., AND HOWARD W. TIPPER
1948 Glaciation in North Central British Columbia. *American Journal of Science* 246:283-310. New Haven.

Arnold, Brigham
1957 Late Pleistocene and Recent Changes in Land Forms, Climate, and Archæology in Central Baja California. *University of California Publications in Geography*, vol. 10, no. 4. Berkeley.

Arnold, J. R., and Walter F. Libby
1950 *Radiocarbon Dates*. University of Chicago Institute for Nuclear Studies, Sept. 1. Chicago.

Aschmann, Homer H.
1958 Great Basin Climates in Relation to Human Occupance. *In* "Current Views on Great Basin Archæology." *Reports of the University of California Archaeological Survey*, no. 42, pp. 23–40. Berkeley.

B

Bada, Jeffrey L.; Roy A. Schroeder; and George F. Carter
1974 New Evidence for the Antiquity of Man in North America Deduced from Aspartic Acid Racemization. *Science* 184:791–93. Washington, D.C.

Barnett, H. G.
1937 Culture Element Distributions: VII Oregon Coast. *University of California Anthropological Records*, vol. 1. Berkeley.
1940 Culture Processes. *American Anthropologist*, n.s., 12:21–48. Washington, D.C.
1942 Invention and Culture Change. *American Anthropologist*, n.s., 44:14–30. Washington, D.C.
1953 *Innovation, The Basis of Cultural Change*. McGraw-Hill, New York.
1955 The Coast Salish of British Columbia. *University of Oregon Monographs, Studies in Anthropology*, no. 4. Eugene.

Baerreis, David A.
1959 The Archaic as Seen from the Ozark Region. *American Antiquity* 24:270–76. Washington, D.C.

Baumhoff, Martin A.
1955 Excavation of Site Teh–1 (Kingsley Cave). *Reports of the University of California Archaeological Survey*, no. 30, pp. 40–73. Berkeley.
1957 An Introduction to Yana Archæology, *Reports of the University of California Archaeological Survey*, no. 40. Berkeley.
1958a Excavation of a Cache Cave in Pershing County, Nevada. *Reports of the University of California Archaeological Survey*, no. 44, pt. 2, pp. 14–25. Berkeley.
1958b Ecological Determinants of Population. *Reports of the University of California Archaeological Survey*, no. 41, pp. 34–41. Berkeley.

Baumhoff, Martin A., and J. S. Byrne
1959 Desert Side-notched Points as a Time Marker in California. *Papers on California Archaeology*, no. 72. *Reports of the University of California Archaeological Survey*, no. 48, pp. 32–65. Berkeley.

Baumhoff, Martin A., and A. B. Elsasser
1956 Summary of Archæological Survey and Excavation in California. *Reports of the University of California Archaeological Survey*, no. 33, pp. 1–27. Berkeley.

Baumhoff, Martin A., and Robert F. Heizer
1958 Outland Coiled Basketry from the Caves of West Central Nevada. *Reports of the University of California Archaeological Survey*, no. 42, pp. 49–59. Berkeley.
1965 Postglacial Climate and Archæology in the Desert West. *In The Quaternary of the United States*, H. E. Wright, Jr., and David G. Frey, eds., pp. 697–707. Princeton University Press, Princeton.

Beals, R. L., and J. A. Hester
1960 A New Ecological Typology of the California Indians. *In Men and Cultures—Selected Papers of the Fifth International Congress of Anthropological and Ethnological Sciences*, Anthony F.C. Wallace, ed., pp. 411–19. Philadelphia.

Beardsley, Richard K.
1948 Culture Sequences in Central California Archæology. *American Antiquity* 14:1–29. Washington, D.C.
1954 Temporal and Areal Relations in Central California Archæology. *Reports of the University of California Archaeological Survey*, nos. 24, 25. Berkeley.

Bedwell, Stephen Ferguson
1969 "Prehistory and Environment of the Pluvial Fort Rock Lake Area of South Central Oregon." Ph.D. dissertation, University of Oregon, Eugene. University Microfilms, Ann Arbor, Mich.
1973 *Fort Rock Basin: Prehistory and Environment*. University of Oregon Books, Eugene.

Bedwell, Stephen Ferguson, and L. S. Cressman
1971 Fort Rock Report: Prehistory and Environment of the Pluvial Fort Rock Lake Area of South-Central Oregon. *In* "Great Basin Anthropological Conference, University of Oregon, 1970, Selected Papers," C. Melvin Aikens, ed. *University of Oregon Anthropological Papers*, no. 1, pp. 1–25. Eugene.

BELOUS, RUSSELL E.

1947   The Central California Chronological Sequence Re–examined. *American Antiquity* 12:341–53. Washington, D.C.

BENNYHOFF, JAMES A.

1950   Californian Fish Spears and Harpoons. *University of California Anthropological Records* 9:295–337. Berkeley.

1956   An Appraisal of the Archæological Resources of Yosemite National Park. *Reports of the University of California Archaeological Survey,* no. 34. Berkeley.

1958   The Desert West: A Trial Correlation of Culture and Chronology. *Reports of the University California Archaeological Survey,* no. 42, pp. 98–112. Berkeley.

BENNYHOFF, JAMES A., AND ROBERT F. HEIZER

1958   Cross-dating Great Basin Sites by California Shell Beads. *Reports of the University of California Archaeological Survey,* no. 42, pp. 60–92. Berkeley.

BERGER, RAINER; REINER PROTSCH; RICHARD REYNOLDS; CHARLES ROZAIRE; AND JAMES R. SACKETT

1972   New Radiocarbon Dates Based on Bone Collagen of California Paleoindians. *Contributions to the University of California Archaeological Research Facility,* no. 12 (VI), pp. 43–49. Berkeley.

BERREMAN, JOEL V.

1944   Chetco Archæology: A Report of the Lone Ranch Creek Shell Mound on the Coast of Southern Oregon. *General Series in Anthropology,* no. 11. George Banta Publishing Company, Menasha, Wisc.

BIRD, JUNIUS B.

1961   B.P.: Before Present or Bad Policy? *American Antiquity* 26:557–58. Washington, D.C.

BOAS, FRANZ

1891   Third Report on the Indians of British Columbia. Report of the Sixty-first Meeting of the British Association for the Advancement of Science at Cardiff in Aug., pp. 408–49.

1895a   Fifth Report on the Indians of British Columbia. Report on the Sixty-fifth Meeting of the British Association for the Advancement of Science at Ipswich in Sept., pp. 522–92.

1895b   Zur Anthropologie der nordamerkanischen Indianer. *Zeitschrift fur Ethnologie,* Sieben und zwanzigster Jahrgang, pp. 366–411.

1896   Anthropometrical Observations on the Mission Indians of Southern California. American Association for the Advancement of Science, *Proceedings* 44:261–69. N.p.

1899   Anthropometry of Shoshonean Tribes. *American Anthropologist,* n.s., 1:751–58. Washington, D.C.

1902   The Jesup North Pacific Expedition. *Proceedings of the International Congress of Americanists,* 13th Session, pp. 91–100. Easton, Pa.

1905   Anthropometry of Central California. *Bulletin of the American Museum of Natural History* 17:347–80. New York.

1940   The Analysis of Anthropometrical Series. *In Race, Language and Culture.* The Macmillan Company, New York. Originally published in *Archiv für Rassen- und Gesellschafts-Biologie* 10 (1913):290 et. seq.

BONNICHSEN, ROBSON

1964   The Rattlesnake Canyon Cremation Site, Southwest Idaho. *Tebiwa,* vol. 7, no. 1, pp. 28–38. Pocatello.

BORDEN, CHARLES E.

1950   Preliminary Report on Archæological Investigations in the Fraser Delta Region. *Anthropology in British Columbia,* no. 1, pp. 13–27. Victoria.

1951   Facts and Problems of Northwest Coast Prehistory. *Anthropology in British Columbia,* no. 2, pp. 35–52. Victoria.

1953– Some Aspects of Prehistoric Coastal–Interior Re-
1954   lations in the Pacific Northwest. *Anthropology in British Columbia,* no. 4, pp. 26–32. Victoria.

1957   Notes and News. *American Antiquity* 23:325. Washington, D.C.

1960a   DjRi 3, An Early Site in the Fraser Canyon, British Columbia. *National Museum of Canada Bulletin* 162, *Anthropological Series,* no. 4, pp. 101–18. Ottawa.

1960b   Notes and News—Northwest. *American Antiquity* 25:628. Washington, D.C.

1961a   Fraser River Archæological Project. *National Museum of Canada Anthropology Papers,* no. 1. Ottawa.

1961b   Notes and News—Northwest. *American Antiquity* 26:584. Washington, D.C.

1961c   Notes and News—Northwest. *American Antiquity* 27:274. Washington, D.C.

1962a   Notes and News—Northwest, British Columbia. *American Antiquity* 27:613. Washington, D.C.

1962b   West Coast Crossties with Alaska. *In* "Prehistoric Cultural Relations Between the Arctic and Temperate Zones of North America," John M. Campbell, ed. *Arctic Institute of North America Technical Paper,* no. 11, pp. 9–19. Montreal.

1968a   New Evidence of Early Cultural Relations between Eurasia and Western North America. *Proceeding of the VIIIth Congress of Anthropological and*

Ethnological Sciences 3:331–37. Science Council of Japan, Toyko and Kyoto.

1968b A Late Pleistocene Pebble Tool Industry of Southwestern British Columbia. *In* "Early Man in Western North America: Symposium of the Southwestern Anthropological Association, San Diego, 1968." *Eastern New Mexico University Contributions in Anthropology,* vol. 1, no. 4, pp. 55–69. Portales, N.M.

BORNS, H. W., JR.

1966 The Geography of Paleo-Indian Occupation in Nova Scotia. *Quaternaria* 8:49–57. Rome.

BOULE, MARCELLIN, AND HENRI V. VALLOIS

1957 *Fossil Man.* Michael Bullock, trans. The Dryden Press, Inc., New York.

BOWERS, STEPHEN

1963a Aboriginal Fish-hooks. *Reports of the University of California Archaeological Survey,* no. 59, pp. 73–76. Berkeley.

1963b Fish-hooks from Southern California. *Reports of the University of California Archaeological Survey,* no. 59, pp. 71–72. Berkeley.

BOYD, WILLIAM C.

1939a Blood Groups. *Tabulae Biologicae,* vol. 10. The Hague.

1939b Blood Groups of American Indians. *American Journal of Physical Anthropology,* n.s., 25:215–35. Philadelphia.

1950 *Genetics and the Races of Man: An Introduction to Modern Physical Anthropology.* D. C. Heath & Co., Boston.

BRAINERD, GEORGE W.

1952 On the Study of Early Man in Southern California. *Reports of the University of California Archaeological Survey,* no. 16, pp. 18–22. Berkeley.

1953 A Re-examination of the Dating Evidence for the Lake Mohave Artifact Assemblage. *American Antiquity* 18:270–71. Washington, D.C.

BRAND, DONALD D.

1938 Aboriginal Trade Routes for Sea Shells in the Southwest. *Association of Pacific Coast Geographers Yearbook* 4:3–10. Corvallis, Ore.

BRIGHT, ROBERT C.

1963 "Pleistocene Lakes Thatcher and Bonneville, Southeastern Idaho." Ph.D. dissertation, University of Minnesota.

1966 Pollen and Seed Stratigraphy of Swan Lake, Southeastern Idaho: Its Relation to Regional Vegetational History and to Lake Bonneville History. *Tebiwa,* vol. 9, no. 2, pp. 1–47. Pocatello.

BRIGHT, ROBERT C., AND MEYER RUBIN

1965 *Guidebook for Field Conference E: Northern and Middle Rocky Mountains.* International Association for Quaternary Research, VIIth Congress, pp. 105–6. Nebraska Academy of Sciences, Lincoln.

BROECKER, WALLACE S.

1957 "Application of Radiocarbon to Oceanography and Climatic Chronology." Ph.D. dissertation, Columbia University.

1965 Isotope Geochemistry and the Pleistocene Climatic Record. *In The Quaternary of the United States,* H. E. Wright, Jr., and David G. Frey, eds., pp. 737–53. Princeton University Press, Princeton.

BROECKER, WALLACE S., AND J. L. KULP

1956 The Radiocarbon Method of Age Determination. *American Antiquity* 22:1–11. Washington, D.C.

1957 Lamont Natural Radiocarbon Measurements IV. *Science* 126:1324–34. Washington, D.C.

BROECKER, WALLACE S.; J. L. KULP; AND C. S. TUCEK

1956 Lamont Natural Radiocarbon Measurements III. *Science* 124:154–65. Washington, D.C.

BROECKER, WALLACE S., AND PHIL C. ORR

1958 Radiocarbon Chronology of Lake Lahontan and Lake Bonneville. *Geological Society of America Bulletin* 69:1009–32. New York.

BROECKER, WALLACE S., AND WILLIAM R. FARRAND

1963 Radiocarbon Age of the Two Creeks Forest Bed, Wisconsin. *Geological Society of America Bulletin* 74:795–802. New York.

BROWN, LIONEL A.

1960 "A Typology and Distribution of Projectile Points from Sauvies Island, Oregon." M.A. thesis, Department of Anthropology, University of Oregon, Eugene.

BRYAN, ALAN LYLE

1965 Paleo-American Prehistory. *Occasional Papers of the Idaho State University Museum,* no. 16. Pocatello.

1966 "Pleistocene of Alberta in Relation to the Problem of Early Men in America." Paper presented at the 1966 Society for American Archæology Meetings, Reno.

BRYAN, ALAN LYLE, AND D. R. TOUHY

1960 A Basalt Quarry in Northeastern Oregon. *American Philosophical Society Proceedings,* vol. 104, no. 5, pp. 485–510. Philadelphia.

BUETTNER-JANUSCH, JOHN

1954 Human Skeletal Material from Deadman Cave,

Utah. *University of Utah Anthropological Papers,* no. 19. Salt Lake City.

Butler, B. Robert

1957 Art of the Lower Columbia Valley, *Archaeology,* vol. 10, no. 3, pp. 158–65. New York.

1958a *Archaeological Investigations on the Washington Shore of The Dalles Reservoir, 1955–57.* Report on a joint archæological project carried out under terms of a contract between the U.S. National Park Service and the University of Washington. Seattle, Mimeographed.

1958b Ash Cave (45WW61), A Preliminary Report. *The Washington Archaeologist,* vol. 2, no. 12, pp. 3–10. Seattle.

1959a Lower Columbia Valley Archæology: A Survey and Appraisal of Some Major Archæological Resources. *Tebiwa,* vol. 2, no. 2, pp. 6–24. Pocatello.

1959b The Prehistory of the Dice Game in the Southern Plateau. *Tebiwa,* vol. 2, no. 1, pp. 65–71. Pocatello.

1960 "The Physical Stratigraphy of Wakemap Mound: A New Interpretation." M.A. thesis, University of Washington, Seattle.

1961a Additional Notes and Comments on Atlatl Weights in the Northwest. *Tebiwa,* vol. 4, no. 1, pp. 29–31. Pocatello.

1961b The Old Cordilleran Culture in the Pacific Northwest. *Occasional Papers of the Idaho State University Museum,* no. 5. Pocatello.

1962a Contributions to the Prehistory of the Columbia Plateau: A Report on Excavations in the Palouse and Craig Mountain Sections. *Occasional Papers of the Idaho State University Museum,* no. 9. Pocatello.

1962b The B. Stewart and the Cradleboard Mortuary Sites: A Contribution to the Archæology of The Dalles Region of the Lower Columbia Valley. *Tebiwa,* vol. 5, no. 1, pp. 30–40. Pocatello.

1963 An Early Man Site at Big Camas Prairie, South-Central Idaho. *Tebiwa,* vol. 6, no. 1, pp. 22–33. Pocatello.

1964a A Recent Early Man Point Find in Southeastern Idaho. *Tebiwa,* vol. 7, no. 1, pp. 39–40. Pocatello.

1964b A Tentative History of Self-handled Mauls at The Dalles of the Lower Columbia. *Tebiwa,* vol. 7, no. 2, pp. 37–41. Pocatello.

1965 A Report on Investigation of an Early Man Site Near Lake Channel, Southern Idaho. *Tebiwa,* vol. 8, no. 1, pp. 1–20. Pocatello.

1967 More Haskett Point Types from the Type Locality. *Tebiwa,* vol. 10, no. 1, p. 25. Pocatello.

Butzer, Karl W.

1965 Artifact from Deposits of Mid-Wisconsin Age in Illinois. *Science* 142:1722–23. Washington, D.C.

Byers, Douglas S.

1959a An Introduction to Five Papers on the Archaic Stage. *American Antiquity* 24:229–32. Washington, D.C.

1959b The Eastern Archaic: Some Problems and Hypotheses. *American Antiquity* 24:234–56. Washington, D.C.

1966a The Debert Paleo-Indian Site. *A Guide for Stop No. 11, Field Trip No. 4,* Geological Association of Canada, Mineralogical Association of Canada. Ms.

1966b The Debert Archæological Project: The Position of Debert with Respect to the Paleo-Indian Tradition. *Quaternaria* 8:33–47. Rome.

Byrne, John V.

1963 Coastal Erosion, Northern Oregon. *In Essays in Marine Geology in Honor of K. O. Emery,* Thomas Clements, ed., pp. 11–33. University of Southern California Press, Los Angeles.

Byrne, John V.; Gerald A. Fowler; and Neil J. Maloney

1966 Uplift of the Continental Margin and Possible Continental Accretion Off Oregon. *Science* 154: 1654–55. Washington, D.C.

C

Caldwell, Warren W.

1953 An Archæological Survey of the Okanagan and
1954 Similkameen Valleys of British Columbia. *Anthropology in British Columbia,* no. 4, pp. 10–25. Victoria.

1956 "The Archæology of Wakemap." Ph.D. dissertation, University of Washington, Seattle.

Campbell, E. W., and W. H. Campbell

1935 The Pinto Basin Site. *Southwest Museum Papers,* no. 9. Los Angeles.

1940 A Folsom Complex in the Great Basin. *The Masterkey,* vol. 14, pp. 7–11. Los Angeles.

Campbell, E. W.; W. H. Campbell; E. Antevs; C. Amsden; J. Barbieri; and F. Bode

1937 Archæology of Pleistocene Lake Mohave. *Southwest Museum Papers,* no. 11. Los Angeles.

Campbell, John M., ed.

1962 Prehistoric Cultural Relations Between the Arctic and Temperate Zones of North America. *Arctic Institute of North America, Technical Paper,* no. 11. Montreal.

Campbell, John M.

1962 Cultural Succession at Anaktuvuk Pass, Arctic

Alaska. *In* "Prehistoric Cultural Relations Between the Arctic and Temperate Zones of North America." *Arctic Institute of North America, Technical Paper*, no. 11, pp. 39–54. Montreal.

CAPES, KATHERINE H.
1964   Contributions to the Prehistory of Vancouver Island. *Occasional Papers of the Idaho State University Museum*, no. 15. Pocatello.

CARLSON, ROY L.
1960   Chronology and Culture Change in the San Juan Islands, Washington. *American Antiquity* 25: 562–86. Washington, D.C.

CARTER, GEORGE F.
1957   *Pleistocene Man at San Diego.* Johns Hopkins University Press, Baltimore.
1958   Archæology in the Reno Area in Relation to the Age of Man and the Culture Sequence in America. *American Philosophical Society Proceedings*, vol. 102, no. 2, pp. 174–92. Philadelphia.
1959   Man, Time, and Change in the Far Southwest. *Annals of the Association of American Geographers*, vol. 49, no. 3, part II, pp. 8–30. Washington, D.C.

CHANG, KWANG-CHIH
1963   Prehistoric Archæology in China. *Arctic Anthropology*, vol. 1, no. 2, pp. 29–61. Madison, Wisc.
1967   *Rethinking Archaeology.* Random House, New York.

CHARD, CHESTER S.
1958   An Outline of the Prehistory of Siberia, Part I: The Pre-metal Periods. *Southwestern Journal of Anthropology* 14:1–33. Albuquerque.

CLARK, JOHN G. D.
1952   *Prehistoric Europe: The Economic Basis.* Philosophical Library, New York.

CLEMENTS, THOMAS, ED.
1963   *Essays in Marine Geology in Honor of K. O. Emery.* University of Southern California Press, Los Angeles.

CLEMENTS, THOMAS, AND LYDIA CLEMENTS
1953   Evidence of Pleistocene Man in Death Valley, California. *Geological Society of America Bulletin*, 64:1189–1203. New York.

COLBERT, EDWIN H.
1937   The Pleistocene Mammals of North America and Their Relations to Eurasian Forms. *In Early Man*, George Grant MacCurdy, ed. J. B. Lippincott Co., Philadelphia and New York.

COLE, DAVID L.
1963   *Interim Report on Excavations in the John Day Dam Reservoir Area, 1962–63.* Submitted to the National Park Service. University of Oregon, Eugene.
1964   *Interim Report 1963–64, John Day Dam Reservoir Project, Part One: Excavations at Wildcat Canyon, Site 35GM9. Area 5.* Submitted to the National Park Service. University of Oregon, Eugene.
1966   *Report on Archaeological Research in the John Day Dam Reservoir Area—1965.* Interim Report to the National Park Service. Museum of Natural History, University of Oregon, Eugene.

COLE, DAVID L., AND L. S. CRESSMAN
1959   *Archaeological Excavations in the John Day Reservoir Area, Oregon: Interim Report for 1958–59.* Submitted to the National Park Service. University of Oregon, Eugene.
1960   *Interim Report on Excavations in the John Day Dam Reservoir Area, 1959.* Interim Report for 1959–60, submitted to the National Park Service. University of Oregon, Eugene.
1961   *Interim Report 1960–61: John Day Reservoir Project, Columbia River.* University of Oregon, Eugene.

COLE, DAVID L., AND FRANK C. LEONHARDY
1964   *Interim Report 1963–64, John Day Dam Reservoir Project, Part Two: Report on Survey and Excavations on Blalock Island.* University of Oregon, Eugene.

COLINVAUX, PAUL A.
1964a The Environment of the Bering Land Bridge. *Ecological Monographs* 34:297–329. Durham, N.C.
1964b Origin of Ice Ages: Pollen Evidence from Alaska. *Science* 145:707–8. Washington, D.C.
1967   Bering Land Bridge: Evidence of Spruce in Late-Wisconsin Times. *Science* 156:380–83. Washington, D.C.

COLLIER, DONALD; ALFRED E. HUDSON; AND ARLO FORD
1942   Archæology of the Upper Columbia Region. *University of Washington Publications in Anthropology*, vol. 9, no. 1. Seattle.

COLLINS, LLOYD R.
1951   "The Cultural Position of the Kalapuya in the Pacific Northwest." M.S. thesis, Department of Anthropology, University of Oregon, Eugene.

COOK, S. F.
1946   A Reconsideration of Shellmounds with Respect to Population and Nutrition. *American Antiquity* 12:50–53. Washington, D.C.

COOK, S. F., AND ROBERT F. HEIZER
1962 Chemical Analysis of the Hotchkiss Site (CCO-138). *Reports of the University of California Archaeological Survey*, no. 57, pt. 1. Berkeley.

COOPER, WILLIAM S.
1958a Coastal Sand Dunes of Oregon and Washington. *Geological Society of America*, memoir 72. New York.
1958b Terminology of Post-Valders Time. *Geological Society of America Bulletin* 69:941–45. New York.

COTTER, J. L.
1937 The Occurrence of Flints and Extinct Animals in Pluvial Deposits near Clovis, New Mexico. *Academy of Natural Science Journal* 89:1–16. Philadelphia.

COWAN, RICHARD D.
1967 Lake Margin Ecologic Exploitation in the Great Basin as Demonstrated by an Analysis of Coprolites from Lovelock Cave, Nevada. *Reports of the University of California Archaeological Survey*, no. 70, pp. 21–35. Berkeley.

CRABTREE, DON E., AND B. ROBERT BUTLER
1964 Notes on Experiments in Flintknapping: 1. Heat Treatment of Silica Minerals. *Tebiwa*, vol. 7, no. 1, pp. 1–6. Pocatello.

CRAIG, B. G., AND J. G. FYLES
1960 Pleistocene Geology of Arctic Canada. *Geological Survey of Canada*, paper 60–10. Department of Mines and Technical Surveys, Canada.

CRANDELL, DWIGHT R.
1965 The Glacial History of Western Washington and Oregon. *In The Quaternary of the United States*, H. E. Wright, Jr., and David G. Frey, eds., pp. 341–53. Princeton University Press, Princeton.

CRANE, H. R.
1956 University of Michigan Radiocarbon Dates I. *Science* 124:664–72. Washington, D.C.

CRESSMAN, LUTHER S.
1931 Some Effects of Thyroid Disorder in Women. *Human Biology*, vol. 3, no. 4, pp. 529–46. New York.
1933 Contributions to the Archæology of Oregon: Final Report on the Gold Hill Burial Site. *University of Oregon Studies in Anthropology*, vol. 1, bull. 1. Eugene.
1936 Archæological Survey of the Guano Valley Region in Southeastern Oregon. *University of Oregon Monographs. Studies in Anthropology*, no. 1, pp. 1–48. Eugene.

1937a The Wikiup Damsite No. 1 Knives. *American Antiquity* 3:53–67. Washington, D.C.
1937b Petroglyphs of Oregon. *University of Oregon Monographs. Studies in Anthropology*, no. 2. Eugene.
1939 Early Man and Culture in the Northern Great Basin Region of South Central Oregon. *Carnegie Institution of Washington*, year book no. 38, pp. 314–17. Washington, D.C.
1940a Studies on Early Man in South Central Oregon. *Carnegie Institution of Washington*, year book no. 39, pp. 300–6. Washington, D.C.
1940b Early Man in the Northern Part of the Great Basin of South-central Oregon. *Proceedings of the Sixth Pacific Science Congress of the Pacific Science Association* 4:169–75. Berkeley.
1944 New Information on South-central Oregon Atlatls. *The Masterkey*, November, pp. 169–79. Los Angeles.
1946 Early Man in Oregon: Stratigraphic Evidence. *Scientific Monthly* 62:43–51. Washington, D.C.
1947 Facts and Comments—Further Information on Projectile Points from Oregon. *American Antiquity* 13:177–79. Washington, D.C.
1948 Facts and Comments—Odell Lake Site: A New Paleo-Indian Camp-site in Oregon. *American Antiquity* 14:57–58. Washington, D.C.
1950 Archæological Research in the John Day Region of North Central Oregon. *American Philosophical Society Proceedings* 94:369–90. Philadelphia.
1951 Western Prehistory in the Light of Carbon 14 Dating. *Southwestern Journal of Anthropology* 7:289–313. Albuquerque.
1952 Oregon Coast Prehistory. *American Philosophical Society Yearbook, 1952*, pp. 256–60. Philadelphia.
1956a Facts and Comments—Additional Radiocarbon Dates, Lovelock Cave, Nevada. *American Antiquity* 21:311–12. Washington, D.C.
1956b Klamath Prehistory. *American Philosophical Society Transactions*, n.s., vol. 46, pt. 4. Philadelphia.
1963a The Archæological Salvage Program in the Round Butte Dam Reservoir, Jefferson County, Oregon. Final report to the Portland General Electric Company. Department of Anthropology, University of Oregon, Eugene. Xeroxed.
1963b "The Development of Archæology in the Pacific Northwest." Paper read at the Northwest Anthropological Conference, Portland, Oregon.
1964 Comments on Prehistory. *In* "The Current Status of Anthropological Research in the Great Basin: 1964," Warren L. d'Azevedo et al., eds. *Desert Research Institute Technical Report Series S-H, Social Sciences and Humanities Publications*, no. 1, pp. 275–93. Reno.

1966b Facts and Comments—Man in Association with Extinct Fauna in the Great Basin. *American Antiquity* 31:866–67. Washington, D.C.

1968 Early Man in Western North America: Perspectives and Prospects. *In* "Early Man in Western North America: Symposium of the Southwestern Archæological Association, San Diego, 1968," Cynthia Irwin-Williams, ed., *Eastern New Mexico University Contributions in Anthropology,* vol. 1, no. 4, pp. 78–87. Portales, N.M.

CRESSMAN, LUTHER S., AND D. L. COLE

1962 *Interim Report 1961 62: John Day Reservoir, Columbia River.* University of Oregon, Department of Anthropology, Eugene. Dittoed.

CRESSMAN, LUTHER S., AND WILLIAM S. LAUGHLIN

1941 A Probable Association of Mammoth and Artifacts in the Willamette Valley, Oregon. *American Antiquity* 6:339–42. Washington, D.C.

CRESSMAN, LUTHER S., AND EDNA C. SPENKER

1933 Notes On Some Quantitative Evidence of the Effect of Thyroid Disorder upon the Birth-rate. *Human Biology,* vol. 5, no. 3, pp. 516–19. New York.

CRESSMAN, LUTHER S.; HOWELL WILLIAMS; AND ALEX D. KRIEGER

1940 Early Man in Oregon; Archæological Studies in the Northern Great Basin. *University of Oregon Monographs. Studies in Anthropology,* no. 3. Eugene.

CRESSMAN, LUTHER S., ET AL.

1942 Archæological Researches in the Northern Great Basin. *Carnegie Institution of Washington Publication,* no. 538. Washington, D.C.

1960 Cultural Sequences at The Dalles, Oregon; A Contribution to Pacific Northwest Prehistory. *American Philosophical Society Transactions,* n.s., vol. 50, pt. 10. Philadelphia.

CREUTZ, E., AND J. MORIARTY

1963 Inferences on the Use Position of San Dieguito Percussion-flaked Artifacts. *American Antiquity* 29:82–89. Washington, D.C.

CRITTENDEN, MAX D., JR.

1963 New Data on the Isostatic Deformation of Lake Bonneville. *U.S. Geological Survey Professional Paper,* 454–E. Washington, D.C.

CURRAY, JOSEPH R.

1961 Late Quaternary Sea Level: A Discussion. *Geological Society of America Bulletin* 72:1707–12. New York.

1965 Late Quaternary History, Continental Shelves of the United States. *In The Quaternary of the United States,* H. E. Wright, Jr., and David G. Frey, eds., pp. 723–35. Princeton University Press, Princeton.

CURRAY, JOSEPH R., AND D. G. MOORE

1964 Pleistocene Deltaic Progradation of Continental Terrace, Costa de Nayarit, Mexico. In "Marine Geology of the Gulf of California: A Symposium," Tjeerd H. van Andel and George G. Shore, Jr., eds. *American Association of Petroleum Geologists Memoir* 3:193–215. Tulsa.

D

D'AZEVEDO, WARREN L., ED.

1963 The Washo Indians of California and Nevada. *University of Utah Anthropological Papers,* no. 67. Salt Lake City.

DAMON, PAUL E., AND AUSTIN LONG

1962 Arizona Radiocarbon Dates III. *Radiocarbon* 4:246. New Haven.

DANIEL, GLYN E.

1950 *A Hundred Years of Archaeology.* Gerald Buckworth and Co., Ltd., London.

DAUGHERTY, RICHARD D.

1952 Archæological Investigations in O'Sullivan Reservoir, Grant County, Washington. *American Antiquity* 17:374–86. Washington, D.C.

1954 Notes and News—Pacific Coast. *American Antiquity* 19:422. Washington, D.C.

1956a Archæology of the Lind Coulee Site, Washington. *American Philosophical Society Proceedings* 100:223–78. Philadelphia.

1956b Early Man in the Columbia Intermontane Province. *University of Utah Anthropological Papers,* no. 24. Salt Lake City.

1958 Notes and News—West Coast and Great Basin. *American Antiquity* 23:453–54. Washington, D.C.

1962 The Intermontane Western Tradition. *American Antiquity* 28:144–50. Washington, D.C.

1963 Current Research—Northwest. *American Antiquity* 29:265–66. Washington, D.C.

1964 Current Research—Northwest. *American Antiquity* 29:554–55. Washington, D.C.

1964 Current Research—Northwest. *American Antiquity* 30:245. Washington, D.C.

1965 Current Research—Northwest. *American Antiquity* 30:541–44. Washington, D.C.

DAUGHERTY, RICHARD D.; BARBARA A. PURDY; AND ROALD FRYXELL

1967 The Descriptive Archæology and Geochronology

of the Three Springs Bar Archæological Site, Washington. *Washington State University Laboratory of Anthropology, Report of Investigations,* no. 40. Pullman.

DAVIS, EMMA LOU

1963   The Desert Culture of the Western Great Basin: A Lifeway of Seasonal Transhumance. *American Antiquity* 29:202–12. Washington, D.C.

DAVIS, JAMES T.

1959   Further Notes on Clay Human Figurines in the Western United States. *Reports of the University of California Archaeological Survey,* no. 48, pp. 16–31. Berkeley.

1960   Archæology of the Fernandez Site, A San Francisco Bay Region Shellmound. *Reports of the University of California Archaeological Survey,* no. 49, pp. 11–52. Berkeley.

1961   Trade Routes and Economic Exchange among the Indians of California. *Reports of the University of California Archaeological Survey,* no. 54. Berkeley.

1962   The Rustler Rockshelter Site (SBr-288), A Culturally Stratified Site in the Mohave Desert, California. *Reports of the University of California Archaeological Survey,* no. 57, pt. 2. Berkeley.

DAVIS, JAMES T., AND A. E. TREGANZA

1959   The Patterson Mound: A Comparative Analysis of the Archæology of site Ala-328. *Reports of the University of California Archaeological Survey,* no. 47. Berkeley.

DAVIS, WILBUR A.

1962   "The Concept of Technological Systems." Ph.D. dissertation, University of Oregon, Eugene.

1964   "Notes on Technologies and Material Cultures of the Great Basin." Paper read at the Great Basin Anthropological Conference, Reno, Sept. 4–5.

DEEVEY, EDWARD S., JR.

1965   Pleistocene Nonmarine Environments. *In The Quaternary of the United States,* H. E. Wright, Jr., and David G. Frey, eds., pp. 643–52. Princeton University Press, Princeton.

DICE, LEE R.

1943   *The Biotic Provinces of North America.* University of Michigan Press, Ann Arbor.

DIEBOLD, A. RICHARD, JR.

1960   Determining the Centers of Dispersal of Language Groups. *International Journal of American Linguistics* 26:1–10. Chicago.

DORT, WAKEFIELD, JR.

1964   Geology of the Midvale Site Complex, Idaho. *Tebiwa,* vol. 7, no. 1, pp. 17–22. Pocatello.

DORT, WAKEFIELD; E. J. ZELLER; M. D. TURNER; AND J. E. VAZ

1965   Paleotemperatures and Chronology at Archæological Cave Site Revealed by Thermoluminescence. *Science* 150:480–81. Washington, D.C.

DOWNS, JAMES F.

1964   "The Significance of Environmental Manipulation in Great Basin Cultural Development." Paper read at the Great Basin Anthropological Conference, Reno, Sept. 4–5.

DRUCKER, PHILIP

1943   Archæological Survey on the Northern Northwest Coast. *Bureau of American Ethnology Bulletin,* no. 133, *Anthropological Papers,* no. 20. Smithsonian Institution, Washington, D.C.

1955a Indians of the Northwest Coast. *American Museum of Natural History Anthropological Handbook,* no. 10. McGraw-Hill, New York.

1955b Sources of Northwest Coast Culture. *In* "New Interpretations of Aboriginal American Culture History," Seventy-fifth Anniversary Volume of the Anthropological Society of Washington, Betty J. Meggers and Clifford Evans, eds., pp. 59–81. Washington, D.C.

DUBOS, RENÉ

1961   *Dreams of Reason.* Columbia University Press, New York.

DUFF, WILSON

1956   Prehistoric Stone Sculpture of the Fraser River and Gulf of Georgia. *Anthropology in British Columbia,* no. 5, pp. 15–151. Victoria.

DUMOND, D. E.

1962   Blades and Cores in Oregon. *American Antiquity* 27:419–24. Washington, D.C.

1968   On the Presumed Spread of Slate Grinding in Alaska. *Arctic Anthropology,* vol. 5, no. 1, pp. 82–91. Madison, Wisc.

DYCK, W.; J. G. FYLES; AND W. BLAKE, JR.

1965   Geological Survey of Canada: Radiocarbon Dates IV. *Radiocarbon* 7:24–46. New Haven.

DYEN, ISIDORE

1956   Language Distribution and Migration Theory. *Language* 32:611–26. Baltimore.

1962   The Lexicostatistically Determined Relationship of a Language Group. *International Journal of American Linguistics* 28:153–61. Chicago.

E

EASTERBROOK, DONALD J.

1963   Late Pleistocene Glacial Events and Relative Sea-level Changes in the Northern Puget Lowland, Washington. *Geological Society of America Bulletin* 74:1465–84. New York.

1966 Radiocarbon Chronology of Late Pleistocene Deposits in Northwest Washington. *Science* 152: 764–67. Washington, D.C.

EBERHART, HAROLD H.

1957 "Time Markers in Southern California Archæology." Ph.D. dissertation, Department of Sociology and Anthropology, University of California, Los Angeles.

ELMENDORF, WILLIAM W.

1965 Linguistic and Geographic Relations in the Northern Plateau Area. *Southwestern Journal of Anthropology* 21:63-78. Albuquerque.

ELSASSER, ALBERT B.

1958a Aboriginal Use of Restrictive Sierran Environments. *Reports of the University of California Archaeological Survey,* no. 41, pp. 27–33. Berkeley.

1958b The Surface Archæology of Site 26-Pe-5, Pershing County, Nevada. *Reports of the University of California Archaeological Survey,* no. 44, pt. 2, pp. 26–51. Berkeley.

1960a The Archæology of the Sierra Nevada in California and Nevada. *Reports of the University of California Archaeological Survey,* no. 51. Berkeley.

1960b The History of Culture Classification in California. *Reports of the University of California Archaeological Survey,* no. 49, pp. 1–10. Berkeley.

ELSASSER, ALBERT B., AND ROBERT F. HEIZER

1963 The Archæology of Bowers Cave, Los Angeles County, California. *Reports of the University of California Archaeological Survey,* no. 59, pp. 1–60. Berkeley.

1966 Excavation of Two Northwestern California Coastal Sites. *Reports of the University of California Archaeological Survey,* no. 67, pp. 1–149. Berkeley.

ELSASSER, ALBERT B., AND E. R. PRINCE

1961 The Archæology of Two Sites at Eastgate, Churchill County, Nevada. I. Wagon Jack Shelter by Robert F. Heizer and M. A. Baumhoff. II. Eastgate Cave by Albert B. Elsasser and E. R. Prince. *University of California Anthropological Records* 20:139–49. Berkeley.

EMERY, K. O., AND LOUIS E. GARRISON

1967 Sea Levels 7,000 to 20,000 Years Ago. *Science* 157:684–87. Washington, D.C.

ENGAR, WALTER D.

1942 Archæology of Black Rock 3 Cave, Utah. *University of Utah Anthropological Papers,* no. 7. Salt Lake City.

EPSTEIN, JEREMIAH F.

1963 The Burin-faceted Projectile Point. *American Antiquity* 29:187–201. Washington, D.C.

EWING, MAURICE, AND W. L. DONN

1956 A Theory of Ice Ages. *Science* 123:1061–66. Washington, D.C.

F

FAIRBRIDGE, R. W.

1958 Dating the Latest Movement of the Quaternary Sea Level. *Transactions of the New York Academy of Sciences,* series II, vol. 20, no. 6, pp. 471–82. New York.

FARRAND, WILLIAM R.

1961 Frozen Mammoths and Modern Geology. *Science* 133:729–35. Washington, D.C.

FENENGA, FRANKLIN, AND FRANCIS A. RIDDELL

1949 Excavation of Tommy Tucker Cave, Lassen County, California. *American Antiquity* 14:203–14. Washington, D.C.

FENNEMAN, NEVIN M.

1931 *Physiography of Western United States.* McGraw-Hill, New York.

FLINT, RICHARD F.

1947 *Glacial Geology and the Pleistocene Epoch.* 4th printing, 1953. John Wiley & Sons, New York.

1957 *Glacial and Pleistocene Geology.* 5th printing, 1966. John Wiley & Sons, New York.

1963 Status of the Pleistocene Wisconsin Stage in Central North America. *Science* 139:402–4. Washington, D.C.

FLINT, RICHARD F., AND MEYER RUBIN

1955 Radiocarbon Dates of pre-Mankato Events in Eastern and Central North America. *Science* 121: 649–58. Washington, D.C.

FORDE, DARYLL

1954 Foraging, Hunting, and Fishing. *In History of Technology,* Charles Singer, E. J. Holmyard, and A. R. Hall, cds., vol. 1, pp. 154–86. Oxford University Press, New York.

FOSTER, GEORGE M.

1965 The Sociology of Pottery: Questions and Hypotheses Arising from Contemporary Mexican Work. *In* "Ceramics and Man," F. R. Matson, ed., *Viking*

Fund Publications in Anthropology, no. 41, pp. 43–61. Aldine Publishing Co., Chicago.

FOWLER, MELVIN L.

1959   Modoc Rock Shelter: An Early Archaic Site in Southern Illinois. *American Antiquity* 24:257–70. Washington, D.C.

FRYE, JOHN C.; H. B. WILLMAN; AND ROBERT F. BLACK

1965   Outline of Glacial Geology of Illinois and Wisconsin. *In Quaternary of the United States,* H. E. Wright, Jr., and David G. Frey, eds., pp. 43–62. Princeton University Press, Princeton.

FRYXELL, ROALD

1962a   Interim Report: Archæological Salvage in the Lower Monumental Reservoir, Washington. *Washington State University Laboratory of Archaeology and Geochronology, Report of Investigations,* no. 21. Pullman.

1962b   A Radiocarbon Limiting Date for Scabland Flooding. *Northwest Science,* vol. 36, no. 4, pp. 113–19. Pullman.

1965   Mazama and Glacier Peak Volcanic Ash Layers: Relative Ages. *Science* 147:1288–90. Washington, D.C.

G

GENOVES, SANTIAGO

1967   Some Problems in the Physical Anthropological Study of the Peopling of America. *Current Anthropology* 8:297–312. Chicago.

GEOLOGICAL ASSOCIATION OF CANADA

1958   Glacial Map of Canada. Toronto.

GEOLOGICAL SOCIETY OF AMERICA

1945   Glacial Map of North America. *Special Papers,* no. 60. First edition. New York.

GEROW, BERT A., AND ROLAND W. FORCE

1968   *An Analysis of the University Village Complex; With a Reappraisal of Central California Archaeology.* The Board of Trustees of the Leland Stanford Junior University, Stanford.

GIFFORD, EDWARD W.

1926   Californian Anthropometry. *University of California Publications in American Archaeology and Ethnology* 22:217–390. Berkeley.

1940   Californian Bone Artifacts. *University of California Anthropological Records,* vol. 3. Berkeley.

GIFFORD, EDWARD W., AND W. EGBERT SCHENCK

1926   Archæology of the Southern San Joaquin Valley, California. *University of California Publications in American Archaeology and Ethnology,* vol. 23. Berkeley.

GILBERT, GROVE K.

1890   Lake Bonneville. *U.S. Geological Survey Monographs,* vol. 1. Washington, D.C.

GONSALVES, WILLIAM C.

1955   Winslow Cave, A Mortuary Site in Calaveras County, California. *Reports of the University of California Archaeological Survey,* no. 29, pp. 31–45. Berkeley.

GOSS, JAMES A.

1965   Ute Linguistics and Anasazi Abandonment of the Four Corners Area. *In* "Contributions of the Weatherhill Mesa Archæological Project," Douglas Osborne et al., *Memoirs of the Society for American Archaeology,* no. 19, pp. 73–81. Washington, D.C.

1968   Culture-Historical Inference from Utaztekan Linguistic Evidence. *In* "Utaztekan Prehistory," *Occasional Papers of the Idaho State University Museum,* no. 22, pp. 1–42. Pocatello.

GRANT, CAMPBELL

1965   *The Rock Paintings of the Chumash, A Study of a California Indian Culture.* University of California Press, Berkeley and Los Angeles.

GRAY, MARGERY P.

1958   A Method for Reducing Non-specific Reactions in the Typing of Human Skeletal Material. *American Journal of Physical Anthropology,* n.s., vol. 16, pp. 135–39. Philadelphia.

GREEN, F. E.

1963   The Clovis Blades: An Important Addition to the Llano Complex. *American Antiquity* 29:145–65. Washington, D.C.

GREENGO, ROBERT E.

1951   Molluscan Species in California Shell Middens. *Reports of the University of California Archaeological Survey,* no. 13. Berkeley.

1961   "An Archæological Sequence on the Middle Columbia River." Paper read at the meeting of the Society for American Archæology, Columbus, Ohio.

GRIFFIN, J. B.

1946   Cultural Change and Continuity in Eastern United States Archæology. *Papers of the R. S. Peabody Foundation in Archaeology* 3:37–95. Andover, Mass.

1960   Some Prehistoric Connections between Siberia and America. *Science* 131:801–12. Washington, D.C.

1967 Eastern North American Archæology: A Summary. *Science* 156:175–91. Washington, D.C.

GRIFFIN, J. B., ED.

1952 *Archaeology of the Eastern United States.* University of Chicago Press, Chicago.

GROSSCUP, GORDON L.

1956 The Archæology of the Carson Sink Area. *Papers on California Archaeology,* nos. 37–43, *Reports of the University of California Archaeological Survey,* no. 33, pp. 58–64. Berkeley.

1957 A Bibliography of Nevada Archæology. *Reports of the University of California Archaeological Survey,* no. 36. Berkeley.

1958 Radiocarbon Dates from Nevada of Archæological Interest. *Reports of the University of California Archaeological Survey,* no. 44, pt. 1, pp. 17–31. Berkeley.

1960 The Culture History of Lovelock Cave, Nevada. *Reports of the University of California Archaeological Survey,* no. 52. Berkeley.

GRUHN, RUTH

1960 The Mecham Site: A Rockshelter Burial in the Snake River Canyon of Southwest Idaho. *Tebiwa,* vol. 3, nos. 1, 2. Pocatello.

1961a The Archæology of Wilson Butte Cave, South-Central Idaho. *Occasional Papers of the Idaho State University Museum,* no. 6. Pocatello.

1961b A Collection of Artifacts from Pence-Duerig Cave in South-Central Idaho. *Tebiwa,* vol. 4, no. 1, pp. 1–23. Pocatello.

1961c Notes on Material from a Burial along the Snake River in Southwest Idaho. *Tebiwa,* vol. 4, no. 2, pp. 37–39. Pocatello.

1964 Test Excavations at Sites 10-OE-128 and 10-OE-129 Southwest Idaho. *Tebiwa,* vol. 7, no. 2, pp. 28–36. Pocatello.

1965 Two Early Radiocarbon from the Lower Levels of Wilson Butte Cave, South-Central Idaho. *Tebiwa,* vol. 8, no. 2, pp. 57. Pocatello.

GUNKEL, ALEXANDER

1961 A Comparative Cultural Analysis of Four Archæological Sites in the Rocky Reach Reservoir Region, Washington. *Theses in Anthropology,* no. 1. Washington State University, Pullman.

GUNNERSON, JAMES H.

1962 Plateau Shoshonean Prehistory: A Suggested Reconstruction. *American Antiquity* 28:41–45. Washington, D.C.

H

HAAG, WILLIAM G.

1962 The Bering Strait Land Bridge. *Scientific American,* vol. 206, no. 1, pp. 112–23. New York.

HALE, KENNETH

1958 Internal Diversity in Uto-Aztecan: I. *International Journal of American Linguistics* 24:101–7. Chicago.

1959 Internal Diversity in Uto-Aztecan: II. *International Journal of American Linguistics* 25:114–21. Chicago.

HALL, ROBERT L.

1964 Current Research: Northern Mississippi Valley. *American Antiquity* 30:239. Washington, D.C.

HAMY, E.

1963 The Fishhook Industry of the Ancient Inhabitants of the Archipelago of California. *Reports of the University of California Archaeological Survey,* no. 59, pp. 61–70. Berkeley.

HANSEN, HENRY P.

1942 The Influence of Volcanic Eruptions upon Post-Pleistocene Forest Succession in Central Oregon. *American Journal of Botany* 29:214–19. Columbus, Ohio.

1946 Early Man in Oregon: Pollen Analysis and Postglacial Climate and Chronology. *Scientific Monthly* 62:52–62. Washington, D.C.

1947 Postglacial Forest Succession, Climate, and Chronology in the Pacific Northwest. *American Philosophical Society Transactions,* n.s., vol. 37, pt. 1. Philadelphia.

1949 Postglacial Forests in West Central Alberta, Canada. *Bulletin of the Torrey Botanical Club* 76:278–89. New York.

1950 Postglacial Forests along the Alaska Highway in British Columbia. *American Philosophical Society Proceedings* 94:411–21. Philadelphia.

1955 Postglacial Forests in South Central and Central British Columbia. *American Journal of Science* 253:640–58. New Haven.

HARDING, M.

1951 La Jollan Culture. *El Museo* 1:10–11, 31–38. San Diego.

HARNER, MICHAEL J.

1953 Gravel Pictographs of the Lower Colorado River Region. *Reports of the University of California Archaeological Survey,* no. 20, pp. 1–32. Berkeley.

1956 Thermo-facts vs. Artifacts: An Experimental Study of the Malpais Industry. *Reports of the*

University of California Archaeological Survey, no. 33, pp. 39–43. Berkeley.

1958 Lowland Patayan Phases in the Lower Colorado River Valley and Colorado Desert. *Reports of the University of California Archaeological Survey*, no. 42, pp. 93–97. Berkeley.

HARRINGTON, MARK R.

1927 Some Lake-bed Camp-sites in Nevada. *Indian Notes, Museum of the American Indian Heye Foundation*, vol. 4, no. 1, pp. 40–47. New York.

1930 Prehistoric Man of the Santa Barbara Coast, by David Banks Rogers (review). *American Anthropologist* 32:693–96. Washington, D.C.

1933 Gypsum Cave, Nevada. *Southwest Museum Papers*, no. 8. Los Angeles.

1948 An Ancient Site at Borax Lake, California. *Southwest Museum Papers*, no. 16. Los Angeles.

1955 A New Tule Springs Expedition. *The Masterkey*, vol. 29, no. 4, pp. 112–14. Los Angeles.

1957 A Pinto Site at Little Lake, California. *Southwest Museum Papers*, no. 17. Los Angeles.

HARRINGTON, MARK R.; IRWIN HAYDEN; AND LOUIS SCHELLBACH

1930 Archæological Explorations in Southern Nevada. *Southwest Museum Papers*, no. 4. Los Angeles.

HARRISON, WILLIAM M., AND EDITH S. HARRISON

1966 An Archæological Sequence for the Hunting People of Santa Barbara, California. *Annual Report of the University of California Archaeological Survey, 1965–1966*, pp. 1–89. Berkeley.

HAURY, EMIL W.

1953 Artifacts with Mammoth Remains, Naco, Arizona. *American Antiquity* 19:1–14. Washington, D.C.

1957 An Alluvial Site on the San Carlos Indian Reservation, Arizona. *American Antiquity* 23:2–27. Washington, D.C.

1958 Evidence at Point of Pines for a Prehistoric Migration from Northern Arizona. *In* "Migrations in New World Culture History," *Social Science Bulletin*, no. 27. University of Arizona Press, Tucson.

1959 Pleistocene Man at San Diego, by George F. Carter (review). *American Journal of Archaeology* 63:116–17. Princeton.

1960 Facts and Comments—Association of Fossil Fauna and Artifacts of the Sulphur Spring Stage, Cochise Culture. *American Antiquity* 25:609–10. Washington. D.C.

HAURY, EMIL W.

1950 *The Stratigraphy and Archaeology of Ventana Cave, Arizona.* University of Arizona Press and University of New Mexico Press, Tucson and Albuquerque.

HAURY, EMIL W.; E. B. SAYLES; AND WILLIAM W. WASLEY

1959 The Lehner Mammoth Site, Southeastern Arizona. *American Antiquity* 25:2–30. Washington, D.C.

HAYDEN, JULIAN D.

1966 Restoration of the San Dieguito Type Site to its Proper Place in the San Dieguito Sequence. *American Antiquity* 31:438–40. Washington, D.C.

HAYNES, C. VANCE, JR.

1964 Fluted Projectile Points: Their Ages and Dispersion. *Science* 145:1408–13. Washington, D.C.

1966 Elephant-hunting in North America. *Scientific American*, vol. 214, no. 6, pp. 104–12. New York.

1967 Carbon-14 Sampling of the Tlapacoya Site, Mexico, and Postscript of January 1968, *Boletin Instituto de Antropología y Historia* 29:49.

1968 Geochronology of Late Quaternary Alluvium. *In Means of Correlation of Quaternary Successions*, Proceedings, VII Congress, International Association for Quaternary Research, Roger B. Morrison and Herbert E. Wright, Jr, eds., vol. 8, pp. 591–631. University of Utah Press, Salt Lake City.

1973 Reply to M. P. Wade's "Artifacts of Early Man in the New World." *Science* 182:1371–72. Washington, D.C.

HAYNES, VANCE C., JR., AND E. THOMAS HEMMINGS

1968 Mammoth-bone Shaft Wrench from Murray Springs, Arizona. *Science* 159:186–87. Washington, D.C.

HEFLIN, EUGENE

1966 The Pistol River Site of Southwest Oregon. *Reports of the University of California Archaeological Survey*, no. 67, pp. 151–206. Berkeley.

HEGRENES, JACK R., JR.

1955 "The Use of Discontinuous Traits in Problems of Divergence and Discrimination in American Indian Crania." M.S. thesis, Department of Anthropolgy, University of Oregon, Eugene.

HEIZER, ROBERT F.

1938 A Complete Atlatl Dart from Pershing County, Nevada. *New Mexico Anthropologist* 2:78–81. Albuquerque.

1939 Some Sacramento Valley-Santa Barbara Archæological Relationships. *The Masterkey* 13:31–35. Los Angeles.

1941 Prehistoric Man of the Santa Barbara Coast, by David Banks Rogers (review). *American Antiquity* 6:372–75. Washington, D.C.

1942 Massacre Lake Cave, Tule Lake Cave and Shore Sites. *In* "Archæological Researches in the Northern Great Basin," L. S. Cressman et al., *Carnegie Institution of Washington Publication,* no. 538, pp. 121–33. Washington, D.C.

1944 Artifact Transport by Migratory Animals and Other Means. *American Antiquity* 9:395–400. Washington, D.C.

1946 The Occurrence and Significance of Southwestern Grooved Axes in California. *American Antiquity* 11:187–93. Washington, D.C.

1949a The Archæology of Central California. *University of California Anthropological Records,* vol. 12. Berkeley.

1949b Curved Single-piece Fishhooks of Shell and Bone in California. *American Antiquity* 15:89–97. Washington, D.C.

1950 History and Circumstances of the Discovery of the (Stanford) Skull. *Reports of the University of California Archaeological Survey,* no. 6, pp. 1–9. Berkeley.

1951a An Assessment of Certain Nevada, California and Oregon Radiocarbon Dates. *In* "Radiocarbon Dating," F. Johnson, ed., *Society for American Archaeology Memoir,* no. 8, pp. 23–25. Washington, D.C.

1951b Preliminary Report on the Leonard Rockshelter, Pershing County, Nevada. *American Antiquity* 17:89–98. Washington, D.C.

1952 A Review of Problems in the Antiquity of Man in California. *Reports of the University of California Archaeological Survey,* no. 16, pp. 3–17. Berkeley.

1953 Sites Attributed to Early Man in California. *Reports of the University of California Archaeological Survey,* no. 22, pp. 1–4. Berkeley.

1956 Recent Cave Explorations in the Lower Humboldt Valley, Nevada. *Papers on California Archaeology,* no. 42, *Reports of the University of California Archaeological Survey,* no. 33, pp. 50–57. Berkeley.

1958a Prehistoric Central California: A Problem in Historical-Developmental Classification. *Reports of the University of California Archaeological Survey,* no. 41, pp. 19–26. Berkeley.

1958b Radiocarbon Dates from California of Archæological Interest. *Reports of the University of California Archaeological Survey,* no. 44, pt. 1, pp. 1–16. Berkeley.

1960a Physical Analysis of Habitation Residues. *In* "The Application of Quantitative Methods in Archæology," Robert F. Heizer and S. F. Cook, eds., *Viking Fund Publications in Anthropology,* no. 28, pp. 92–124. Quadrangle Books, Chicago.

1960b A San Nicolas Island Twined Basketry Water Bottle. *Reports of the University of California Archaeological Survey,* no. 50, pp. 1–3. Berkeley.

1964 The Western Coast of North America. *In Prehistoric Man in the New World,* J. D. Jennings and E. Norbeck, eds., pp. 117–48. University of Chicago Press, Chicago.

HEIZER, ROBERT F., AND M. A. BAUMHOFF

1961 The Archæology of Two Sites at Eastgate, Churchill County, Nevada. I. Wagon Jack Shelter, by Robert F. Heizer and M. A. Baumhoff. II. Eastgate Cave by Albert B. Elsasser and E. R. Prince. *University of California Anthropological Records* 20:119–38. Berkeley.

1962 *Prehistoric Rock Art of Nevada and Eastern California.* University of California Press, Berkeley.

HEIZER, ROBERT F., AND ALBERT B. ELSASSER

1953 Some Archæological Sites and Cultures of the Central Sierra Nevada. *Reports of the University of California Archaeological Survey,* no. 21 Berkeley.

HEIZER, ROBERT F., AND F. FENENGA

1939 Archæological Horizons in Central California. *American Anthropologist,* n.s., 41:378–99. Washington, D.C.

HEIZER, ROBERT F., AND GORDON L. GROSSCUP

n.d. Archæology of Site Ch-15, Churchill County, Nevada. Unpublished ms.

HEIZER, ROBERT F., AND H. KELLEY

1962 Burins and Bladelets in the Cessac Collection from Santa Cruz Island, California. *American Philosophical Society Proceedings* 106:94–105. Philadelphia.

HEIZER, ROBERT F., AND ALEX D. KRIEGER

1956 The Archæology of Humboldt Cave, Churchill County, Nevada. *University of California Publications in American Archaeology and Ethnology,* vol. 47. Berkeley.

HEIZER, ROBERT F., AND E. M. LEMERT

1947 Observations on Archæological Sites in Topanga Canyon, California. *University of California Publications in American Archaeology and Ethnology,* vol. 44. Berkeley.

HEIZER, ROBERT F., AND W. C. MASSEY

1953 Aboriginal Navigation off the West Coasts of Upper and Baja California. *Bureau of American Ethnology Bulletin,* no. 151, pp. 285–311. Washington, D.C.

HEIZER, ROBERT F., AND J. E. MILLS

1952 *The Four Ages of Tsurai: A Documentary History of the Indian Village on Trinidad Bay.* University of California Press, Berkeley.

HEIZER, ROBERT F., AND DAVID M. PENDERGAST

1955 Additional Data on Fired Clay Human Figurines from California. *American Antiquity* 21:181–85. Washington, D.C.

HENRY, THOMAS R.

1955 Ice Age Man, the First American (with eight paintings by Andre Durenceau). *The National Geographic Magazine,* vol. 108, no. 6, pp. 781–806. Washington, D.C.

HERSKOVITZ, MELVILLE J.

1948 *Man and His Works.* Alfred A. Knopf, New York.

HESTER, JAMES J.

1962 Early Navajo Migrations and Acculturation in the Southwest. *Museum of New Mexico, Papers in Anthropology,* no. 6. Santa Fe.

1966 Origins of the Clovis Culture. *Actas y Memorias* vol. 36. Congreso Internacional Americanistas, Madrid

HEUSSER, CALVIN J.

1960 Late Pleistocene Environments of North Pacific North America. *American Geographical Society Special Publication,* no. 35. New York.

1965 A Pleistocene Phytogeographical Sketch of the Pacific Northwest and Alaska. *In The Quaternary of the United States,* H. E. Wright, Jr., and David G. Frey, eds., pp. 469–83. Princeton University Press, Princeton.

HEWES, GORDON W.

1946 Early Man in California and the Tranquility Site. *American Antiquity* 11:209–15. Washington, D.C.

HIBBARD, C. W.; D. E. RAY; D. E. SAVAGE; D. W. TAYLOR; AND J. E. GUILDAY

1965 Quaternary Mammals of North America. *In The Quaternary of the United States,* H. E. Wright, Jr., and David G. Frey, eds., pp. 509–25. Princeton University Press, Princeton.

HILL-TOUT, CHARLES

1895 Later Prehistoric Man in British Columbia. *Proceedings and Transactions,* Royal Society of Canada, second series-1, meeting of May 1895.

HINDES, M. G.

1962 The Archæology of the Huntington Lake Region in the Southern Sierra Nevada. *Reports of the University of California Archaeological Survey,* no. 58. Berkeley.

HOIJER, HARRY

1956 The Chronology of the Athapaskan Languages. *International Journal of American Linguistics* 22:218–32. Chicago.

HOLLAND, STUART S.

1964 Landforms of British Columbia, A Physiographic Outline. *British Columbia Department of Mines and Petroleum Resources Bulletin,* no. 48. Victoria.

HOLMES, W. H.

1901 Review of the Evidence Relating to Auriferous Gravel Man in California. *Smithsonian Institution Annual Report, 1899,* pp. 419–72. Washington, D.C.

HOPKINS, DAVID M.

1959 Cenozoic History of the Bering Land Bridge. *Science* 129:1519–28. Washington, D.C.

HOPKINS, DAVID M., ED.

1967 *The Bering Land Bridge.* Stanford University Press, Stanford.

HOPKINS, DAVID M.; F. S. MACNEIL; R. L. MERKLIN; AND O. M. PETROV

1965 Quaternary Correlations Across Bering Strait. *Science* 147:1107–14. Washington, D.C.

HOPKINS, NICHOLAS A.

1965 Great Basin Prehistory and Uto-Aztecan. *American Antiquity* 31:48–60. Washington, D.C.

HORBERG, LELAND

1952 Quaternary Volcanic Ash in Southern Alberta, Canada. *Science* 115:138–319. Washington, D.C.

HOWARD, EDGAR B.

1935 Evidence of Early Man in North America, Based on Geological and Archæological Work in New Mexico. *The Museum Journal,* vol. 24, nos. 2, 3. University of Pennsylvania, Philadelphia.

HOWELLS, W. W.

1966 Population Distances: Biological, Linguistic, Geographical, and Environmental. *Current Anthropology* 7:531–40. Chicago.

HRDLIČKA, ALEŠ

1906 Contribution to the Physical Anthropology of California. *University of California Publications in American Archaeology and Ethnology,* vol. 4, no. 2. Berkeley.

1908 Physiological and Medical Observations among the Indians of Southwestern United States and Northern Mexico. *Bureau of American Ethnology Bulletin,* no. 34. Washington, D.C.

1909 On the Stature of the Indians of the Southwest

and of Northern Mexico. *In Putnam Anniversary Volume*, pp. 405–26. G. E. Stechert & Co., New York.

HUBBS, CARL L.

1955 Water, Fish, and Man in Southern California, Abstract. *Southern California Academy of Sciences Bulletin*, vol. 54, no. 3, pp. 167. Los Angeles.

1961 "Some Highlights from the Natural Radiocarbon Datings of the La Jolla Laboratory." Paper read at Meetings of the National Academy of Science, La Jolla, October 29.

HUBBS, CARL L.; GEORGE S. BIEN; AND HANS E. SUESS

1962 La Jolla Natural Radiocarbon Measurements II. *Radiocarbon* 4:204–38. New Haven.

1963 La Jolla Natural Radiocarbon Measurements III. *Radiocarbon* 5:254–72. New Haven.

1965 La Jolla Natural Radiocarbon Measurements IV. *Radiocarbon* 7:66–117. New Haven.

HUBBS, CARL L., AND R. MILLER

1948 II. The Zoological Evidence: Correlation between Fish Distribution and Hydrographic History in the Desert Basins of Western United States. *In* "The Great Basin, with Emphasis on Glacial and Postglacial Times." *Bulletin of the University of Utah*, vol. 38, no. 20, *Biological Series*, vol. 10, no. 7, pp. 17–166. Salt Lake City.

HULSE, FREDERICK S.

1955 Blood-types and Mating Patterns among Northwest Coast Indians. *Southwestern Journal of Anthropology* 11:93–104. Albuquerque.

1957 Linguistic Barriers to Gene-flow: The Blood-groups of the Yakima, Okanagon and Swinomish Indians. *American Journal of Physical Anthropology*, n.s., 15:235–46. Philadelphia.

1960 Ripples on a Gene-pool: The Shifting Frequencies of Blood-type Alleles Among the Indians of the Hupa Reservation. *American Journal of Physical Anthropology*, n.s., 18:141–52. Philadelphia.

HUMPHREY, ROBERT L.

1966 The Prehistory of the Utakok River Region, Arctic Alaska. *Current Anthropology* 7:586–88. Chicago.

HUNT, ALICE P.

1960 Archæology of the Death Valley Salt Pan, California. *University of Utah Anthropological Papers*, no. 47. Salt Lake City.

HUNT, ALICE P., AND DALLAS TANNER

1960 Early Man Sites Near Moab, Utah. *American Antiquity* 26:110–17. Washington, D.C.

HUNT, CHARLES B.

1965 Quaternary Geology Reviewed (review of *The Quaternary of the United States*, Wright and Frey, eds.). *Science* 150:47–50. Washington, D.C.

HUNT, C. G.; H. D. VARNES; AND H. E. THOMAS

1953 Lake Bonneville: Geology of Northern Utah Valley, Utah. *U.S. Geological Survey Professional Paper*, no. 257–A. Washington, D.C.

HYMES, D. H.

1957 A Note on Athapaskan Glottochronology. *International Journal of American Linguistics* 23:291–97. Chicago.

1960 Lexicostatistics So Far. *Current Anthropology* 1:3–39. Chicago.

I

INTERNATIONAL ASSOCIATION FOR QUATERNARY RESEARCH, VII CONGRESS

1965 *Guidebook for Field Conference E: Northern and Middle Rocky Mountains*, p. 106. Nebraska Academy of Sciences, Lincoln.

IRVING, WILLIAM N.

1962 A Provisional Comparison of Some Alaskan and Asian Stone Industries. *In* "Prehistoric Cultural Relations between the Arctic and Temperate Zones of North America," John M. Campbell, ed., *Arctic Institute of North America Technical Paper*, no. 11. Montreal.

IRWIN-WILLIAMS, CYNTHIA

1967a Picosa: The Elementary Southwestern Culture. *American Antiquity* 32:441–57. Washington, D.C.

1967b Association of Early Man with Horse, Camel, and Mastodon at Hueyatlaco, Valsequillo (Puebla, Mexico). *In* "Pleistocene Extinctions, The Search for a Cause," Paul S. Martin and H. E. Wright, Jr., eds. *Proceedings VII Congress, International Association of Quaternary Research*, vol. 6, pp. 337–47. Yale University Press, New Haven.

IRWIN-WILLIAMS, CYNTHIA, ED.

1968 Early Man in Western North America: Symposium of the Southwestern Anthropological Association, San Diego, 1968. *Eastern New Mexico University Contributions in Anthropology*, vol. 1, no. 4. Portales, N.M.

IVES, P. C.; BETSY LEVIN; R. D. ROBINSON; AND MEYER RUBIN

1964 U.S. Geological Survey Radiocarbon Dates VII. *Radiocarbon* 6:37–76. New Haven.

J

JACOBS, MELVILLE
1937 Historic Perspectives in Indian Languages of Oregon and Washington. *Pacific Northwest Quarterly* 28:55–75. Seattle.
1959 The Content and Style of an Oral Literature: Clackamas Chinook Myths and Tales. *Viking Fund Publications in Anthropology,* no. 26. Wenner–Gren Foundation for Anthropological Research, New York.

JAMESON, SYDNEY J. S.
1958 Archæological Notes on Stansbury Island. *University of Utah Anthropological Papers,* no. 34. Salt Lake City.

JELINEK, ARTHUR J.
1966 An Artifact of Possible Wisconsin Age. *American Antiquity* 31:434. Washington, D.C.

JENNESS, DIAMOND
1932 The Indians of Canada. *Department of Mines, National Museum of Canada Bulletin,* no. 65. Ottawa.

JENNINGS, JESSE D.
1956 The American Southwest: A Problem in Cultural Isolation. *In* "Seminars in Archæology: 1955," Robert Wauchope, ed., *American Antiquity,* vol. 22, no. 2, pt. 2. *Society for American Archaeology Memoir,* no. 11, pp. 59–127. Washington, D.C.
1957 Danger Cave. *University of Utah Anthropological Papers,* no. 27. Also released as *Society for American Archaeology Memoir,* no. 14, *American Antiquity,* vol. 23, no. 2, pt. 2. Reprint 1970. Salt Lake City.
1964 The Desert West. *In Prehistoric Man in the New World,* Jesse D. Jennings and Edward Norbeck, eds., pp. 149–74. University of Chicago Press, Chicago.
1966 Early Man in the Desert West. *Quaternia* 7:81–89. Rome.

JENNINGS, JESSE D., AND EDWARD NORBECK
1955 Great Basin Prehistory: A Review. *American Antiquity* 21:1–11. Washington, D.C.

JENNINGS, JESSE D., AND EDWARD NORBECK, EDS.
1964 *Prehistoric Man in the New World.* University of Chicago Press, Chicago.

JOHANNESSEN, CARL L.
1964 Marshes Prograding in Oregon: Aerial Photography. *Science* 146:1575–78. Washington. D.C.

JOHNSON, FREDERICK, AND JOHN P. MILLER
1958 Pleistocene Man at San Diego, by G. F. Carter (review). *American Antiquity* 24:206–10. Washington, D.C.

JOHNSTON, W. A.
1933 Quaternary Geology of North America in Relation to the Migration of Man. *In The American Aborigines,* Diamond Jenness, ed. University of Toronto Press, Toronto.

JONES, PHILIP MILL
1956 Archæology Investigations on Santa Rosa Island in 1901. *University of California Anthropological Records,* 17:201–80. Berkeley.

K

KELLEY, J. CHARLES
1959 The Desert Cultures and the Balcones Phase: Archaic Manifestations in the Southwest and Texas. *American Antiquity* 24:276–89. Washington, D.C.

KELLY, ISABEL T.
1932 Ethnography of the Surprise Valley Paiute. *University of California Publications in American Archaeology and Ethnology,* 31:67–210. Berkeley.

KENASTON, MONTE RAY
1966 The Archæology of the Harder Site, Franklin County, Washington. *Washington State University Laboratory of Anthropology, Report of Investigations,* no. 50. Pullman.

KENNEDY, KENNETH A. R.
1959 The Aboriginal Population of the Great Basin *Reports of the University of California Archaeological Survey,* no. 45. Berkeley.

KIDD, ROBERT STUART
1964 "A Synthesis of Western Washington Prehistory from the Perspective of Three Occupation Sites." M.A. thesis, University of Washington, Seattle.
1967 The Martin Site, Southwestern Washington. *Tebiwa,* vol. 10, no. 2, pp. 13–38. Pocatello.

KING, ARDEN R.
1950 Cattle Point: A Stratified Site in the Southern Northwest Coast Region. *Society for American Archaeology Memoir,* no. 7. Washington, D.C.

KING, PHILIP B.
1965 Tectonics of Quaternary Time in Middle North America. *In The Quaternary of the United States,* H. E. Wright, Jr., and David G. Frey, eds., pp. 831–70. Princeton University Press, Princeton.

KLUCKHOHN, CLYDE
1940 The Conceptual Structure in Middle American Studies. *In The Maya and Their Neighbors,* C. L.

Hay et al., eds., pp. 41–51. D. Appleton-Century Company, New York and London. Reprint 1962. University of Utah Press.

KOWTA, M.

1961 Excavations at Goleta, Artifact Description; Chipped Lithic Material. *University of California Archaeological Survey Annual Report, 1960–1961*, pp. 349–83. Berkeley.

KRIEGER, ALEX D.

1958 Pleistocene Man at San Diego by G. F. Carter (review). *American Anthropologist*, n.s., 60:974–78. Washington, D.C.

1964 Early Man in the New World. *In Prehistoric Man in the New World*, J. D. Jennings and E. Norbeck, eds., pp. 23–81. University of Chicago Press, Chicago.

KRIEGER, HERBERT W.

1927 Archæological Investigations in the Columbia River Valley. *Smithsonian Miscellaneous Collections*, vol. 78, no. 7, pp. 187–200. Washington, D.C.

1928a Prehistoric Inhabitants of the Columbia River Valley. *Explorations and Field Work of the Smithsonian Institution in 1927*, pp. 133–40. Washington, D.C.

1928b A Prehistoric Pit House Village Site on the Columbia River at Wahluke, Grant County, Washington. *U.S. National Museum Proceedings* 73:1–29. Washington, D.C.

KROEBER, ALFRED L.

1923 American Culture and the Northwest Coast. *American Anthropologist*, n.s., 25:1–20. Washington, D.C.

1925 Handbook of the Indians of California. *Bureau of American Ethnology Bulletin*, no. 78. Washington, D.C.

1936 Prospects in California Prehistory. *American Antiquity* 2:108–16. Washington, D.C.

1939 Cultural and Natural Areas of Native North America. *University of California Publications in American Archaeology and Ethnology*, vol. 38. Berkeley.

1940 Stimulus Diffusion. *American Anthropologist*, n.s., 42:1–20. Washington, D.C.

1948 *Anthropology: Race, Language, Culture, Psychology, Prehistory*. Harcourt, Brace, New York.

1955 Linguistic Time Depth Results So Far and Their Meaning. *International Journal of American Linguistics* 21:91–104. Chicago.

KULP, J. LAURENCE

1961 Geologic Time Scale. *Science* 133:1105–14. Washington, D.C.

L

LAGUNA, FREDERICA DE

1956 *Chugach Prehistory*. University of Washington Press, Seattle.

LAMB, SIDNEY M.

1958 Linguistic Prehistory in the Great Basin. *International Journal of American Linguistics* 24:95–100. Chicago.

1964 The Classification of the Uto-Aztecan Languages: A Historical Survey. In "Studies in Californian Linguistics," William Bright, ed. *University of California Publications in Linguistics* 34:106–25. Berkeley.

LANNING, EDWARD P.

1963 Archæology of the Rose Spring Site, INY-372. *University of California Publications in American Archaeology and Ethnology* 49:237–336. Berkeley.

1967 *Peru before the Incas*. Prentice-Hall, Inc., Englewood, N.J.

LATHRAP, DONALD W., AND DICK SHUTLER, JR.

1955 An Archæological Site in the High Sierra of California. *American Antiquity* 20:226–40. Washington, D.C.

LAUGHLIN, WILLIAM S.

1941 Excavations in the Calapuya Mounds of the Willamette Valley, Oregon. *American Antiquity* 7:147–55. Washington, D.C.

1943 Notes on the Archæology of the Yamhill River, Willamette Valley, Oregon. *American Antiquity* 9:220–29. Washington, D.C.

1948 Peabody Museum Aleutian Expedition, 1948. Unpublished data.

1962 Bering Strait to Puget Sound: Dichotomy and Affinity between Eskimo-Aleuts and American Indians. *In* "Prehistoric Cultural Relations between the Arctic and Temperate Zones of North America," John M. Campbell, ed., *Arctic Institute of North America Technical Paper*, no. 11, pp. 100–125. Montreal.

1963 Eskimos and Aleuts: Their Origin and Evolution. *Science* 142:633–45. Washington, D.C.

LAYRISSE, MIGUEL, AND JOHANNES WILBERT

1960 El antigeno del sistema sanguineo Diego. La Fundacion Creole y la Fundacion Eugenio Mendoza. Caracas, Venezuela.

LEATHERMAN, KENNETH E., AND ALEX D. KRIEGER
1940   Contributions to Oregon Coast Prehistory. *American Antiquity* 6:19–28. Washington, D.C.

LEE, THOMAS E.
1955   The Second Sheguiandah Expedition, Manitoulin Island, Ontario. *American Antiquity* 21:63–71. Washington, D.C.

LEONHARDY, FRANK C.
1961   "The Cultural Position of the Iron Gate Site." M.A. thesis, University of Oregon, Eugene.

LEONHARDY, FRANK C., AND DAVID G. RICE
1970   A Proposed Culture Typology for the Lower Snake River Region, Southeastern Washington. *Northwest Anthropological Research Notes*, vol. 4, no. 1, pp. 1–29. Moscow, Idaho.

LÉVI-STRAUSS, CLAUDE
1956   The Family. *In Man, Culture and Society*, H. L. Shapiro, ed., pp. 261–85. Oxford University Press, New York.

LIBBY, WILLARD F.
1951   Radiocarbon Dates II. *Science* 114:291–96. Washington, D.C.
1952   *Radiocarbon Dating*. University of Chicago Press, Chicago. Second edition 1955.
1954   Chicago Radiocarbon Dates V. *Science* 120:733–42. Washington, D.C.

LILLARD, JEREMIAH B.; ROBERT F. HEIZER; AND FRANKLIN FENENGA
1939   An Introduction to the Archæology of Central California. *Sacramento Junior College Department of Anthropology Bulletin*, no. 2. Sacramento.

LINTON, RALPH
1936   *The Study of Man: An Introduction*. D. Appleton-Century Company, New York.

LOUD, LEWELLYN L., AND MARK R. HARRINGTON
1929   Lovelock Cave. *University of California Publications in American Archaeology and Ethnology*, vol. 25, no. 1, pp. 1–183. Berkeley.

LOWIE, R. H.
1923   The Cultural Connection of Californian and Plateau Shoshonean Tribes. *University of California Publications in American Archaeology and Ethnology* 20:145–56. Berkeley.

M

MACDONALD, G. F.
1966   The Technology and Settlement Pattern of a Paleo-Indian Site at Debert, Nova Scotia. *In Quaternia* 8:59–73. Rome.

MACNEISH, RICHARD S.
1962   Recent Finds in the Yukon Territory of Canada. *In* "Prehistoric Cultural Relations between the Arctic and Temperate Zones of North America," John M. Campbell, ed., *Arctic Institute of North America Technical Paper*, no. 11, pp. 20–26. Montreal.

McCOWN, THEODORE
1950   The Stanford Skull: The Physical Characteristics. *Reports of the University of California Archaeological Survey*, no. 6, pp. 10–17. Berkeley.

McGEE, W. J.
1955   An Obsidian Implement from Pleistocene Deposits in Nevada. *Reports of the University of California Archaeological Survey*, no. 32, pp. 30–38. Berkeley.

MALDE, HAROLD E.
1964a   Environment and Man in Arid America. *Science* 145:123–29. Washington, D.C.
1964b   Ecologic Significance of Some Unfamiliar Geologic Processes. *In* "The Reconstruction of Past Environments," *Fort Burgwin Research Center Publication*, no. 3, pp. 7–13. Assembled by James J. Hester and James Schoenwetter. Fort Burgwin Research Center, Ranches of Taos, N.M.
1965   Snake River Plain. *In The Quaternary of the United States*, H. E. Wright, Jr., and David G. Frey, eds., pp. 255–63. Princeton University Press, Princeton.
1968   The Catastrophic Late Pleistocene Bonneville Flood in the Snake River Plain, Idaho. *Geological Survey Professional Paper*, no. 596. Washington, D.C.

MALDE, HAROLD E., AND CYNTHIA IRWIN-WILLIAMS
1967   Preliminary Report on Radiocarbon Dates from the Valsequillo Area, Puebla, Mexico. Released by the Peabody Museum of Archaeology and Ethnology, Harvard University. Paper read at the annual meetings of the Society for American Archæology, Ann Arbor, Michigan, May.

MALDE, HAROLD E., AND D. E. TRIMBLE
1965   *Guidebook for Field Conference E: Northern and Middle Rocky Mountains*. International Association for Quaternary Research, VII Congress. Nebraska Academy of Sciences, Nebraska.

MALOUF, CARLING; CHARLES E. DIBBLE; AND ELMER R. SMITH
1950   The Archæology of the Deep Creek Region, Utah. *University of Utah Anthropological Papers*, no. 5. Salt Lake City.

MARSHALL, NEIL F., AND JAMES R. MORIARTY

1964 Principles of Underwater Archæology. *Pacific Discovery*, vol. 17, no. 5, pp. 18–25. San Francisco.

MARTIN, PAUL S.; JAMES SCHOENWETTER; AND BERNARD ARMS

1961 *The Last 10,000 Years.* Geochronology Laboratories, University of Arizona. Tucson.

MARTIN, PAUL S., AND H. E. WRIGHT, JR., EDS.

1967 Pleistocene Extinctions, the Search for a Cause. *Proceedings, VII Congress, International Association for Quaternary Research,* vol. 6. Yale University Press, New Haven.

MASON, OTIS T.

1902 Aboriginal American Harpoons, A Study in Ethnic Distribution and Invention. *Annual Report of the Smithsonian Institution, 1900,* pp. 189–304. Washington, D.C.

MASON, RONALD J.

1962 The Paleo-Indian Tradition in Eastern North America. *Current Anthropology* 3:227–78. Chicago.

MASSEY, WILLIAM C.

1947 Brief Report on Archæological Investigations in Baja California. *Southwestern Journal of Anthropology* 3:344–59. Albuquerque.

1961 The Cultural Distinction of Aboriginal Baja California. *In Homenaje a Pablo Martinez del Rio en al 250 anniversario de la primera edicion de "Los Origenes Americanos,"* pp. 411–22. Mexico.

MASSEY, WILLIAM C., AND CAROLYN OSBORNE

1961 A Burial Cave in Baja California, The Palmer Collection, 1887. *University of California Anthropological Records* 16:339–64. Berkeley.

MATHEWES, R. W.; C. E. BORDEN; AND G. E. ROUSE

1972 New Radiocarbon Dates from the Yale Area of the Lower Fraser River Canyon, British Columbia. *Canadian Journal of Earth Sciences,* vol. 9, no. 8, pp. 1055–57. Ottawa.

MATSON, FREDERICK R., ED.

1965 Ceramics and Man. *Viking Fund Publications in Anthropology,* no. 41. Aldine Publishing Company, Chicago.

MATTHES, FRANÇOIS E.

1939 Report of Committee on Glaciers, April 1939. *Transactions of the American Geophysical Union,* pt. 4, pp. 518–23. Washington, D.C.

MEIGHAN, CLEMENT W.

1953a Archæology of Sites Nap-129 and Nap-131. *University of California Anthropological Records* 12: 315–17. Berkeley.

1953b Preliminary Excavation at the Thomas Site, Marin County. *Reports of the University of California Archaeological Survey,* no. 19, pp. 1–14. Berkeley.

1954 A Late Complex in Southern California Prehistory. *Southwestern Journal of Anthropology* 10:215–27. Albuquerque.

1955a Archæology of the North Coast Ranges, California. *Reports of the University of California Archaeological Survey,* no. 30, pp. 1–39. Berkeley.

1955b Excavation of Isabella Meadows Cave, Monterey County, California. *Reports of the University of California Archaeological Survey,* no. 29, pp. 1–30. Berkeley.

1955c Notes on the Archæology of Mono County, California. *Reports of the University of California Archaeological Survey,* no. 28, pp. 6–28. Berkeley.

1959a California Cultures and the Concept of an Archaic Stage. *American Antiquity* 24:289–318. Washington, D.C.

1959b The Little Harbor Site, Catalina Island: An Example of Ecological Interpretation in Archæology. *American Antiquity* 24:383–405. Washington, D.C.

1965 Pacific Coast Archæology. *In Quaternary of the United States,* H. E. Wright, Jr., and David G. Frey, eds., pp. 709–20. Princeton University Press, Princeton.

MEIGHAN, CLEMENT W., AND C. VANCE HAYNES, JR.

1968 New Studies on the Age of the Borax Lake Site. *The Masterkey* 42:4–9. Los Angeles.

MEINZER, OSCAR E.

1922 Map of the Pleistocene Lakes of the Basin-and-Range Province and Its Significance. *Geological Society of America Bulletin* 33:541–52. New York.

MERRIAM, JOHN C.

1939 Paleontology, Early Man, and Historical Geology. *Carnegie Institution of Washington,* year book no. 38, pp. 301–10. Washington, D.C.

1941 Paleontology, Early Man, and Historical Geology. *Carnegie Institution of Washington,* year book no. 40, pp. 316–33. Washington, D.C.

MERRIAM, JOHN C., AND ASSOCIATES

1938 Paleontology, Early Man, and Historical Geology. *Carnegie Institution of Washington,* year book no. 37, pp. 340–64. Washington, D.C.

MICHAEL, HENRY N., AND ELIZABETH K. RALPH, EDS.

1971 *Dating Techniques for the Archaeologist.* MIT Press, Cambridge, Mass.

MICHELSSON, TRUMAN

1930 Note on Shoshonean Anthropometry. *Proceedings of the Twenty-third International Congress of Americanists,* p. 856. Mexico City.

MILLER, WICK R.

1966 Anthropological Linguistics in the Great Basin. *In* "The Current Status of Anthropological Research in the Great Basin." *Desert Research Institute Technical Report Series S-H, Social Sciences and Humanities Publications,* no. 1, pp. 75–112. Reno.

MILLS, JOHN E.

1950 Recent Developments in the Study of Northwestern California Archæology. *Reports of the University of California Archaeological Survey,* no. 7, pp. 21–25. Berkeley.

MILLS, JOHN E., AND CAROLYN OSBORNE

1952 Material Culture of an Upper Coulee Rockshelter. *American Antiquity* 17:352–59. Washington, D.C.

MITCHELL, DONALD H.

1965 Preliminary Excavations at a Cobble Tool Site DjRi 7) in the Fraser Canyon, British Columbia. *Anthropology Papers, National Museum of Canada,* no. 10. Ottawa.

1968a Microblades: A Long-Standing Gulf of Georgia Tradition. *American Antiquity* 33:11–15. Washington, D.C.

1968b "Archæology of the Gulf of Georgia Area, a Natural Area and Its Culture Types." Ph.D. dissertation, Department of Anthropology, University of Oregon, Eugene.

MORIARTY, JAMES R.

1966 Culture Phase Divisions Suggested by Typological Change Coordinated with Stratigraphically Controlled Radiocarbon Dating at San Diego. *Anthropological Journal of Canada,* vol. 4, no. 4, pp. 20–30. Ottawa.

1967 Reports: Transitional Pre-Desert Phase in San Diego County, California. *Science* 155:553–56. Washington, D.C.

MORIARTY, JAMES R.; G. SHUMWAY; AND C. N. WARREN

1959 Scripps Estates Site I (SDi-525): A Preliminary Report on an Early Site on the San Diego Coast. *University of California Archaeological Survey Annual Report, 1958–1959,* pp. 187–216. Los Angeles.

MORRISON, ROGER B.

1961a Correlation of the Deposits of Lakes Lahontan and Bonneville and the Glacial Sequences of the Sierra Nevada and Wasatch Mountains, California, Nevada, and Utah. *U.S. Geological Survey Professional Paper,* no. 424-D, pp. 122-124D. Washington, D.C.

1961b New Evidence on the History of Lake Bonneville from an Area South of Salt Lake City, Utah.

U.S. Geological Survey Professional Paper, no. 424-D, pp. 124-127D. Washington, D.C.

1964 Lake Lahontan: Geology of Southern Carson Desert, Nevada. *U.S. Geological Survey Professional Paper,* no. 401. Washington, D.C.

1965 Quaternary Geology of the Great Basin. *In The Quaternary of the United States,* H. E. Wright, Jr., and David G. Frey, eds., pp. 265–85. Princeton University Press, Princeton.

1966 Predecessors of Great Salt Lake. *In Guidebook to the Geology of Utah,* W. L. Stokes, ed., no. 20, pp. 77–104. Utah Geological Society, Salt Lake City.

MORSS, NOEL M.

1931 The Ancient Culture of the Fremont River in Utah: A Report on the Explorations Under the Claflin-Emerson Fund, 1928–29. *Papers of the Peabody Museum of American Archaeology and Ethnology,* vol. 12, no. 3. Cambridge.

MULLER-BECK, HANSJURGEN

1966 Paleohunters in America: Origins and Diffusion. *Science* 152:1191–1210. Washington, D.C.

MULLINEAUX, DONALD R.; H. WALDRON; AND MEYER RUBIN

1965 Stratigraphy and Chronology of Late Interglacial and Early Vashon Glacial Time in the Seattle Area, Washington. *U.S. Geological Survey Bulletin,* no. 1194-0. Washington, D.C.

MULLOY, WILLIAM

1954 The McKean Site in Northeastern Wyoming. *Southwestern Journal of Anthropology* 10:432–60. Albuquerque.

1958 A Preliminary Historical Outline for the Northwestern Plains. *University of Wyoming Publications,* vol. 22, no. 1. Laramie.

N

NAMAIS, JEROME

1965 Short-period Climatic Fluctuations. *Science* 147: 696–706. Washington, D.C.

NELSON, CHARLES M.

1966 A Preliminary Report on 45CO1, a Stratified Open Site in the Southern Columbia Plateau. *Washington State University Laboratory of Anthropology, Report of Investigations,* no. 39. Pullman.

NELSON, NELS C.

1909 Shellmounds of the San Francisco Bay Region. *University of California Publications in American Archaeology and Ethnology* 7:309–56. Berkeley.

1910 The Ellis Landing Shellmound. *University of California Publications in American Archaeology and Ethnology* 7:357–426. Berkeley.

1936 Notes on the Santa Barbara Culture. *In Essays in Anthropology Presented to A. L. Kroeber in Celebration of His Sixtieth Birthday, June 11, 1936,* pp. 199–209. University of California Press, Berkeley.

NEUMANN, GEORGE K.

1956 The Upper Cave Skulls from Choukoutien in the Light of Paleo-Amerind Material. *American Journal of Physical Anthropology, Proceedings of the Twenty-fifth Annual Meeting of the American Association of Physical Anthropologists,* n.s., 14: 380. Philadelphia.

NEWMAN, RUSSELL W.

1957 A Comparative Analysis of Prehistoric Skeletal Remains from the Lower Sacramento Valley. *Reports of the University of California Archaeological Survey,* no. 39. Berkeley.

NEWMAN, THOMAS M.

1959 "Tillamook Prehistory and Its Relation to the Northwest Coast Culture Area." Ph.D. dissertation, University of Oregon, Eugene.

1966 Cascadia Cave. *Occasional Papers of the Idaho State University Museum,* no. 18. Pocatello.

NICHOLS, HARVEY

1967 Pollen Diagrams from Sub-Arctic Central Canada. *Science* 155:1665–68. Washington, D.C.

O

OETTEKING, BRUNO

1930 *Craniology of the North Pacific Coast.* Memoir of the American Museum of Natural History; Publications of the Jesup North Pacific Expedition, vol. 11, pt. 1. E. J. Brill, Ltd., Leiden, Netherlands. G. E. Stechert & Co., New York.

OLSON, EDWIN A., AND W. S. BROECKER

1959 Lamont Natural Radiocarbon Measurements V. *American Journal of Science Radiocarbon Supplement* 1:1–28. New Haven.

OLSON, RONALD L.

1930 Chumash Prehistory. *University of California Publications in American Archaeology and Ethnology* 28:1–21. Berkeley.

OPPENHEIMER, J. ROBERT

1954 *Science and the Common Understanding.* Simon and Schuster, New York.

ORR, PHIL C.

1952a Preliminary Excavations of Pershing County Caves. *Nevada State Museum, Department of Archaeology Bulletin,* no. 1. Carson City.

1952b Review of Santa Barbara Channel Archæology *Southwestern Journal of Anthropology* 8:211–26. Albuquerque.

1953 Speleotherm Age Dating. *Texas Archaeological Society Bulletin* 24:7–17. Austin.

1956a Pleistocene Man in Fishbone Cave, Pershing County, Nevada. *Nevada State Museum, Department of Archaeology Bulletin,* no. 2. Carson City.

1956b Radiocarbon Dates from Santa Rosa Island, I. *Santa Barbara Museum of Natural History, Department of Anthropology Bulletin,* no. 2. Santa Barbara.

1960 Radiocarbon Dates from Santa Rosa Island, II. *Santa Barbara Museum of Natural History, Department of Anthropology Bulletin,* no. 3. Santa Barbara.

1962 On New Radiocarbon Dates from the California Channel Islands. *Observations,* no. 8. Western Speleological Institute, Inc., Museum of Natural History, Santa Barbara, California, and Nevada State Museum, Nevada. Mimeo.

1964 Pleistocene Chipped Stone Tool on Santa Rosa Island, California. *Science* 143:243–44. Washington, D.C.

1967 Geochronology of Santa Rosa Island, California. *Proceedings of the Symposium on the Biology of the California Islands,* pp. 317–25. Santa Barbara Botanic Garden, Santa Barbara.

1968 *Prehistory of Santa Rosa Island.* Santa Barbara Museum of Natural History, Santa Barbara.

ORR, PHIL C., AND RAINER BERGER

1966a The Fire Areas on Santa Rosa Island, California, I. *Proceedings of the National Academy of Science* 56:1409–16. Washington, D.C.

1966b The Fire Areas on Santa Rosa Island, California, II. *Proceedings of the National Academy of Science* 56:1678–82. Washington, D.C.

OSBORNE, DOUGLAS

1950 An Archæological Survey of the Benham Falls Reservoir, Oregon. *American Antiquity* 16:112–20. Washington, D.C.

1956 Evidence of the Early Lithic in the Pacific Northwest. *Research Studies, State College of Washington* 24:38–44: Pullman.

1957a Excavations in the McNary Reservoir Basin near Umatilla, Oregon. *Bureau of American Ethnology Bulletin,* no. 166. Washington, D.C.

1957b Pottery in the Northwest. *American Antiquity* 23:28–34. Washington, D.C.

1958 Western American Prehistory—An Hypothesis. *American Antiquity* 24:47–52. Washington, D.C.

1959 Archæological Tests in the Lower Grand Coulee,

Washington. Washington State University, Pullman. Mimeo.

OSBORNE, DOUGLAS; ALAN BRYAN; AND ROBERT H. CRABTREE
1961 The Sheep Island Site and the Mid-Columbia Valley. *Bureau of American Ethnology Bulletin,* no. 179, pp. 267–306. Washington, D.C.

OSBORNE, DOUGLAS; WARREN W. CALDWELL; AND ROBERT H. CRABTREE
1956 The Problem of Northwest Coastal-Interior Relationships as Seen from Seattle. *American Antiquity* 22:117–28. Washington, D.C.

OSBORNE, DOUGLAS, AND ROBERT H. CRABTREE
1961 Two Sites in the Upper McNary Reservoir. *Tebiwa,* vol. 4, no. 2, pp. 19–36. Pocatello.

OSBORNE, DOUGLAS; ROBERT H. CRABTREE; AND ALAN BRYAN
1952 Archæological Investigations in the Chief Joseph Reservoir. *American Antiquity* 17:360–73. Washington, D.C.

OSGOOD, CORNELIUS
1940 Ingalik Material Culture. *Yale University Publications in Anthropology,* no. 22. New Haven.
1951 Culture: Its Empirical and Non-empirical Character. *Southwestern Journal of Anthropology* 7: 202–14. Albuquerque.

OSMUNDSON, JOHN, AND CHRISTOPHER HULSE
1962 Preliminary Report on an Archæological Survey of the Bruces Eddy Reservoir, North Central Idaho, 1961. *Tebiwa,* vol. 5, no. 1, pp. 11–29. Pocatello.

OWEN, ROGER C.
1964 Early Milling Stone Horizon (Oak Grove), Santa Barbara County, California: Radiocarbon Dates. *American Antiquity* 30:210–13. Washington, D.C.
1967 Assertions, Assumptions, and Early Horizon (Oak Grove) Settlement Patterns in Southern California: A Rejoinder. *American Antiquity* 32:236–41. Washington, D.C.

OWEN, ROGER C.; FREDDIE CURTIS; AND DONALD S. MILLER
1964 The Glen Annie Canyon Site, SBa142, An Early Horizon Coastal Site of Santa Barbara County. *University of California Archaeological Survey Annual Report, 1963–1964.* Los Angeles.

P

PANTIN, A. M., AND ROBERT KALLSEN
1953 The Blood Groups of the Diegueño Indians. *American Journal of Physical Anthropology,* n.s., 11:91–96. Philadelphia.

PATTERSON, J. T.
1937 Boat-shaped Artifacts of the Gulf Southwest States. *University of Texas Bulletin,* no. 3732, *Anthropological Papers,* vol. 1, no. 2. Austin.

PECK, STUART L.
1955 An Archæological Report on the Excavation of a Prehistoric Site at Zuma Creek, Los Angeles County, California. *Archaeological Survey Association of Southern California Paper,* no. 2. Los Angeles.

PECK, STUART L., AND G. A. SMITH
1957 The Archæology of Seep Spring. *San Bernardino County Museum Quarterly,* vol. 4, no. 4. San Bernardino.

PÉWÉ, TROY L.; DAVID M. HOPKINS; AND J. L. GIDDINGS
1965 The Quaternary Geology and Archæology of Alaska. *In The Quaternary of the United States,* H. E. Wright, Jr., and David G. Frey, eds., pp. 355–74. Princeton University Press, Princeton.

PILLING, ARNOLD R.
1955 Relationships of Prehistoric Cultures of Coastal Monterey County, California. *Kroeber Anthropological Society Papers,* no. 12, pp. 70–87. Berkeley.

PLAFKER, GEORGE
1965 Tectonic Deformation Associated with the 1964 Alaska Earthquake. *Science* 148:1675–87. Washington, D.C.

PORTER, STEPHEN C.
1964 Antiquity of Man at Anaktuvuk Pass, Alaska. *American Antiquity* 29:493–96. Washington, D.C.

POURADE, RICHARD F., ED.
1966 *Ancient Hunters of the Far West.* The Copley Press, Los Angeles.

POWERS, HOWARD A., AND RAY WILCOX
1964 Volcanic Ash from Mount Mazama (Crater Lake) and from Glacier Peak. *Science* 114:1334–36. Washington, D.C.

PRESTON, R. S.; E. PERSON; AND E. S. DEEVEY
1955 Yale Natural Radiocarbon Measurements, II. *Science* 122:954–60. Washington, D.C.

PUTNAM, FREDERICK W.
1879 *Vol. VII—Archaeology, Report upon United States Geographical Surveys West of the One Hundredth Meridian, In Charge of First Lieut. Geo. M. Wheeler.* Government Printing Office, Washington, D.C.

R

RANDLE, KEITH; GORDON G. GOLES; AND LAURENCE R. KITTLEMAN
1971 Geochemical and Petrological Characterization of Ash Samples from Cascade Range Volcanoes. *Quaternary Research* 1:261–82. New York.

RAY, VERNE F.
1932 Pottery on the Middle Columbia. *American Anthropologist,* n.s., 34:127–33. Washington, D.C.

1939 Cultural Relations in the Plateau of Northwestern America. *Publications of the Frederick Webb Hodge Anniversary Publication Fund,* vol. 3. The Southwest Museum, Los Angeles.

REDFIELD, ALFRED C.
1967 Postglacial Change in Sea Level in the Western North Atlantic Ocean. *Science* 157:687–92. Washington, D.C.

REICHLEN, HENRY, AND ROBERT F. HEIZER
1964 The Scientific Expedition of Leon de Cessac to California, 1877–1879. *Reports of the University of California Archaeological Survey,* no. 61, pp. 9–23. Berkeley.

RICE, DAVID G.
1972 The Windust Phase in Lower Snake River Region Prehistory. *Washington State University Laboratory of Anthropology, Report of Investigations,* no. 50. Pullman.

RICE, H. S.
1965 The Cultural Sequence at "Windust Cave." M.A. thesis. Washington State University, Pullman.

RICHMOND, GERALD M.
1961 New Evidence of the Age of Lake Bonneville from the Moraines in Little Cottonwood Canyon, Utah. *U.S. Geological Survey Professional Paper,* no. 424-D, pp. 127–128D. Washington, D.C.

1964 Glaciation of Little Cottonwood and Bells Canyons, Wasatch Mountains, Utah. *U.S. Geological Survey Professional Paper,* no. 454-D. Washington, D.C.

1965 Glaciation of the Rocky Mountains. *In The Quaternary of the United States,* H. E. Wright, Jr., and David G. Frey, eds., pp. 217–30. Princeton University Press, Princeton.

RICHMOND, GERALD M.; ROALD FRYXELL; GEORGE NEFF; AND PAUL WEIS
1965 The Cordilleran Ice Sheet of the Northern Rocky Mountains and Related Quarternary History of the Columbia Plateau. *In The Quaternary of the United States,* H. E. Wright, Jr., and David G. Frey, eds., pp. 231–42. Princeton University Press, Princeton.

RIDDELL, FRANCIS A.
1956a Archæological Research in Lassen County, California. *Reports of the University of California Archaeological Survey,* no. 33, pp. 44–49. Berkeley

1956b Final Report on the Archæology of Tommy Tucker Cave. *Reports of the University of California Archaeological Survey,* no. 35, pp. 1–25. Berkeley.

1958 The Eastern California Border: Cultural and Temporal Affinities. *Reports of the University of California Archaeological Survey,* no. 42, pp. 41–48. Berkeley.

1960 The Archæology of the Karlo Site (LAS-7), California. *Reports of the University of California Archaeological Survey,* no. 53. Berkeley.

RIDDELL, FRANCIS A., AND DONALD F. MCGEEIN
1969 Facts and Comments—Atlatl Spurs from California. *American Antiquity* 34:474–78. Washington, D.C.

RIDDELL, HARRY S.
1951 The Archæology of a Paiute Village Site in Owens Valley. *Reports of the University of California Archaeological Survey,* no. 12, pp. 14–28. Berkeley.

RIDDELL, HARRY S., AND FRANCIS A. RIDDELL
1956 The Current Status of Archæological Investigations in Owens Valley, California. *Reports of the University of California Archaeological Survey,* no. 33. Berkeley.

RIGG, GEORGE B., AND HOWARD F. GOULD
1957 Age of Glacier Peak Eruption and Chronology of Postglacial Peat Deposits in Washington and Surrounding Areas. *American Journal of Science* 255:341–63. New Haven.

RITCHIE, WILLIAM
n.d. The Northeastern Archaic—A Review. Mimeo.

ROBERTS, FRANK H. H., JR.
1935 A Survey of Southwestern Archæology. *American Anthropologist,* n.s., 37:1–35. Washington, D.C.

1961 River Basin Surveys Papers, Numbers 21–24. *Bureau of American Ethnology Bulletin,* no. 179. Washington, D.C.

ROBINSON, E.
1942 Shell Fishhooks of the California Coast. *Bernice Pauahi Bishop Museum, Occasional Papers,* vol. 17, no. 4. Honolulu.

ROGERS, D. B.
1929 Prehistoric Man of the Santa Barbara Coast. Santa Barbara Museum of Natural History, Santa Barbara.

ROGERS, MALCOLM J.

1929 The Stone Art of the San Dieguito Plateau. *American Anthropologist,* n.s., 31:454–67. Washington, D.C.

1939 Early Lithic Industries of the Lower Basin of the Colorado River and Adjacent Desert Areas. *San Diego Museum Papers,* no. 3. San Diego.

1941 Aboriginal Culture Relations between Southern California and the Southwest. *San Diego Museum Bulletin,* vol. 5, no. 3. San Diego.

1945 An Outline of Yuman Prehistory. *Southwestern Journal of Anthropology* 1:167–98. Albuquerque.

1958 San Dieguito Implements from the Terraces of the Rincon-Patano and Rillito Drainage System. *Kiva,* vol. 24, no. 1, pp. 1–23. Tucson.

ROMNEY, A. KIMBALL

1957 The Genetic Model and Uto-Aztecan Time Perspective. *Davidson Journal of Anthropology,* vol. 3, no. 2, pp. 35–41. Seattle.

ROSCOE, ERNEST J.

1967 Ethnomalocology and Paleoecology of the Round Butte Archæological Sites, Deschutes River Basin, Oregon. *Museum of Natural History Bulletin,* no. 6. University of Oregon, Eugene.

ROSS, RICHARD E.

1963 "Prehistory of the Round Butte Area, Jefferson County, Oregon." M.A. thesis, University of Oregon, Eugene.

ROSTLUND, ERHARD

1952 Freshwater Fish and Fishing in Native North America. *University of California Publications in Geography,* vol. 9. University of California Press, Berkeley.

ROUSE, IRVING

1939 Prehistory in Haiti: A Study in Method. *Yale University Publications in Anthropology,* no. 21. New Haven.

1958 Childe, Vera Gordon—1892–1957 (obituary). *American Antiquity* 24:82–84. Washington, D.C.

1960 The Classification of Artifacts in Archæology. *American Antiquity* 25:313–23. Washington, D.C.

1965 The Place of "Peoples" in Prehistoric Research. *Journal of the Royal Anthropological Institute of Great Britain and Ireland,* vol. 95, no. 1, pp. 1–15. London.

ROUST, NORMAN L.

1968 Archæological Materials from Winnemucca Lake Caves. *Reports of the University of California Archaeological Survey,* no. 44, pt. 2, pp. 1–13. Berkeley.

1966 Archæology of Granite Point, Pershing County, Nevada. *Reports of the University of California Archaeological Survey,* no. 66, pp. 37–72. Berkeley.

RUBIN, MEYER, AND CORRINNE ALEXANDER

1958 U.S. Geological Survey Radiocarbon Dates IV. *Science* 127:1476–86. Washington, D.C.

1960 U.S. Geological Survey Radiocarbon Dates V. *American Journal of Science Radiocarbon Supplement* 2:129–85. New Haven.

RUDENKO, S. I.

1961 *The Ancient Culture of the Bering Sea and the Eskimo Problem.* Arctic Institute of North America Anthropology of the North. Translations from Russian sources, no. 1, Paul Tolstoy, trans. University of Toronto Press, Toronto.

RUDY, JACK R

1953 Archæological Survey of Western Utah. *University of Utah Anthropological Papers,* no. 12. Salt Lake City.

RUSSELL, ISRAEL C.

1885– Geological History of Lake Lahontan. *U.S. Geolog-*
1886 *ical Survey Monographs,* pp. 10–11. Washington, D.C.

S

SANGER, DAVID

1964 Excavations at Nesikep Creek (EdRk:1), A Stratified Site Near Lillooet, British Columbia: A Preliminary Report, *National Museum of Canada Bulletin,* no. 193, *Anthropological Series,* no. 61, pp. 130–61. Ottawa.

1966 Excavations in the Lochnore-Nesikep Creek Locality, British Columbia: Interim Report. *Anthropology Papers, National Museum of Canada,* no. 12. Ottawa.

1967 Prehistory of the Pacific Northwest Plateau as Seen from the Interior of British Columbia. *American Antiquity* 32:186–97. Washington, D.C.

1968a Seven Thousand Years of Prehistory in the Interior of British Columbia. *The Beaver, Magazine of the North.* Winnipeg.

1968b Prepared Core and Blade Traditions in the Pacific Northwest. *Arctic Anthropology* 5:92–120. Madison, Wisc.

SAPIR, EDWARD

1916 Time Perspective in Aboriginal American Culture, A Study in Method. *Anthropological Series,* no. 13, Memoir 90. Department of Mines, Geological Survey, Canada. Government Printing Bureau, Ottawa.

SAYLES, E. B.

1965 Late Quaternary Climate Recorded by Cochise Culture. *American Antiquity* 30:476–80. Washington, D.C.

SAYLES, E. B., AND ERNEST ANTEVS

1941 *The Coshise Culture.* Gila Pueblo Medallion Papers, no. 29. Globe, Ariz.

SCHENCK, W. EGBERT

1926 The Emeryville Shellmound Final Report. *University of California Publications in American Archaeology and Ethnology,* vol. 23, no. 3, pp. 123–46. Berkeley. Reprint 1965, Kraus, New York.

SCHENCK, W. EGBERT, AND ELMER J. DAWSON

1929 Archæology of the Northern San Joaquin Valley. *University of California Publications in American Archaeology and Ethnology,* vol. 25. Berkeley.

SCHUMACHER, PAUL

1874 Remarks on the Kjökken-Möddings on the Northwest Coast of America. *Smithsonian Institution Annual Report, 1873,* pp. 354–62. Washington, D.C.

1960a The Manufacture of Shell Fish-hooks by the Early Inhabitants of the Santa Barbara Channel Islands. *Reports of the University of California Archaeological Survey,* no. 50, pp. 23–24. Berkeley.

1960b Observations Made in the Ruins of the Villages of the Original Inhabitants of the Pacific Coast of North America. *Reports of the University of California Archaeological Survey,* no. 50, pp. 19–23. Berkeley.

1963 The Method of Manufacture of Several Articles by the Former Indians of Southern California. *Reports of the University of California Archaeological Survey,* no. 59, pp. 77–82. Berkeley.

SEARS, WILLIAM H.

1964 The Southeastern United States. *In Prehistoric Man in the New World,* J. D. Jennings and E. Norbeck, eds., pp. 259–87. University of Chicago Press, Chicago.

SHAPIRO, H. L., WITH THE FIELD ASSISTANCE OF FREDERICK S. HULSE

1939 *Migration and Environment.* Oxford University Press, London, New York, Toronto.

SHEPARD, FRANCIS P.

1963 Thirty-five Thousand Years of Sea Level. *In Essays in Marine Geology in Honor of K. O. Emery,* T. Clements, ed., pp. 1–10. University of Southern California Press, Los Angeles.

1964 Sea Level Changes in the Past 6000 Years: Possible Archæological Significance. *Science* 143:574–76. Washington, D.C.

SHEPARD, FRANCIS P., AND H. E. SUESS

1956 Rate of Postglacial Rise of Sea Level. *Science* 123: 1082–83. Washington, D.C.

SHEPARD, FRANCIS P.; J. R. CURRAY; W. A. NEWMAN; A. L. BLOOM; N. D. NEWELL; J. I. TRACEY, JR.; H. H. VEEH

1967 Holocene Changes in Sea Level: Evidence in Micronesia. *Science* 157:542–44. Washington, D.C.

SHEPPE, WALTER, ED.

1962 *First Man West: Alexander Mackenzie's Journal of His Voyage to the Pacific Coast of Canada in 1793.* University of California Press, Berkeley.

SHIMER, JOHN A.

1960 *The Sculptured Earth: The Landscape of America.* Columbia University Press, New York.

SHINER, JOEL L.

1961 The McNary Reservoir: A Study in Plateau Archæology. *Bureau of American Ethnology Bulletin,* no. 179, pp. 149–266. Washington, D.C.

SHUMWAY, G.; C. L. HUBBS; AND J. R. MORIARTY

1961 Scripps Estate Site, San Diego, California: A La Jolla Site Dated 5460 to 7370 Years Before the Present. *New York Academy of Sciences Annual* 93:37–132. New York.

SHUTLER, RICHARD, JR.

1968 Tule Springs: Its Implications in Early Man Studies in North America. *In* "Early Man in Western North America," C. Irwin-Williams, ed., pp. 19–26. *Eastern New Mexico University Contributions in Anthropology,* vol. 1, no. 4. Portales, N.M.

SILSBEE, JOAN M.

1958 Determining the General Source of California *Olivella* Shells. *Reports of the University of California Archaeological Survey,* no. 41, pp. 10–11. Berkeley.

SIMPSON, RUTH D.

1956 An Introduction to Early Western American Prehistory. *Southern California Academy of Sciences Bulletin,* no. 55, pp. 61–71. Los Angeles.

1958 The Manix Lake Archæological Survey. *The Masterkey,* vol. 32, no. 1, pp. 4–10. Los Angeles.

1961 Coyote Gulch. *Archaeological Survey Association of Southern California Paper,* no. 5. Los Angeles.

SMILEY, TERAH L., ED.

1955 Geochronology with Special Reference to Southwestern United States. *Physical Science Bulletin,* no. 2, *University of Arizona Bulletin Series,* vol. 26, no. 2. University of Arizona Press, Tucson.

SMITH, CLARENCE E., AND W. D. WEYMOUTH
1952 Archæology of the Shasta Dam Area, California. *Reports of the University of California Archaeological Survey*, no. 18. Berkeley.

SMITH, ELMER R.
1952 The Archæology of Deadman Cave, Utah: A Revision. *University of Utah Anthropological Papers*, no. 10. Salt Lake City.

SMITH, G. A.; S. SCHUILING; L. MARTIN; R. SAYLES; F. JILLSON
1957 Newberry Cave, California. *San Bernardino County Museum Quarterly*, vol. 4, no. 3. San Bernardino.

SMITH, HARLAN I.
1909a Archæology of the Gulf of Georgia and Puget Sound. *Memoirs of the American Museum of Natural History*, vol. 4, pt. 6, pp. 55–76. G. E. Stechert, New York.
1909b Shell-heaps of the Lower Fraser River, British Columbia. *Memoirs of the American Museum of Natural History*, vol. 3, pt. 4, pp. 133–92. New York.

SMITH, HARLAN I., AND GERARD FOWKE
1909 Cairns of British Columbia and Washington. *Memoirs of the American Museum of Natural History*, vol. 4, pt. 2, pp. 55–76. New York.

SMITH, M. W.
1946 Petroglyph Complexes in the History of the Columbia-Fraser Region. *Southwestern Journal of Anthropology* 2:306–22. Albuquerque.
1950 Archæology of the Columbia-Fraser Region. *Society for American Archaeology Memoir*, no. 6, pp. v–46. Menasha, Wis.
1956 The Cultural Development of the Northwest Coast. *Southwestern Journal of Anthropology* 12:272–94. Albuquerque.

SMITH, PHILIP S.
1937 Certain Relations between Northwestern America and Northeastern Asia. *In Early Man*, George Grant MacCurdy, ed., pp. 85–92. J. B. Lippincott Company, Philadelphia and New York.

SNYDER, LAURENCE H.
1926 Human Blood Groups: Their Inheritance and Racial Significance. *American Journal of Physical Anthropology*, n.s., 9:233–63. Philadelphia.

SPAULDING, ALBERT C.
1953 Statistical Techniques for the Discovery of Artifact Types. *American Antiquity* 18:305–313. Washington, D.C.
1957 *Method and Theory in American Archaeology: An Operational Basis for Culture-Historical Integration*, by Philip Phillips and G. R. Willey, and *Method and Theory in American Archaeology II, Historical-Developmental Interpretation*, by Gordon R. Willey and Philip Phillips (review). *American Antiquity* 23:85–87. Washington, D.C.
1960 The Dimensions of Archæology. *In Essays in the Science of Culture; In Honor of Leslie A. White*, Gertrude E. Dole and Robert L. Carneiro, eds., pp. 437–56. Thomas Y. Crowell Co., New York.

SPINDEN, HERBERT JOSEPH
1908 The Nez Percé Indians. *American Anthropological Association Memoir*, vol. 2, no. 3. Menasha, Wisc.

SQUIER, ROBERT J.
1953 The Manufacture of Flint Implements by the Indians of Northern and Central California. *Reports of the University of California Archaeological Survey*, no. 19, pp. 15–44. Berkeley.
1956 Recent Excavation and Survey in Northeastern California. *Reports of the University of California Archaeological Survey*, no. 33, pp. 34–38. Berkeley.

STALKER, A. MacS.
1969 Geology and Age of the Early Man Site at Taber, Alberta. *American Antiquity* 34:425–28. Washington, D.C.

STEEN, VIRGINIA, AND ROALD FRYXELL
1965 Mazama and Glacier Peak Pumice Glass: Uniformity of Refractive Index after Weathering. *Science* 150:878–80. Washington, D.C.

STEEN-MCINTYRE, VIRGINIA; ROALD FRYXELL; AND HAROLD MALDE
1973 Unexpectedly Old Age of Deposits at Hueyatlaco Archæological Site, Valsequillo, Mexico, Implied by New Stratigraphic and Petrographic Findings. *Geological Society of America Abstract*, vol. 5, no. 7, pp. 820–21. Boulder, Colo.

STEWARD, JULIAN H.
1937 Ancient Caves of the Great Salt Lake Region. *Bureau of American Ethnology Bulletin*, no. 116. Washington, D.C.
1938 Basin-Plateau Aboriginal Sociopolitical Groups. *Bureau of American Ethnology Bulletin*, no. 120. Washington, D.C. Reprint 1970, University of Utah Press, Salt Lake City.
1940 Native Cultures of the Intermontane (Great Basin) Area. *In* "Essays in Historical Anthropology of North America," *Smithsonian Miscellaneous Collections* 100:445–502. Washington, D.C.
1955 *Theory of Culture Change*. University of Illinois Press, Urbana.

STEWART, T. D.

1960 A Physical Anthropologist's View of the Peopling of the New World. *Southwestern Journal of Anthropology* 16:259–73. Albuquerque.

STOCK, CHESTER

1924 A Recent Discovery of Ancient Human Remains in Los Angeles, California. *Science* 60:2–5. Washington, D.C.

STRONG, EMORY

1959 *Stone Age on the Columbia River.* Metropolitan Press, Portland.

1966 The McClure Atlatls. *Screenings,* vol. 15, no. 5, pp. 1–4. The Oregon Archæological Society, Portland.

STRONG, WILLIAM D.; WILLIAM E. SCHENCK; AND JULIAN H. STEWARD

1930 Archæology of The Dalles-Deschutes Region. *University of California Publications in American Archaeology and Ethnology* 29:1–154. Berkeley.

STUCKENRATH, R., JR.

1966 The Debert Archæological Project, Nova Scotia: Radiocarbon Dating. *Quaternia* 8:73–80. Rome.

SUESS, HANS E.

1954 U.S. Geological Survey, Radiocarbon Dates I. *Science* 120:467–73. Washington, D.C.

1956 Absolute Chronology of the Last Glaciation. *Science* 123:355–58. Washington, D.C.

SUTTLES, WAYNE, AND WILLIAM W. ELMENDORF

1963 Linguistic Evidence for Salish Prehistory. *Symposium on Language and Culture: Proceedings of the Annual Spring Meeting of the American Ethnological Society,* pp. 40–52. Seattle.

SWADESH, MORRIS

1949 The Linguistic Approach to Salish Prehistory. *In* "Indians of the Urban Northwest," Marian W. Smith, ed., pp. 161–73. *Columbia University Contributions to Anthropology,* no. 36. AMS Press, New York.

1950 Salish Internal Relationships. *International Journal of American Linguistics* 16:157–67. Chicago.

1952 Lexico-statistical Dating of Prehistoric Ethnic Contacts with Special Reference to North American Indians and Eskimos. *American Philosophical Society Proceedings* 96:452–63. Philadelphia.

1953 Mosan I: A Problem of Remote Common Origin. *International Journal of American Linguistics* 19:26–44. Chicago.

1954 Time Depths of American Linguistic Groupings. *American Anthropologist,* n.s., 56:361–77. Washington, D.C.

1954– Algunas fechas glotocronolgicas importantes para
1955 la Prehistoria Nahua. *Revista Mexicana de Estudios Antropologicos,* Tomo Decimocuarto, Mexico, D.F.

1956 Problems of Long-range Comparison in Penutian. *Language* 32:17–41. Baltimore.

1959 Linguistics as an Instrument of Prehistory. *Southwestern Journal of Anthropology* 15:20–35. Albuquerque.

1964 Linguistic Overview. *In Prehistoric Man in the New World,* J. D. Jennings and Edward Norbeck, eds., pp. 527–56. University of Chicago Press, Chicago.

SWANSON, EARL H., JR.

1956 "Archæological Studies in the Vantage Region of the Columbia Plateau, Northwestern America." Ph.D. dissertation, University of Washington, Seattle.

1958 The Schaake Village Site in Central Washington. *American Antiquity* 24:161–71. Washington, D.C.

1959a Archæological Survey of the Methow Valley, Washington. *Tebiwa,* vol. 2, no. 1, pp. 72–76. Pocatello.

1959b Whiskey Dick Shellmound, Washington, *American Antiquity* 25:122–23. Washington, D.C.

1961 Preliminary Report on Archæology in the Birch Creek Valley, Eastern Idaho. *Tebiwa,* vol. 4, no. 1, pp. 25–28. Pocatello.

1962a Early Cultures in Northwestern America. *American Antiquity* 28:151–58. Washington, D.C.

1962b An Introduction to Birch Creek: A Foreword to Glacial and Soil Studies in the Lemhi Range. *Tebiwa,* vol. 5, no. 2, p. 1. Pocatello.

1962c A Note on Early Artifacts at the Schaake Site, Washington. *Tebiwa,* vol. 5, no. 2, pp. 23–28. Pocatello.

1962d The Emergence of Plateau Culture. *Occasional Papers of the Idaho State University Museum,* no. 8. Pocatello.

1964 Geochronology of the DjRi3 Site, British Columbia, 1959. *Tebiwa,* vol. 7, no. 2, pp. 42–52. Pocatello.

SWANSON, EARL H., JR., AND ALAN BRYAN

1954 An Archæological Survey of Caves in Washington. *American Antiquity* 19:387–89. Washington, D.C.

1960 Carved Stone Objects from the Columbia Plateau. *Tebiwa,* vol. 3, nos. 1, 2, pp. 39–40. Pocatello.

1964 Birch Creek Papers No. 1: An Archæological Reconnaissance in the Birch Creek Valley of Eastern Idaho. *Occasional Papers of the Idaho State University Museum,* no. 13. Pocatello.

SWANSON, EARL H., JR.; ALAN BRYAN; AND ROGER POWERS

1962 Archæological Explorations in Southwestern

Idaho. Manuscript on file, Idaho State College Museum, Pocatello.

SWANSON, EARL H., JR., AND B. ROBERT BUTLER

1962 The First Conference of Western Archæologists on Problems of Point Typology. *Occasional Papers of the Idaho State University Museum,* no. 10. Pocatello.

SWANSON, EARL H., JR.; B. ROBERT BUTLER; AND ROBSON BONNICHSEN

1964 Birch Creek Papers No. 2: Natural and Cultural Stratigraphy in the Birch Creek Valley of Eastern Idaho. *Occasional Papers of the Idaho State University Museum,* no. 14. Pocatello.

SWANSON, EARL H., JR.; ROBERT POWERS; AND ALAN BRYAN

1964 The Material Culture of the 1959 Southwestern Idaho Survey. *Tebiwa,* vol. 7, no. 2, pp. 1–27. Pocatello.

SWANTON, JOHN R.

1952 The Indian Tribes of North America. *Bureau of American Ethnology Bulletin,* no. 145. Washington, D.C.

SWARTZ, BENJAMIN K.

1964 "Archæological Investigations at Lava Beds National Monument, California." Ph.D. dissertation, University of Arizona, Tempe.

T

TAYLOR, DEE C.

1954 The Garrison Site. *University of Utah Anthropological Papers,* no. 16. Salt Lake City.

TAYLOR, D. W.

1965 The Study of Pleistocene Nonmarine Mollusks in North America. *In The Quaternary of the United States,* H. E. Wright, Jr., and David G. Frey, eds., pp. 597–611. Princeton University Press, Princeton.

TAYLOR, HERBERT C., JR.

1964 Contributions to the Prehistory of the Columbia Plateau, by Robert Butler (review). *American Antiquity* 30:230–31. Washington, D.C.

TAYLOR, WALTER W.

1948 A Study of Archæology. *American Anthropological Association Memoir,* no. 69. Menasha, Wisc.

1961 Archæology and Language in Western North America. *American Antiquity* 27:71–81. Washington, D.C.

TEN KATE, HERMAN F. C.

1892 Somatological Observations on the Indians of the Southwest. *A Journal of American Ethnology and Archaeology* 3:117–44. Boston.

TERASMAE, J.

1961 Notes on Late-Quaternary Climatic Changes in Canada. *Annals of the New York Academy of Science* 95:658–75. New York.

THIEME, FREDERICK P., AND CHARLOTTE M. OTTEN

1957 The Unreliability of Blood Typing Aged Bone. *American Journal of Physical Anthropology,* n.s., 15:387–97. Philadelphia.

THIEME, FREDERICK P.; CHARLOTTE M. OTTEN; AND H. ELDON SUTTON

1956 A Blood Typing of Human Skull Fragments from the Pleistocene. *American Journal of Physical Anthropology,* n.s., 14:437–43. Philadelphia.

THOMPSON, RAYMOND H.

1958 Modern Yucatecan Maya Pottery Making. *Memoirs of the Society for American Archaeology,* no. 15. Washington, D.C.

THOMPSON, RAYMOND H., ED.

1958 Migrations in New World Culture History. *Social Science Bulletin,* no. 27. University of Arizona Press, Tucson.

TING, PETER

1967 A Pyramid Lake Surface Artifact Assemblage Located at or Near the 3800 Foot Elevation. *The Nevada Archaeological Survey Reporter,* no. 8, Aug. 1967, pp. 4–12. University of Nevada, Reno.

TOUHY, DONALD R.

1956 Shoshoni Ware from Idaho. *Davidson Journal of Anthropology,* vol. 2, no. 1, pp. 55–72. Seattle.

TOUHY, DONALD R., AND EARL H. SWANSON, JR.

1960 Excavation at Rockshelter 10-AA-15, Southwest Idaho. *Tebiwa,* vol. 3, nos. 1, 2, pp. 20–24. Pocatello.

TREGANZA, ADAN E.

1942 An Archæological Reconnaissance of Northeastern Baja California and Southeastern California. *American Antiquity* 8:152–63. Washington, D.C.

1947 Notes on the San Dieguito Lithic Industry of Southern California and Northern Baja California. *University of California Publications in American Archaeology and Ethnology* 44:253–55. Berkeley.

1952 Archæological Investigations in the Farmington Reservoir Area, Stanislaus County, California. *Reports of the University of California Archaeological Survey,* no. 14. Berkeley.

1954 Salvage Archæology in the Nimbus and Redbank Reservoir Areas, Central California. *Reports of the University of California Archaeological Survey,* no. 26. Berkeley.

1958 Salvage Archæology in the Trinity Reservoir Area, Northern California. *Reports of the University of California Archaeological Survey,* no. 43, pt. 1. Berkeley.

1959 Salvage Archæology in the Trinity Reservoir Area, Northern California—Field Session 1958. *Reports of the University of California Archaeological Survey,* no. 46. Berkeley.

TREGANZA, ADAN E., AND A. BIERMAN

1958 The Topanga Culture: Final Report on Excavations, 1948. *University of California Anthropological Records,* no. 20, pp. 45–86. Berkeley.

TREGANZA, ADAN E., AND ROBERT F. HEIZER

1953 Additional Data on the Farmington Complex, A Stone Implement Assemblage of Probable Early Postglacial Date from Central California. *Reports of the University of California Archaeological Survey,* no. 22, pp. 28–38. Berkeley.

TREGANZA, ADAN E., AND G. G. MALAMUD

1950 The Topanga Culture. First Season's Excavation of the Tank Site, 1947. *University of California Anthropological Records,* vol. 12. Berkeley.

TREGANZA, ADAN E.; C. E. SMITH; AND W. D. WEYMOUTH

1950 An Archæological Survey of the Yuki Area. *University of California Anthropological Records,* vol. 12, pp. 113–28. Berkeley.

TRIMBLE, DONALD E., AND WILFRED J. CARR

1961 Late Quaternary History of the Snake River in the American Falls Region, Idaho. *Geological Society of America Bulletin* 72:1739–48. New York.

TRUE, D. L.

1958 An Early Complex in San Diego County, California. *American Antiquity* 23:255–63. Washington, D.C.

TUTHILL, CARR, AND A. A. ALLANSON

1954 Ocean-bottom Artifacts. *The Masterkey* 28:222–32. Los Angeles.

U

UHLE, MAX

1907 The Emeryville Shellmound. *University of California Publications in American Archaeology and Ethnology* 7:1–106. Berkeley.

UNITED STATES ARMY, CORPS OF ENGINEERS

1952 Columbia River and Tributaries, Northwestern United States, in Eight Volumes. *House Document* no. 531, 81st Congress, 2nd Session, vol. 1. Government Printing Office, Washington, D.C.

UNITED STATES DEPARTMENT OF AGRICULTURE

1941 Climate and Man. *Yearbook of Agriculture.* United States Government Printing Office, Washington, D.C.

UPSON, J. E.

1949 Late Pleistocene and Recent Changes of Sea Level along the Coast of Santa Barbara County, California. *American Journal of Science* 247:94–115. New Haven.

V

VOEGELIN, CARL F.

1958 The Dispersal Factor in Migrations and Immigrations of American Indians. *In* "Migrations in New World Culture History," Raymond H. Thompson, ed., pp. 47–62. *Social Science Bulletin,* no. 27. University of Arizona Press, Tucson.

VOEGLIN, F. M., AND E. W. VOEGLIN

1941 Map of North American Languages. *American Ethnological Society Publication,* no. 20. New York.

VOEGLIN, F. M., AND CARL F. VOEGLIN

1966 Map of North American Indian Languages. *American Ethnological Society.* Printed by Rand McNally. New York.

VOGEL, J. C.

1966 Comments. Pradel: Transition from Mousterian to Perigordian. *Current Anthropology* 7:46–47. Chicago.

W

WADE, M. P.

1973 Artifacts of Early Man in the New World. *Science* 182:1371. Washington, D.C.

WAHRHAFTIG, J. H., AND J. H. BIRMAN

1965 The Quaternary of the Pacific Mountain System in California. *In The Quaternary of the United States,* H. E. Wright, Jr., and David G. Frey, eds., pp. 299–340. Princeton University Press, Princeton.

WALDRON, H. H.; D. R. MULLINEAUX; AND D. R. CRANDELL

1957 Age of the Vashon Glaciation in the Southern and Central Parts of the Puget Sound Basin. *Geological Society of America Bulletin* 68:1849–50. New York.

WALKER, DEWARD E., JR.

1967 Mutual Cross-utilization of Economic Resources in the Plateau: An Example from Aboriginal Nez Percé Fishing Practices. *Washington State Uni-*

versity Laboratory of Anthropology, Report of Investigations, no. 41. Pullman.

WALKER, EDWIN F.

1947 Excavation of a Yokuts Indian Cemetery. Kern County Historical Society, Bakersfield, California.

1952 Five Prehistoric Archæological Sites in Los Angeles County, California. *Published by the S. W. Hodge Anniversary Publication Fund*, no. 6. Los Angeles.

WALLACE, WILLIAM J.

1951a The Mortuary Caves of Calaveras County, California. *Archaeology*, vol. 4, no. 4, pp. 199–203. New York.

1951b The Archæological Deposit in Moaning Cave, Calaveras County. *Reports of the University of California Archaeological Survey*, no. 12, pp. 29–41. Berkeley.

1954 The Little Sycamore Site and the Early Milling Stone Cultures of Southern California. *American Antiquity* 20:112–23. Washington, D.C.

1955 A Suggested Chronology for Southern California Coastal Archæology. *Southwestern Journal of Anthropology* 11:214–30. Albuquerque.

1958 Archæological Investigations in Death Valley National Monument, 1952–1957. *Reports of the University of California Archaeological Survey*, no. 42, pp. 7–22. Berkeley.

1962a Archæological Explorations in the Southern Section of Anza-Borrego Desert State Park. *Archaeological Report*, no. 5. California State Department of Parks and Recreation, Sacramento.

1962b Prehistoric Cultural Development in the Southern California Deserts. *American Antiquity* 28:172–80. Washington, D.C.

1963 Current Research—Great Basin. *American Antiquity* 29:267–68. Washington, D.C.

WALLACE, WILLIAM J., AND DONALD W. LATHRAP

1952 An Early Implement Assemblage from a Limestone Cavern in California. *American Antiquity* 18:133–38. Washington, D.C.

WALLACE, WILLIAM J., AND EDITH S. TAYLOR

1952 Excavation of Sis-13, a Rockshelter in Siskiyou County, California. *Reports of the University of California Archaeological Survey*, no. 15, pp. 13–39. Berkeley.

1955a Archæology of Wildrose Canyon, Death Valley National Monument. *American Antiquity* 20:355–67. Washington, D.C.

1955b Early Man in Death Valley. *Archaeology*, vol. 8, no. 2, pp. 88–92. New York.

1956 The Surface Archæology of Butte Valley, Death Valley National Monument. *Contributions to California Archaeology*, no. 1. Los Angeles.

1958 An Archæological Reconnaissance in Bow Willow Canyon, Anza-Borrego Desert State Park. *The Masterkey* 32:155–66. Los Angeles.

1960a The Indian Hill Rockshelter, Preliminary Excavations (Anza-Borrego State Park). *The Masterkey* 34:66–82. Los Angeles.

1960b Surface Archæology of Anza-Borrego Desert State Park, California. *The Masterkey* 34:4–18. Los Angeles.

WARNICA, JAMES N.

1966 New Discoveries at the Clovis Site. *American Antiquity* 31:345–57. Washington, D.C.

WARREN, CLAUDE N.

1960 Housepits and Village Patterns in the Columbia Plateau and Southwestern Washington. *Tebiwa*, vol. 3, nos. 1, 2, pp. 25–28. Pocatello.

1967a The San Dieguito Complex: A Review and Hypothesis. *American Antiquity* 32:168–85. Washington, D.C.

1967b The Southern California Milling Stone Horizon: Some Comments. *American Antiquity* 32:233–36. Washington, D.C.

WARREN, CLAUDE N.; ALAN BRYAN; AND DONALD TOUHY

1963 The Goldendale Site and Its Place in Plateau Prehistory. *Tebiwa*, vol. 6, no. 1, pp. 1–21. Pocatello.

WARREN, CLAUDE N., AND ANTHONY J. RANERE

1968 Outside Danger Cave: A View of Early Man in the Great Basin. *In* "Early Man in North America; Symposium of the Southwestern Anthropological Association, San Diego, 1968," C. Irwin-Williams, ed., pp. 6–18. *Eastern New Mexico University Contributions in Anthropology*, vol. 1, no. 4. Portales.

WARREN, CLAUDE N., AND D. L. TRUE

1961 The San Dieguito Complex and Its Place in California Prehistory. *University of California Archaeological Survey Annual Report, 1960–1961*, pp. 246–91. Los Angeles.

WARREN, CLAUDE N.; D. L. TRUE; AND ARDITH A. EUDEY

1961 Early Gathering Complexes of Western San Diego County: Results and Interpretations of an Archæology Survey. *University of California Archaeological Survey Annual Report, 1960–1961*, pp. 1–108. Los Angeles.

WARREN, CLAUDE N.; CORT SIMS; AND MAX G. PAVESIC
1968 Cultural Chronology in Hells Canyon. *Tebiwa*, vol. 11, no. 2, pp. 1–37. Pocatello.

WEDEL, WALDO R.
1941 Archæological Investigations at Buena Vista Lake, Kern County, California. *Bureau of American Ethnology Bulletin*, no. 130. Washington, D.C.

WELLS, PHILIP V.
1966 Late Pleistocene Vegetation and Degree of Pluvial Climatic Change in the Chihuahuan Desert. *Science* 153:970–75. Washington, D.C.

WELLS, PHILIP V., AND RAINER BERGER
1967 Late Pleistocene History of Coniferous Woodland in the Mohave Desert. *Science* 155:1640–47. Washington, D.C.

WENDORF, FRED
1966 Early Man in the New World: Problems of Migration. *American Naturalist* 100:253–70. Tempe, Ariz.

WENDORF, FRED; A. D. KRIEGER; C. C. ALBRITTON; AND T. D. STEWART
1955 *The Midland Discovery: A Report on the Pleistocene Human Remains from Midland, Texas*. University of Texas Press, Austin.

WHEAT, JOE BEN
1967 A Paleo-Indian Bison Kill. *Scientific American*, vol. 216, no. 1, pp. 44–52. New York.

WHEELER, RICHARD P.
1952 A Note on the "McKean Lanceolate Point." *Plains Archaeological Conferences News Letter*, vol. 4, no. 4. Norman, Okla.

1954 Selected Projectile Point Types of the United States, I, II. *Oklahoma Anthropological Society Bulletin*, vol. 2, no. 4, pp. 1–6. Oklahoma City.

WHEELER, S. M.
1942 *Archaeology of Etna Cave, Lincoln County, Nevada*. Nevada State Park Commission, Carson City.

WHEELER, S. M., AND GEORGIA N. WHEELER
1944 *Cave Burials near Fallon, Churchill County, Nevada*. Nevada State Park Commission, Carson City.

WHITMORE, FRANK C., JR.; K. O. EMERY; H. B. S. COOKE; AND DONALD J. P. SWIFT
1967 Elephant Teeth from the Atlantic Continental Shelf. *Science* 156:1477–81. Washington, D.C.

WILCOX, RAY E.
1965 Volcanic-ash Chronology. *In The Quaternary of the United States*, H. E. Wright, Jr., and David G. Frey, eds., pp. 807–16. Princeton University Press, Princeton.

WILLEY, GORDON R., AND PHILIP PHILLIPS
1958 *Method and Theory in American Archaeology*. University of Chicago Press, Chicago.

WILLIAMS, HOWEL
1942 The Geology of Crater Lake National Park. *Carnegie Institution Publication*, no. 540. Washington, D.C.

1944 Volcanoes of the Three Sisters Region, Oregon Cascades. *University of California Publications Bulletin of the Department of Geological Sciences* 27:37–84. Berkeley.

WILMSEN, EDWIN M.
1964 Flake Tools in the American Arctic: Some Speculations. *American Antiquity* 29:338–44. Washington, D.C.

WINGFIELD-STRATFORD, ESMÉ
1930 *The History of British Civilization*. 2nd rev. ed. Harcourt Brace & Company, Inc., New York.

WITTHOFT, JOHN
1952 A Paleo-Indian Site in Eastern Pennsylvania: An Early Hunting Culture. *American Philosophical Society Proceedings* 96:464–95. Philadelphia.

WOO, JU-KANG
1958 Tzeyang Paleolithic Man—Earliest Representative of Modern Man in China. *American Journal of Physical Anthropology*, n.s., 16:459–71. Philadelphia.

1959 Human Fossils Found in Liukiang, Kwangsi, China. *Vertebrata Palasiatica*, vol. 3, no. 3, pp. 109–23. Academia Sinica. Peking.

WOO, JU-KANG, AND RU-CE PENG
1959 Fossil Human Skull of Early Paleoanthropic Stage Found at Mapa, Shaoquan, Kwantung Province. *Vertebrata Palasiatica*, vol. 3, no. 4, pp. 176–83. Academia Sinica. Peking.

WOODWARD, A.
1937 Atlatl Dart Foreshafts from the La Brea Pits. *Southern California Academy of Sciences Bulletin*, vol. 36, no. 2, pp. 41–60. Los Angeles.

WORMINGTON, H. M.
1955 A Reappraisal of the Fremont Culture. *Denver Museum of Natural History Proceedings*, no. 1. Denver.

1957 Ancient Man in North America. *Denver Museum of Natural History Popular Series*, no. 4. Denver. 4th ed.

1962   A Survey of Early American Prehistory. *American Scientist* 50:230–42. New Haven.

WORMINGTON, H. M., AND RICHARD G. FORBIS

1965   An Introduction to the Archæology of Alberta, Canada. *Denver Museum of Natural History Proceedings,* no. 11. Denver.

WRIGHT, HERBERT E., JR., AND DAVID G. FREY, EDS.

1965   *The Quaternary of the United States: A Review Volume for the VII Congress of the International Association for Quaternary Research.* Princeton University Press, Princeton.

Z

ZEUNER, FRIEDRICH E.

1950   *Dating the Past: An Introduction to Geochronology.* Methuen & Co., Ltd., London.

ZINGG, ROBERT M.

1939   *A Reconstruction of Uto-Aztekan History.* G. E. Stechert, New York.

Index

Prehistory of the Far West was set in Intertype Granjon with handset Garamond foundry display type by the University of Utah Printing Service. Text paper is Beckett Offset, end-sheets are Strathmore Americana, and the cover is Roxite Buckram. This book was printed by the University of Utah Printing Service and bound at Mountain States Bindery. Dust jacket design by Bailey-Montague & Associates.